Novelist

Antonia White

(Eirene Botting)

1899–1980

LIVED HERE
1899–1921

Nothing to Forgive

The end-papers at the back and front of this book show the plaque commemorating Antonia White at 22 Perham Road, London W14, her home for the first 22 years of her life, and the fictional childhood home of the heroines of her novels.

Nothing to Forgive

A *Daughter's Story of Antonia White*

Lyndall Passerini Hopkinson

Chatto & Windus

LONDON

Published in 1988 by
Chatto & Windus Limited
30 Bedford Square
London WC1B 3RP

A CIP catalogue record for this book is available
from the British Library.

ISBN 0 7011 2969 7

Photoset in Linotron Sabon by
Rowland Phototypesetting Limited
Bury St Edmunds, Suffolk
Printed and bound in Great Britain by
Mackays of Chatham PLC, Chatham, Kent

Contents

Acknowledgements

The person who deserves most thanks is my father Tom Hopkinson. Not only did he entrust me with the originals of his notebooks from 1932–43, but he also gave me constant encouragement while I was writing this book and he approved the part of the manuscript concerning his early life and marriage to my mother, where his notebooks and love-letters are often quoted.

I am grateful to my half-sister Susan Chitty for having given me photocopies of my father's, Eric Earnshaw-Smith's and Bertrand Russell's letters to our mother when she first knew I was writing this book, and, more recently, for sending me a copy of a letter from Lyn Cosgriff, part of which I quote; also to her and to Carmen Callil as my co-literary executors of Antonia White's estate for permission to quote from unpublished works.

Thanks are also due to Mary Hitchcock Palmer, Richard Temple Muir and Lyn Cosgriff for phrases quoted from their letters, and to Mary for photographs. And to Ian Henderson who talked very frankly to me about his relationship with my mother. I would also like to thank my editor, Alison Samuel.

I also wish to acknowledge the following publishers for quotations from published works: The Enitharmon Press, *Journal 1936–1937* by David Gascoyne; Hutchinson & Co. Ltd, *Of This Our Time* by Tom Hopkinson; and The Virago Press for the published works of Antonia White (*Frost in May, The Lost Traveller, The Sugar House, Beyond the Glass, Strangers, The Hound and the Falcon* and *As Once in May*).

I would like to thank my half-sisters, Nicolette and Amanda Hopkinson, for permission to use photographs taken by their mother, Gerti Deutsch (nos. 15, 19, 20); and the Borough of Hammersmith and Fulham Libraries and Archives department for their help and for permission to reproduce the commemorative plaque used as end-papers and the photo of Perham Road.

Lyndall Passerini Hopkinson
Cortona, 1988

To
VALERIA AND BELINDA

'whose friendship I value so
much and without whose encouragement
this book might never have been written'

Antonia White, 1954

Prologue

The Easter of 1980 was unusually bright for England. The cloudless days were mild, but the moonlit nights were cold. There would even be a frost in May that year; but by then Antonia White, my mother, had been buried in a Sussex cemetery fifteen miles across country from the Catholic nursing home where she lay that sunny April.

No one had told me Mother was dying.

What intuition or instinct in February had urged me to leave central Italy, where I live, to drive across a wintry Europe with my semi-invalid husband, Lorenzo, sleeping most of the way on a bunk-bed in the back of our little van? Was it my mother's longest silence in our sporadic correspondence between England and Italy which alerted me that something might be wrong? Then why had I not just flown over alone for a fleeting visit to allay my suspicions? I had often done so in the past few years, when a strange telepathy, which had evolved so late in our uneasy relationship, had again and again compelled me to leave for England just when Antonia most needed someone, although she had never appealed for help. Whatever it was that brought me from Tuscany to the surprisingly cheerful room in Sussex where my mother lay kept me there as winter warmed into spring.

I had not seen my mother since All Saints' Day when her other daughter, my half-sister Sue, and I had settled her in at St Raphael's, the home run by Catholic nuns in Danehill, Sussex. That day, after all our misgivings that she might be miserable or refractory or both, surprisingly she had said, 'I'm so happy!', releasing me to return to Italy less worried about her than I had been for the previous four years, in which she had been suffering from osteoporosis and cancer and had broken a hip. At different times she had been in public hospitals, a private nursing home, a geriatric ward, or, when she could bear institutions no more (or vice versa), at home with a rota of agency nurses. Finally, the trundling back and forth was over and she was in good hands, apparently content to be so, not even lamenting having had to leave her London flat.

When she had arrived at St Raphael's, her body had not completely capitulated to the assaults that disease had made on it. With help she could move painfully from bed to desk. She was still *compos mentis* – indeed more so than at many other stages of her life.

Now, four months later, as I went into her room with Sue, I was shocked: no one had warned me that she was completely bed-ridden and could no longer read or write. Nor was I prepared for the fact that, though she could still talk a little, her words were either senseless ramblings, or filled with obsessive fears and fantasies that people were angry with her. She insisted the nuns had broken her front tooth (one that had in fact been missing for ages). 'They hit me on the head with a board. They do it every morning. They're quite right. I'm very naughty.' Most of the time she did not recognise us, her only children. Only once did she seem to connect with the present: a nun had brought in an elegant tray with steaming coffee, cream and biscuits for which Sue and I were too profusely thankful. 'Window dressing!' said Antonia sharply before wandering back into the labyrinths of confusion.

The next visit, with a friend of hers, Senta Marnau, was even more distressing. She seemed to be in physical pain; and her mind in a state of torment. She was seeing ghastly apparitions and hearing demons screeching. A howling gale blowing in from the coast twenty miles away bent and twisted the tops of the bare trees outside the window, adding an apocalyptic atmosphere to the eerie scenes she kept describing. People were rising from their graves – among them her father's old pupil, Compton Mackenzie, carrying an umbrella. 'Can't you hear the terrible screams?' she kept asking.

As if she were a sick child assailed by nightmares, Senta and I took turns holding her hand – soothing words only added to her confusion. Once, when her infernal visions seemed more fearful than ever, I stroked her head and said, 'Don't worry. Everything's all right.' Startled at having been drawn back to reality for a moment, she looked at me as if I were a stranger and asked crossly, 'What's all right?', true to the fiery Antonia I had always known.

There was one breakthrough of recognition when, slowly, doubtfully, she scanned my name in two monotonous syllables: 'Lyn – dall?'

I nodded. She asked me about a wounded stray cat I had written to her about. I told her the vet had had to amputate his front leg, but assured her he was now more lively and wily than before. 'I wish I were brave like him,' she said.

Every time Senta and I got up to leave Antonia became so agitated that we lingered on, though it meant driving back to London in the storm after dark. And when finally we did part, we were all so racked with misery, that when I went to say goodbye to the Reverend Mother, and she asked, 'And how did you find your dear mother?', I burst into tears. She told me kindly, 'It's marvellous really, her going through all this remorse now so that she'll be ready to meet the Lord.' As someone who has never been a Catholic, these mathematics of mercy were incalculable to me: did it mean there was a hope that any torments of hell my mother might have to face after death would be lessened by what she was undergoing now?

All I could do was to come from London as often as possible to sit with her. It was not easy because Lorenzo was not well enough to make the journey repeatedly, and could not be left for long; also he had started a long and painful course of dental treatment in London.

At every visit Antonia looked more hunched and shrunken, filling less and less of the narrow bed. Usually she was too weak or too confused to speak. She seldom recognised me, though when I told her who I was, she would stare at me in a kind of disbelieving wonderment. Sometimes she thought I was Sue, her favourite daughter, a Catholic and a writer like herself, and who was away doing research for a book on Gwen John. Whoever she thought I was, my voice and touch seemed to comfort her. Once when I was stroking her she insisted I was 'touching filth' as if she were pleading forgiveness. But although I *had* forgiven her, I was afraid to say so, for she might still have leapt back fiercely and demanded, 'Forgiven me for what?' And I would have been too cowardly to answer, 'For the way you never bothered to find out who I really was, because you ignored me in babyhood, terrorised me in childhood and slighted me in adolescence.'

The last day of March was Antonia's eighty-first birthday.

When I arrived a nun was feeding her, telling her over and over again to swallow, as she patiently held a spoonful of custard to her lips. After a while the nun gave up. 'I'm afraid it's pretty hopeless,' she said and retreated with the bowl still full, leaving us alone. It did not seem possible for anyone to go on existing like that; yet, only a few days before, the doctor had cheerily predicted she might survive another couple of months, even though the cancer had spread to her lymphatic system and was causing swellings.

That afternoon Antonia was particularly troubled. I thought it might be the sunlight spilling through the window-panes onto her bed, so I pulled the curtains to keep it off her face, but still she kept trying to shift her head as if to avoid invisible blows, and talked of the threatening screams again. I wondered whether it was her way of describing pain, remembering how, when I was in the throes of my worst migraine headaches as a child, pain had transposed itself into other guises, such as a ship tossed on high seas, or an insoluble equation. When at last she sank into stillness or sleep, I – who until so recently had not believed in anything – flung all the frustrated spiritual fervour of years of agnosticism into pleading with God: 'Please don't let her suffer any more. Please let her die now, in her sleep, on her birthday with the sun shining, her hand in mine. Surely she's made amends enough. *Please*, PLEASE . . .' But her irregular, laboured breaths continued to mock my prayers. God was as stubborn as Antonia that day and in no mood for simple endings.

On waking she asked, 'Have I been crying again? It's become a bad habit.'

I had caught the habit.

I cried because I could not assuage her present agony and fear; nor annihilate her past struggles against devastating depression, anxiety and loneliness; nor attenuate her dread of what the eternal future held for a Catholic guilty of many sins. I cried for what had been, for what had not been and for what might have been: for the mental suffering her almighty ego had inflicted on herself and others, particularly on her two children. I see now there was as much self-pity as commiseration in my tears.

Since there could no longer be any doubt that she was nearing the end, Lorenzo agreed to come to Sussex for the Easter weekend so that I could be constantly beside my mother.

During the long watch by my mother's death-bed, as I contemplated her frail hand lying so still and trusting in mine, which looked grotesquely rough around the pale softness of hers, which had never pulled up a weed or cleaned a stable, it seemed incredible that for the first time I should feel an overwhelming love for this emaciated human being who, for so many years, had aroused only terror in me. It was not the kind of love I imagine a normal daughter feels for a normal mother, but the concerned, protective love a mother might feel for her child – something neither of us, for different reasons, had ever known.

My youngest half-sister, Amanda Hopkinson, whose own mother had died in her arms only a few months before, understood my strange bewilderment. When she came to say her farewell to Antonia, of whom she had always been fond, she told me, 'It's odd how much one can love them when they can't harm one any more.'

At the time I had been shocked at her saying this aloud. It seemed somehow profane to utter such a sad truth in front of someone so fragile and defenceless for whom change was now too late. Also, I suspected some part of my mother might still be capable of understanding, even if she couldn't answer back any more.

The nuns by now had given up putting on her spectacles with the heavy cataract lenses; and her pink plastic hearing-aids lay abandoned on the spotless white chest-of-drawers. No longer hidden behind the glasses, one could see how emaciated her face had become. Although Antonia cannot have seen much through those unfocused eyes, oddly she seemed to see and hear better without these trappings of old age. Every so often she would look around the room with innocent wonderment, or turn her face in the direction of someone walking into the room. She would react with a shudder if a door slammed, and start at the scream of any passing jet; even the tinkle of a teaspoon on a saucer could make her open her eyes wide in astonishment.

Occasionally she seemed to want to speak, the lips trembled but no words escaped from her dry mouth. I asked if she were thirsty. She nodded. But she no longer had the strength to swallow – and anyway her head, too heavy now for her slender neck, drooped and lolled so that the water spilled over the bed. All one could do was to dampen her tongue with wet cotton-wool. Once I asked if she was in pain, and told her to squeeze my hand if she wanted me to ask for a pain-killer: to my horror, her almost weightless hand shifted slightly in mine, like a fledgling stirring in its nest.

And all those long and weary days the sun kept shining. From all around came the sounds of life. Next door the television jangled away every afternoon, reaching a cacophonic climax on Easter Saturday with the commentary on the Boat Race. Further up the corridor someone in a wistful mood would play 'When I Grow Too Old To Dream' over and over again on a scratched 78 record – it had been the first song our Nurse, Mary, had taught us in the 1930s when she was in love.

At intervals a nun would bring in tea or coffee with cake or biscuits, exquisitely served on a silver tray. Although I wasn't hungry and felt there was something almost unseemly in crunching up biscuits with Death hovering so close, perhaps part of me was establishing that I at least still sided with the living, as I gratefully polished off the lot.

When my mother seemed awake – or was she only stirring in her sleep? – I would read or talk to her. Was there something I should be saying to ease her into death and liberate her from hanging on to a life to which she clung because of a terror that a Catholic hell lay in wait for her? I tried to remember the words of the prayer that my father's father, the Archdeacon of Westmorland and arch-disapprover of my mother, used to say at the end of evensong, but could get no further than 'Lord, now lettest thou thy servant depart in peace according to thy word.'

There was a Bible by her bed, but as I read it aloud the Old Testament sounded too heartless, and there was little consolation for her situation in the New. I tried reciting the few poems I knew by heart, but soon broke off: lines learnt in the fifth form are not chosen for someone struggling with death – 'Shall I compare thee to a summer's day?' Jumbled snatches of the text from Verdi's *Requiem* – *Agnus Dei, qui tollis peccata mundi, dona eis requiem* – *Salva me, fons pietatis* – *Libera me, Domine, de morte aeterna* – *dona eis, Domine, et lux perpetua* – seemed more suitable, but with a Latin abandoned since schooldays, I feared my pronunciation might offend her, the daughter of a classical scholar.

So I stopped quoting and told her I loved her. Was I being hypocritical? Even during those recent years of her broken health, when the parent-child relationship had been reversed and she had depended on me for help, my feelings had been like her own when her mother had been ill: 'She could not remember ever having loved her mother and what she felt now was mainly pity.' How could I be sure this new emotion was not compassion in disguise? Certainly I had never been able to love all those unhappily conflicting personalities who had once combined to make up my impatient, hot-tempered mother. But that mother was as unrecognisable in this helpless wreck on the bed as she was in the pretty eager girl on the poster advertising the Virago edition of the works of Antonia White which someone had pinned to the wall over her bed. That photograph had been taken long before I existed, when she was still Eirene Botting, the name she was born with. It was impossible to see in that untroubled face the seeds of the madness that was soon to come, and would haunt the rest of her life.

If Père Boulogne is right that 'De temps à autre, on est soi, un instant', in which brief moments between 31 March 1899 and April 1980 had Eirene/Antonia been her true self? *Whom* then did I now think I loved?

In the middle of my thoughts she murmured the last words I would ever hear her say: 'Which one?'

For a second I hesitated: should I pretend to be Sue, who might not get back before our mother died?

Why end on a lie? I had told her so many in the past to protect her feelings or mine.

'It's Lyndall,' I said.

I'm glad I told the truth. She squeezed my hand lightly with the one that always rested there; then very, very slowly dragged her other one towards it across the humps and hollows in the duvet. When it finally reached mine, she started to lift my hand, but if it had been made of lead it could not have cost her more effort. I tried to help by following the direction she was taking it upwards. She halted at her mouth – 'Perhaps she's trying to show me she's thirsty,' I thought – then she pressed (if such a word can describe the action of someone so weak) my hand to her lips and held it there a long time before kissing it. Then she let it drop, worn out and panting from such exertion.

It took all my efforts not to let her hear my sobs. With one gesture, which seemed to convey affection and remorse, gratitude and apology, she had placated the past by acknowledging me finally as her own.

But even so, she excluded me from her death.

From Good Friday until the Wednesday after Easter I had sat with her constantly by day as Lorenzo whiled away the tedious hours listening to the radio in the van or drinking tea in the nuns' parlour. Luckily he liked sleeping in the van: it reminded him of his pioneering days in Africa, long before we knew each other. By night, as the frost painted the van white, we slept on the two narrow bunks, swathed in sleeping bags, and wearing thick woollen socks and knitted ski caps, our breath turning to frozen mist on the windscreen as the thermometer sank lower and lower. The nuns had promised to call me if my mother's condition should change. It didn't.

Then we had to leave for London where Lorenzo had another appointment with his dentist. We told the nuns we would be back on Friday morning.

At nine o'clock on the Thursday evening, 10 April, the nun who sat sewing in Antonia White's room heard a little sob. Looking up, she realised that Eirene Adeline Botting's soul was freed at last from the prison of the crumpled body that lay discarded on the convent bed.

CHAPTER 1

A Letter from the Grave

*Philanthropists are usually execrable company; so are
'unselfish' mothers and world reformers.*
Antonia White, 27 June 1937

I received a letter from my mother after she was dead. It had been
handed to my sister by a nun at St Raphael's the day after Antonia's
death but she had forgotten to pass it on until after the funeral. Our
names on the envelope were written in a shaky travesty of the familiar
neat hand, and much of the page-long note, dated three months before
she died, was hard to decipher: but the meaning of those unfinished
sentences in straggly lines was clear: our mother was asking to be
forgiven for her 'selfishness and thoughtlessness' about us as children.
She said she had come to love us when we grew up and hoped there
would be 'nice things as well as ones horrid to remember'.

There was nothing new in Antonia's admission of having been an
inadequate mother: she had made it publicly fifteen years before in a
published correspondence with a man called Peter Thorpe, *The Hound
and the Falcon*, in which she confessed, 'I was a hideously selfish and
incompetent mother to them when they were little'; and she had
repeated it in letters she wrote to me when I was grown up.

But this tormented letter from the grave begging forgiveness stirred
me as no lifetime confession had done. Although I thought I had
forgiven her when she lay dying, I wondered whether it had been with
my whole heart or only with my mind? To know the answer I would
have to make sense of our troubled relationship and see if I could find
out why I believed she had always slighted me.

The first thing I did on getting home to Italy was to re-read my
mother's printed works. The task was not a long one, for she had
written only six novels (two of which were about cats) and a book of
short stories, besides the collection of letters. A quartet of novels were

the story of her life from the age of nine, when she became a convert to Catholicism, to the time when she was released from Bedlam in 1923 after nine months of complete insanity following the collapse of her first marriage. By then she was only twenty-four.

Apart from the first novel, *Frost in May*, which established her reputation as a writer in 1933, and the description of her madness in the last one, *Beyond the Glass* published in 1954, I had never been very enthusiastic about them. And *The Hound and the Falcon*, which should have interested me because it talked of people I knew, had always disturbed me by its sins of omission.

When Antonia had started that 'hectic exchange of letters' with Peter Thorpe in 1940 they were strangers to each other. He had written to her after reading *Frost in May* and she had been intrigued enough by his letter to want to know more about him. Within six weeks she had altered her openings from 'Dear Mr Thorpe' to 'Darling Peter' and confessed 'I have done a great many odd things in my life but I have *never* fallen in love by post before.' And like most people in love she tried to present herself in a good light. This not only affected the verity of some of her descriptions of her internal wrestling match against the dictates of the Catholic Church, which she had abandoned long before the correspondence began, and to which she returned before the letters dwindled to silence after only a year, but toned down some of the tougher facts of her personal life to sentimental half-truths.

This was particularly true when she tried to present herself as a reformed mother. My sister and I were eleven and nine at the time, and only in the previous two years had she begun not to regard her children as 'hostile strangers', yet she told Peter:

> I adore them both and more as they get older . . . If I had to part from Lyndall, it would be a great grief, but if I had to part from Sue, I'd never get over it . . . Sue might be a saint. She has enough violence and intensity to be. But Lyndall, as a Catholic or anything else, seems pretty obviously destined to be a charming and devoted wife and mother. I don't think she'll ever 'go to the bad'. But Susan will go to one extreme or the other.

Re-reading that in 1980 it was difficult not to feel amused. Aged nearly fifty and childless, I had been twice-married, once divorced, had no fixed religion and a past that it would need some courage to reveal. Whereas Sue, a writer of biographies and a lukewarm Catholic, was still married to the man she had met as a virgin student at Oxford and had four children by him. But, I had to remember, my mother did once admit to Peter, 'Not being one hundred per cent woman, I can't rely on female intuitions.'

Strangers, the collection of Antonia's short stories first published in 1954, was the book I had always preferred. Each time I read one of her stories I was proud to be her daughter and gratified that the book was dedicated to me, although I knew it was a spurious dedication: the best stories had been written for my father, Tom Hopkinson, before I was born, or about him after my parents broke up, and they all predated the last three novels published before them, one of which had been dedicated to Sue.

The only 'revelation' while re-reading my mother's books came from recognising how similar some of her feelings for her mother were to mine about her in my teens, though she was not afraid of her as I was, instead she despised her mother and treated her in a dismissive way. Of course I knew that Antonia, like me, had preferred her father: it was the recurring theme in her novels, and her morbid feelings for him had been the cause of many of her neuroses in later life.

Having re-read Antonia's printed works, I searched for any letters from her I might have kept. After growing up I had usually enjoyed getting her letters, though when I saw my mother's handwriting on the envelope my instinctive reaction had always been that of the child over-sensitive to adult criticism: 'What have I done wrong?' At boarding-school I had sometimes carried her letters around for days before steeling myself to read them. If a letter began 'My darling' or 'Darling' it was safe to read on; 'My dearest' and 'Dearest' could mean danger, but better face it at once; 'My dear' or, worst of all, 'Dear' signalled serious trouble ahead, and it sometimes took days to find enough courage to bare my breast to the finely sharpened words of wrath that followed because of something I had said or done unintentionally – for I would never have dared intentionally to upset my fiery mother.

I discovered I had kept over two hundred of her letters from a correspondence that had begun in 1952 soon after a critical point in both our lives: she was estranged from her favourite daughter who for the next few years would refuse any communication, and I had just abandoned a fiancé and fled to Rome on a single ticket.

The first of these letters I received from my mother, flustered from being left to deal with the aftermath of my 'Italian fugue' and 'reeling from shock' at the trail of lies I had left behind me, was an indignant 'Dearest Lyndall' one. But after getting my letter of apology and explanation, she had sent a long, reassuring 'My darling Lyndall' letter; and from then on, with a thousand miles of land and sea separating us, we found a smoother path, though she trod it more cautiously than I at first. I found writing to her easier than conversation because I did not have to censor every sentence.

After a while she began to acknowledge similar traits in our natures. One she underlined was '*fear of rebuff*'. She was right in saying it was 'extraordinarily painful to people like us'. And she offered condolences for our shared faults:

> We have one awful thing in common: the need for outside stimulus, particularly from a *person*. People don't realise we collapse when they aren't there and are fundamentally unself-confident and *not* self-starters.

Now that we were beginning to know and trust each other more, my mother attempted to make amends for having belittled me in the past. She used a two-fold path to try to instil in me the self-confidence I lacked because of her always having emphasised my sister's superiority in looks and talent and integrity. First she began by acknowledging there was a streak of me in her as well as of Sue, 'but an absolutely different streak'. Then she said:

> I don't think I *could* write to Sue now if I tried because half Sue just isn't there. But if I write to you, at least I know I am writing to a real person.

The second way was to insist that I, as well as Sue, was prettier than she had been in her 'palmiest days'. She passed on any favourable comments, such as one made by 'a funny little man called Miron Grindea' after she had shown him a photograph of me: 'So beautiful, so profoundly disturbing.' But nothing she said now could ever persuade me I might be attractive, and I would continue to be amazed and flattered when anyone liked me or fell in love with me.

I had forgotten too that she had tried to encourage me to write. It astonished me to read that she had said when I was twenty-one, 'You happen to have this rather rare gift of "attention" which is one reason why I think you may turn out to be a writer.' Many times she praised me for my letters, suggesting I should turn some anecdote from them of my life in Rome into an article for *Lilliput* or *Punch*; but since she destroyed all my letters before going to St Raphael's, I do not know whether she was just being kindly encouraging.

But the main effect of re-reading all those letters from my mother was to underline to me how sad and solitary the last third of her life had been. From 1952 until Sue's truce with her in 1957, it was overshadowed by 'the sorrows of being deserted by my beautiful daughter or the horrors of financial crises or just the general unbearability of the world of today'. Then, for her remaining quarter of a century on earth, she struggled with a recurrence of religious doubts, depressions over a perpetual writing block, the 'eternal money' worries; and, for the last few years, ill-health. And yet, in an interview given six years before she died, Antonia had said it was the happiest period of her life because all the 'ghastly crises' were over. But she did admit, when the interviewer asked whether she considered her life had been a happy one, that 'interesting' might be a more appropriate description.

After reading those letters I saw clearly, with a line of vision no longer obstructed by worries about her physical, mental and material welfare, that despite her moanings – usually humorous – she was a brave woman.

But so far I had only re-trodden known ground.

The period of most of those 'ghastly crises' was the one she had been blocked from recounting in novels, though she had tried with many false starts. Of course she had often told my sister and me from too early an age most of what had happened between coming out of the asylum in 1923, and coming back to the Church in 1941, for discretion was not one of her virtues. In those eighteen years she had lost her faith; had several affairs, marriages and divorces; had two abortions and two children; and had nearly gone out of her mind a second time. But the full impact of what she had gone through, and put other people through, would only hit me when I read her unpublished notebooks, to which, as one of her literary executors, I would soon have access. She had kept these notebooks almost uninterruptedly from 1933 to 1979.

Near the end of her life, when I came across some of these variegated notebooks when tidying up for my mother, she warned me, 'You may be shocked by what you read there one day,' adding rather crossly, 'I'm afraid I can't help that!' In one of the later notebooks she had written:

I know that it seems conceited to imagine that anyone might ever want to publish any extracts. And I can most truly say that nothing in all these volumes & volumes . . . has been written with any idea of publication . . . I ought perhaps to have put in my will that they should all be burnt at my death. On the other hand, if anything of my writing survives, other writers might find things of interest to them . . . All I can say is that they are a record, absolutely spontaneous, and not in any way dressed up, of what I was thinking and feeling at the time . . . There are things in them which it would hurt Sue, and perhaps Lyndall, to read . . . And I know they are a rather horrible exposure of myself . . .

But I was not shocked or hurt by what I read so much as disturbed, for in those notebooks the dark side of Antonia's nature often took control of her pen. Reading them was like undertaking a journey to the outskirts of hell, and I often had to put them aside and go for a long walk in the country to reassure myself a safer world existed outside my mother's mind.

In her notebooks she wrote almost exclusively of her changeable attitude to herself and those close to her. Once a problem, an idea or a person became ensnared in the machinery of her mind it risked becoming an obsession and being transformed. This had happened with her father, writing, money, her jealousy over my father's mistress, some of her lovers, religious concepts and, later, with Sue. The advantage of mattering less to her was that one was in less danger of being put on trial by those advocates of God and the devil which were forever at war in her schizophrenic brain.

But the notebooks are also a chronicle of what it feels like to be losing your mind and to have it saved at the last minute by undergoing over four hard years of Freudian analysis. Through them one follows my mother's gradual return, after tempests of rage and hate, to a calmer state of mind, which enabled her to write again – for a while at least – and to practise again the religion of her childhood, despite fluctuating convictions; and to try to accept some responsibility for her children.

After the taming of her ego, she became less self-centred and more aware that others suffer and have needs too. And by the time she was in her mid-fifties she had become a fairly coherent person, though seldom free of some obsession, and would remain so for the last twenty-five years of her life, despite having to battle twice more to hang on to her reason, in 1952 and 1965.

Naturally I was curious to see any references to my half-sister and myself in the diaries. In the beginning these were conspicuous by their absence, whereas my father's notebooks of the early thirties are full of anecdotes about Sue and me as small children. The first rare mentions of us felt like blows below the belt, even though they only confirmed what I had always known in my heart.

One of the results of a self-admitted 'radical defect' in her nature as a woman made Antonia dislike motherly and wifely ways. (Her prediction to Peter Thorpe that I would be a devoted wife and mother was the most damning she could have made.) But I discovered in the notebooks that, despite her dislike of children as children, she had had an admiration for Sue as a person almost from the start, and sometimes quoted something profound Sue had said when still a small child. So I wondered whether it was what I lacked, rather than what I did, which had vexed her when I was young, and made her write the day after my sixth birthday, when she and my father had finally decided to part for good, 'I wish I could have Susan and not Lyndall.'

But it was only when I read the blunt statement 'I always resented the birth of my second child' that I realised I had been sentenced to rejection by my mother in her womb. It was not as simple as being just one more of the world's unwanted children, after all she had had an abortion seven years before I was born, and would have another one seven years later. Perhaps then, there had been something wrong not with the child but with the mother who could not accept her child before even being acquainted with it. If I could come to understand what had happened between her conception and mine, perhaps I would discover what lay behind some of those troubling words my mother had written in her notebooks, and be able to make sense of her different attitude to her two children by different fathers.

Antonia White's Parents

I do not think anyone could have had an odder pair of
parents.
Antonia White, 11 November 1970

My mother's father, Cecil George Botting, first set eyes on Christine Julia White at a tennis club in Dulwich when they were both twenty-two. He fell in love at once.

He had been as charmed by the little continental bow she had given him when they were first introduced as by her Latin good looks – an olive skin, coppery brown hair, and great dark eyes which gave her a wistful expression. The fact that she also 'talked Pessimism', a philosophy that queried the sense of an existence which led only to death, then fashionable in Germany where she had just returned from being a governess, must have made her seem an exotic flower among the English roses of a suburban tennis club.

Even though the only thing they seem to have had in common was good reason for being pessimistic, whatever attracted her to this very opposite of her dream prince that summer afternoon of 1893 would keep them together until his death thirty-six years later.

Cecil's parents were of solid yeoman and artisan stock which for generations had lived in Sussex. He was born there on the very day that an eighteen-month-old sister died of croup, consigning to him the burden of being an only child who would be cherished and cosseted by his mother far beyond infancy.

Christine was the youngest of eight. Both her parents, who were in fact related, descended from gentry who could boast a coat-of-arms—something which consoled her throughout her life for lack of wealth and position. Her mother died soon after she was born. Perhaps because she was a romantic child who shut out reality by creating a fantasy world, she claimed she had not particularly minded being motherless and was not attached to her twice-widowed father whose chief concern was for his own comfort. Henry White had a formidable temper; any request from his children for money invoked his worst rages, for he considered his duty to them ended with their education. So, like her brothers and sisters before her, his favourite, Christine, had been expected to support herself from the age of eighteen as a governess in Hamburg.

By the time she returned from Germany four years later, the weaver of fantasies who had dreamed of one day being adored by a handsome, rich and aristocratic husband, was beginning to fear she would end up unmarried like her older sisters, Connie and Bee.

When Christine met Cecil he had more reason for being pessimistic than she, having just survived the most miserable year of his life.

On coming down from Cambridge Cecil had become a 'mere usher' at a 'charnel house' – his way of describing his post as a junior schoolmaster at Colet Court, the preparatory school for St Paul's – and found it a 'most soul-destroying' profession at first. It would be his sudden love for Christine that turned a drudgery into a vocation and made him come to terms with being a schoolmaster. She became 'an object in life which I shall not count ten years of hard work too high a price to pay'.

In fact he achieved his goal of earning enough to be able to marry her in half that time by taking on private pupils as well. In throwing his heart and soul into teaching he had set himself on the path to becoming a 'brilliant, conscientious schoolmaster'. Soon, so many of his pupils had won scholarships to St Paul's that he was invited to join the staff as a junior Classics master. He was to slave away there for thirty years. By the time he took early retirement because of ill health, Cecil Botting's Greek and Latin textbooks, written jointly with A. E. Hillard, were in use in most of the public schools of England, but any money they might have made, he seems to have invested unwisely.

Cecil's mother, Adeline Jeffery (Ada), had been a short, dumpy girl, with onyx-rimmed brown eyes stuck in her doughy face 'like raisins in a scone'. It is to be hoped Fred Botting married her for her sweet nature, and not because she would come into the lion's share of Binesfield, a sixteenth-century cottage with farmlands. Though the plainest of three sisters, Ada was the only one to find a husband. The other two, Agnes and Clara, were the spinster aunts, Leah and Sophy, affectionately described in *The Lost Traveller*. Agnes, frail and bed-ridden, I remember from childhood visits to Binesfield.

Fred and Ada Botting settled down in Storrington where Cecil was born on 25 September 1870. His childhood was dull. His mother's over-protectiveness made his contemporaries ridicule him and turned him into a solitary child. By the age of seven Cecil had taken refuge in teaching himself Latin and Greek from textbooks bought from a market stall with his precious pocket-money.

His father, who ran a grocery and drapery shop in Storrington, did not idolise him as much as his mother did, yet Cecil was fonder of him and touchingly protective towards him. This may have been because of Fred Botting's handicap of having been deaf since childhood, when a schoolmaster had dealt him a savage blow first on one ear and then on the other; or because early on he discovered his father had another problem. Whenever little Cecil hid under the counter of 'Botting's Stores' pretending that he owned it, he noticed his father often knocked things over and slurred his words. This aroused ridicule in some customers. Too young to realise this odd behaviour was caused by drinking, Cecil resolved to make the world respect him and George Frederick Botting instead of laughing at them. From then on he threw himself into studying with such determination that he won a scholarship to Dulwich College, just as the family business was on the verge of bankruptcy. In order to be with their thirteen-year-old son, his parents moved to a house in London that was 'Lilliputian and in a slum', and opened a new store near the school.

Until this enterprise went bankrupt, too, Cecil had to endure the humiliation of delivering the groceries to the back doors of his school-fellows' houses. He must have been thankful when his father gave up the struggle to be a shopkeeper and embarked on the career of a clerk. But Fred's office jobs, alas, always ended in dismissal when he insulted someone in authority during one of his drinking spells, or failed to turn up for work when hungover.

Cecil never complained about his father. Freed from the grocery round, he willingly helped to pay off some of his parents' debts by charging fellow pupils half-a-crown an hour for coaching in Latin and Greek, while studying hard to achieve his ambition of a classical scholarship to Cambridge – which he won in 1889.

Away from home for the first time, and from that suffocating devotion which had been his reward for being the mainstay of a feckless father and a meek mother, another side of Cecil began to emerge when he went up to Emmanuel College.

He was befriended at once by a second-year student, Nevinson (Toby) de Courcy, who became his mentor. Still smarting from the mortifications he had suffered as a schoolboy, Cecil was as perplexed as he was flattered that someone so well-born, who was close in line of succession to an Irish peerage, should pick the son of a grocer-manqué as his protégé.

Toby was charming and witty. He had a social ease and sophistication which at once captivated gauche young Cecil and would remain his beau ideal for life. He modelled himself on a character from Meredith's *The Egoist*.

The works of Meredith, as well as of Oscar Wilde and Walter Scott, Kipling and Pater, were only some of the revelations for which Cecil had to thank Toby. Under his influence, Cecil became a gourmet with a discriminating taste in wines. And he became very clothes-conscious, indulging in an abundance of overcoats and waistcoats, silk socks and scarves, which he could ill afford and were of little help in refining his stolid plebeian appearance.

Compton Mackenzie, who was one of Cecil Botting's first pupils, referred to those coats in his autobiography: 'I can see him divesting himself of those greatcoats and hanging them up in our hall seventy years ago as clearly as I can see the words I am writing.' He also said his tutor was then 'a very plump young man with a pink face and a small fair waxed moustache'.

It was at Cambridge that Cecil, who had been raised as a pious Protestant, became first a cynical atheist, and then a tolerant agnostic. Toby, who was a cradle Catholic but did not practise his faith, occasionally took Cecil to a High Mass to enjoy the 'aesthetics of high-church rituals'. The fact that people like his parents considered Roman Catholic services as sinister and decadent, suitable only for foreigners, added a sense of daring to attending the rites.

The only time Cecil ever slacked was at Cambridge. He came down with a second instead of the first that everyone had predicted. Far worse, he left Cambridge with a 'morbid view of life' and in a state of turmoil about who he really was. An idle hedonist born in him there aroused guilt in the diligent puritan of the past who, though liberated now from any religious creed, was searching for an abstract truth.

His post-university days were further blighted by the struggle to pay off debts to Cambridge tailors and restaurateurs greater than his entire first year's salary of £120. He could not afford to have his watch repaired, a torment for so punctual a man, or his boots re-soled – 'water has entered into my boots even as the iron has entered into my soul' he told Toby.

Cecil grew more and more despondent as he realised he had to abandon the hedonist. The hedonist was used to dining out in style with a bottle of good French wine, whereas the poor schoolmaster often had to make do with a Bath bun for lunch.

In his choice of a wife, Cecil made one great and lasting concession to the hedonist. And getting engaged to Christine was one of the very few decisions Cecil ever made which upset his mother. Although she never dared to criticise his future bride to his face, she confided to everyone else that Christine was far too vain and undomesticated a young lady to make a good wife. While secretly envying her future daughter-in-law's tiny waist, she made disparaging remarks about her figure, implying it was unhealthy to be so thin and that she was not structured for child-bearing. The sallow complexion boded ill, she thought, and the lovely hands were too fragile and pampered to perform wifely duties.

Christine had taken just as immediate a dislike to her future mother-in-law but made no effort to conceal it. Everything about her repelled Cecil's fiancée, who prided herself on being an aesthete: her name; her Sussex accent; her table manners; and, worst of all, her looks. Nearing fifty, Ada was by now a homely frump. She wore a wig and her body was no longer just dumpy, but grotesque. Whenever Christine was particularly aggrieved by something Cecil had done, she would refer scathingly to his 'peasant' origins. Fortunately she liked his father and conceded that he looked 'surprisingly aristocratic'.

During their long engagement they had many lovers' tiffs. Each was quick-tempered and their natures were very different. Cecil was pathologically neat and tidy; his handwriting small and regular, his wardrobe always in immaculate order. Christine was chaotic in everything; her large handwriting sprawled over ink-splotched pages. She dressed for dramatic effect, pulling her latest acquisitions out from the untidy drawers where they lay jumbled together with old clothes she could not be bothered to mend or discard. He was meticulously punctual: she was so vague about time that she would often still be dilly-dallying over what to wear while he was already waiting impatiently in the hall, gloved and hatted, to escort her somewhere. He was scrupulously honest and never lied: she could be a fibber when altering the truth might avert a scene, and was not above a little cheating at croquet or bridge. She was full of fantasy: he had no inventive imagination. He punctilious: she scatterbrained. Almost everything about him was predictable; almost nothing about her was. Since she thought she was sublimely reasonable, quite unaware that her behaviour was often impenetrable to a logical mind, it distressed her that someone as intelligent as Cecil often failed to see her point of view.

However much Cecil loved Christine, it was with his heart more than his head. She could never replace his Cambridge soul-mate, Toby, who was everything Cecil 'would wish to be and never can be', and whom he had reassured in a rueful letter, written on the eve of the wedding day, 18 April 1898, '*Ich habe geliebt und gelebt* . . . I have never allowed *anything* to come between us and nothing ever shall.' Toby, who had been responsible for the happiest years of Cecil's life, also married later. They continued to correspond until Toby's death abroad in 1919.

After a brief honeymoon in Paris, Cecil and Christine settled down in the house in Perham Road, West Kensington, where he had been living with his parents since his promotion to nearby St Paul's. He had had the good sense to move his parents into a small flat close by before the wedding, even though it would mean the young Bottings had to take a lodger in order to pay the older Bottings' rent. It also meant they could not afford to redecorate, so poor Christine had to live with her predecessors' ugly furniture, as well as being saddled with their hideous wedding present to her and Cecil. Chosen with Ada's unerring bad taste, it was an 'uncompromising middle-class late-Victorian bed, solid in workmanship and repulsive in design; planned to bear the weight of pregnancies, long illnesses and dead bodies'.

The bed's services to travail began a year after the wedding when, on 31 March 1899, Christine was delivered of a daughter after a long and agonising labour – because she had bronchitis at the time, the doctor had refused to give her chloroform.

Three months before my mother was born, around Christmas time, Christine had tried to kill herself. Cecil had come home very drunk after a convivial evening with his old Cambridge friends and had done something which so distressed his wife that she had taken an overdose. She never revealed what it was he had done, but this episode of Cecil's drunkenness remained one of her pet grievances, flaring up at intervals to 'blaze with as fierce a flame of resentment as if the injury had been inflicted only yesterday'. From it stemmed a disillusionment with her marriage that made her return to seek in a realm of make-believe the romance missing in her life; until the day would come, after she was widowed, when she could barely distinguish reality from illusion. By the time I knew her, although she was over sixty while pretending to be half that age, what Antonia called a 'barrier of near insanity' had made it almost impossible to get through to her. But when we went to stay with her, we thought it quite fun to have to treat our grand-mother as if she were royalty and curtsey to her, though it puzzled me that anyone playing at being regal wore such a grease-stained dress with a moth-eaten piece of ermine round the collar.

The agonies of childbirth would take Christine 'down to the gates of hell' three more times in that detested bed, but only her first-born would live for more than twenty minutes.

A single first survivor, followed by babies unable to hold onto life, is typical of the progeny of a mother whose blood group is incompatible with the father's. As I, Christine's grandchild, have rhesus negative blood, it probably came through her, whereas Cecil probably belonged to a rhesus positive blood group, as do 85 per cent of the world's population. But the effects of conflicting blood groups were not known in those days, so Cecil's mother could continue to entertain her pet theory that her daughter-in-law was not built for child-bearing.

Cecil only allowed his child to be baptised a Protestant as a con-cession to his parents, for he was still a 'sincere disbeliever'. But he overruled his wife's wish to call the baby Cynthia by giving her a classical name, Eirene, to be put before Adeline, his mother's Christian name which Christine disliked as much as the person who bore it.

As soon as Eirene Adeline Botting reached school age she came to detest her name as much as her mother did, and was pleased that in private her mother called her 'Tony' – why I do not know. And when Eirene started writing and needed a pen name, she lengthened Tony to Antonia and added on her mother's maiden name, hence Antonia White.

CHAPTER 3

∾

Antonia White's Childhood

*It seems I had a shock in childhood which paralysed me
emotionally.*
Antonia White, 24 June 1938

My mother's first four years are recounted in sixteen chapters of an
unfinished autobiography published posthumously in *As Once in May*.
The most traumatic event of her childhood is described at the end of
Frost in May, where the tribulations of the young heroine, Nanda
Grey, are identical to her own at a convent school. Both books,
like her unpublished notebooks, reveal how her father's influence
overshadowed her whole life.

Cecil Botting was in his twenty-ninth year when his daughter was
born. He regarded children as a 'rather tiresome usual consequence of
marriage', though he would have liked a son to follow in his footsteps.
Having suppressed his disappointment at having a daughter, he hoped
that the ambitions he had cherished for a boy might be fulfilled by an
intelligent girl.

Antonia sensed that he was not interested in her as a child, but was
only looking ahead towards what he hoped she might become: 'He
wanted me to develop fast mentally. To obey unquestioningly, be a
good pupil, keep in my place.' She suspected he loved her only when
she pleased him, not for what she was in herself.

Her first vivid personal memory of him dated back to when she was
three: she is standing in his study being taught the first line of the *Iliad*
by ear. But other early memories of her father, more menacing and
tinged with fear, went deep in her unconscious until they were dredged
up in her thirties by a psychoanalyst.

The schoolmaster father bred in Antonia a dread of making mistakes
and a need for approval. Besides teaching her Latin and Greek so
young, he spent hours correcting her natural tendency to write

backhand. When he scolded her if she made a slip in her homework she felt sick with terror, and his rages could paralyse her into idiocy.

He became in her mind the archetype of a 'Disapproving Adult', always lying in wait to censure her, to wreck her happiness and arouse her guilt. Yet it did not stop her from behaving outrageously at times. Even as a child, while fearing his disapprobation more than anything else in the world, she took gigantic risks in wilfully doing things she knew would infuriate him, hoping, of course, he would not find out.

There was one memorable occasion when not only was her crime discovered, but she had the audacity to deny she had committed it.

At the age of four she had drawn an enormous noughts and crosses plan in the dining room, knowing full well that scribbling on the wall, even of her own nursery, was absolutely forbidden.

When her parents came into the room, Cecil demanded sternly if she were the culprit, and she was foolhardy enough to say, 'No'.

'You impudent little liar!' he thundered.

He dragged me into the study and shut the door behind us. Then, pushing me into the narrow space between the spare desk and the bookcase surmounted by the bust of Athene, he stationed himself in front of me, blocking me in. He picked up a ruler from the desk and fingered it. His face was flushed and his eyes glinted with anger yet he was wearing a curious one-sided smile as if he were in some way pleased, as well as angry. When he spoke, his voice was unexpectedly quiet.

'This time you've gone rather too far, Eirene . . . You see this ruler? . . . I'm going to take down your knickers and beat you with it.'

I was too horrified to obey. What horrified me was not the idea of being beaten though, as I had never been beaten before, I imagined it would be extremely painful, but those dreadful words, 'I'm going to take down your knickers'. No one except the maid who acted as my nurse ever saw me naked. I should have been shy of being seen with nothing on even by my mother. Certain parts of my body were 'rude' and must always be kept covered up, except in my bath, by my knickers. The thought of these most secret and shameful areas being exposed bare to the person I most revered, and not even accidentally, but by his own hand, was so shocking that I felt I should never survive such shame.

After that, my mind is a blank. Perhaps my look of horror softened his heart, perhaps my mother intervened, perhaps the doorbell rang announcing the arrival of a pupil. All I know is that he did not carry out his dreadful threat.

Antonia suspected her father would also disapprove of one of the games she played with Gérard Sinclair-Hill.

Again Antonia was four at the time: Gérard, the step-nephew of a friend of her mother, was seven and also an only child. When they first met by the Round Pond in Kensington Gardens Gérard gave Antonia a solemn kiss. She fell in love at once and was even more delighted when Gérard told her how pretty she was and suggested, 'Shall we be sweethearts?'

Their childish betrothal quickly developed into something which both of them took very seriously. It lasted for several years with many of the characteristics of an adult love affair, 'ecstasy, jealousy, mutual (and often justified) accusations of infidelity'.

In Antonia's unfinished autobiography, a whole chapter is devoted to this infant love affair which became a secret 'marriage' a couple of months after their first meeting. Their married names were Mr and Mrs John Barker, the rich owners of the grandest shop in Kensington High Street. Sometimes when they were alone in Antonia's nursery, 'Mr Barker' would suggest he and his wife should go to bed, and they would lie down together under the table. The warmth of Gérard's body and his 'ardent' kisses 'melted' Antonia into 'a state of rapture', but she could never give herself up wholly to this sensual pleasure because she was too aware of her father's presence in his study next door.

Some notes on Gérard written in a diary more than thirty years later said: 'Strong fear of displeasing him. Almost orgasm when he put his arm round me. Feeling of a rare, delicious & forbidden pleasure which my father would deprive me of if he knew about it. Always in fantasy he was tortured and mutilated & I intervened at last to save & comfort him.'

Antonia's father, even without knowing what went on in the nursery, did not approve of his little daughter's friendship with an older boy. He had upbraided his mother when she once referred to Gérard as 'Eirene's sweetheart' and asked her never to use such an idiotic expression again; and he told Christine she should find little girls for their child to play with.

When the children were not 'flirting' – the word Gérard used for the Barkers' goings-on under the table – they acted out stories they had read or made up. They also had surprisingly serious discussions for their age, one of the chief topics being another discovery of four-year-old Mrs Barker: religion.

Antonia had become fascinated by God just before meeting Gérard, when her grandparents had taken her for her memorable first visit to the family cottage in Sussex, Binesfield. There, Aunt Agnes had been shocked, and Aunt Clara astounded, that their little great-niece had only been to church once to be a bridesmaid and thought churches were just places for getting married in. They set things right by teaching her to say prayers, and explaining that God was no ordinary mortal.

She had accepted at once the existence of God and Christ. And if, on returning home, they seemed less real than at Binesfield, she was still careful about remembering to say her prayers before bed, 'because I knew I would not go to heaven if I didn't'.

But Gérard had not made up his mind whether he believed in God or not. His step-grandmother, he told Antonia, did believe in Him; his stepfather, Osman Edwards, who was a 'lot brainier than Granny', used to, but didn't any longer. This set Antonia wondering whether her father believed in God, for she was sure he was much brainier than Mr Osman Edwards and Aunt Agnes had told her that only wicked people did not believe in God. But she did not dare to ask him, because if her father had said he did not she would have been in 'an agonising quandary. His opinion would have had tremendous weight with me.'

This quandary would be resolved when Antonia's agnostic father became a convert to Catholicism in his mid-thirties.

Already Cecil Botting's word was 'absolute law' in the family. Whenever her parents had one of their fearful scenes, with Cecil 'almost foaming at the mouth, stamping and shouting', he usually won. After he had the added weight of God and the Catholic Church behind him, he was raised to omnipotence in his daughter's eyes.

Cecil Botting's conversion had come about swiftly. He was influenced by one of his favourite pupils, a beautiful nineteen-year-old Catholic, Dorothy Seaton (later to become Lady MacAlister), who had given him some Catholic Truth Society pamphlets to read in order to rectify many erroneous ideas he held about Roman Catholicism. Three months later he was seeking admission to the Catholic Church.

Cecil told his pupil he felt it nothing short of miraculous that after a fifteen-year-long 'honest search after truth' he should find himself receiving instruction in the Faith from Father Sydney Smith: 'During all those years I have been trying to open a lock & at last I have found the key.' He felt he ought to atone for years of disbelief by writing about Roman Catholicism, to allay some of the suspicions and doubts about it which then existed in many English minds. But instead, aware that he was not a writer, he set about trying to bring his own family into the papal fold.

This caused his parents much pain. But his wife went quite cheerfully into the Roman Catholic Church with him; and his small daughter was conditionally baptised a few weeks later.

When Antonia came of age spiritually at seven she was fully baptised, and thus set firmly on the thorny path she would pursue through life. 'Of course my father was "God" to me. I *still* wonder if I would have become a Catholic on my own' she wrote in middle age. How Antonia felt at being 'forcibly converted' is best described in her own words, written later:

> When I was told I was to become a Roman Catholic I was very shocked inside but of course told no one . . .
>
> I got to be quite proud of being a Catholic: it was like learning something rather difficult & of course it was gratifying to know one was *right* and everybody who wasn't a Catholic was wrong. But I felt isolated, too . . . I didn't like the few Catholics I met very much. They seemed rather condescending and it was always 'Catholics don't do things that way'. But I did genuinely like the idea of Our Lady & my guardian angel and pictures and statues and miracles happening here and now . . .
>
> I came to think of Protestants (contemporary ones) as not so much bad but *stupid*. I understood that my father had become a Catholic because he was so *clever*: if a person had a good intellect and did not want to lead a bad life he would *have* to become a Catholic.

Antonia's relationship with her mother for those first seven years was quite different from that with her father, although Christine too was strict and did not spoil her only child. In fact she did not spend much time with Antonia, who was brought up mainly by the cook and housemaid.

Her mother was much less important to Antonia than her father: 'She hadn't the power to hurt me because I didn't love her enough.'

She had started life finding Christine quite 'an agreeable companion'. In *As Once in May* there is a charming description of their almost daily shopping expeditions to the North End Road, enlivened by their pretence that they were on horseback. Antonia was about three at the time; a pretty child with a sensuous round face and long fair hair. But as she grew older, little poison darts from Ada, who doted on her only granddaughter as much as on her only son, made Antonia begin to look at her mother more critically. She adored her grandmother, and purred with pleasure every time Ada Botting called her 'Daddy's girl', yet there were times when she was ashamed of being too sympathetic a listener to those jibes against her mother.

Looking back over her life, Antonia decided her pre-school days at Perham Road were not unhappy, merely 'excessively monotonous'. As the only creature of its kind in the household she felt at times either 'oddly diminished' by the grown-ups, who appeared to belong to a different species, or 'conceitedly unique', so that she swung from despair to presumption and would continue to do so for the rest of her life.

But from the age of seven, when she started to turn 'into a critical little prig of a schoolgirl' at her Froebel school, Antonia was terrified of the impression her eccentric mother might make on her friends, and found her refusal to look or behave like other people's mothers shameful and embarrassing. This was exactly how I felt about *her* on those thankfully rare occasions when she came to take me out from boarding-school in Oxford. But, whereas she developed a superior, sneering attitude towards her mother which she later regretted – 'I only *hope* she did not realise I despised her' – my chief feeling for her, which echoed hers for her father, was fear.

Christine, living so out of touch with reality, seemed unaware that her husband considered her a beautiful nitwit, and that her child felt contempt for her. She filled her dull existence with bridge parties, losing more than she won, and reading. She also played the piano a little, leaving out the difficult passages, and occasionally made what her daughter saw as 'pathetic attempts' at painting and writing. She was long since buried when Antonia, aged sixty-seven and still ruminating about her father, accepted 'I am my mother's child as well as his,' and acknowledged that her writing side might have come from Christine: 'My father obviously wrote much better . . . But my mother's imaginative, intuitive side, her interest in people, even her romanticising were much more the qualities of a writer of fiction than my father's. She was spontaneous, unconventional, could let herself go as he never could.'

Two years after her reception into the Catholic Church, Antonia was sent to the Sacred Heart Convent in Roehampton a few miles away. Her five years there are the story of *Frost in May*. She never doubted that her father thought he was doing what was best for her, stretching his meagre means to pay her full fees as a boarder; but once again it was his will, not hers, he was satisfying with his sacrifice, and she who paid the victim's price.

Estrangement from a part of herself had already begun under her father's rule. Not only had he forced her naturally untidy backhand writing into a neat forward-slanting script, but he was always criticising her and looking for faults, in his attempt to make her become what she was not by nature, and to mould her into a perfect replica of himself.

Now the nuns of the Sacred Heart would set to work, too, to stamp out the faults in this little convert's character. They were the same ones of which she had been accused by her parents and teachers – self-wilfulness and obstinacy, untidiness, being argumentative – to which were added vanity and desire for admiration.

At Roehampton fear became her daily bread. The constant repetition that she was a sinner turned her fear of having committed some mortal sin into an obsession. The 'hair-splitting "examinations of conscience"' which the children had to make every night increased this fear. And each time Antonia went to confession came an added fear that she might commit 'sins of omission'. The terror of dying 'unprepared' and being condemned to hell for ever began to haunt Antonia.

A cruel incident connected with the breaking of Antonia's will is not recounted in *Frost in May*. It took place when she had been at Roehampton for three years, but was still haunting her, fifty years later, on the anniversary of her First Communion. At the last minute the Reverend Mother had stopped Antonia from making her First Communion with her friends on the summer feast of Corpus Christi, on the grounds that she had talked too much in the corridors. Instead she had to take it alone on 21 November, which had made her feel disgraced and different from the others whom she so desperately wanted to be like: 'I *still* can't help feeling, if I'd been an Ambassador's daughter she wouldn't have so cruelly disappointed both me and my parents.'

The nuns were so concerned with suppressing their charges' faults that they seem to have ignored two of their own: snobbery and intolerance. By never allowing Antonia to forget she was a mere middle-class convert, they created in her a yearning to belong among the élite. In spite of always being top of the class she felt inferior because she was not a well-born cradle Catholic; and because she did not excel in any of the things most praised by her schoolfellows, like being good at games or physically courageous, she developed a fervent admiration for people who 'cut a figure' or who were popular.

Next the nuns found fault with her choice of friends: 'I notice that you choose your friends rather for such superficial attributes as cleverness and humour and even for the still more unworthy and frivolous reasons of mere "good looks" and a social position above your own' one of the nuns told the lowly convert in *Frost in May*. But it was her friends who made Roehampton more bearable for Antonia, especially one who came of old and wealthy Catholic lineage, Charlotte d'Erlanger (Léonie de Wesseldorf in *Frost in May*). And since the nuns had not yet succeeded in their aim of breaking Antonia's will and re-setting it 'in God's own way', she continued her friendship with the much admired Charlotte.

Instead of wiping out this lively child's faults, the nuns merely drove them temporarily underground, where they remained life-long scourges, and taught her to hate herself.

But Antonia was not unhappy at Roehampton; any rebelliousness was directed against the convent's methods of systematically educating her 'to mistrust and check every natural impulse' and not against the Catholic Church in which she still believed passionately. In fact when she was fourteen, and her father's small resources were being drained by her mother's ill-health – Christine's fifth pregnancy had ended in a miscarriage which nearly cost her her life – so that Antonia was threatened with having to leave Roehampton, she suddenly realised that her roots were there and she had become dependent on its unique atmosphere. She pleaded so hard with her father in the holidays to let her stay on that he brought his parents back to live under his roof at Perham Road to save the rent on their flat, and persuaded the nuns to reduce their fees for Antonia's education.

He pampered her in other ways those Christmas holidays. Christine was still confined to her bed, so he asked Antonia to accompany him to hear his favourite opera *Tannhäuser* at Covent Garden. Afterwards they dined in the style of his Cambridge days. Antonia had never seen this side of her father, extravagant and indulgent. On returning home he gave her a lingering goodnight kiss, and stroked her hair while she tried to tell him what a wonderful evening it had been.

Father and daughter would soon regret that first time her will had won over his, because before the next term was over Antonia had been asked to leave Roehampton.

Already ambitious to become a writer, she was secretly writing a cautionary tale about a set of wicked people who practised nameless vices – nameless because Antonia did not know any – but who would be brought to repentance. The profligate hero, for example, was destined to become a Trappist monk. Unfortunately she had only reached the stage of painting her characters as black as possible, in order that their conversion might be the more spectacular, when Charlotte persuaded her to let her read what she had written so far. Charlotte hid the few chapters entrusted to her in a French exercise book in her desk.

On a routine inspection of desks, a nun found the manuscript.

Two days of agony followed their disappearance. For two long nights she lay awake, 'sobered and shivering', as she remembered passage after passage which would require a good deal of explanation in any nun's eye, such as the hero's having 'pressed a kiss of burning passion' on the heroine's 'scarlet mouth'. How would she ever manage to convince them that there were going to be 'magnificent repentances and renunciations' which would make her novel striking propaganda for the Faith?

But it was not to Reverend Mother Bradshaw she would have to defend her writing, but her irate father, to whom the manuscript had been sent. In *Frost in May* the scene her father made took place on Nanda's fourteenth birthday, Easter Sunday. In real life it took place on a Sunday in Lent, two days before Antonia's fifteenth birthday.

Brushing aside Antonia's attempts to explain, her father only wanted to know if his daughter had written those vile and degrading chapters without help or suggestion from anyone else. When she admitted she had, he slammed his hand on the table and exploded: 'Then I say that if a young girl's mind is such a sink of filth and impurity, I wish to God that I had never had a daughter.'

What followed is described in Nanda's experiences in *Frost in May*:

She burst into a storm of convulsive, almost tearless sobs that wrenched all her muscles and brought no relief. The whole world had fallen away and left her stranded in this one spot alone for ever and ever with her father and those awful words. She felt her mother touch her sleeve and shook her off, blindly, mechanically, hardly knowing that she was there . . . If he had stripped her naked and beaten her, she would not have felt more utterly humiliated. Never, never, could things be the same. Never again would he believe in her. Never again could she love him in the old way.

The consequences, her father told her, were to be that she must leave the convent for ever. That though she was not officially expelled, her dismissal had all the stigma of expulsion. That Mother Bradshaw had even suggested she might be removed to another house of the Order, but that he had refused.

It was Mother Bradshaw who rescued her from her father's wrath, and putting an arm round her shoulders led her away, speaking soothing words to her. And when her tears were spent, told her they had been good tears:

'I have waited for them and prayed for them . . . I have seen you growing up, intelligent, warm-hearted, apparently everything a child should be. But I have watched something else growing in you, too – a hard little core of self-will and self-love . . . I am only acting as God's instrument in this. I had to break your will before your whole nature was deformed . . . Yours is a nature with a great capacity for good and evil; you are gifted but wayward; obstinate, yet easily led. You have one quality which I think will help you through life. I believe you are fundamentally honest. But there was a quality you needed more. We tried to teach you by easy ways, but today you have had to learn it by hard ones – the quality of humility.'

Antonia did not learn all the facts about her 'expulsion' from Roehampton until seventeen years after the publication of Frost in May, by which time her father had been dead for twenty years, for it was a subject he rigidly refused to discuss even when she was grown up. In a notebook of 1950 she recounts that while talking to Mother Bradshaw at a 'Child of Mary' meeting, it came out that it had been her father who wanted her to leave Roehampton. In an interview with Mother Bradshaw, before his confrontation with his daughter, he had said, 'If this is how she is spending her time, the sooner she comes home and works with me the better.' Antonia began to suspect he had used the situation for his own ends, since he had wanted her to go to St Paul's the year before.

This probably explains why, on her return home, her father was unexpectedly genial, and made no reference to their terrible last encounter. But whatever the true facts, the manner of Antonia's leaving Roehampton took on the proportions of a crucifixion in her mind, an unjust judgement with terrible retribution, which is perhaps why in the novel it takes place over an Easter weekend, with her agony beginning on Good Friday. And one thing is certain, from that day on the relationship between father and daughter changed: each had lost trust in the other.

But even before leaving Roehampton Antonia had sensed something was changing in her. It was not just puberty, though that *had* come as a shock – she had lived through months of terror and shame because she thought the growing of pubic hair meant she was being turned into an animal as a result of inadvertently having committed some terrible sin – but an uneasy awareness that a 'mysterious stranger' was growing inside her. This is described in Antonia's second novel, *The Lost Traveller*, where the heroine, now named Clara, looking at herself in the mirror feels some part of her has broken loose and judges differently from the rest. It is someone her old self does not approve of, and she wishes she could disown this stranger in the glass.

The first time Antonia was aware of this other self was on the evening when she pleaded with her father not to make her leave Roehampton and go as a day-girl to St Paul's. Her old nature saw the sense of his reasoning, as it always did, and wanted to comply with his wishes; yet she heard herself protesting with a violence she did not consciously feel, like someone possessed. The force of that unknown voice in her vanquished only temporarily her father's almighty will, since within a few months he had his way and she was a pupil at St Paul's.

But rebellion still seethed inside her and, though she avoided open confrontations, she took to *not* doing the things that would have pleased him.

Since she knew he still entertained dreams of her becoming a school-mistress, she deliberately refused to take school-work seriously, doing only enough work in the subjects she really cared about, English and French literature, to satisfy her own pride and walk off with the prizes. Her determination not to become a schoolmarm made her develop the flighty side of her nature so firmly held at bay in the convent. Money, or rather the lack of it, began to take on an exaggerated importance for her.

At first she vaunted her Catholicism at St Paul's, festooning herself with medals and scapulars and dating her homework by the feasts of the Catholic Church. But, at heart, she felt *déclassée* and an exile, particularly when she visited Roehampton again. Although the nuns received her very kindly, the situation was false and strained: 'It was a relief when the heavy door shut behind me and I was back again in the suburban lane, in the world to which I, an outsider from first to last, really belonged.'

The medals disappeared inside her clothes. Though she still went to Mass, Antonia tried to avoid going alone with her father because she was 'painfully aware' of his presence and felt it an intrusion of privacy. She preferred her mother to be there too: 'her much looser attitude towards religion, though I priggishly despised it, was a great relief to me.' Religion, which had been the pivot of her life for seven years, came to have less and less meaning for her, yet she minded not being able to 'put God first' any more, even though she was relieved that she need no longer live in terror of discovering she might have a vocation.

Perhaps Cecil's attention was not focused on trying to alter this newly-emerging Antonia because he had had two other blows in 1914 besides his daughter's disgrace.

That year his father died at the age of seventy. Although Cecil had thought he was prepared for the worst – the old man had had a stroke three years before and had been like 'a living doll' ever since – it had been a terrible blow. That childhood love for his father had never diminished and not one of the three women in his family could console him for the loss of the only other male Botting.

And that summer war was declared.

The Great War would bring Cecil constant sorrow as the news came in of one after another of his ex-pupils having been killed.

Yet Antonia, despite the war and her fall from grace, her anxiety at the stranger she was becoming to herself and her fading beliefs, her grandfather's death and her father's despondency, was far from gloomy. 'I think the happiest time of my life, when I was least afraid of public opinion, was at St Paul's' she decided on reviewing the first half of her life in 1939.

Stranger still, her father's outburst in the nuns' parlour at Roehampton against her vulgar prose did not at first put Antonia off writing – that would only come much later with one of the severest cases of writer's block ever recorded.

At St Paul's she contributed pieces to the school magazine. She even managed to earn some money from her pen by writing advertising copy for Dearborn's, a manufacturer of beauty products, after having suggested to them ways of improving their publicity. She made a second attempt at writing a novel and, strangest of all, read it to her father 'with no misgivings'. Apparently he was 'not at all unsympathetic' about this second book, but it did not win the approval she had been hoping to regain: 'obviously he judged me by too high standards and felt that if I weren't George Meredith full grown at 16 I was no good.'

Instead of going to university as Cecil had hoped, she left school at seventeen and took a job. She always said that the only reason she left St Paul's to become a governess was because she had been 'dazzled by the prospect of £10 a term'.

Money would be of key importance to Antonia throughout her long life. As an old woman, re-reading all her old notebooks, she was shocked at how many times 'eternal money problems' came up, and her 'incessant preoccupation' and anxiety about it. She acknowledged that she was the child of both her parents in being money-conscious and extravagant; but whereas her mother wanted money only for clothes and adornment – to win admiration – her father used it more for power.

Money was an incessant topic of conversation at Perham Road. All the major rows she could remember between her father and mother were about it: 'My parents worked out their drama in terms of money.'

Cecil was certainly not a mean man. He coached many of his poorer pupils for nothing, and was conscientious about helping relatives in need. Yet his daughter maintained her father was generous only in giving people what *he* wanted them to have. He gave his wife presents, but little spending money; and gave his child what he thought she needed, but Antonia was never asked what *she* wanted and never dared to suggest what she would like.

As a child Antonia had often been upbraided by her father about over-spent pocket money. He always made her save any money she was given as presents from friends or relatives, depriving her of the pleasure of going with her mother to blow them in the North End Road. She developed a conviction that her father did not want her to have money, whereas he was probably trying to discourage her from becoming an overspender who would then be burdened by the misery of being in debt, as he had been after Cambridge. But he did not achieve this for, as Antonia was the first to admit, she was never ever able to save, and was in debt for most of her life.

'What does money most represent to me?' Antonia once asked

herself. The answer was 'freedom'. It also gave her a sense of adequacy. Yet if she had any money, she seemed compelled to get rid of it by overspending, so that it never bought her relief from anxiety. She added, 'It is very exciting to me to make money by my own efforts.'

Antonia took that first job to taste freedom, but did not shake the dust of Perham Road from her feet for long. After six months as a governess, she came to live at home again, but continued to earn her own living, first by teaching, then as a clerk in the Ministry of Pensions. When she was eighteen Dearborn's gave her a regular contract for £250 a year to write advertisements – more than the entire amount her parents had had to live on during their first year of marriage. As she was also beginning to have stories accepted in magazines under the name of Antonia White, she soon realised she could afford to pay her way through acting school. Since she admitted that she was 'a singularly poor actress, feeble of voice and constrained of gesture', this decision seems to have come once again from a desire to defy her father who 'simply hated' her acting 'if there was anything like an audience'. He had once made a furious scene after she had performed in a 'little show for charity', and had said 'I would rather see you dead than an actress', though the next day 'he was ruefully sweet, almost loverlike' towards her.

Soon after starting at the Academy of Dramatic Art (now RADA) in 1919, Antonia fell romantically in love with a fellow student, Philip Reeves. Up till then she had only had what she called 'silly flirtations', though she had once had a proposal of marriage from a medical student, but when he had tried to explain the facts of life she had fled in alarm, preferring to preserve intact her hazy convent-girl notions about what went on between men and women. Yet one of the things she dreaded most was remaining a spinster.

Philip Reeves, on whom the character of the actor Stephen Tye is based in Antonia's third novel, *The Sugar House*, was the first man for whom Antonia felt sexual desire. But they did not have an affair, partly because he was less attracted to her than she to him.

Antonia abandoned the Academy with two terms of her course still to run. She left because she could not resist the temptation of an offer of a small part in a play called *The Private Secretary* that was to go on tour. Life on that tour in the early 1920s is described in an essay called 'The First Time I Went on Tour'; and in *The Sugar House* she compares the closeness and rivalries of the players on tour to the 'changing feuds and friendships' at Roehampton: 'Here, as there, she found herself both accepted and a little apart. She was beginning to wonder if there were any place where she did perfectly fit in.'

Before going on tour Antonia had met a young man at a theatre club who had been courting her assiduously ever since. His name was Reginald Green-Wilkinson. She was flattered by the attentions of this gangling, overgrown schoolboy, a year younger than she was, who might one day inherit a fortune, and became very fond of him as well as being gratified by his dog-like devotion.

Reggie was the black sheep of his family, despised by his father, the despair of his adoring mother. Sweet natured and unambitious, he had no desire to enter any of the family businesses. Instead, being mildly stage-struck, he hung around theatrical companies in the hope of getting a job to eke out his allowance, which was minimal because his family were trying to curb his drinking. But he continued to drink, merely getting into debt to pay for it; so his father, sick of his son's requests for money, packed him off to South America to work for an uncle.

Reggie was heart-broken at leaving Antonia with whom he was by then in love. She went to see him off at the station. Just as the train for Southampton was pulling out of the station he called out of the window, 'Will you marry me?', and she heard herself screaming back above the hissing steam, 'Yes!'

All the way home she felt elated. Now she could show her father that she was not going to remain a spinster. As a child he had kept rubbing it in that the reason she must study hard to become a schoolmistress was that she might never marry, and since she thought then that women were married entirely for their looks, she assumed that meant that she was not attractive. She had become even more convinced she was plain at Roehampton because the nuns constantly called attention to her defects, and told her she had ugly teeth so that she became afraid to smile.

Reggie's simple directness had always moved Antonia. She hoped against hope that one day she might feel something more passionate than sisterly affection, for he filled the gap of the younger brother whom as a lonely only child she had always wanted. At most she loved him protectively, though he towered above her in spite of his slouch. His face had a curiously 'unfinished look', irregular features, and deep-set dark blue eyes that drooped downward, giving him a hangdog expression.

By accepting Reggie's proposal, Antonia had won back her father's approval and made up for all the pain she had caused him over the past seven years, for Cecil liked his future son-in-law. He was impressed by his having been to Eton and his double-barrelled name, and the fact that one of his uncles was a peer, and another was a well-known aeroplane manufacturer. Christine was less enthusiastic; her female intuition sensed something was wrong, but she could give no logical reason for preventing the wedding from taking place, nor could she stop her husband from spending far more than he could afford on it when Reggie returned from South America.

Marriage and Madness

*Love of the theatre was the one thing Reggie and I had
in common.*
Antonia White, 15 September 1937

To Antonia, her wedding on 28 April 1921 in Brompton Oratory
seemed as unreal as a dream. She walked up the aisle 'only hazily
aware of organ music, turning heads and the candle-lit altar at the
foot of which stood a red-headed man, so unfamiliar in his formal
clothes that at first she did not recognise him'.

But despite his formal apparel the familiar unkempt Reggie was
definitely there. In the wedding photograph his tie is crooked, his
trousers too short, and his huge feet, twice the length of hers, splayed
apart. Antonia, looking far older than her twenty-two years, barely
reaches his shoulder. There is something innocent and touching about
their timid smiles and awkward stances; as if they are playing at getting
married. In fact, as they stood side by side during the ceremony,
stumbling over their vows so that the old priest patiently had to keep
prompting them, she felt they were 'like children who have forgotten
the answers in catechism class'. She had to remind herself there was
nothing childish in the solemn promises they were making in front of
God, and thought with panic, 'Do we really know what we are doing?'

It would soon become clear that neither of them knew then what
they were doing.

Antonia's knowledge of the facts of life was still fairly vague.
Whenever her mother had tried to bring up the subject, she waved it
aside, pretending to know more than she did. She told me that while
she was changing into her going-away clothes after the reception, her
mother had come into the room. Christine then told her that something
so appalling was going to happen that night, she could only pray to
God and make sure there was a glass of milk and biscuits by her bed
to console herself with when it was all over.

Although she knew her mother often over-dramatised, Antonia set off with dread for her honeymoon. And the atmosphere of the country house, Horsley Towers, lent to them by one of Reggie's aunts for their honeymoon, heightened this feeling of impending doom. Reggie was uneasy too.

Their first evening as husband and wife is described in Antonia's short story, 'The Rich Woman', where the young couple feel they are actors in a play being watched by the servants.

After dinner, tired as they both were, Reggie insisted they should dance. With limbs loosened by champagne, she found herself enjoying dancing with him, and echoed his wish that it would be wonderful to go on all night; but tiredness finally overcame her.

When Antonia said she must go to bed, for a moment Reggie had looked almost angry; but he quickly recovered his smile and kissed her on the cheek saying, 'Run along, my darling old thing. I'll just go and have a nightcap. Positively only one.'

This is my mother's account to me of what then happened.

She went up to bed and waited in a state of rigid apprehension for Reggie to join her; but tired out from the strain of the long and emotional day, sleep overcame fear.

She was awakened by Reggie's stumbling against the bed. He gave her a bleary-eyed glance before noticing the milk and biscuits on the bedside table. 'Biscuits. Oh good!' he mumbled, and ate the lot before clambering, fully dressed, on top of the bed and falling asleep. Antonia didn't know whether to feel relieved or annoyed at having been cheated of the experience her mother had predicted would befall her that night. 'You see, darling,' she told me, 'although I was petrified, I was also curious to know what happened. I had only the haziest ideas of the facts of life, although I had read Thomas Hardy and other authors which had given me some intimation of what went on between men and women. But I had no idea what had to go where for children to be conceived, and had some vague idea that it was connected with some particular way of kissing. And of course I'd never seen a naked man, except in statues, and knew nothing about – er – *phallus erectus*.'

After three months of marriage, Antonia still knew nothing about *phallus erectus*. Whether it was drink that made Reggie impotent, or whether he drank because he was impotent, the result was the same: within a short time they were both wretched. Soon they would add to their miseries by being in debt.

The main reason for their getting into debt was that, on Antonia's insistence, they had rented a tiny furnished house in Chelsea, opposite the Catholic Church on the corner of Cheyne Row, which was way above their means. Thirty-eight Glebe Place is the 'sugar house' in Antonia's novel of that name; she calls herself Clara, and Reggie is Archibald Hughes-Follett, though, according to Antonia, the portrait of him was 'idealised'. *The Sugar House* had the worst and most contradictory reviews of any of her novels when it came out in 1952, yet it was the author's favourite because she felt it portrayed so exactly her mood during her marriage to Reggie.

Antonia's choice of accommodation turned Cecil Botting's contentment to disapproval again. He considered Chelsea a hive of iniquity, where free love flourished between long-haired artists and shingled flappers, and he could not understand why West Kensington, where a large flat would have cost half the price, was not good enough for the young married couple.

Antonia had chosen Chelsea precisely because its pleasant streets of variegated houses did not remind her of Perham Road and the drably uniform terraces of West Kensington. And it was the thought of those very artists which had lured her to the area because of a romantic notion that to live surrounded by painters and writers working away in their studios might be an incentive for her to become a serious writer one day, instead of just being a 'messy amateur'. In anticipation of this she had put down 'authoress' as her profession on her marriage certificate.

But her ambition to become a serious writer was not realised while Antonia was married to Reggie; in fact her muse dried up so completely that she could not write even one story for a magazine. Her contribution to their inadequate income came from her advertising copy for the faithful Dearborn's – except when she played a small part in a Komisarewsky production at the Stage Society. Reggie soon lost the job he recorded on their marriage certificate – 'secretary, Anglo Continental Film Studios' – as he would all his future jobs, which ranged from bit parts on stage to driving a delivery van for Lyons. When he came home after having been fired, he was either drunk and incoherent, or hungover and penitent.

The only thing that consoled them for their failures was playing with toy soldiers, a passion Antonia had had from early childhood. They kept a small attic room exclusively for this, leaving their opposing armies arrayed there in permanent battle.

The summer which followed their wedding was unusually hot. The little house became claustrophobic as one airless day after another turned it into a 'stifling box'. Antonia grew more and more tired and languid until she became so apathetic that she could not bring herself to get dressed, but sat about in a dressing-gown with her hair loose and unbrushed.

She was incapable of writing: even advertising copy no longer came easily. Despondent at her inability to write, which continued long after the heatwave was over, Antonia bought a stout black notebook, exactly like one her father used to record his lecture notes in, and began to keep a secret diary.

Into this notebook went 'reflections on her own character, severe exhortations to herself, scraps of conversation overheard in the street, descriptions of rooms or faces; dreams, speculations about religion and life, curious names which she might one day use in a story'. It was one of those she was persuaded to destroy in 1948, but she says it had soon degenerated into 'mere maunderings of self-analysis and self-pity'.

As summer turned to winter, Antonia felt more isolated than ever before, yet if old friends wanted to visit her, some obscure impulse drove her to find excuses as to why it was not possible. The more she was alone, the more she became conscious of her own emptiness. Like Clara in *The Sugar House*, she looked into mirrors to make sure she still existed, and was always horrified at how vacant her expression had become.

Antonia, who till now had had a normal figure, began to grow fat, which made her parents hope she was pregnant. When she assured her mother she was not, Christine said, 'I hope you're not doing anything the Pope wouldn't approve of, darling.' Although this remark puzzled Antonia, who knew nothing about birth control and had no need of it anyway, she had answered sharply, 'Of course not!'

Antonia's state grew worse. Like Clara she wandered aimlessly about the house, 'stopping now and then to stare for long spells at an old newspaper whose meaning she could not take in, smoking cigarettes, mechanically combing her hair and eating, if she ate at all, with a strange compulsive greed; stuffing herself with anything she could find; sponge cakes, chocolates, old heels of bread and cheese, like a ravenous child'.

Reggie alternated feeling remorse and annoyance over his young wife's strange behaviour: she swung from compassion to resentment over his. But she cast aside any thought of leaving him; partly because, as a Catholic, she thought she was committed for life, and partly because she had nowhere to go. It would have been too humiliating to go back to Perham Road: to have to face her father's questions and her mother's triumphant sympathy.

When she visited her parents, if Reggie was not too drunk or hungover to come with her, they made a huge effort to appear a happy couple. Having put some clothes in order, she would dress and make up with as much care as if she were preparing for a stage part, and he would hide his usual slovenliness by shaving and putting on a clean shirt. Their disguise was so convincing that during these visits Antonia momentarily managed to distance the fear that her life was broken, and even felt a glimmer of hope that her state of 'paralysed drifting' might not go on for ever. But as soon as she re-entered the front door of 38 Glebe Place, she was trapped again by isolation and wretchedness.

Before Antonia had sunk so low, Reggie and she had sometimes pulled themselves together enough to dine with friends at some cheap dive in the King's Road. On one of these occasions they were introduced to a man who now would act as a catalyst in her life.

Eliot Seabrooke was a painter, nearly twice Antonia's age, whose morals confirmed Cecil Botting's worst fears of what a Chelsea artist was like. In *The Sugar House*, under the name of Marcus Grundy, he is described as tall and heavily built with a lithe body; he had an impressive head with crow's feet round his grey eyes, and there was an 'oddly youthful delicacy' about his plump, full-moon face.

On meeting Antonia again by chance in the street, he noticed at once something was wrong, and suspected her marriage was not going well. Although her looks had deteriorated rapidly those past few months, she was still attractive enough to arouse a seducer's instincts. He suggested she should come to his studio one day, saying he would like to do a portrait of her.

She was delighted that the first real artist she had met should find her interesting enough to want to paint her, and dreamt of this leading her into the world of art at last. But after Antonia walked into his studio, she was soon disillusioned. Eliot wanted to talk about love, not art, and having made one quick sketch, set about trying to seduce her.

Eliot Seabrooke did not seduce Antonia, not because she had been unwilling to get into his bed, but because he took pity on her hysterical sobbing and withdrew from the fray, angry and astonished, when he found she was still a virgin. However he had reawakened such strong feelings in her – feelings that had lain dormant since the time she had been in love with Philip Reeves – that when she calmed down, it was she who wanted Eliot to kiss and embrace her again. But he had the decency not to persist in making love to her: instead he made them both a cup of tea.

He told her that, even though she was a Catholic, her marriage could be dissolved. Until then she had not known that the non-consummation of a marriage was grounds for an annulment – indeed she still did not fully understand what the word 'consummation' meant.

She walked back to the 'sugar house' in a state of dismay and turmoil. Reggie, on seeing her swollen face, asked what was wrong. He admitted he had known for some time they had grounds for an annulment, but had been too afraid of losing her to say so.

For the first time since they had married Reggie now made a decision. Though she pleaded against it, convinced she could force him back into being the child she had always dominated, he insisted that they must part.

Reggie left Glebe Place that very evening. She spent the night alone in the house she had once so desired and had now come to hate, too shattered to weep or pray.

The next morning she telephoned her father and asked him to come and fetch her.

Antonia was surprised by the ease with which she returned to her childhood home almost as if she had never left it. The punctual meals and the routine chores she had always found so dull prevented her from falling into the drifting apathy of the past months. But she lacked all desire and had become incapable of thought.

Her father treated her as if she were an invalid convalescing from an illness. Sometimes when he spoke to her, a word or phrase would lodge in her brain and go on repeating itself like a record when the needle sticks, distracting her from hearing the rest of what he was saying. The only time she reacted to something her father said was when he suggested she might like to coach some of his younger pupils since she was doing nothing with her time. The very idea brought back all her old terror of being a schoolmistress, and she burst into tears. They were the first ones she had shed since leaving Reggie, and stopped Cecil from ever repeating that suggestion again.

The only other time she felt any emotion during that period was the last time she saw Reggie. She had to identify him through a glass door in a lawyer's office as the husband against whom she was bringing proceedings in the nullity suit. On returning home she developed a blinding headache.

Later Antonia felt no stress while being examined by two court doctors to check that her marriage had truly not been consummated; in fact she was so completely detached emotionally from what was going on that her body no longer seemed to have any connection with her. But a headache as violent as the one she had felt after seeing Reggie struck her afterwards, and all the way home her right temple throbbed painfully to the words 'virgo intacta, virgo intacta'.

Antonia had been living at Perham Road in this impassive state for many weeks, when two men came into her life who pulled her out of the void into the world of the living.

The first was Eric Earnshaw-Smith. With him she would have an 'extraordinary relationship' for the next fifty years. The other was a man called Robert, whose surname she never mentions. In the three weeks she knew him he would be the innocent cause of a terrible upheaval that overshadowed the rest of her life. Both are described in her last novel, *Beyond the Glass*, where Eric is Clive Heron, and Robert is Richard Crayshaw.

Antonia had already met Eric briefly when she was at drama school. He had been a friend of her first love, Philip. He worked in the Foreign Office and was a cat-like person who walked by himself, hating commitments and detesting intrusion, yet Antonia had always felt a 'peculiar pleasure' at seeing him whenever they ran across each other.

On this particular October afternoon in 1922, when twenty-three-year-old Antonia chanced to meet Eric taking his regular Saturday constitutional, he paid her the rare compliment of inviting her back to his rooms. She wondered whether it was wise to go alone to a man's house, but accepted because she sensed that there would be no danger of Eric behaving like Eliot Seabrooke, for he was 'neither masculine nor feminine' in manner or looks. He is described in her writings as being tall and 'preternaturally slender' with a small and pale 'delicately featured' face which seemed too frail to support the weight of the pince-nez that protected his 'childishly blue' eyes. And that is exactly how I remember him from my childhood.

They spent the afternoon listening to classical music on his wind-up gramophone and discussing religion, on which they disagreed – he thought God was 'an unnecessary hypothesis' – and cats, about which they were in absolute agreement. From then on Eric became the one person with whom Antonia could discuss anything – 'he always chose the topic' – and he would have more influence on her mind than anyone else, including her father.

At the end of the evening, by which time he knew of her separation from Reggie, and they had agreed that as fellow neurotics they would henceforth treat each other with cat-like circumspection, he put out a tentative suggestion to take her to a party in a few days' time – with the proviso of course that if at the last minute he could not face it the invitation would be withdrawn.

Fortified by a whisky beforehand, Eric took Antonia to the party. There she met Robert.

Robert was an army officer in a Scottish regiment stationed in Ireland. He was on a month's leave and staying with his sister who was giving the party for him in her Chelsea studio.

When Eric and Antonia walked into the candle-lit studio the guests were seated on the floor listening to a Beethoven sonata. Shortly after lowering herself onto a cushion she became aware that someone was trying to attract her attention, yet everyone was facing the pianist and no one was looking at her. She tried to concentrate on the music, but someone kept impinging on her mind. After a while she tried throwing back a stern thought to this intruder, 'I don't *want* to be disturbed', and was astonished to hear an inner voice, a man's, say teasingly, 'You may as well give in. My will's stronger than yours.'

When the sonata was finished, a stranger helped her to her feet. Although they had never met before, she recognised him from a photograph of an extraordinarily good-looking young subaltern with a slightly mischievous air Eric had shown her not long before. She also knew without doubt that he was the 'intruder' in her mind. It was Robert.

They danced. They fell in love. Within a few hours Robert had thrown away the ring his Irish fiancée had given him.

A physical and psychic rapport between Antonia and Robert had erupted with such force that they did not need words to communicate. If they parted without planning their next meeting, she became so expert at their game of telepathy that he had only to will her and she went instinctively to the right place at the right time. A sense of heightened perception she had felt the moment they danced together, remained with her when they were apart. The most trivial words and objects were charged with extraordinary significance: everything had its own language and conveyed a secret meaning. She felt free of anxiety when he was not around, and '*completely* alive' when they were together, driving in sunlight or fog, dancing at the Palais, or 'wrestling' in her father's study. Her religion 'dropped back into unquestioning faith'. Every morning she arose with a lighter body; in three weeks she lost over a stone.

At the end of those three weeks she had gone out of her mind.

When my mother first told me this story I was eight. I thought it meant that if you are too happy you go out of your mind. Although, when I grew up, I realised that happiness was not the cause of my mother's madness, somewhere I must still fear it, for I find it almost impossible to feel great joy.

Antonia and Robert's brief encounter, and her madness, are described in *Beyond the Glass*. While working on the book in 1953–4, Antonia found writing the first half the usual hard labour; but as soon as she came to the part about Robert it seemed as if someone else was writing it. She worked with a speed and intensity she had never known before: 'it was almost like being possessed & not consciously working it out.'

Of course there is something abnormal about the state of being in love, but reviewing how she had felt about Robert, Antonia realised later she had been manic at the time. One of the symptoms had been a 'wild and utterly baseless optimism about money – telling my father that I'd allow him £1000 a year'; another was delusions about writing. She was certain she only need convey this 'dazzling new intensity of vision' in a book to write a unique masterpiece.

The moment of Antonia's going out of her mind is also described in 'The House of Clouds', a short story written seven years after the event – 'no pain whatever in writing it, in fact it took the "haunting" away'.

This is what happened. Robert had to leave to spend a few days with his parents in Wiltshire. The evening before, they dined as usual with his sister, Dorothy, and her lover in the studio. After dinner, Antonia had suddenly walked out of the house, gone down a narrow passage that led to the Thames, and walked into the water without knowing why, for she was still in a state of perfect bliss. Luckily Robert had followed her and grabbed her from behind before she drowned – for my mother, to her chagrin, had never managed to learn to swim.

The evening of the next day, after Robert had left, Antonia behaved oddly again. She was at home, lying on the sofa, when she fell into a cataleptic state in which she knew that she was 'being mysteriously prepared for something'. Suddenly she felt impelled to go to Dorothy's studio. Dorothy and her lover were about to have dinner when she arrived; they asked Antonia to join them, but she sat apart by the fire, and asked for bread and salt to keep away evil spirits. She sat there in silence for some time, then, suddenly, became hysterical, crying and babbling like a child. They put her to bed and telephoned her parents.

Antonia lay on the little camp bed in which Robert had so recently slept, alternating delirious ravings with singing an incantation to keep the evil spirits at bay. In that bed she also had her last psychic contact with him. 'Take care!' she had cried as her mind's eye saw Robert's car hurtling down a country lane towards an oncoming lorry. The crash came. She screamed; but soon calmed down on seeing him climbing out from the wreckage. 'Thank God he's not hurt,' she told Dorothy, who was sitting beside her waiting for the Bottings to arrive. It was later confirmed that Robert had had a collision at that time; his car had been badly damaged, but he had been unharmed.

Her father arrived with the family doctor. To her he appeared as a monk in a brown habit. When he tried to kiss her, she pushed him away, choked by a physical horror of this monk who she knew was really the devil in disguise. The doctor could not get through to her either. She talked to him in a child's voice about her money-box, but became violent when he tried to give her an injection of morphine. They stayed with her all night. The next morning she was still confused and raving, so they moved her to a nursing home.

After a day or two, when her condition had not improved, her father signed the certificate of insanity that committed her to a public asylum for the insane – Bethlem, the Hospital of St Mary of Bethlehem, better known by its notorious name of Bedlam.

There seemed to be no clinical explanation for Antonia's madness. Her parents were told by Dr Percy Smith, who saw her first on 16 November 1922, that she might never recover.

In fact Antonia was out of her mind for less than a year. Most of that time she was experiencing intense fantasies, some hellish, some beatific, into which any real-life happenings, such as being force-fed through the nose, were absorbed. An example of this comes in 'The House of Clouds', where she describes being trapped in the padded cell:

> The only thing she was sure of was that the rubber room came after she had been changed into a salmon and shut up in a little dry, waterless room behind a waterfall. She lay wriggling and gasping, scraping her scales on the stone floor, maddened by the water pouring just beyond the bars that she could not get through. Perhaps she died as a salmon as she had died as a horse, for the next thing she remembered was waking in a small, six-sided room whose walls were all thick bulging panels of grey rubber.
>
> She knew without being told, that the rubber room was a compartment in a sinking ship, near the boiler room, which would burst at any minute and scald her to death. Somehow she must get out. She flung herself wildly against the rubber walls as if she could beat her way out by sheer force. The air was getting hotter. The rubber walls were already warm to touch. She was choking, suffocating . . .

Once she was Lord of the World; another time she was a flower growing in a stream. The water flowing through her flower throat made her sing a repetitive little song, 'Kulallah, Kulallah'.

After a few months, between the changing hallucinations, a small patch of reality became permanent: in it people and objects remained stable. The nurses grew familiar; some of what they said even made sense, though she wished they would not keep calling her by a name she was sure belonged to someone else: Eirene.

Then one spring day she noticed the pattern on the rim of a plate formed perplexing words: BETHLEM HOSPITAL. Now that she could read, the nurses lent her magazines, and she was even more puzzled to see they were dated 1923, for she was sure it was 1922. With her mind working overtime trying to understand who and where she was, she remembered she had once had a father and a home. With great difficulty, for the words she formed kept coming out mirror-wise and she had to remind herself that in the world where her father lived people wrote the other way round, she sent him a short note asking him to try and find her. She had no idea that he had been coming regularly to Bethlem, though she had often been too violent for him to be allowed near her.

By August 1923 Antonia was allowed out of Bedlam, on the

condition she did nothing strenuous and went to bed not later than ten. Her father came to fetch her, and on the way home in the taxi Cecil and Antonia 'hugged and kissed each other like reunited lovers'. The next day he took her to Binesfield.

After the excitement of rejoining her family calmed down, there were moments when she wished she was back in that world 'beyond the glass', inhabited by that other self she had first glimpsed in the mirror as an adolescent, because her oldest tormentor, boredom, had returned with renewed intensity. 'In the asylum I was never bored,' she claimed in one of her notebooks.

Her family tried to keep her amused by endless games of croquet and walks, but they refused to discuss the only thing that really interested her: Robert. The most she managed to extract from her parents, who always changed the subject, was that he had come to see them as soon as he had heard she was in an asylum, but on learning that she would probably never recover her sanity, had asked to be stationed abroad. They denied knowing his whereabouts. They also did not tell her he had married the girl he had been engaged to before they met. She only learned that from Eric much later.

In notes Antonia made for her never-to-be-finished fifth novel, she said of Robert's desertion, 'Queer. I seem to have *accepted* Robert's disappearance.' She also wrote, 'Sense of a totally blank future,' but clarified this as being in no way similar to the 'dead' state she had been in before meeting Robert.

Cecil Botting indulged his twenty-four-year-old daughter after she returned from the asylum. He heaped presents on her, and when they returned to London he satisfied one of her oldest childhood dreams: he bought her a riding-habit and paid for her to have riding lessons. He also allowed her to attend Spanish classes and to go out with men he considered safe escorts, as long as she respected the ten o'clock curfew imposed by the Bethlem doctor.

Eric came into this category. More surprisingly so did a man she had met at the riding stables. His name was Dougal and he had a limp.

Looking back, Antonia wondered what had duped her father into accepting Dougal so meekly. Perhaps it was partly because the younger man was an accomplished flatterer, and partly because Cecil was impressed by his bravery in the war, where, he told them, he had been seriously wounded, hence the limp. Cecil soon came to hope his daughter would marry Dougal, who had proposed to her, when her annulment came through.

When Antonia agreed she might one day marry Dougal, she did not love him. Robert's desertion had convinced her she would never fall in love again. She had only become interested in Dougal when she learned he was 'on the fringes of Fleet Street'. He was amusing to go out with and told many fascinating stories about the war which made it clear he was a man of courage. She called him her 'wounded hero'.

One night, after Dougal had dined at Perham Road, he and her father stayed talking until so late that Cecil invited him to spend the night. Antonia had long since gone to bed. When Dougal crept into her bedroom wearing one of her father's old dressing gowns, she thought she was dreaming, since she had no idea he was still in the house. But after he climbed into her bed it became clear he was no phantasm.

Antonia never succeeded in explaining to herself why she had not protested at what he did next. She had resisted Robert, her greatest love whom she had desired so passionately, so why did she let this intruder make love to her in her father's house? 'I can only say, the whole thing suddenly seemed to me so meaningless that I felt it didn't matter whether I resisted or not.'

The morning after losing her virginity, Antonia woke with the sense of uneasiness which follows an unpleasantly realistic dream. At breakfast she noticed distasteful things about Dougal; and at their next encounter she found him so repellent that she refused to let him make love to her again. Two weeks later she received a letter from a woman who claimed to be Dougal's wife, saying she had just borne his baby, and warning Antonia he was a beguiler. She said he had never fought in the war because he was a cripple who had had polio as a child. Antonia refused to see him again.

'Dougal. The liar: the man who got me on false pretences. The first physical lover. I conceived a child at once,' states a diary entry of Antonia's in 1952.

A doctor confirmed Antonia's suspicion that she might be pregnant. Her first reaction had been of 'utter panic' that her father would have to know. This made Antonia do something she rarely did: she confided the dreadful news to her mother. Her mother courageously relayed it to her father. The scene he made, Christine told her daughter, was the most violent she had ever witnessed, but his rage was all directed against

Dougal, and not against Antonia. Had he known his whereabouts, she really believed he would have killed Dougal.

When Antonia heard that her father did not blame her for the situation, she faced it calmly, indeed, she was surprised by her lack of emotion.

Twenty-five years later she recounted in her notebook what then happened.

Her father was in 'a terrible state' and said she could not have the baby at home. He wanted to send her to Spain to have it secretly: 'what was to happen to it, I don't know'. Antonia could not face going there alone and through Eliot Seabrooke met a woman, Wyn Henderson, who knew an abortionist in London.

Although Cecil officially opposed her decision to abort, he lent her the money to pay for a course of injections to induce a miscarriage. He must have known that he was committing a sin almost as grave as murder for a Catholic, and risking eternal damnation; but, according to Antonia, he told her it was her responsibility and she who was committing a grave sin. I think my mother put more blame on her father than was fair; he had already suffered so much on her account. She admitted he was sweet to her when the pain started – 'If he had been my husband, he could not have been kinder' – and accompanied her to the nursing home to have the miscarriage.

Antonia was very upset when they told her it had been a boy:

> I was a practising Catholic then but I did not seem to feel guilt about having had an abortion but just human sorrow because I had killed my little boy.

Yet Antonia remembers feeling 'perfectly serene and unguilty' after the abortion in March 1924. She read Proust and felt 'completely free' in her mind. However, she did go to Confession, something she had refused to do beforehand because she had feared a priest might arouse her 'religious moral conscience'. Only much later would her conscience trouble her: 'Of course the guilt is mine' she wrote at the age of fifty-one.

Dougal, like Reggie and Robert, joined those she would never see again except in dreams.

In April her father took her to Paris. Antonia described their short stay there alone as 'a sort of honeymoon' and wondered if it was a reward for not having kept her child. On that holiday she tried to bring up the subject of their final scene at Roehampton. He refused to discuss it and she never dared to mention it again.

On their return Cecil confessed that, while she had been in Bedlam, Reggie's father had given him £500 for her. When Cecil handed over the money, he deducted half for what he claimed was 'compensation' for expenses connected with the asylum, and the cost of her stay in Paris, and the full £30 fee for the abortionist.

Antonia continued to be in the state of mind she had been in since coming out of the asylum: 'light-hearted and detached, not exactly cynical but not taking herself very seriously and incapable of any violent emotion.' She went back to her Spanish classes, but not to riding. She started to earn money again with copywriting and renewed her friendship with Eric Earnshaw-Smith.

Eric introduced her to a friend of his from Cambridge days called Alan Walker, who was in the Diplomatic Service.

Encouraged by Eric and her father, who approved of Alan, they got engaged. But while motoring through Italy with her and Eric that summer, he threw such a tantrum about some minor mishap that Antonia realised she could never marry such a 'peculiar character'. She broke off the engagement to Alan and became engaged to Eric instead.

Antonia had always held Eric in awed admiration. When he asked her to marry him, she was too honoured to refuse, brushing away a fleeting doubt that it was 'against nature', although he had not yet explained he was a homosexual. She had always been convinced he was a confirmed bachelor, which in most ways he was and would continue to be after their marriage.

CHAPTER 5

ॐ

Marriage and Folly

My relationship with him [Eric] was unique . . . a kind
of mental blood-tie if there is such a thing . . . I really
married him in order to be able to see enough of him!
Antonia White, 8 September 1974

When Antonia married Eric Earnshaw-Smith in the Church of the
Holy Trinity, Brook Green, in the spring of 1925, after the annulment
of her marriage to Reggie had at last been sanctioned by the *Sacra
Rota*, she finally left her father's house for good. She was just twenty-six
at the time, and Eric was nearly thirty-two.

Their 'Platonic' marriage, for they would never attempt a sexual
relationship, began very happily, although they were extremely un-
alike: 'he is almost all pure intelligence and wit, the most civilised,
balanced and lucid person I have ever met, whereas I am half a romantic
barbarian.'

Apart from being a *mariage blanc*, the Earnshaw-Smiths' marriage
was unusual in many ways. Neither was possessive of the other: he
never objected if she went to parties or dined out alone with other
men; she respected his privacy if he wanted to spend an evening at
home in male company. Together they went to theatres, concerts and
films.

When Eric brought his bride to Paultons Square to live with him
and his black cat, Mr Pusta, she became his 'other pussy cat', and
purred with pleasure. And she treated him as a cat too, never invading
his territorial rights and 'allowing him to go through the rituals
which surrounded all his actions'. Antonia was not allowed to change
anything in the rooms without Eric's permission; and the way the
household functioned was dictated by him – which was just as well
since she was untidy and undomesticated even when in her right mind.

Their domestic routine seldom varied. They breakfasted at home while Eric read *The Times*. Since each worked – shortly before marrying, Antonia had landed a full-time job as a copywriter in W. S. Crawford's advertising agency, and Eric was still in the Foreign Office – they did not see each other again until the evening. Then, having changed, they would have a pre-dinner drink. If neither had a social engagement, they dined together in a little restaurant nearby. Over dinner Eric read the evening paper – handing his wife the pages he had finished with – and only with the arrival of coffee was any conversation allowed to start. Back under their own roof, Eric would either continue their conversation, if he thought it worthy of pursuit, or he would choose a record with great care, place two chairs at the exact distance from the gramophone to ensure the best sound effect, and spend the rest of the evening listening to music with her. Before they retired to their separate bedrooms, Mr Pusta was given his nightcap of 'milkie'.

Antonia always said those first years with Eric, and the two at St Paul's, were the most carefree times she knew. He was the only person she ever submitted to willingly and unquestioningly. Looking back, she wondered if she had let him dominate her too much by handing over 'the keys of my conscience to him'.

Eric replaced her father as Antonia's mentor, and became her new 'God'. But there was a 'blessed difference': there was no guilt in her relationship with him and he never imposed anything on her mind, as her father did, but would always take into consideration her point of view in any discussion, so that it never became an argument. 'I defied my father only when I had Eric to back me up.'

The most important outcome of Antonia's second marriage was that she gave up Catholicism. But, as she later told Peter Thorpe, her husband was in no way to blame for this: 'He never tried to stop me from practising (we were married in a Catholic Church), never mocked my religion or tried to reason me out of it.'

Eric was a thinking disbeliever, well-read in philosophy and theology. The philosopher whose ideas were closest to his own was George Santayana, so it was natural that he would introduce Antonia to his works. She was at once attracted to Santayanan ideas, but had difficulty accepting the theory that the teachings of the Church are only 'poetically true'. Eric then encouraged her to explore other philosophies and suggested she should attend a course of lectures Bertrand Russell was giving every Monday evening.

In January 1926 Antonia boldly wrote inviting her lecturer and his wife, who lived in nearby Sydney Street, for a drink. In his reply of acceptance, Russell explained that his wife was out of London giving political speeches and confessed he had been hoping to become acquainted with her since the first lecture.

Over the next two years it is clear from the sporadic correspondence between Bertie and Tony that he would have liked to have an affair with her, but, though she thoroughly enjoyed occasional dinners *à deux* with him, over which he did not only 'try to epitomize the teachings of philosophy', she would not sleep with him. Yet *she* seems to have been the one who kept their correspondence alive when he moved out of London. In the few letters he wrote to Antonia between 1926 and 1928, he is always thanking her for hers – 'You *do* write good letters' – using work as the excuse for not having answered them. At the time he was writing *Analysis of Matter* at a constant rate of 2500 words a day.

It sounds as if Antonia, besides being the more prolific correspondent, made provocative remarks in her letters to keep the flirtation alive, taunting the older man with descriptions of the way young men were treating her. In one she must have teased him that she was thinking of becoming a lesbian, for he replied, 'My heart is wrung to think that men should be so foolish & blind as to drive you to contemplate the sad alternative you mention – would that I were at hand to present arguments on the other side!'

On one occasion, 'delectable Tony' seems to have responded less coldly to the advances of her 'devoted Bertie'. His last letter to her, before a year of silence, the only one which begins 'My darling', said: 'I was quite intoxicated by your kindness to me yesterday . . . I keep wondering whether it was just a mood, or whether you feel the same way still?' He asked if she would dine with him the next time he came to London and stay with him till morning: 'You know how long I have wanted you, & now hope makes me dumb & shy.'

My mother told me she did not sleep with Bertrand Russell, and this seems confirmed by his name not being included in either list of past lovers she made in her notebooks, in 1954 and 1958. She admitted she had considered the possibility before that dinner, but his fervour in the taxi afterwards, where he fell on his knees to plead with her to spend the night with him, bleating like a sheep 'Please, *p-l-e-e-a-s-e*', made it seem preposterous.

Years later I would be reminded of this story when an elderly Italian philosopher slowly creaked onto his knees in front of me. I thought he was searching for something on the floor, until he clasped me round the calves and moaned in a trembly voice, 'Ti prego, *ti pre-e-go*.' As I hauled him to his feet, I wondered whether this was the way of all philosophers' wooing?

Antonia did not start having affairs until she had been married to Eric for two years, by which time Russell had been in pursuit for more than a year. Her fear that it might have been her passionate desire for Robert which had driven her mad, combined with revulsion over her one and only sexual experience, made her repress the strongly sensual side of her nature.

But the first stirring of that other side began when she went on holiday to Paris in 1926. There she wrote the only one of her earlier notebooks which she did not later burn. It describes her first flight in an aeroplane, where she notes that a newly married couple in front of her are reading *Tit Bits* and *Country Life* while she watches the landing with fascination.

In the short 'Paris' notebook of 1926 Antonia is consciously showing-off her talent for writing; but she also unconsciously reveals her fascination with homosexuality:

> There is a clever little Eton cropped thing called Muriel who plays the piano at the Boeuf. She got up and danced the Charleston among wild applause, hiking up her soft dull rose frock to show a pair of sinewy knees in rolled stockings. She was joined later by a pretty languid little American in chartreuse green. They jigged opposite each other in the exasperating double time of the Charleston while the fairies clapped the tune, until they fell into each others arms kissing frantically from sheer exhaustion.

She was tempted to take a job in Paris, but could not bring herself to abandon Eric with whom she was still very happy. She returned to London and her 'dishonest' job in Crawford's, about which she would always have ambivalent feelings, recognising that advertising, if it is to sell goods, cannot afford to be over-truthful.

On her next holiday in France, in the spring of 1927, Antonia began her first love-affair. She was by now twenty-eight.

His name was Yvon. He was a poor and handsome young man from Martinique, 'slender and small boned' and younger than she.

On returning to Eric, she wrote for him a fictionalised account of their liaison, altering the girl slightly, but not Yvon, whose body she described as being like that of 'a very young girl'.

'Mon pays c'est la Martinique', was published in *As Once in May* after her death. What is interesting about this earliest surviving piece of Antonia's writing is that it distinguished the two sides of her nature: the controlled, 'harsh and haughty' Convent-educated girl and the 'girl in the glass'. The latter is clearly shown as the sensual, instinctive side of her nature – the one which was in fact repressed by her stern Catholic upbringing.

Over the next two years Antonia had half-a-dozen short affairs. Eric knew; he also knew her attachment to him remained the most important and stabilising thing in her life. Justifying her behaviour later to a Catholic friend, she said 'All that leaping into bed that used to go on in Bloomsbury and Chelsea was pretty trivial . . . only an exaggerated reaction against the old taboos.'

Although Antonia may have *thought* she felt no guilt at flouting old taboos, having renounced her religion and denied her father, who was 'no longer a terrifying figure', she was frigid. By 1928 something was going wrong again. Until then, apart from 'off-days' and occasional headaches and a feeling of restlessness, she had had no reason to be anxious about herself. Her only qualms had been about the meaning-lessness of her affairs and her 'silly job' in advertising. But now she started to put on weight rapidly again. She felt listless and had lost the ability to write.

In July Antonia went on holiday to Austria, ostensibly to visit her maiden aunt, Bee, Christine's sister, who was a governess in Vienna. Her father, who was retiring early due to ill health, was hurt that she would be away for his last speech day at St Paul's; but he aroused her guilt less easily now that she had Eric to sustain her.

The Earnshaw-Smiths had odd relationships with their respective parents and parents-in-law. They sometimes dined with the Bottings, but the two men did not get on. There was an undeclared rivalry between Cecil and Eric; it would have been stronger if Cecil had known that Eric sometimes addressed Antonia as 'My dear daughter'. Her father had been deeply upset by Antonia's desertion of the Catholic Church and suspected his son-in-law was partly responsible. But Eric and Christine liked each other: he was charmed and amused by her.

Eric's parents lived in Cambridge with a youngest son, Lel. As seldom as possible Eric would force himself to visit them. He was on one of these visits when Antonia announced she was leaving for Vienna.

His letter telling her what to instruct the char before leaving gives an idea of their domestic set-up:

My dear Wife

I have just consumed an ice with our little Lel, & am feeling the usual sickness in consequence; observe and pardon my shakey handwriting. How are my poor deserted pussy cats getting on? I will pray for you (to WHAT?) as the hour draws near for your departure. I don't know how you can face it – I was overwhelmed with nausea merely by my journey to Cambridge . . . It is uncertain how long I can stand home-life, but equally uncertain how to escape therefrom. However if the weather continues fine the river offers a very agreeable solution, & keeps me out of doors & away from Mama . . .

I hope you'll have a really good time on your voyagings, and come back to Master with a lovely glossy fur and renovated whiskers.

I cannot restrain myself from appending a list of instructions: you know how I love them, so bear with me.

1. [Asks for five ties to be sent to him with some laundry.]

2. Would you initiate Nancy [the substitute char] into the workings of Domestic Economy, particularly impressing on her (a) the importance of keeping the bedroom door & window open as much as possible and (b) the imperative necessity of leaving the kitchen window so that Mr Pusta & friends can come & go. Also to feed the darling on her return in the evening, taking care that the said friends do not snatch his viands, & give him milkie before retiring.

3. Have you paid the Olde Candye Shoppieyie?

4. [More instructions for charlady.]

With these few precepts I close, heaping blessings & love on your dear head.

I trust you will *never* desert

Mr Micawber

What happened that summer in Austria is not revealed in any notebook, nor in Antonia's unfinished novel about that period, *Clara IV*.

There was a lover, her fifth according to a list in a notebook. He was an Austrian called Edo, and his name is followed by one word: 'Demoralisation'. An extract from *Clara IV* shows the heroine's state of mind on the train as she returns to her husband, Clive, after some sort of emotional débâcle in Austria:

The first thing she was going to tell him was that never again was she going to go off on her own without him. These last two weeks in Austria had proved that, away from him, she could not be trusted to behave like a rational human being. There were things she had thought and done in these past two weeks she would be ashamed to tell even to Clive who understood and condoned everything . . .

The chaotic state of her suitcases reflected all too shamefully the way she had let herself go, physically, morally and mentally in the last half of her holiday . . . there had been one or two days in the past fortnight when . . . she had wondered whether she were not going out of her mind again or had not even already done so . . . But she knew she could count on finding him waiting for her at Caroline [i.e. Paultons] Square; her saucer of milk and her basket ready to welcome back a pussy-cat who, this time, had strayed so alarmingly far from her master that she had dreaded she would never find her way back to him.

Under Eric's protection again, Antonia managed to pull herself together again — on the surface at least.

It was unfortunate for a young man named Rudolph Glossop that he walked into her life shortly after her return from Austria, for he would soon find himself in a more demoralised state than she was.

CHAPTER 6

·ᕯ·

A Birth and a Death

*The Silas time, except for a few ecstatic moments, certainly
was not happy.*
Antonia White, 8 October 1952

Silas, the name by which Rudolph Glossop was known to his friends, was a mining engineer of twenty-six who had recently returned from prospecting in Canada. His profession, his stolid background – his father was a bank manager and his mother a Scottish Calvinist – his public school education leading to a London degree in mine engineering might have deceived people into thinking him conventional. But he was as much interested in poetry and music as in mathematics and mining, and when he returned to England to take up a post as a lecturer at the University of Birmingham, that side of him which been starved during those three years in Canada was in need of nourishment.

Since there was not much intellectual stimulation at home in Bakewell, Derbyshire, Silas used to come to London where he had many friends and where his favourite sister lived.

His best friend at the time was a painter, Frank Freeman. It was to his flat that Silas went one 'fateful Tuesday' afternoon in mid-September 1928, feeling so despondent about his future in England that he had decided he would probably go back to prospecting in Canada at the end of the winter. Maybe to cheer him up, Frank took him to 52 Paultons Square to meet his friends the Earnshaw-Smiths.

When Silas met Antonia he was struck by her deceptively feminine looks and ways. She was excellent company, well-read and a witty conversationalist. She had recently begun a part-time job on Desmond MacCarthy's literary review, *Life and Letters*, having cut down to half-time at Crawford's, and was at last on the fringes of the world she most admired: Bloomsbury. Outwardly she epitomised the free-thinking, free-loving, agnostic spirit of the 1920s.

By the time Silas returned to Bakewell three days later he had fallen in love with Antonia, and she with him.

Silas was three years younger than Antonia; tall, firmly built and good looking, he was a contrast to the people of indeterminate sex with whom she usually mixed, yet he was not alarmingly male. Although there was nothing effeminate about him, he once admired an attractive girl sighted in a mirror before realising it was his own reflection. He had a sensitive, intuitive poet's mind which was often overshadowed by the logical scientist in him.

It was not the polarities in their natures, but what they had in common, which was to cause them trouble one day. They were emotionally immature, and each thought the other was the more sophisticated and the more self-assured. Both were moody and given to depression and accidie and headaches. Both needed reassurance.

Silas invited Antonia to spend a weekend with him in Birmingham, explaining to his landlady that she was a cousin, Mrs Smith.

His preparations to receive the woman he hoped would become his first mistress were touching. He wrote asking what she would like for breakfast – tea or coffee or cocoa – and which was her favourite brand of marmalade? And did she need a hot-water bottle? He tried to make order of the bachelor chaos in his rooms by clearing up 'an astonishing collection' of books, which ranged from Whitehead's *Introduction to Mathematics* to *Les Fleurs du Mal*, for Silas was a prodigious reader. In the fifty letters he wrote to Antonia over the next three months, among the names of authors he was reading were Beddoes, Blake, Samuel Butler, Pepys, Aldous Huxley, Nietzsche, Defoe, Santayana, Yeats, Shakespeare, Shaw and Beatrix Potter.

To the sound of the lady in the room below struggling with a piece by Chopin, and with frequent interruptions to feed shillings into the gas meter, Silas and Antonia passed their first weekend as lovers. If it was not the 'transcendental experience' both had hoped it would be, each concealed their disillusionment from the other.

'Emotions always have a delayed action with me,' Silas explained in a letter he wrote to Antonia immediately after their first weekend together. Reading only his side of their correspondence, one gets the impression that she must often have chided him for not showing his feelings, for he is always excusing himself and explaining how hard it is for him 'to be open', because of having had to suppress his emotions all his life.

In November, during the third weekend they spent together in Birmingham, Antonia conceived a child. Her life now took what she afterwards called its 'sensational "wrong turning"'.

As soon as she realised, she broke the news that she was pregnant to Silas over a weekend in early December. To judge from a letter he wrote to her afterwards, he must have gone through a hellish couple of days. She made a scene over how the child, already named 'Francis' in anticipation of its being a boy, was going to be supported, having apparently misunderstood Silas's intentions – which were honourable, as he explained again in that letter, adding 'if you will only trust me & remember that I love you, I'm sure we'll find a solution.'

The next time they met was in London, where Silas went to be near Antonia during his Christmas vacation. He now began to see another side of her nature – her vicious temper and fits of sulking, her wild extravagance and irresponsibility with money – but persuaded himself her erratic behaviour was brought on by the worry of being pregnant, and the dilemma of whether to break off with Eric, or stay married to him and let him become the child's official father, as he had offered.

Before Christmas Silas was summoned home to Bakewell because his father had had a stroke, and on the night of 21 December Mr Glossop died.

By then Antonia had made up her mind to seek an annulment of her marriage to Eric, again on the grounds of non-consummation, and to marry Silas: 'Eric begged me to wait a little, but being impetuous and very much in love, I wanted to marry my lover and live an ordinary "natural" life.' While waiting for the annulment, the law required that she move away from her safe haven under Eric's roof. She rented a room in the nearby King's Road where she was lonely and miserable. Silas was by now back in Birmingham.

At the end of the spring term Silas felt he had no alternative but to return to Canada. At first Antonia protested, but she accepted when he pointed out it was the only way he could hope to earn enough money to support a child and a wife. With her extravagant tastes he knew they would never manage on his £400-a-year as a university lecturer. A dining-room table she had set her heart on had already cost him more than a month's salary.

When Silas left for Canada in the spring of 1929 Antonia had already received ninety letters from him since their meeting the previous autumn. Though these letters were hardly cheerful, and often spoke of his black moods, they seem joyful compared to the ones he wrote from Canada, as he roamed from one to another of the Huronian Belt Mining Company's silver mines in the hope of being given a settled job – for he needed some sort of permanency before bringing out his future wife and future baby. In these letters the descriptions of his physical hardships and, far worse, his mental state, and the bleakness of his prospects are heart-breaking. A place which had seemed to him the worst imaginable 'hell-hole' shortly after his arrival, Timmins, had become a desirable haven after a few months.

Almost every letter spoke of money, or rather lack of it, for however much he managed to send back to Antonia from his irregular earnings, she was never satisfied. Some unexpected expense always cropped up, such as the 'rapacious' doctor's bills when she caught measles shortly after Silas's departure, in the sixth month of her pregnancy. He promised somehow to send her £50 as soon as the firm he worked for was 'in funds' again, hoping she would keep some of it to pay the hospital fees when the time came.

Antonia left her job with *Life and Letters* and took unpaid leave from Crawford's. She gave up her rented room and went, in July, to spend the last weeks of her confinement at Binesfield.

Since Cecil's early retirement from St Paul's the previous summer, the Bottings had moved permanently to Sussex. He was suffering from diabetes and high blood pressure, and the family doctor had hoped that if he gave up work, and moved to the country, his life could be prolonged. Although Cecil had argued that it was worry, not work, that killed a man, he had been pleased to return to his beloved Sussex. But he did not escape from worry there, thanks mainly to his daughter who later confessed, ten years after his death, that her father would have enjoyed his brief retirement more 'if I hadn't ruined it for him'.

First Antonia upset him by showing no interest whatsoever in the improvements he was carrying out at Binesfield, which she would one day inherit. Then, when she at last came down to see him six months after his retirement, it was not to admire the works, but to inform him she was pregnant by a lover. He was of course horrified. Eventually he came round, 'reluctantly', to the idea of her one day marrying Silas, after having met him.

Then, a few weeks before the birth of her child, his daughter turned up in Sussex, penniless, and with no definite plans yet to join Silas, although her annulment would soon be through. In fact Antonia was so broke that she asked her father to lend her £30 for her forthcoming hospital expenses – the £50 Silas had promised had still not arrived and she would discover only later that this had not been his fault, but the result of 'complete turmoil' in the accounts department of the silver-mining firm where he worked. There ensued one of the most painful scenes that ever took place between them, during which Antonia felt extremely bitter that her father had been more prepared to lend her money for the abortion five years ago than he was now for the birth of a child. Yet, in the end, he not only lent her the money for the hospital, but also agreed that the baby, plus a nurse, could stay at Binesfield until she could take it with her to join Silas.

Just before the baby was due, Antonia returned to London to stay with a friend called Addy. When labour started on the afternoon of Friday, 16 August, she went into the Royal Northern Hospital.

That Friday night, Eric, who was still officially her husband, went to his club and drank himself 'silly with whisky' while waiting for news from the hospital. He wrote Antonia a note which ended, 'I wish it were all over – and so do you I expect . . . I am thinking of you all the time, & can only send as much love as possible.'

But it was a long and difficult labour, and the baby was not born until the morning of Sunday, 18 August 1929. Eric wrote from the Cavendish Club that he was relieved, but wished yet another woman had not been added 'to the army of sinners'.

The name registered on the child's birth certificate was Susan Earnshaw-Smith.

When Silas returned to base on 20 August, after a prospecting trip that had been uneventful, 'beyond nearly colliding with a bear', he found cables waiting for him announcing the birth of a daughter. Immediately he sent Antonia a telegram and a letter.

The telegram never reached her. Because she was already angry about the £50 not having arrived, she refused to believe he had sent it. When, twenty-six years later, she was struggling with *Clara IV*, in which Silas would have to be portrayed, and going through old papers connected with that period, she told me in a letter that she had come to the conclusion that the telegram she had waited for 'so agonisingly' in the hospital had been sent to Binesfield and been destroyed by her father: 'If I had had that telegram, things *might* have turned out differently.'

The letter Silas wrote to her expressing his pleasure at his daughter's birth, said that once again his plans had fallen through. In a previous letter he had told her he hoped he had persuaded his firm to allow him to study geology at the Massachusetts Institute of Technology in Boston in the winter while keeping him on half pay. Now, instead of Boston which would have been tolerable, he was talking about a place called Wa Wa where it snowed all winter, and added, 'I long to see Tony on snowshoes.' The letter reached her two weeks after the birth of Susan, when she was upset about many things and not in a frame of mind to be amused by the idea of wearing snowshoes in Wa Wa.

Antonia was upset that the baby had not been a boy; the birth of a daughter had been a double blow, for as she explained to me once, her father had told her that if she had had a son, it would have wiped out his distress about the whole thing. She was recovering from a long and difficult labour, and was also cross that her attempts to breast-feed the baby were so disastrous that she quickly gave up. She felt guilty about not having any maternal feelings for Sue, and wrote about this to Bertrand Russell, who had agreed to be the child's 'pagan godfather' by sending a silver mug *before* the birth – he would never do anything for it again. He told her not to worry: 'You will find that affection will grow; it is a result, not a cause, of the care one takes of the child.'

On coming out of hospital Antonia went back to Binesfield, taking the baby with a nurse there, too. But it vexed her that she was still being judged, and found guilty, by her father who disapproved of the way she handled everything. Nothing she said could justify to him her refusal to have the child baptised.

In a letter Antonia wrote me in her mid-fifties she talked of

Silas's real hatred of Christianity. I must have had it too then. You can see the really savage rebellion of the 'twenties against everything that seemed to them stuffy and hypocritical and Victorian. And yet how conscientious Si was in spite of all his bravado of being a 'free spirit' and a 'Nietzschean wild man'.

As soon as the civil dissolution of her marriage to Eric came through that autumn (the religious annulment would take longer) Antonia went back to London to live under his roof again, leaving her father to reign over a household of females ranging from the month-old baby to the two old aunts, who were now in their eighties. (His mother had died by then.)

Although she was happy to be back with Eric, who would remain her closest friend, things had changed at 52 Paultons Square in the eight months she had been away. Also Eric had 'openly reverted to homosexuality', whereas during their marriage he had always been extremely discreet about it – far more than she had been over her lovers.

That autumn of 1929 Silas was having a tough time. The great slump had begun and the Huronian Belt Mining Company, like so many other businesses, was running into trouble. His only hope of a settled job was to accept being sent back to Timmins in Ontario, since the offer of Wa Wa had been withdrawn. Timmins was the one place he had always hoped not to inflict on her, with its 'unwanted priests' and 'revolting nuns'. He was also 'in a lamentable condition' after receiving a fierce letter from Antonia who still had not forgiven him for the £50 that had gone astray, although he was now sending her £20 a month to pay for the nurse at Binesfield. He had been tempted to remove her photograph from the walls of his shared hut, and had scarcely dared to open her next letter. But he did, and answered it with a cry, 'Oh Tony, Tony, how long will it be till we can tell our sinister fates to go to hell.'

His only consolation was the thought of his baby daughter for whom, on learning that she had been ill, he had suddenly realised he had strong paternal feelings.

But the worst was yet to come. With the Wall Street crash at the end of October, the Huronian gave all its geologists one month's notice. The first letter he wrote to Antonia after this disastrous piece of news had the words 'De Profundis' written under the address. He told her he had wanted to write her a joyful letter, having just received the first photograph of Susan, which had moved him deeply; instead it was a letter full of woe. If he could not find another job, he wondered if she could somehow support herself and Sue for two months, allowing him time to go to South Africa, '3rd class', to look for work there.

In November Antonia went back to her job at Crawford's part-time. Much to her annoyance, during her absence her office had been occupied by a copywriter several years her junior. He had been at Crawford's for over a year, so she already knew him by sight and reputation. It was difficult not to: in the women's cloakroom, where confidences were exchanged, she had often heard secretaries gossiping about this handsome newcomer. These female twitterings irritated her: she could see nothing special about him, in fact she had always disliked what she knew of him.

She assumed this intruder would now return to his old place and was furious when she was told she had to share her office with him. His name was Tom Hopkinson.

'He was the first person who challenged my unique position at Crawford's. Till he appeared, I was acknowledged cock (or hen!) of the social, intellectual & literary walk.' Tom and Antonia began to treat each other with polite rudeness, 'and immensely enjoyed scoring off each other'.

On 17 November 1929, three months after the birth of his grand-child, Cecil Botting died of a cerebral haemorrhage.

When she saw her father's dead body lying on his bed at Binesfield, Antonia was seized by an extraordinary desire to strip him naked: 'that strange temptation . . . to which mercifully I did not yield. I don't really think it was a wish to do something wrong – I cannot analyse it. Perhaps I wanted to see for myself that my father was a man like other men.'

It would be many years before Antonia mourned her father's death. At the time she could only feel relief at what she hoped was the death of her conscience. When planning *Clara IV*, which would have been about the Eric/Silas period and the death of her father, Antonia wrote in her notes for it: 'There is the marriage that is not a physical marriage; the escape from the father that is no escape, even when he dies.'

The news of Cecil's death took a month to reach Silas. He immediately sent an affectionate note, followed by another one two days later in which he said he hoped 'young Su' would not now become a nuisance.

Perhaps the person most affected by Cecil Botting's death was Sue, though she was not aware of it. Christine had always found the presence of the baby and its nurse tiresome, and now that Cecil, with his stern sense of duty, was no longer around, there was no one in England who seemed much to care about the poor little creature's fate. At the time, for whatever reason, Antonia did not try to make a home for the child and nurse with her. Sue was put into a children's home in London.

The person who was kindest to Antonia after her father's death was Tom. She told a friend, 'he was very sweet to me when I came back rather shaken after the funeral.' Within two months she had become Tom's mistress.

Antonia was now thirty; Tom was twenty-four. It was seven months since she had last seen Silas.

CHAPTER 7

The Hopkinsons

I could do real violence to the whole Hopkinson family.
Antonia White, 2 December 1939

Tom Hopkinson, my father, came from that social order which used to provide Britain with her worthy professional classes. However, one of his great great grandfathers had been a renegade at the beginning of the nineteenth century, and Tom would become one, too.

This ancestor, John Lomax, had lived 'in sin' with Alice, the daughter of Thomas Hopkinson, a stone mason from Bury, after his father, who owned cotton mills in Lancashire, threatened to cut him off if he married her. They had had five children: their only son, John Hopkinson, would become Mayor of Manchester and marry a wealthy Miss Dewhurst from Yorkshire.

My father's father, Henry, was one of John Hopkinson's grandsons. He was born in 1876 in Manchester where his father was Professor of Law at Owen's College. His first contact with London, like Cecil Botting's, was as a pupil at Dulwich College, when his father entered politics in 1889. It is unlikely that Henry would have met Cecil at Dulwich – for Botting was six years the older. Yet, despite their very different backgrounds, my two future grandfathers had many things in common besides having been educated at the same school.

Henry Hopkinson, like Cecil Botting, suffered humiliation at Dulwich: he had to endure ruthless teasing because of his northern accent, which he would never lose, and a stammer. He also read Classics at university (but at Oxford, not Cambridge); and, odder still, in his late thirties he took a decision connected with religion that would change his life and that of his family. At thirty-six Cecil had turned to Catholicism: at thirty-seven Henry abandoned a professorship in archaeology to become a clergyman, a calling at which he would earn much less money for much more work.

My father, Henry's second son, talks much of his childhood and the effect that his father's becoming a clergyman had on the whole family in his autobiography, *Of This Our Time*. He was born three weeks after Antonia's sixth birthday. Unlike Antonia, who says in one of her notebooks 'The first thing I remember wanting to be as a child was *good*!!', Tom's earliest memories are of having goodness thrust upon him right from the start by his stern mother.

Evelyn Fountaine, Henry's wife, who was a clergyman's daughter, had set about dealing with her second child's wilfulness at once – a problem she had been spared with her firstborn, Jack. In his autobiography, Tom describes his mother telling him how she used to wheel him through Victoria Park in Manchester, little Jack trotting obediently alongside the pram, as he screamed himself purple protesting against some piece of maternal authority. Despite the horrified looks of passers-by, Evelyn let him howl himself to a standstill in order, as she put it, to '"break his will" for the child's future good'.

She told him of many other struggles between them, always with satisfaction in her voice for she had always been the victor; and described how, before he was even two, he used to sit in his cot rehearsing for these rows, carefully going over his lines: 'Thomas never hasn't . . . Thomas never doesn't . . . Thomas never *won't*'.

Henry Hopkinson took no part in this contest of wills between his wife and small son; he had a horror of arguments or conflict of any kind. If pressed to take sides, he would delay any decision by saying with solemnity he must first 'th-th-think' the matter over.

After Tom, who was only fourteen months younger than Jack, a future lawyer, came Paul and Stephan and, finally, Esther, her father's favourite who became an Anglican nun. Paul, when he grew up, joined the regular army, and Stephan – the rebel, the most brilliant of them all – much to Tom's disgust and his parents' relief, unexpectedly became a clergyman.

When they were small, the five young Hopkinsons grouped their parents together as 'father 'n' mother' assuming they thought as one on every issue. But Tom began to realise that his mother was the dominant figure. By that time he had reached an age when he could have used more persuasive words than 'won't' or 'shan't' to fight a less one-sided battle against her, but he chose instead to lay down arms. It wasn't that he had been won over to believing that always putting others first was the correct way to live, as his mother did, but just that he felt it wiser to keep such thoughts to himself.

Next Tom discerned a deeper understanding and sounder judgement in his father than in his mother, and wished he would assert some authority, instead of always sitting there passively, head slightly tilted to one side as if to avoid the force of his wife's convictions, and bowing to her wishes even if they were surely not his own. If only his father would deal in a more masterful way with his family, Tom felt his mother might shed her forceful tactics and be more feminine. He longed for her to release that tenderness he knew was locked up inside her like a miser's treasure, because she had let him see glimpses of it whenever he was ill. Then she tended him lovingly, arousing in him ineffable longings for more such treatment.

There was another important female figure in Tom's early childhood, even harsher than his mother, who was employed by her to help look after the children before they went away to school. Her name was Hilda Frances Moore but they called her 'Mim'. Sometimes days would pass without her saying a friendly word to her charges. When he was grown-up, and kept notebooks like Antonia's, Tom would say of Miss Moore:

> She was small, slight, anaemic, thin wispy hair, a sallow fallen face, nose the most prominent feature, greyish green eyes, a mole with hairs growing from it. Genteel, angular . . . nagging, unloving. It seems to me the strongest criticism of my mother that she should ever have put such a woman over us . . . I wonder sometimes if my longing for a woman's affection – a weak, exaggerated longing – is not partly due to the person who looked after us when we were small.

Tom's happiest early recollections all concern Wales where his grandfather, Sir Alfred Hopkinson, had given Henry and Evelyn a small holiday house near Aber on the edge of the Menai Straits: Glen Afon. It faced both sea and mountains, and a little river flowed through the garden.

In the room Tom shared with Jack at Glen Afon, the ceiling was covered with a patterned paper. As he lay on his bed looking up at it, Tom turned each shape into a character. One was 'a good little fairy'; another shape was a witch who ill-treated him and set him tasks to do. He always bore her cruelty with 'the utmost patience & docility', indeed always asked for more.

Tom's earliest memories are recounted in the same notebook of 1943. He was about three:

I am standing by the side-board in the big dining-room of our house at Aber . . . wearing a dark blue smock. This smock is intended to button up at the front with two or three round white buttons like pyjama buttons. It has short sleeves, and smocking front and back. And, here is the point, I have put my smock on back to front to make myself look like a girl.

My second memory is of a cherished doll. I called her 'Helen' . . . Helen was not my baby, as I think most children's dolls are to them. She was both my wife and myself. I imagine that I kept Helen until I was about five.

Mim, who was given to repeating tales about each child which she knew it did not wish to hear, told every newcomer that Tom put his smock on like a girl and played with a doll. The way he silenced her was to become suddenly so outwardly boyish that these stories became palpably unsuited to him. 'My girlishness went underground and partly survived as a lack of real courage and conviction about being boyish.'

Tom's first memory of exerting toughness also took place at Aber when he was five or six. A much older boy had come to tea. Tom noticed how Mim treated him with respect. After tea the visitor challenged Jack and Tom to fight him in turn. Jack thought it a silly game and merely pretended to spar; but Tom threw himself into the fray with such fervour that his opponent declared, 'He's the hero. He does at least try to fight.' From then on, particularly for any show of physical courage, admiration and approval would become as important to Tom as they were to Antonia.

It was about this time that Jack and Tom were sent away to a prep school called Lawrence House. When assailed by homesickness during his first two terms at boarding school, Tom would imagine himself back at Aber, lying alone in the overgrown garden watching the insects in the long grass, or gazing up at the seagulls that circled the bay.

During the summer term Tom decided he must overcome 'his failing' of feeling homesick, and try to master cricket which he detested. Having got over his fear of being struck by the hard ball, he discovered he could play well enough to gain respect in that world where till now he had felt an inferior outsider. Since studying came easily to him, he soon began to wonder if he did not fit in better at school than at home. This was particularly true after a dramatic change in his parents' style of living took place when he was nine.

At the end of the summer holidays of 1914 Henry Hopkinson assembled his whole family. He solemnly asked each one for their approval about a decision he intended to make. He wanted to give up his academic career and become a clergyman. It would mean having to move out of their comfortable quarters provided by the university, and living modestly without servants. He expected them all to help with the housework.

To the five children, this was far more shattering news than the declaration of war only a few days before.

Appalled as he was by his father's decision, Tom gave his consent with the rest. But inwardly he was against it and feared that what he already considered his mother's 'exaggerated concern for other people' would now be boundless. He was proved right. And there was something much worse he had not foreseen: as a result of clergymen being short of time, as well as money, there would be no more holidays at Aber.

The boys would have had to leave boarding school, too, if a generous uncle, Austin Hopkinson, MP, had not offered to pay their fees.

When Tom was older, he questioned his parents about his father's renunciation of the academic work he had loved to enter the Church. He was told by his father, who had always been very religious, that he had once listened to such an unimpressive sermon that the only explanation he could find for its hardly making sense was that the speaker must have been extremely tired from overwork, 'meaning there must be a great need for men in his calling'. Whereas his mother said it was because Henry had such a horror of the dirt and squalor in the slums of Manchester that he thought he ought to get over it by working among the poor.

The first effects of this decision were felt by the elder boys only when they came home for the Christmas holidays of 1914. By then their father had been appointed to his first ecclesiastical post as junior curate of a small parish in Colne. His living quarters, although larger than most of the houses in that industrial town in East Lancashire, were too small for a family of seven. The only place where the children could play on rainy days – and it always seemed to be raining in Colne – was in the cellar, where any rowdiness would not disturb their busy father in his small study.

The father who emerged from that study to greet his sons on their return from school was wearing the uniform of his new servitude to God: a dark clerical suit and a white 'dog collar'. From then on it would be the way they would always see him dressed as he progressed, over the next twenty years, from junior curate to venerable Archdeacon of Westmorland.

Home life was austere for the five children for the next seven years as the family moved from one bleak industrial area to another each time Henry was appointed to a new parish. But at least in term-time Tom was happy, particularly after he moved to his public school, St Edward's in Oxford.

At first he was bitterly disappointed on being sent to St Edward's; since a small boy he had set his heart on joining the navy and, with this in mind, had wanted to go to the Royal Naval College at Osborne. But the First World War put an end to Tom's dream of becoming a sailor.

Early in 1918 his father joined the Royal Army Medical Corps as a private, although he disapproved of killing fellow human beings. The war was going so badly for Britain that, after having been assured he need not fight but could be a stretcher-bearer behind the lines, Henry decided he ought to enlist.

Tom was pleased and proud of this 'different' father in uniform. He had never doubted that his father had physical courage: as a small boy he had watched him separate two fiercely fighting dogs, and only a year before he had seen him rescue a drunken man from a pack of louts who were taunting him. To Tom, who had always longed for his father to exert more authority over his domineering mother, the second episode had proved what he had always suspected: his father could assert himself when he wanted to.

In the army his father seemed rejuvenated. He stood up straighter and looked taller. His quiet sense of humour, much repressed since joining the clergy, returned and, to his thirteen-year-old son, he even appeared to stammer less.

The Armistice was signed before Henry had finished his training. But he was so disgusted by the horrors and suffering caused by the Great War, without even having seen them, that he could not allow one of his sons to devote his life to a career that glorified war. So again Tom followed in Jack's footsteps to become Hopkinson minor at St Edward's, having won a scholarship which paid most of the fees.

Once he became used to its Spartan ways, he settled in and became very happy there. But, he realised later, it was 'an unthinking happiness', based entirely on being approved of by others: 'If there were some who did not approve, I could think, as I feel Father often feels,

that they were wrong – not just mistaken, but valuing wrong things.'
The approval that accounted for his happiness and popularity at St
Edward's came from his success at games; 'I should have got very little
pleasure out of being good at rugger and cricket if the "School" had
been most interested in the Eleusinian Mysteries.'

In a later notebook Tom recorded:

> But, I remember so well, I was conscious of something *not* there which
> ought to be . . . I remember this would most come over me in Hall at
> supper in the evening . . . As everybody about me talked and chattered, I
> would subtract myself from them. I just loosed my moorings & let go, &
> always at such times the thought of the person I was fondest of was a sort
> of cushioning lifebelt & enshrouding mist.
>
> How many of those who have filled this role for me had any idea of the
> part they played? If one disappeared, through too long absence, through
> snubbing me sharply in some way, I found another. Always there was
> someone. Their name became a kind of talisman to me. A form of reassur-
> ance. In moments of fear, above all of humiliation, I would find myself
> saying it over to myself.

This absolute need for someone to be fond of would stay with Tom
all his life: 'somebody to relate my existence to, a secret confider and
approver'. His first of those talismans had been his doll, Helen; then
a succession of friends at school; then, as a grown man, he sought it
in woman after woman.

When Tom had been at St Edward's nearly four years, his father's
health broke down under the strain of overwork. On their doctor's
insistence, Evelyn persuaded his clerical superiors to move Henry from
Manchester to a place where the work would be less arduous. His new
parish was in the village of Burneside in Westmorland. Living in the
country put fresh vigour into all the family, and finally they were
compensated for the loss of holidays at Aber.

Tom, who was sixteen at the time, still practised the Protestant
religion which was always heavily enforced at home and at school.
But he had begun, in his mind, to question some tenets of Christianity,
and, having once heard a story about someone who had had a previous
life, he became interested in the theory of reincarnation.

Besides the outer change of moving to Burneside that took place in
his mid-teens, something was also changing inside Tom. It was his
attitude to his father.

In answer to a request for money to buy a hockey stick, his father had sent him a mildly exhortative letter, suggesting between the lines that perhaps he should spend more time on work and less on sport. In spite of an apologetic ending, 'It's a dreadful thing to have a father who slips too easily into the pulpit,' the letter had irritated him, and made him aware of the ever-widening gap between his parents' way of thinking and his own. After all, he was ahead of most of his contemporaries, getting good end-of-term reports – which showed that playing in the school's rugger and cricket teams was not detrimental to his school-work – so why should he take his father's advice of 'renouncing of other things' to slog harder at Greek and Latin syntax?

Looking back, he dated having ceased to be a child from the time he rejected the advice given by his father in that letter. From then on he began, inwardly, to question many of his father's opinions – something he already did with all of his mother's.

As the time drew near for Tom to leave St Edward's he had to decide on a career. Having a talent for drawing he thought about becoming an architect. Then, after winning ten shillings in an essay competition, he wondered whether to become a writer. It was the warden of St Edward's who insisted he ought to go up to Oxford. The idea appealed to him because it meant he could put off deciding what to do in life for a few more years. His father agreed, but only on the condition that he won a scholarship, which, much to his astonishment, he succeeded in doing.

The reason for this was that his future tutor, Robin Collingwood, thought Tom's English essay one of the best he had ever come across, and told fellow examiners at Pembroke College, who had protested that the other papers were not up to the required standard, that if scholarships were not to be awarded for outstanding work on the rare occasions when it turned up, he could not see the point of holding scholarship examinations at all. The remaining money needed for Tom to attend university was provided once again by Austin, his father's younger brother.

Tom had learned more about his Uncle Austin when he had been to stay with him at his imposing Victorian mansion, Ryecroft Hall in Lancashire, a year before. Once he had grown accustomed to his blunt, sardonic manner, Tom became fond of this unmarried uncle who had made a fortune out of designing a machine for cutting coal, but was not interested in riches. By the time Tom went to Oxford, Austin had given away his handsome house to the local council to help solve the post-war housing shortage; and had changed from smoking cigars to smoking a pipe because he had worked out that by so doing he could save enough to support a working family for a year. 'The important thing in life,' he told his nephew, 'is to *have* everything – but not want any of it. If you've never had it, you're bound to miss it. But if you've got everything and *don't* want it, you're a free man!'

When Tom thanked him for his kindness in helping him go up to Oxford, Austin had said, 'Learn to be arrogant! That's the purpose of going to university.'

When Tom replied by suggesting that his uncle, who besides running a successful engineering firm was an aggressive Independent Member of Parliament, had seemed to manage very well without having gone to university, the older man answered gruffly, 'I'm not arrogant – I'm just rude. You must learn to go one better.'

So, in the autumn of 1923, Tom started his life as an Oxford scholar studying Latin, Greek and philosophy for a degree in Greats.

Until deciding whose approval he wished to win, Tom was not as happy at University as he had been at school. But he says he settled down to four of the happiest years of his life as soon as he found 'a compromise which secured as many approvals as I could reasonably expect to win and gratified as many different sides of myself as possible'.

He gained a place in the university rugby team, and won the approval of the hearty set, yet they sensed he was not really one of them. When celebrating with them at victory dinners, he would drift off as he used to in Hall at St Edward's, distancing himself from their drinking and rowdiness.

Tom also found favour in one of the factions of the undergraduate intelligentsia: it included Cecil Day-Lewis, Rex Warner and Charles Fenby. They founded a society, 'The Jawbone', and a short-lived magazine called the *Broad*, to which Tom contributed, as well as to the better-established *Cherwell*.

Yet in this world, too, he was regarded with some suspicion because of his other life on the football field. Cecil Day-Lewis in particular never trusted him after a wisecrack Tom made during a poetry-reading at the Jawbone. When the title was announced of one of the poems Cecil was to recite, 'Naked Woman with Kotyle', Tom was heard to comment, 'Lucky chap, old Kotyle!' It was not the jocose jibe of an experienced womaniser, as Cecil may have thought, but of a young

man as unversed in matters of sex as the poet himself – for both these
sons of clergymen were still virgins.

Tom did not fall in love until the spring of 1927, during his last year
at Oxford. Until then he had only secret longings or undeclared
passions for girls, because of a slight received the first time he had
plucked up the courage to say 'I love you.' He had been about six at
the time, and the nursery maid to whom he had said these 'momentous
words' had merely smiled and continued to put on his socks.

Next came an experience which would often be repeated in his life:
'to be strongly attracted to a woman or girl, perhaps even to "fall in
love" with her, for a single quite unimportant characteristic'. The first
time had been when he was twelve, on a 'ramble' in Colne:

> When it came to tea-time I sat ... opposite an older girl, about 16,
> dark-skinned & black-haired – and I fell in love with her for the way she
> ate a tomato. I watched her, entranced.

By the time he went up to Oxford, he still could not bring himself
to make a pass at a girl, even if she made it clear such a move would
not be taken amiss.

And even when he was twenty-two, and about to leave Oxford,
Tom did not manage to have an affair with the young woman he had
fallen in love with shortly before leaving Oxford:

> Pam, if she had been articulate, would have said that I led her on to the
> point where she was willing to sleep with me – and then indignantly refused
> to have anything more to do with her on the grounds that she would
> not ... The only excuse is that *I did not know how* to get any further.

The approval Tom had coveted the most at Oxford came from his
tutor, Robin Collingwood. It was the kind of benign approval he
always desired from people older and wiser than himself. 'He was the
father of my mind' he wrote when he heard of Collingwood's death
in 1943.

Confronted with the question of how he was to earn his living, Tom
came face to face with the opposing aspects of himself: 'the conforming
and the nonconforming, the practical and the side that wished to be
creative'.

Tom felt drawn to writing, and Collingwood encouraged him, but
at home endless discussions took place with his father about the choice
of a more stable career. They also discussed religion over which father
and son were now far apart in their views, for Tom had become an

agnostic at university, though he still went to church at home to please his family.

The evening before returning for his last term at Oxford, son and father had had a ponderous discussion about Tom's wish to become a writer which had, as always, been like 'a slow-motion verbal wrestling match'. By the end of the discussion, the most Henry would concede was that Tom should become a schoolmaster, and during the holidays he could live at home free of charge and try his hand at writing.

By the time Tom left Oxford, his closest friend, Charles Fenby, who had gone down the year before and landed a job on the *Westminster Gazette*, had arranged an interview for Tom with his editor. It had gone well, and Tom was confident there would be a job for him if he went to London. Reluctantly, his father gave him £25 and said he should return home if things did not work out.

At the beginning of September 1927, aged twenty-two, Tom set off for London determined to make his living as a journalist.

Although the full-time job did not materialise until Tom had been in London for three months, Charles took him under his wing. He found him a cheap room in the squalid lodging house in Bayswater where he boarded, and helped him get short pieces placed in the paper's diary at ten shillings a time. When the job at last came through, Tom thought he was on the road to becoming a journalist.

On New Year's Eve he took Pam, who was in London, to the cinema. He still had not succeeded in sleeping with her. When Tom returned to his room with the usual sense of frustration he felt after seeing Pam, Charles broke the news that Tom had been fired. The *Westminster Gazette* was to be amalgamated with another liberal paper, and last-comers on the staff were to be the first to go.

In despair, Tom turned to his uncle Austin, who arranged a meeting with a man from *The Times* and another from the *Scotsman*. Nothing came of either.

'No shorthand, no chance,' said the man from the *Scotsman*.

But Austin's intervention helped to solve a different problem. Henry Hopkinson came to London, ostensibly to visit his parents who lived in Holland Park, and walked over to Bayswater to see how his second son was faring in the big city. Tom was out when his father arrived:

Something about the look of the place must have aroused his suspicion. Could it have been one or two of the cards stuck against the row of antiquated bell pulls by our front door? Did it cross his mind that Baroness Flogge on the first floor might be indicating a speciality, rather than displaying a hereditary title from some German principality? . . . Some breath of suspicion, coupled with concern for his son's welfare, evidently caused him to make inquiries, dressed in that clergyman's uniform which gave my fellow tenants as much cause for suspicion as their supposed activities gave him . . . when I got home in the evening the house was in uproar, and Charles, returning before I did, had faced general indignation – which he rapidly passed on to me.

Tom was now roofless as well as jobless. But Austin offered the use of the second floor in his pleasant eighteenth-century house in Great Smith Street. There was room for Charles, too, who was also hunting for new lodgings. At first he hesitated – 'he did not intend to come under the general supervision of the Hopkinson family, one experience of which had been quite enough' – but the house's central position in Westminster, plus the luxury of a bathroom, overcame his resistance, particularly as Austin was asking only the same rent as they had paid in Bayswater: a pound a head a week.

The problem of a job was not so easily solved. After three months, during which he had succeeded only in placing a couple of short pieces in the *Manchester Guardian* at three guineas a time, he was broke, despite a further £10 from his father. The time had come when he must take any kind of work while waiting to find a toehold in journalism in London.

Tom went to see the Oxford Appointments' Committee. All they could offer was a possible vacancy for a trainee copywriter with an advertising agency.

Tom started work as a copywriter at W. S. Crawford's in March 1928, at a salary of £4 a week. What he would come to think of the advertising world is described in his autobiography, in which he says that during his four years there, he never lost the feeling that he was serving a prison sentence.

The first time Tom saw Tony White, the name by which Antonia was known at Crawford's where she had been for three years, she did not see him. He was walking past the lift shaft on one of the upper floors when he heard the sharp tapping of high heels below. Looking down he saw a neat, slightly plump young woman in a green knitted suit hurrying down a lower corridor:

From her chin thrust forward, and the way she set each foot down as though wanting to knock a hole in the tiles with her heel, the impression I took in was of smouldering indignation. The sharpness of that instant impression remains, as though in it I had seen an essential aspect of her personality, but at the time no doubt I put it on one side since there were plenty of day-to-day reasons for anyone working in Crawford's to be angry.

Two years later she became his first mistress.

CHAPTER 8

༄

A 'Forbidden' Marriage

*I always felt there was a 'curse' on our marriage: my
father's curse presumably.*
Antonia White, November 194(8?)

During the second half of her life, when she was trying to make sense
of the first half, Antonia wrote in a notebook that she could hardly
believe anyone could have 'so messed and muddled it' as she had from
1924 to 1930. But although people supposed she led a wild sexual life
while married to Eric, in fact, until having 'genuine affairs' with Silas
and Tom, she had had only four or five 'sporadic' ones.

Searching for some justification for having started her affair with
Tom, whom she had always rather disliked and not even found
attractive, she decided it had something to do with her father's death
at the end of 1929. After it Tom had assumed for her a 'violent, almost
compulsive importance'. He suddenly stood for 'security, respect-
ability, a *family*' and she wished she could spend Christmas with him
and his family. Then, at a Christmas party at Crawford's, a drunken
man looked as if he were about to push Tom out of the window.
Antonia was so furious that she rushed to his defence like 'an animal
defending its mate'. Afterwards she was astonished she had felt so
strongly about him: up to then it had been little more than an 'agreeable
flirtation'.

When Silas's last month with the Huronian was over at the end of
November, he had not left North America after all, because there was
a chance he might be offered prospecting work in Mexico. And shortly
after Antonia and Tom began their affair, he had an offer of work
from an American-run copper mine in Los Pilares de Nacozari; but by
the time he had reached Mexico, all explorations had been suspended
there, too, because of the recession. The only job they could find for
him at Los Pilares was *jefe de los muestras* (head of the mine sampling
department) on far lower pay than he had been expecting. By the

spring he had realised, however frugally he lived, he could not afford to bring Antonia and Sue to live there. He started to save the little he could from what was left of his salary after deducting the monthly contribution of £20 for Sue's upkeep. With it he intended to buy a boat ticket back to England in order to marry his 'fiancée' and legitimise his daughter, since Antonia's full annulment had finally come through.

Silas knew nothing of Tom; but Tom knew something of Silas. Antonia had told him she had a daughter by a man who was abroad who, she insisted, was uncertain of his feelings. He also knew there was a possibility that she might one day join that man in Canada or Mexico, and that he could not count on a lasting relationship, as one of his earliest love letters shows:

> Oh, Tonita . . . I try to remember always those Americas that will, it seems, slide in between us, and I try while remembering them, not to have them so very much in mind – it *is* wrong, Tony, just to steal you for as long as possible . . . It is wrong and I shall do it.

Tom's early letters also show how much he admired and was in awe of his first mistress. He may have thought he was in love, and he was drawn to Antonia sexually, but to someone reading those letters fifty years later, there is a false note in his overdeclared passion and terms of endearment – 'my saving grace', 'my wood pigeon', 'my golden locks' – which give the impression he is trying to convince himself, more than her, of his love. Could he really have had such a romantic vision of my mother that first summer, when she was away staying with friends, as to imagine her 'idling on a punt in mauve most refreshing to look at, doing nothing in a garden all cool in silk, lovely to touch and the colour of condensed milk', or was he projecting an unconscious desire to find a woman the antithesis of his mother, who dressed in plain clothes and was never idle?

It must be remembered that twenty-four-year-old Tom had not yet seen certain aspects of Antonia in love. The person she loved became the centre of her life, and she was only happy when she was in a 'state of grace' with them. But the deeper she fell in love, the worse she handled her lovers: 'I take offence at the smallest thing, I stay too long, I become a bore and then suddenly a black curtain of melancholy descends and I feel shut in, cut off.'

But a bond which would hold Tom and Antonia together was their shared 'phobia for writing'. Right from the start each would read to the other whatever they were working on in the evening in front of the fire in Great Smith Street, or at Paultons Square where Antonia still lived under Eric's roof.

Early on in their relationship, Tom over-praised her letter-writing as well as her femininity. But he has not kept most of those letters which he once found so 'simple and beautiful' where, he said, the thoughts of her heart had come clear to him from her writing 'like a person talking across water in the evenings', as she did his.

Antonia wrote for Tom some of her finest work, starting with the short story about madness, 'The House of Clouds', which she wrote for him as an overture to their affair; it would appear in *Life and Letters* shortly after. Her impotence where writing was concerned seemed to be cured at last, something not even the patiently encouraging Eric had been able to help her achieve, for she had published nothing during their marriage. She also liked parts of a novel Tom had started writing when he was unemployed. She thought it showed he had the makings of a good writer and made him continue with it.

In the summer of 1930, when their affair had been going on for six months, Tom and Antonia went on holiday together. She chose Cassis in the south of France, which was then in vogue with artists and writers.

It was a holiday marred by problems. Not long before their departure Silas had written to say he would soon be returning to England, so Antonia was constantly fretting over whether she should marry him or not. She was also worried about her job. One of Crawford's directors, Florence Sangster, who had never liked her, was annoyed about Antonia's half commitment to the firm, and had issued an ultimatum that by the time she returned from holiday she must either become full time again, or leave.

Antonia was nervous, which made her irritable. She had unconsciously started doing what she would later recognise she always did: as soon as she began to feel joy she felt compelled to turn it into sorrow. She realised this was a 'fearful "sell"' for her lovers: 'They're always attracted because I seem so gay and then I proceed to make their life and mine a perfect hell of torment.'

But Tom, with gentle amenability, managed to pacify her, and when the holiday was over, and they had returned to their separate dwellings, he assured her that, 'whatever there was to worry us, I had a happy blessed holiday, and it was you who made it out of a few railway tickets and some rather stuffy hotels and one or two nice cafés.'

The first thing Antonia did on her return from France, at the beginning of August 1930, was to hand in her notice to Crawford's. Tom, who was still working there, relayed back to her the day-to-day reactions of Florence Sangster, who had never believed she would leave, and by the end of August was wishing she could get her back. After a month, Antonia too was regretting her hastiness, realising it was not going to be as easy to earn her living as a freelance writer as she had hoped. She had placed nothing since leaving Crawford's and was living on a loan from Tom.

In September Silas returned from Mexico.

Antonia went to meet him at Waterloo. In the taxi taking him to lodgings she had found for him, she blurted out that she was having an affair with another man.

There now followed two months of chaos while Antonia tried to make up her mind whether she was going to marry Silas or Tom, who had made an offer of marriage shortly before Silas's return.

After long discussions with Silas, she returned to the original plan of marrying him, though she assured Tom it was not what she wished, but for Susan's and Silas's sakes. She emphasised the sacrifices she was making, particularly that she and Silas were penniless and unemployed.

Tom ceded her, without jealousy, to Silas in a letter of 26 September:

It will be hard for you to-day, to-morrow, & next month – but . . . so many things would have torn at you & me . . .

Oh Tony you are going to be all right because you must. We have shot the lovely albatross, my dear, & you must make something out of what we have done . . . I shall be all right, Tony. It will take me time . . . You are the only person who has ever known what I was trying to do . . . The book will be yours . . . I will say so in the front . . . Though now I can't read [it] to you I will be doing it for you alone.

I will do anything I can for you & him [Silas] . . . You must remember I have money . . . Soon I shall be making more than I use . . . For the small amount of mine you have – please cross it off . . . Try to stay in England. Something for Silas will come . . .

Always, always, remember you & me,

Tom

Was it a question of money that then made Antonia change her mind and decide to marry Tom after all, for she says in one of her notebooks that she thinks one of the reasons she married Tom was that he had 'a regular job and £100' in the bank? Or was it that she could not bear to renounce their writing bond, to which he had alluded in his letter?

Whatever the reason, it was Tom whom she now decided to marry.

Tom told his parents he was engaged. When his father learnt some of the facts of the past of his son's future wife, he was scandalised and distressed. Overworked as he was, Henry Hopkinson made the long journey from Carlisle to London to meet Antonia and found her even less suitable for a daughter-in-law than he had feared. He offered to disentangle his son from her clutches, but was assured it was not necessary; Tom intended to marry Antonia with or without his family's agreement. In his autobiography he says that only later, thinking over his father's abhorrence for emotional scenes, did he come to appreciate how much this offer must have cost him.

Antonia noticed Tom was glum after his father's departure and fussed about it. 'You're not to worry,' he told her, 'I am only anxious to begin our new life as soon as ever we can.'

A few days later, on Trafalgar Day, 21 October, they went to the opening of a Noël Coward play. In the interval Antonia again brought up his disapproving parents and made a scene. Tom broke off their engagement. She fled from the theatre, hailed a taxi and rushed round to Silas's rooms. She fell into his arms, telling him that she and Tom had parted for good and that he was the one she was going to marry. The result of this 'headlong flight' to Silas after Tom's rejection was, as she coyly put it, that she 'came closer to Silas' than ever before.

The next day Tom called on Antonia at Paultons Square, for she was still living in Eric's house. He was contrite; he begged her forgiveness; he said that of course he still wanted to marry her.

She began to waver again.

There followed a couple of weeks of frenetic indecision. By the end of it, Antonia had again opted for marrying Tom. She said later it was Eric, 'who obviously stood for a substitute father', who influenced her, when she was too exhausted to know what she felt. Eric now offered to swap living quarters with Tom, giving Antonia the opportunity to see how she felt about living with his successor, and he and Mr Pusta moved to Great Smith Street.

She wrote a note to Silas telling him she would not be marrying him after all. Yet they had spent the afternoon before reading Shakespeare's sonnets together, and in the evening, he told my sister, she had been kind and sympathetic, gay and fond. She had made no mention of the decision she had reached.

'I did damage him then,' admitted Antonia long afterwards, 'but I could not down my feeling for Tom.'

Tom's father made one last desperate attempt to prevent the marriage. Having failed to dissuade his son on moral grounds from marrying a twice-divorced woman six years older than himself and the mother of an illegitimate baby, he suggested that her past madness might result in her bearing unbalanced children; and insisted a certificate must be produced to prove her type of insanity was not hereditary.

Tom traced the doctor, R. Percy Smith, MD, FRCP, who had treated her in Bedlam but his attestation, dated 22 November 1930, was in Antonia's favour. He said her 'acute mental illness' in 1922 had been 'the result of prolonged mental stress' and he knew of no family history of mental disease. He pointed out she had given birth to a child in 1929, which he understood to be 'quite normal mentally'. The ending of the document must have pleased Tom when he showed it to his father:

> There is no special reason to expect that her children will inherit a tendency to mental disease, but I have no information as to the family history of her prospective husband.

The irony was that when Tom's father asked for that certificate, they had already conceived a child, though neither was aware of it.

Defeated and despondent, Henry Hopkinson could only insist his son be married in a church. Tom, although an atheist now, conceded, not wanting to disappoint his father further; and Antonia was too worn out to care any more. Later she insisted she had not realised that getting married in a Protestant church would excommunicate her from the Catholic religion.

My parents were married in Carlisle Cathedral in November 1930, early on a cold morning when there was nobody about, with my disapproving grandfather, then Canon in residence of the cathedral, officiating. No friends, and none of my mother's relatives, were present. She wore a blue hat with too flimsy a dress, and shivered and shook from beginning to end. All through the ceremony, she was aware that had her father been alive she would not have dared to marry Tom. She was sure that Cecil would have approved of Tom as a person, 'at least of his conventional side', but she knew he would have considered him a 'forbidden husband': an idea that remained implanted in her mind.

My mother had a 'kind of attack' in the hotel after the wedding, and looked so pale and ill that Tom told her afterwards he had been afraid she was going to die. She thought it was due to the cold and to nervous exhaustion. Only on returning to London, after a sombre honeymoon on the Solway Firth, did she discover that she was pregnant again. The honeymoon did not shake off another uneasy feeling she had had in Carlisle Cathedral: that in renouncing her independent life with Eric she had come right up against the 'old disapproval of the elders' in Tom's conventional bourgeois family, and felt an outcast.

Silas – the loser who turned out to have been the winner – stayed in London for a while. He even saw Antonia and Tom occasionally, and, more frequently, his daughter who was now living with a foster mother. The reason for this was that before Silas's return, Tom had made Antonia take him to meet Sue. When he saw that her feet sticking out from the blanket wrapped around her were blue with cold, he had suggested to Antonia there must be some better way of having her cared for. And so, after eight months in the institution, a foster home had been found for Sue.

Lack of work would drive Silas abroad again, this time to West Africa. But by the time he left, Susan had been brought to live with Tom and Antonia after my birth to become one of their family. Her surname, which had never been Glossop anyway, would be changed to Hopkinson, and the Hopkinson clan would accept her in a way they never accepted her mother.

The full weight of remorse about the way she had behaved to Silas would not fall on Antonia's shoulders until many, many years later, in 1955, while re-reading his letters for *Clara IV*, to try and get back to the period and understand how it must have looked to him. She then wrote me two letters, written only two days apart, telling me how depressed and '*guilty*' she felt after reading those letters, which had made her see how '*much* too demanding and selfish' she had been by not taking into account the hardships Silas had been suffering.

> It is awful at the end where his letters suddenly become terribly sad & affectionate & homesick & he complains for the first time that I don't write so often & that his friends write & say how 'radiant' I'm looking. Of course all that meant – Tom!

Antonia had always thought Silas had stopped loving her while he was abroad; the letters show clearly that he had not.

Tom, too, would feel penitent. When his marriage to Antonia was over he wrote:

> I made use of Tony, not, I think, knowingly – though I did know quite clearly that I was in love with Pam, and did know that Tony belonged to someone who was not there to protect his property – to secure the knowledge I needed. I secured the knowledge. For the two offences against love and honour which I committed I had an exceedingly heavy price to pay.

But before talking about the end of my parents' marriage, we must see how it began.

The place Antonia had found for her and Tom to live was not a house in Bloomsbury or Chelsea, as she had hoped, but even so the rent of the large, sprawling reversed-L-shaped flat in Kensington was more than they could afford. It was off the then unfashionable Fulham Road in a block called Cecil Court. (Before a Freudian analyst pointed it out, Antonia denied having noticed the connection with her father.)

In the front of 18 Cecil Court were three light and airy rooms with balconies overlooking Fawcett Street, and at the back four small and dingy ones, plus accessories. Tom brought what few possessions he had from Great Smith Street, and Antonia came with a small dowry of furniture bought over the past year from the hard-earned money Silas had been sending home to support his child. But the two most important pieces were two identical desks made of plywood, which they bought for £5 each and installed side by side in the living room to start their married life as two writers.

Cecil Court was soon less sparsely furnished. Antonia kept ordering furniture which they could not pay for out of Tom's salary and her negligible earnings from freelancing. Tom who was never stingy, but hated being in debt and was wise with money, suffered from Antonia's extravagant ways. Tom described in his autobiography how their money problems began immediately:

> My small capital of about £100 had gone before our honeymoon ended, all except £30 which we were reserving 'for desperate emergencies', but the first of these arrived within three days of moving into our new home.
>
> 'There's a man at the door wanting to see you,' Tony said to me at breakfast.

'What kind of a man?'

'A rather beagledy man.' This was a word she and Eric used, meaning shabby or down at heel. He proved to be the foreman of the firm which had done the decorating, and he thrust a bill into my hand.

'But it's the agents you want to see,' I told him. 'They undertook to redecorate . . .'

'These are *additional* decorations, sir. Outlining the panels of the doors and painting the skirting boards in different colours like the lady ordered . . .'

The bill was for £27, and from that moment we lived on a system of post-dated cheques, carefully spaced out against hoped-for earnings.

There were other differences between them besides money. Antonia did not share Tom's need for physical exercise or his love of the country. From the way she had talked about Binesfield and been anxious to show it to him, he had thought she liked country life but, he says in his autobiography, he soon discovered, to his sorrow, that for her 'the country was endurable as a place to sit in when the sun was shining, though even fine weather brought drawbacks, since she felt in constant danger of being stung or bitten.'

Another difference was that Antonia enjoyed social life. She was gay and a brilliant conversationalist on her best days, whereas at parties Tom grew more and more morose as he searched for something witty or profound to say to her friends which would make them appreciate him in his own right, and not just as a handsome adjunct to his older, more worldly wife. But this became a problem only after my birth, since for the first year of her marriage Antonia was in no mood for parties.

Antonia, who had married Tom 'with a cold, exhausted' heart, hated being pregnant. She found it acutely uncomfortable and disfiguring. She avoided her friends because they made her feel like 'a member of a lower species, a mere breeding rabbit'. She suspected Tom did not like pregnant women and did not want her to have his child because of his parents' hostility towards her and his father's cold disapproval that they were adding to their responsibilities. 'When I love a man, I nearly always want a child by him,' wrote Antonia after I was born, 'I didn't with Tom.'

So, although the circumstances of my birth should have been less distressing than those surrounding Sue's (after all she was married to the father and her own father was no longer alive to censure the act),

Antonia said it was worse because she was no longer in love with Tom, whereas 'I loved Si and I wanted Susan, in spite of all the difficulties.' However, it was not Sue she had wanted, but a child by someone she loved.

There is little record of what she and Tom were feeling during the first months of their marriage – Tom did not start keeping a notebook until 1932, and hers of that period are among those she destroyed. But occasionally they wrote letters to each other, though living under the same roof. He posted his from the office; she left hers on his desk. Here is part of a letter Tom wrote to his wife when she was nearing the end of her pregnancy in May 1931:

> Dearest and only Tony,
>
> I have been reading your letter & reading it again . . . so full of you it almost makes me cry to read.
>
> . . . you're not silly to wish us to have time to see things & one another, and I wish to God we had. And oh you must be tired of always having someone else sitting on your chest. It is such a load for you that it is quite hard to remember this monster may even be an actual positive source of happiness to us.
>
> You're not to abuse yourself & say you're getting tired & dead & useless. You're bound to be tired easily at present, sweetheart . . .
>
> Remember too Tony that your sadness is for want of your own self again, & I do guess how you must long to have it. I do too. And when you have that you will find far more pleasure in our lovely house & in going about & meeting people on fair & equal terms & in building up your book – which will be a real building made of proper bricks.

Her mother came to stay at Cecil Court for the birth, and Tom was summoned to the nursing home in Courtfield Gardens when, much overdue, I at last plucked up the courage to meet my angry and resentful mother face to face by emerging from the uneasy shelter of her womb at midnight between 22 and 23 July 1931.

The actual birth was less difficult than Sue's. The only time in her life Antonia got drunk, she compared the experience to childbirth, saying that in each case one was completely at the mercy of one's body.

They were both disappointed it was not a boy, though Antonia was less so than the first time. The next day Tom wrote to her trying to raise her low post-partum spirits:

> Oh my darling cat I do want you back. There is a nice swept hearth & warm coals & a boiling kettle, and blue & white chintz curtains, and

everything except the one essential puss. Shall I ever cease to bear a grudge against my own descendant for taking up so much of you & your time. . . . Take care of yourself & bless you & our interfering brat. Always your lover Tom.

But the 'brat' came home before its mother. It took her much longer to recover from this birth than from the first:

Funny how I literally retained my second child and was ill for long after . . . I recovered completely from Susan. I think I accepted the experience of having Susan in a way I was unable to accept the experience of having Lyndall. I think I regard both children as having robbed me of something vital.

While Antonia had been in the nursing home waiting impatiently for me to face being born, a young woman came to see her. She had been sent by Tom's boss's nanny, who had told her 'the Hopkinsons wanted a nurse for a two-year-old girl and a new baby'.

Mary Hitchcock was in her early twenties. She had been in service since the age of fourteen and worked in a Dr Barnado's Home before going to her present post, where she was not happy. Antonia engaged the pretty young girl, with her quiet yet decisive manner, on the spot.

Less than a week after I was born, 'Nurse', as Sue and I would call Mary, took me back to Cecil Court. My mother had not even attempted to give me her milk, remembering the 'terror and pain and *repulsion*' of trying to breast-feed Sue.

I now had a substitute mother, something my half-sister never really had, even though, according to Mary Hitchcock, when Sue came to Cecil Court a few days after our arrival, she was brought by a woman who had been taking care of her whom she called 'Mummy' and who seemed jealous when she handed Sue over to Nurse.

The months immediately following my birth were the happiest of my parents' marriage, despite my mother's weak health and the worsening financial problems caused by more mouths to be fed. They were lovingly disposed towards one another, for Antonia had to admit that 'both Silas and Tom loved me more after I had had their children than before. That was the point where I failed each of them.'

When Antonia finally left the nursing home, although she was still feeling low, they went on holiday to Collioure in the south of France where a painter friend lent them a house.

At the beginning of November, Tom was diagnosed as having

appendicitis and sent to the Hampstead General Hospital. While there, he heard that his salary at Crawford's had been reduced by ten per cent, but this was fortunately compensated for by Antonia's having begun a trial job in the advertising department of Harrods.

A less self-centred side of Antonia emerged when Tom was ill. Tired and run down as she still was, she visited him in hospital every day after work, although it was a long journey across London. She arrived, according to one of Tom's letters to her, looking 'pleasant and maidenly and wifely and delicious and domestic and charming', bearing so many gifts bought out of £10 sent by his family as a contribution for medical expenses, that he had to plead with her to stop.

It was a strange and unexpected feature of Antonia's complex make-up that physical or mental distress in others brought out a tender side in her nature. When she was very small one of her favourite fantasies about her friend Gérard had been that he was tortured and she intervened to save and comfort him. Also, as a child, she had sometimes wished something terrible would happen to her father so that she could prove how much she loved him. Her strongest feeling for Reggie had been protectiveness; and she had fallen in love with Tom when he had needed protecting from the office rowdies. The only pleasant episode in my childhood connected with my mother was when she nursed me through an illness in my teens. But the danger of her need to comfort and protect, as Tom would soon discover, was that it could lead her to hurt people in order to have the 'exquisite pleasure' of being 'sweetly kind and tender' afterwards: 'Yes, I have a torturer's nature. And yet the person I torture most of all is myself.'

Before going to work part-time in the Advertising Department of Harrods, Antonia had had another short story published in *Life and Letters*. She told Tom that Logan Pearsall Smith had sent her such a complimentary letter about it that she was considering taking up work on a book she had abandoned after Sue's birth. Tom was pleased, but nevertheless sent her from his hospital bed some tactful advice on her writing:

> 'The Saint' is an utterly delightful story. It is in every way the work of a subtle & artistic mind. If you add to that, as you are planning, more ease & felicity in the stringing of sentences so that you can amble half way down a page, if you want, & still be as lucid & straightforward as you are at present, there is no reason why you should stop anywhere.

In order to write 'The Saint', Antonia had unearthed some half-written chapters of what Bertrand Russell had called, in 1926 when she had started work on them, her 'convent memoirs'. On coming out of hospital, Tom saw this unfinished material and was very impressed. Every day, having first done her bread-winning stint in 'Hell!', i.e. Harrods, he made her work on turning those early recollections into a novel, which she found a chore whose only pleasure was in reading it chapter by chapter to Tom.

At the beginning of 1932 both Tom and Antonia changed jobs. He went from Crawford's to the publicity department of Odhams Press: she returned to the purgatory of Crawford's having left the hell of Harrods. At weekends they both sat writing 'dutifully' at their twin desks; Antonia working on what would become *Frost in May*, and Tom on an equally autobiographical novel about a young man in advertising who really wanted to be a journalist.

On Sunday afternoons they would interrupt their writing either to go for a walk, or for Antonia to give one of her tea parties – since they could not afford drinks parties. According to Geoffrey Grigson's *Recollections*, these were attended by 'moderately able, moderately distinguished but at least independent writers and painters'.

Tom preferred the walks, but he admitted that the people who came to the tea parties were interesting. Besides Geoffrey Grigson and his American wife, Frances, who were planning to launch a new poetry magazine at the time, the guests included John Summerson, already a respected writer on architecture, Alick Schepeler, a handsome woman who had been Augustus John's model and mistress and now worked on *Vogue*, Eliot Seabrooke and another painter, Frank Freeman, with his wife Joan Soutar-Robertson who painted a mural of the Hopkinsons in the hall at Cecil Court which fascinated me as a child – more for the cat in the corner than for my virtually naked parents – and which must have dismayed Tom's relatives when they came to call.

One of the habituées at those teas was a mountain of a woman called Wyn Henderson. She played a strange role in my mother's life for about twenty years, from 1924 when Eliot Seabrooke introduced Antonia to her as someone who knew an abortionist. Divorced and bringing up two sons and a daughter, her voluptuous looks attracted many lovers whom she seemed perfectly willing to share with others. There were many things for which Antonia had to be grateful to Wyn:

she had introduced her to some of the people who became her closest friends, in particular Emily Coleman and Djuna Barnes when they were in London.

Both Emily and Djuna were Americans who wrote and painted in Europe, particularly France, in the 1930s. Like Antonia, they were both uncertain of their femininity and sexuality and suspected that the roles of woman and artist were irreconcilable. Emily usually flung herself into aggressively heterosexual affairs with younger men, one of whom described her as 'boyish physically and female psychologically'; whereas Djuna was at that time part of a lesbian circle in Paris, though when Emily once asked her if she was 'really lesbian', she had replied, 'I might be anything. If a horse loved me, I might be that.'

Of the two, Emily became the closer friend. She was convinced that suffering elevated people, and saw herself and Antonia as champions of spiritual and mental suffering, and told Tom he would never be a great artist until he had learned to suffer more. Like Antonia she had known madness. After the birth of her only child, she had spent two months in an asylum with the *idée fixe* that she was God. Her novel, *The Shutter of Snow*, describing her experience in the asylum had been published not long before, in 1930.

Whenever Emily appeared at the Hopkinsons' tea parties there was no danger of it being a dull afternoon. Djuna once told her she would be marvellous company 'slightly stunned'.

While Antonia was working on *Frost in May* she had a recurring dream, sometimes for two or three nights running, that Tom deserted her under circumstances of peculiar heartlessness. Recounting it in April 1932 Tom added: 'She wakes up hurt and miserable, and it is quite hard for me to convince her that I have not been ill-using her.' The dream had stopped by the time she finished the book.

In December Antonia sent the manuscript to a publisher, Heinemann, before going with Tom to spend Christmas with his family in Cumberland.

His father had been made Archdeacon of Westmorland a year before and had moved to a parish south-west of Carlisle. She found the new vicarage at Cockermouth bleak and spent a 'gloomy' Christmas there: 'the awful cold, the cheerless meals and untuned piano'. Although the whole Hopkinson family had made an effort to be friendly, Antonia found being with Tom's father an acute strain:

I wish he would come out with open hostility instead of this gentle, insulting Christian tolerance. He is gentle, but inflexible. Apparently kind and sensitive, but with that curious frosty chill underneath that seems so characteristic of believing protestant clergymen.

Tom's attitude to his father had changed since he had last been home. He had been shocked by his coldness and lack of encouragement over my birth and his continued disapproval of Antonia. Six months before that dismal Christmas visit he had written that his love for his father, 'one of the guiding principles of my life', had turned sour:

> From thinking him the perfect man, I ask exasperatedly whether he is one at all? He will not ever understand the mixture of mind & bodily feelings which tie me so close to Tony, & which seem to grow stronger every month.

The new year, 1933, did not begin well for Antonia: at the end of January she heard that Heinemann, as she had expected, had turned down her book. Since finishing it, she had lost the discipline of regular writing which Tom had helped her keep, and was beginning to waste time while trying to decide to which of three projects to give precedence:

(1) The Carlyle-Lawrence chimera
(2) The 'Period' generally (roughly 1780–1850)
(3) Vague plans for a new novel.

The novel was connected with the idea of doing a book about her father, about whom she had always wanted to write a 'sort of memoir'.

This uncertainty increased until she was back to her pre-Tom state of the 'old, perpetual trouble. Reading C[arlyle] one feels that *nothing* is worth writing, least of all my own tiny things.'

In February she had a bad attack of flu, followed by tonsillitis. Headaches returned, and the nightmares started.

The first nightmare recorded by Antonia is one she used later in a short story, 'The Moment of Truth'. In it she was at a ball in the house where Reggie and she had spent their honeymoon. It ended with her noticing a little door which had 'MURDER' printed on it; and a man 'with the most awful waxen face and bolting eyes', who was carving ham at the buffet, whispering to her, 'I know MURDER.' 'I woke up then, really terrified, though it doesn't look bad on paper.'

While she was ill in bed her one enjoyment was reading the love letters of Carlyle and his future wife, Jane Welsh. She found herself becoming fascinated by Jane's character, 'passionate, melancholy, impatient, fame-hungry and nervous', and decided she was like her, particularly when she discovered that Jane, after not having seen Carlyle for months, and having only a couple of hours to spend with him, wasted the precious time by forcing a quarrel she did not want.

Antonia did not write in her notebook for four months; and when she did, at the beginning of June 1933, she made no mention of the fact that *Frost in May* was due to come out shortly. Wyn Henderson had recommended it to a rich young man setting up as a publisher. It would be one of the very few books Desmond Harmsworth published, for he grew bored so quickly with publishing that he gave up before printing a needed second edition.

Just before the publication of the book Antonia went to Binesfield to take her mother a copy. Her father had been dead for nearly four years, and Aunt Clara had died, too. Only Aunt Agnes, bed-ridden by now, was left at the cottage with Christine. In her notebook Antonia described her feelings:

> The garden at Binesfield rots slowly away; the lawn covered with 'soldiers' and plantains, the lupins tangled and bedraggled. The walnut tree blighted. I love it still. As soon as I go there I feel contracted to a child again, lazy, restless, half asleep, waiting for something that never happens ... I am always thinking of someone else.

Was that 'someone else' Robert, with whom she had once gone to visit the aunts there? Or her father, who was very much in her mind now that she was trying to write about him? 'The thought of the second book depresses me terribly,' she wrote on coming back.

Later that summer Tom and Antonia were invited to stay with Peggy Guggenheim, an American millionairess and a self-styled 'art addict', for whom Wyn Henderson was running an art gallery in London. Hayford Hall, which came to be known as 'Hangover Hall', was a handsome mansion on the edge of Dartmoor, not far from the sea; Peggy had rented it to satisfy a whim of her latest lover, an English writer called John Holms. She had met him in the South of France through Emily who had been having an affair with him. Although Emily had once given Peggy a black eye in a fight over him, the rift had been mended and Emily, with her small son, was a permanent guest at Hangover Hall. Another permanent guest was Djuna Barnes who wrote much of *Nightwood* there.

Among the casual guests, as well as the Hopkinsons, was William Gerhardie with his current mistress. Gerhardie later described what it was like to stay there in his best-known novel, *Of Mortal Love*.

By day the guests could play tennis and swim and ride on the moors, which Tom enjoyed. In the evening there was drinking and lively conversation over dinner, which suited Antonia much better. After dinner came the moment of 'Truth', a devilish game in which everyone wrote a paragraph on everyone else present about a specific feature agreed beforehand, such as looks or faults or sex appeal. The compositions remained anonymous and were read out by one of the party afterwards, when each, in turn, came under ruthless fire from their fellow guests.

One evening, after everyone had said goodnight, Djuna came downstairs and found Emily sitting cross-legged on the floor with the contents of the waste paper basket spread around her. She was trying to piece together the torn and crumpled scraps of paper to identify from the handwritings who had said what about her that evening in 'Truth'.

Although Antonia was fascinated by the goings-on at Hangover Hall, while there she jotted down only half a page of disjointed notes, probably meaning to elaborate them later.

Antonia stayed on in Devon after Tom had returned to London, and while she was there *Frost in May* came out. The reviews were excellent. Tom sent them all to Devon and passed on Wyn's bulletins from Desmond Harmsworth on how sales were going:

> She sees no reason why you should not go to 2,000 and a second edition. She says all the indications are splendid, and, as she also remarks, you could not have had a greater 'succès d'estime' if you had sold 100,000 copies. Yes. I know we want cash as well!

Yet still Antonia did not mention *Frost* in her diaries. In her first entry after returning from Devon, dated 28 August, she talks only of the next novel on which she was 'completely paralysed'. She had made two false starts and was 'horrified at the niggardly mess'.

That autumn she was lionised in the literary world because of the book's success. Wyn Henderson gave a huge party for her; and the 'literary' Hopkinson – Tom's uncle Martin Hopkinson who owned a publishing house which bore his name – suggested Tom bring her down for a weekend to his country house at Bovingdon in September.

There, says Antonia, Tom 'electrified' the dinner table with an excellent short discourse on the political situation. The other guests had taken 'the splendid line that the rich always take':

(a) Poverty is so good for people. It makes them more spiritual.
(b) Nearly all the unemployed don't want to work.
(c) How disgraceful it is when the poor won't work.
Nothing said about the rich.

The above is one of the extremely rare occasions when one of Antonia's notebooks shows an awareness of what is going on in the world outside her mind; whereas Tom's notebooks were much more factual, and were soon filled with anecdotes about Sue and me, now that we had begun to express ourselves in words. One of the differences between my mother and father was that Antonia wanted 'children as children' and then ignored them; whereas Tom may not have wanted children, but when they were there he could not have been a kinder father. We looked forward to his visits to our nursery end of the flat, where we lived with Nurse and the cook, and dreaded our mother's rare appearances in our domain.

Antonia wrote very little in her notebook that autumn of 1933, but whenever she did there was no mention of *Frost* or whether its excellent reception had given her any satisfaction, but only of the agony of the work in hand, and how she was clutching at any excuse not to get down to the book:

Wonderful what will do it – letters, telephone calls, the need to set my hair or even to make a note here . . . Last week an intermittent headache & malaise, probably psychogenic in origin, made excellent 'reason'. Again I feel 'if only' . . . if only I could make up my mind once & for all about religion – if only I had some green typing paper – if only I had planned & bought my clothes for the autumn etc. The worst thing about being mad in my particular way is that all these things seem of equal importance.

The first of the very few mentions of her children in her notebooks comes just after this where she says that we have become interested in death and like pretending to be dead: 'Susan lying quite still and Lyndall waving her arms and shouting "I'm dead too."'

Then all is silence for a while, not because Antonia had been working on the book, though she did manage to write a piece for a collection called *The First Time I . . .*, but because she had been 'opening connections' for freelancing again, having decided to leave Crawford's for the second time after being given a contract for a book on the Carlyles.

In December she spent a cold week in foggy Edinburgh doing research on Jane Carlyle. While she was there, Tom wrote and told her that *Frost* had been mentioned in all lists of best novels of the year.

He, too, had just had a book published by Victor Gollancz, though not the novel he had been working on, which had been rejected. His was an illustrated political satire against the Prime Minister, Ramsay Macdonald, called *A Strong Hand at the Helm*. It was well reviewed in many papers, and the *Daily Herald* praised it as a 'biting exposure of the "National" Government's incompetence, inconsequence and inconsistency'.

On New Year's day 1934 Antonia finally made an indirect reference to *Frost in May* in her notebook, and, despite the recent return of writing problems and headaches, was able to say in summing up 1933 that it had at least been a year that saw her started off where she should have been years ago: 'No repinings: the thing is to keep on the road.'

On returning from Edinburgh, she took to her bed. She wrote how much she hated the early days of almost every New Year because she was usually ill. This year she had a very sore throat and was husky in the chest; and, she also noted, Sue and I both had chicken-pox.

When she had been ill at the beginning of the previous year she had enjoyed Jane Carlyle's love letters: now, sick again and re-reading them, she was repelled by them, and found Jane 'maddening with her archness – her flirtations and her sham high-browism and her "wee, wee Cicero"'.

By the end of the year the book on Jane Welsh Carlyle would have become such a burden that she abandoned it. Logan Pearsall Smith had told her she should make a 'scholarly job' of it, taking years to write it. She commented that there was nothing she would have liked better, but not having a private income, as he had, she could not afford the luxury of being a serious scholar.

Having spent the advance, she had also been trying to eke out a living by reviewing plays for a literary-political magazine, *Time and Tide*, but this proved too much for her and was another reason why she eventually dropped the book. She observed in her notebook:

The keeping up of an income on freelance work is a strain. I am too friendly to people; too much stung by remorse (probably vanity disguised) if I do not answer letters, talk on the telephone, lunch and ask them to my house.

One of the most ruthless wasters of her time early in 1934 was Alexander Keiller, who was as 'unscrupulous' about other people's time as he was about their tastes or feelings. She had been introduced to this forty-year-old many times divorced heir to a marmalade dynasty by Wyn Henderson. He was notoriously mean. On one occasion he excused himself for taking Antonia to a cheap restaurant because he said he was broke, and then over dinner described a mansion he had just bought and complained it was costing him nearly a million pounds to excavate Glastonbury, for he was a respected amateur archaeologist. Antonia found him most odd: 'Reputed a sadist: but the most sentimental man I know. Yet I enjoy being with him in spite of egoism, bombast, self-pity, merciless boredom.' Less than a month afterwards she changed her tune: 'Thank goodness I am free of AK.' She told me she refused to go out with him again after he had tried, first with pleading, then with bribery, to make her play sexual games with him. He wanted her to climb into a large laundry basket, wearing only a mackintosh, and let him poke her with an umbrella through the wickerwork. When she had reported this indignantly to Wyn, who was enormously fat and always short of money, she had retorted, 'If he can find a large enough basket, and pay enough money, I'll do it for him!'

The one and only time Tom showed jealousy of Antonia was over this eccentric millionaire with whom she was not having an affair. On waking at two o'clock one morning, and not finding his wife in bed beside him, he had taken a taxi to Keiller's flat in Mayfair to bring Antonia home. In that brief glimpse of the flat, he was astonished to see that Keiller, who prided himself on his masculinity and was a champion skier, had a large collection of toy teddy bears.

In March Antonia was ill again with tonsillitis and the profound depression that always accompanied any physical illness. As she lay in bed, feeling as if her head would burst and with her bowels 'tied into an iron knot', she mused on her age. She was about to be thirty-five and the change in her looks since her first marriage weighed heavily on her. Although she thought herself 'no uglier than in those days', she noticed younger women had 'a moisture of skin and lip, a sheen on the hair' she would never have again:

As soon as I feel well enough to make the effort I use up my first strength on combing my hair, creaming my face, rouging my lips. What does it all mean? It's out of all proportion. I have never, I think, expected very much of my appearance. I have always been surprised and delighted when anyone told me I was pretty . . .

Powder & face-cream have come to acquire a value for me which I cannot explain – it is almost like a lust or a kleptomania . . . My first thought – on hearing of the revolution – would be if I'd still be able to get face powder.

In this entry Antonia acknowledges for the first time that she is not in a good mental state. Soon afterwards she consulted Robb, a psychologist suggested by Wyn, but would not go to him for regular treatment. She was afraid that if she were cured of her infantile reactions, she might lose 'a kind of acuteness of perception and feeling' useful to a writer.

At least, she consoled herself, her mental state was not yet so bad as to block her writing completely. Although she could still not bring herself to touch the novel about her father, or write in her notebook over the next three months, she managed to continue as theatre critic for *Time and Tide*, and to write fashion articles for the *Daily Mirror* under the name of Ann Jeffrey – a variation of her grandmother's maiden name, Jeffery. She also wrote two short pieces: 'A Child of the Five Wounds' about Roehampton for a collection edited by Graham Greene, *The Old School*; and an essay about Brighton for an anthology, *Beside the Seaside*.

But by the time they appeared Antonia was in such a bad state that Tom said she must give up attempting to work and get away for a while. In late June, she went to stay in The Old Mill Guest House at Aldermaston to be near Logan Pearsall Smith and his friend Robert Gathorne-Hardy. With Logan, as always, she discussed writing. He insisted she should keep up her notebooks, although she had come to wonder if they served any purpose even as a 'sketchbook'. The few times she had incorporated extracts from them into her writing – as in 'Mon pays c'est la Martinique' – she felt had been a failure.

In July she went to stay with Peggy Guggenheim who had rented a different country house – Warblington Castle on the Sussex-Hampshire border. Since the previous summer there had been a tragedy in Peggy's life, the death of John Holms after a riding accident. Although Peggy had fallen in love with another 'frustrated poet', Douglas Garman, who was one of the guests at Warblington, she had a bad conscience about it and did not want anyone to know. So she kept an isolated room in the tower for herself and her lover, far from the other bedrooms, thinking her secret affair would not be discovered. But she tells in her memoirs how Antonia came up there one day and saw a pair of his grey flannel trousers lying on the bed. In order to keep her secret, she came down to dinner wearing the trousers, although they were several sizes too big.

Antonia wrote a long letter to Tom describing life at Warblington Castle:

> Without John to control us emotion runs high & there are Pretty Doings. The only male here is my old enemy Douglas Garman & we had a really frightful scene at dinner last night when Emily flung a full wine glass all over the table, completely lost her temper and screamed at Garman (I am a perfect Minnie Mouse compared to E. in a rage) & slammed out of the room . . .
>
> It is even madder than Hangover Hall but it takes your mind off of yourself & though it's exasperating & you can't get any breakfast or tea or get your shoes cleaned or find a match or hear yourself speak, I rather enjoy it. I've had bad nightmares though . . . Darling I do want to see you again.
>
> I will write again perhaps, only there's nowhere to write & no posts & no anything. Love to the pussies. We took 100 fleas off the dog this afternoon while Emily played Mozart. It is all like that!
>
> Much, more, most love from Tony

'The pussies' were not sue and i, but our parents' two cats: Fury, a white-and-ginger splotched ex-tomcat who lived up to his name, particularly since the arrival of Vanya, a Russian Blue kitten with more beauty than brains. We were at Cecil Court with Nurse and Tom, and would soon be going to stay with Tom's parents in Cumberland for the summer holidays, where we would have our fifth and third birthdays.

Tom wrote to Antonia at Warblington, assuring her he loved her and talking of a three-week holiday he was planning for them in Brittany.

As 1934 grew worse for Antonia, it improved for Tom. As a result of his book, *A Strong Hand at the Helm*, he was finally launched on a career in journalism. He had been moved from the advertising department of Odhams Press to the post of assistant editor on one of their weeklies, the *Clarion*. His financial situation, which in 1933 had reached desperation point after receiving a back tax demand for £70, had been temporarily solved by his uncle Austin who, grudgingly, had bought back some stocks in his firm which he had laid aside for Tom some years before. Although Austin gave Tom only half their value, it was a godsent windfall and paid off all their debts. Tom even allowed himself and Antonia £50 each spending money. She used hers on clothes: he bought a boat.

On their Saturday afternoon walks along the embankment Tom had often looked longingly at the little pleasure craft on the river, wishing that he could one day own one. Now he had *Scud* and set about repairing her and teaching himself to sail at weekends. He mentions *Scud* in a letter he sent Antonia while she was away that summer, 'as you will have guessed I spent all yesterday and all today on the boat'. What he did not tell her was that the day after she left for Aldermaston he had taken Frances Galt, Geoffrey Grigson's wife, out sailing, and fallen in love with her.

CHAPTER 9

༄

Jealousy and Nightmares

Envious and jealous I am – though not often accused of it.
Antonia White, 1 July 1954

When Antonia returned from Warblington, she and Tom set off for their holiday in Brittany. It was the end of July 1934 and she felt her mental state was as bad as it had been during her marriage to Reggie. But on their arrival in St Malo, on a sunny Sunday morning, she suddenly felt happy. She was pleased to be in France again after three years, and pleased to be with Tom whom she had hardly seen for the past six weeks.

They set off, with a guidebook to Brittany, in search of a place to stay by the sea. They spent their first night in St Cast, which Antonia found 'unspeakable', and quickly moved on to the Baie de la Fresnaye. There they found a secluded inn, formerly a sea-mill, which was almost encircled by water when the tide came in. They decided to spend their holiday in one of its rooms perched high over the rocks with a view across the bay, happy to find solitude and no other guests, even though there was something disquieting about the 'Madame' who ran the place. She was full of strange observations like '*Il ne faut pas dormir l'après midi: ça alourdit le sang,*' and kept bursting in on Antonia when she was trying to write to tell her gloomy tidings, such as how *méchante* the sea was looking, or that a black hen she had bought for their dinner had flown away.

Antonia seemed to be recovering. Tom took her for long walks along the strand when the tide was out which brought colour into her cheeks and gave her an appetite. And, despite Madame's interruptions, during the first week she managed to write three letters – to Eric, Emily and her mother – and two long entries in her notebook, in which she said that, although she still found it impossible to work, the 'actual business of driving a pen over paper was less difficult than it had been'. But the third entry, which began 'The black hen which escaped was eaten by dogs' and continued with some quotes from Santayana's *Reason in Common Sense*, was the last she made in Brittany. Some of the quotes she picked out from Santayana are significant in the light of what was about to happen:

> 'There may well be intense consciousness in the total absence of rationality. Such consciousness is suggested in dreams, in madness and may be found, for all we know, in the depths of universal nature.'
> 'We speak of people being "out of their senses" when they have in fact fallen back into them; or of those who have "lost their mind" when they have lost merely that habitual control over consciousness which prevented it from flaring into all sorts of obsessions and agonies.'

A few days later Antonia began to go out of her mind again.

At the beginning of the holiday she had noticed a slight change in Tom. His face, which had always seemed 'gentle, controlled, almost too anxious to please', sometimes now looked 'defiant, even a little dissolute'. When she told him he seemed different in some way, he said jestingly it was probably because, having just been apart for the longest time ever since they had met five years before, she had forgotten what he was like!

What happened on this holiday Antonia would one day turn into a short story, 'The Moment of Truth', in which she called herself 'Charlotte', and Tom 'Richard'. At the beginning of the story, Charlotte keeps trying to provoke scenes, just as Antonia used to with Tom; and Richard, like Tom, refuses to be roused.

One evening, in the middle of the holiday, Antonia was not feeling well and stayed in bed instead of going down to dinner. Wishing she had something light to read, she remembered Tom had brought a detective story and searched until she found it in the pocket of his coat. Out of the book fell an envelope with a Spanish stamp, addressed to Tom at a poste restante address. Inside was a letter from Frances.

When Tom came up to bed, she cross-examined him until he was forced to admit that he had slept once with its writer when Antonia had been away at Aldermaston, but that he had not seen Frances again. The scene Antonia made, ending with her first attempt to kill herself, is described in 'The Moment of Truth', for, as she wrote two months later, she could not bring herself to write about it at the time because it had brought about complete disintegration, 'physical, mental, nervous and emotional':

It is less actual to me than the asylum which has now acquired a kind of poetic intelligibility for me. This had something of the same quality as the asylum but, in a way, it was worse because it all went on in actual life and ordinary surroundings.

In 'The Moment of Truth', on learning that her husband has been unfaithful, Charlotte flings herself at him, 'tearing at his coat, butting his chest with her head', before falling back exhausted on the bed. Then she breaks into a quiet monologue in which she has changed to 'coldly, ferociously accusing herself'. He cannot bear to listen, hiding his face in his hands. Suddenly, the raving ceases. Before he has time to realise what she is up to, she has gone over to the window and is hoisting herself on to the outside ledge. Richard rushes to grab her:

> They stood for a moment in a grotesque embrace; then, with the force of an uncoiling spring, Charlotte threw herself forward, nearly dragging him with her. Lurching half over the sill, he could see far below the dark masses of slippery, jagged rock, half-bared by the ebbing tide.

She struggles furiously to get free and drops down over the sill, disappearing from sight, except for her two clinging hands whose grip is slowly relaxing:

> 'I want her to die,' he said to himself.
> In the overwhelming relief of acknowledging it, his muscles suddenly asserted themselves . . . He made a dive forward from his hips, reached down, caught Charlotte under the armpits and dragged her up through the window.

Antonia continued to be in such a weak, confused state after learning of Tom's love for someone else, that they cut short their holiday and hurried back to England to seek Eric's advice, for Eric, who was very fond of Tom too, had become a father figure to both of them since their marriage.

Eric was having a quiet holiday near the sea at Shaldon in Devonshire. It was decided that Antonia should stay with him there for a while to see if his calming influence could help her to recover.

Tom, who had a week of his annual holiday left before returning to Odhams, where he had recently become assistant editor of a new magazine, *Weekly Illustrated*, spent it alone at Cecil Court. The flat was empty because Nurse had taken Sue and me to stay with Tom's parents, and the cook was still on her annual holiday. He passed the time writing the fourth chapter of a book he had started earlier that summer, redecorating the flat and varnishing his beloved boat.

He also saw Frances again. She had just come back from Spain and came twice to Cecil Court where they spent a 'few stolen hours' together. After that they never made love again, although they continued to see each other until her death.

There was a *Grand Meaulnes* quality about Tom's love affair with Frances Galt. When it was over, he wrote a short story based on it, called 'The Third Secretary's Story', where that quality of something tasted, then lost, never to be refound is very poignant.

When he had first met Frances at one of Antonia's Sunday tea parties, Tom had found her 'like a long glass of cold water' and been almost rudely offhand: in fact Antonia had reprimanded him afterwards, saying, 'You might at least be decently polite to her, after all she is a friend of mine.'

Recently he described her to me: 'She was a tall American girl, with broad shoulders like a boy, and a very open face and dark hair. She had a slightly stiff American manner, as if not entirely at ease in the European world, and a slim straight body which she had not the least idea how to manage.'

One day, my father told me, when he had known Frances distantly for over three years, they found themselves at the same party given by Wyn Henderson. 'At this party,' he said, 'for the first time, I thought she looked very interesting – besides thinking she looked very pretty, which she always did. I was feeling a bit carefree – we'd just got our £500 from Austin and I wasn't feeling as oppressed as I had been – and I started making up to Frances a bit. Then I wandered off to talk to other people. After a while I saw her going and I went back to say "You mustn't go", but she insisted she had to – she was on her own – so I said, "I'll see you to a taxi".

'When we got to the bottom of an enormous flight of stone steps, we both turned towards each other absolutely . . .', here Tom's voice broke, and it was some time before he could go on, '. . . well, anyway, there was a kind of alcove under the steps, so I drew her into this alcove – because people were coming up and down the stairs – and we fell into an embrace and kissed passionately. After a while she said, "I really must go," so I took her to a taxi and said to the man, "Drive very, very carefully". After that – it was the time Antonia was beginning to go barmy – I didn't know what to do. All we could do was meet occasionally for lunch.'

Over those lunches Tom learned that Frances had recently had pleurisy, that the Grigsons were 'loosely related' and Geoffrey was away in Spain for a while. She had had a short affair with someone else and Geoffrey had had several, in fact their closest connection at that time was *Poetry*, a magazine they ran together.

While Antonia was away in June, Tom rang Frances and invited her out to dinner and a theatre. Afterwards they went back to her flat in Hampstead and spent the night together.

That night was the happiest of Tom's life until then; but as they lay contentedly in each other's arms after making love, Tom told Frances, 'You know that we shall have to pay for this,' and she said quietly, 'Yes, I know.'

In the morning they had got up very early to go out on Tom's new boat. While Tom was rowing out to fetch *Scud*, he saw Frances sitting on the embankment steps that went down to the water, her hands round her ankles and looking very sad. He had the feeling this was 'a critical moment'.

It was a fine June morning and he would have liked to spend the whole day with Frances, but he had to go to work. He was confident they would see each other again that night. But when the time came to part, and he asked, 'Where shall we meet later?' she told him that she had promised Geoffrey to join him in Spain and was booked to leave that very afternoon.

He felt desolate, but dared not ask her not to go away. And after her return, Frances told him, 'I would never have gone out to Geoffrey if you had asked me not to.'

The Grigsons had still been away in Spain when the Hopkinsons left for their holiday in Brittany, but the two couples returned at about the same time. When Frances came to Cecil Court for the second stolen meeting, she told Tom she had conceived a child in Spain with Geoffrey. Tom tried to convince himself it was a good thing because he knew how much she wanted a child, and there could be no coming together for them as he was responsible for Antonia and us children. But although he did not see Frances again for several months, they corresponded, and he wrote in his notebook that he thought constantly of their love-making.

Tom also wrote to Antonia at Shaldon apologising for having made their Brittany holiday so unhappy: 'I have been mad, but I love you Tony and want you to be here.'

During the time Antonia spent with Eric in Shaldon she managed to write in her notebook one afternoon when Eric was out. The rain was driving in sheets outside the window; inside she felt the terrible depression that had overwhelmed her in Brittany welling up again: 'I hardly care what I do; whether Tom & I rediscover our happiness, whether I work or don't work in the future.'

Not only was she even more despondent than before about her writing and convinced she did not have any creative genius, but she could not even settle down to reading. For the next few weeks the only book she occasionally dipped into was Keats's letters from which she sometimes copied out a random quote.

She was still suffering violently from jealousy and acknowledged that it was a 'terrible destroying impulse which had always been very strong in her'.

Antonia returned to Cecil Court in September. Ahead of her and Tom lay a difficult autumn, followed by a worse winter.

A month after her return to London, Antonia recorded in her notebook a surprising moment of optimism and dared to hope that she might cohere again. She was managing to do some hack work, though she was still frightened of attempting any creative writing. Also, to her surprise, men were showing an interest in her.

But Antonia did not write in her notebook again until December, and, according to Tom, those three unchronicled months were alarming. Less than a month after Antonia had hoped her nerves were steadier, Tom wrote, on 23 October: 'Tony has been upset in her mind the last ten days after three weeks of peace and quiet.' The night before she had dreamt of herself as the crazy-looking heroine in a film called *Sanity Crise*.

The real nightmares began again and violent headaches returned. She made further attempts at suicide, rushing for the high window, as in Brittany. Tom would haul her back to bed and lie there, exhausted and trembling, with Antonia in his arms. He tried to soothe her by blaming himself and saying how bad he was for her:

'No, you're not. No, you're not' Tony would say. 'I'm bad for you. I'm so awful and attacking. Something just seems to seize me. Oh Tom, darling, do please kill me. I wouldn't mind a bit.' And she would be soft and convincing as a pleading child, 'Really Tom, it would be much the best thing you could do.'

So with our madness when Tony had reached breaking-point and I had fought with her, it was as if some barrier were lifted, some sort of cloud had gone.

She had many rows with Tom that autumn, and constantly threatened to leave him. Immersed in her own suffering, Antonia did not seem to recognise how much Tom was suffering, too. He yearned for Frances and felt bitter about being shut out of her life so soon after entering it. But he did not give in to despair because he wanted to hold his peculiar marriage together. Also his new job on *Weekly Illustrated* kept his mind fully occupied by day. After one of their rows he wrote to Antonia from the office:

> Pain to your pride, & there must have been much of it, is being avenged. But I know very well that is not all that has been hurt between us . . . I feel very bad about it, and a little desperate . . . I feel that if we could only slide over thin ice we would soon be on firm ground – oh Tony, do bear with me a little longer.

The letter ended, 'If you ever loved me – help.'

They clung on together. By November Antonia was so ill with depression and headaches that she often stayed in bed all day. She had turned against Cecil Court because she suspected Tom had made love to Frances there when she had been at Eric's; and she found the presence of Sue and me painful reminders that she was not free of responsibilities. Her weekly article for the *Daily Mirror*, her only source of income, had become an almost unbearable agony to write. Tom wrote her encouraging notes begging her to rest and not to worry about trying to earn a living, saying that he would provide for us all somehow if she could help by being less extravagant.

However, it was Tom who now took a step which would get him into debt. At his wits' end, he had gone to see Eric to discuss the problem of Antonia. Eric had said 'Do something mad for her sake.' Tom knew that the 'mad' gesture he ought to make was to give up Cecil Court. He fought against it because he was writing well and knew that a major upheaval would upset this. Now, smothering his resentment – 'I'm a person too' – he acted. He sent us away with Nurse to his parents; he put Cecil Court in the hands of renting agents, and took a little furnished house in Godfrey Street, off the King's Road in

Chelsea. They took Kitty the housekeeper with them, the two cats and their twin desks.

Antonia knew the rent of 16 Godfrey Street was far more than Tom could afford, but her first act on moving in was to go out to buy smoked salmon for Fury in order to lure him out of hiding in her desk.

The first week at Godfrey Street, at the end of November, they were both happy. But then things changed. A letter Tom wrote to Antonia when they had been there only two weeks shows that they were considering she might have to go into a clinic. He promised to find 'somewhere human' for her, and to 'come continually' to see her. The letter ended: 'Tony, bear up for a little more.'

Soon after Tom had invited some friends to dinner. When he came home from the office, instead of finding his wife, he found a pencilled note from her on his desk:

Tom dear if I am not in by 8 please do not wait for me for dinner. I will try not to do anything stupid.

You are not responsible for the effect things you have done may have on me. I know my head is not good & I don't see things clearly. But will it ever be?

I am so ashamed of my appearance. If I don't come in to dinner it may be because I don't want to expose myself to your friends & make you ashamed of me. Clothes are no good even if I could afford nice ones because you know the truth. Talent even if I had it does not matter. Nothing counts beside beauty.

I have got your letter with me. Perhaps it would make me happier if I could read it right. But even if I am cured I have only a mutilated life to look forward to.

I don't know what's going to happen to-day. I fight to be self-controlled but this is very strong. Tony.

The time had come to get outside help. Tom took Antonia to see an eminent psychologist and hypnotherapist, William Brown, who had gained renown after the First World War for his success in treating shell-shocked soldiers.

At the first session she felt a 'sense of ease and letting go: complete reassurance'. Because she was calmer afterwards, and because Tom was having to pay two rents since no one had taken Cecil Court, she agreed that they should give up Godfrey Street.

After returning to Cecil Court for Christmas she even managed to write in her notebook again, not having put one word in it during the stay in Chelsea; and, more remarkable, reconsidered the book on her father. She resolved not to be afraid of writing about him any more since it was 'a pure accident' that they were father and child: 'I have a right to look at him; yes, sexually too.'

She also said she felt less indifferent to Tom physically. But with the return of feeling came the return of 'the Frances theme', particularly as Tom had been to see her for the first time since he had learned five months before that she was pregnant. Antonia felt terribly her lack of beauty compared to Frances, and jealousy that Tom had experienced with Frances a physical passion he had never known with Antonia. She acknowledged that there was a 'flaw' in her which might mean she would never have a satisfactory physical relationship with any man, and that it was unfair to go on blaming Tom endlessly for what had happened. After all, she admitted, she had been 'mentally unfaithful' before he had been physically unfaithful: 'I know it is petty to cry out, but I do, I do.' Antonia felt Tom had been jealous of any small success in writing she may have had, yet had shown no jealousy when she had been interested in other men: 'But of course I haven't given my love to anyone else.'

She asked herself what she really felt for Tom.

Although there was 'much to love and admire' in him, she often found him exasperating. She knew she was being unreasonable in minding that he had given his love to another person, since there were times when she actually hated him for being too charitable and considerate: 'He's so smug.'

Antonia's dilemma over what she felt for Tom and what she wanted from him would continue for many years. With her schizophrenic nature, it was almost impossible for her to be constant in her feelings for anyone: her angry ego, warring with that side of her which had once longed to be good, could manipulate her mind into destroying the affections of people who might have been able to save her from herself. Instead, everyone who was close to her would at some stage come under her mental dissecting knife and be harmed by it in some way.

Two days after dissecting her feelings for Tom, Antonia made the first of the lists that would become a feature of her notebooks. She made lists of her joys and miseries of one day; of how her money had been spent or would be spent; of her faults and virtues; of her ex-lovers; of those who wished her dead or who were glad she was alive. This first list, written on 30 December 1934, was of her '*Likes, Hates, and What I would Like to Happen*'. Among the thirty-six hates were:

> Being pregnant.
> People who automatically ask first 'How are the children?'

In the list of '*What I would Like to Happen*', most of which concerned money and writing, were: 'Tom to fall in love with me and realise how he's hurt me', and 'To be free for ever from the idea of eternal damnation'. Among the twenty-four *Likes* was 'Brown's treatment'.

But soon the visits to Brown began to go less well. She could not go under when he tried hypnosis and she was beginning to find the whole thing ridiculous. She told Tom that while 'bumbling away' to her to be 'calmer, more contented, more capable, more spontaneous in your sexual life', Brown would stumble over the fire-irons each time he came to pop his head over the screen behind which she lay to see if she was under yet.

By 6 January she was writing that she was 'sick of the high priest attitude of the psychoanalysts'. And three days later she lashed out directly against her hypnotherapist: 'Too much cant about old Brown. So bloody pleased with himself . . . parental instinct, self-sacrifice – pheugh. Bloody lot of self-sacrifice for him with £5000 a year.'

The headaches started again, accompanied by languor; and at the next treatment she burst into tears for no reason, and wrote afterwards that she felt like a horse ridden on a curb, longing to shake its head free and bolt: 'But where to?'

Her dreams became more frightening and the suicidal impulses returned. Besides trying to fling herself off the balcony at Cecil Court, she took to getting up in the night and running out of the flat half-dressed to head for the Thames. She left messages for Tom in 'looking-glass writing' on his desk, a warning that her other self, which she called 'the beast', was taking over.

Her urge to flee became so strong that she went away for a few days. Tom told her to ring up if she needed comfort: 'I don't want you to be cut off from warmth just because there is some barrier between us physically.' And there was a letter from him waiting for her at Cecil Court on her return, which said he loved her but would not expect her to make love with him until she wanted to, nor need she fear that he would one day go back to making love with Frances.

A few days after her return, Brown admitted defeat and said she needed a proper long analysis. Frances had suddenly become a terrify-ing image. 'The beast' raged against her as well as Tom in Antonia's notebooks. She had given way to a violent impulse to ring up her rival and demand to see her. Frances had been cool, but quite affable, finding the excuse that she was too busy that week, but might be free the one following.

Whenever the image of Frances hovered in her mind Antonia became conscious of her own looks. She imagined Francs's beauty had 'set a standard' for Tom which nothing else could ever equal, and felt ugly and inadequate in her 'wretched body' with its tendency to put on weight when she was unhappy. And yet she had to admit many people had been attracted to her physically. She raged against Tom, but when she then listed points 'Against' and 'For' him, there were twice as many in his favour, among which was 'Because he is so good to and for the children'.

Four days later she noted that she and Tom had been very happy over a weekend. But there had been sadness too: 'He will so seldom talk to me; it is always I who talk to him.' She resented her illness forcing her into an artificial dependence on him and felt it was 'always some future me or some me in the past that Tom seems to love, not me as I am here and now'.

Three weeks later she started sessions with Dennis Carroll, a Freudian psychoanalyst recommended by Brown, and she would be his patient for the next four years.

By now her nightmares had reached such a high pitch of horror that she used to wake Tom up after them for comfort. In one of the early ones she had dreamt that she was eating her brains served cooked to her on a plate. 'And that,' she told Tom, 'is exactly what I am doing day and night.'

After Antonia had been going to Carroll for a month she felt calmer, although the nightmares continued. She had managed to finish an article and had started to write in a notebook again – a new one, because Tom had read the old one without asking permission. On discovering this she had made a terrible scene and during the bitter quarrel that ensued, Tom said to her, 'You're made of iron.' But she soon relented, and for over a year kept two notebooks, sometimes making an entry in both on the same day on the same subject.

The birth of Frances's baby early in March was chronicled in each notebook. In the 'old' one she said she had first heard of it before Tom from a mutual friend, and had discovered it had happened the same night that she had had a terrible nightmare about a man with a deformed face. When she passed on to Tom the news that Frances had had a daughter, her teeth chattered just as they did after the nightmare. According to the second notebook, the nightmare had been so horrific that she woke up gasping and cold with fright. She could not even bring herself to go down the passage to the lavatory alone after it, and asked Tom to accompany her and left the door open.

There were other results at the beginning of Carroll's analysis besides resuming the notebooks again. Antonia decided to lose weight. She managed to stick to her diet and even found pleasure in doing her slimming exercises. She also managed to hold onto herself when having scenes with Tom, instead of trying to kill herself or attacking him physically. In mid-March she was able to write that they had been able to talk without 'lacerating' each other, and, relieved that she had declared a 'truce', Tom had been very tender and kind. She even accepted he might not only have to see Frances, but even make love to her again one day, in order to confirm, or destroy, 'her image in him'.

Thinking that he now had Antonia's permission to see Frances, Tom went to the nursing home in Ladbroke Terrace where her daughter had been born a week before. As he was leaving Frances said, 'When you were standing by the window, I could see that you were crying.'

What Antonia called the 'truce' did not last long.

On Thursday 14 March, Antonia read Tom's black notebook when he had left for the office: 'I had no right to perhaps, but he has read mine and I did.' She was horrified to find how much there was about Frances in it: the last words had been that he had seen Frances the previous day. The few references to Antonia seemed to show that he saw her as 'a pathetic person' for whom he felt only tenderness and pity.

Although her first reaction was to think 'My life is over', she had pulled herself together and made herself behave as if she had not read Tom's notebook, confessing however, 'If I were still religious, I would pray for strength and courage.' She did her exercises, dressed carefully and finished a couple of odd jobs, but she still felt so rasped and on edge that she had to go out, although it was a dark, cold day with snow threatening.

Putting one of her notebooks in her handbag she wandered from café to café writing interminably, as one cup of coffee after another grew cold. She felt 'nervous yet almost exalted' and by the end of the day had written over three thousand words about Tom and Frances and herself.

Antonia wrote that it was not Tom's unfaithfulness she minded so much 'though goodness knows I do mind it', but such falseness in him. He had always denied with 'truth shining out of his eyes' that Frances was important to him. 'Yet all those pages written only last night are Frances, Frances, Frances. A mention of one week – and one week only at Godfrey St – when he was happy and his mind was only on me.'

Why, she asked herself, had she clung to the hope that she and Tom might have been able to make something of their marriage, in spite of her humiliation, misery, exasperation and boredom, when she had loved and admired other men more and had stronger physical feelings for them?

> Yet to no other man have I been faithful for five years, endured things I hate, domesticities, monotony, a dull unvaried life. I have a child by him, yet Lyndall, if she means anything to me, means something as an odd little person in her own right, not as the child of the man I love. I wish I loved my children more.

She wondered whether the time had come to leave Tom and move out of Cecil Court?

She had to interrupt her paragraphless stream of writing to go to her daily session with Carroll. There she broke down and sobbed herself nearly into convulsions, biting her handkerchief and tearing at the pillowcase on the analyst's couch.

After analysis she found another café to sit in and continued her reflections:

> My strength & my weakness both keep natural love away from me. Men are afraid of me because part of my mind is rough & tough, and appalled when they find how wincing, frightened & unprotected my nature is . . . There is a lion & a lamb inside me – and they *won't* lie down side by side.

Although she now said she wished she had a lover, and was not dependent on Tom for 'physical peace', she did not wish it enough to take one. Two men were eager to have an affair with her at the time. One was John Summerson the architect; the other a Jamaican sculptor called Ronald Moody who was modelling her head: 'Both tell me my face is beautiful, but they see me with a sculptor's and an architect's eye. I only see the faded remains of mere prettiness.' She told herself she ought to be less fastidious and consider taking a lover before it was too late.

Once, while she had sat for Ronald in his studio, he had told her he was sure that one day she would leave Tom of her own accord, because he had never accepted her wholeheartedly for what she was.

She now wrote a twenty-page soliloquy on 'To go or not to go', with a microscopic examination of Tom's character. She said she wished him no ill, but wanted to be her own property again:

> But then what am I to do about the children? They love him & he is so good to them. Emotional disturbances are so bad for them. I suppose it must come in the end to 'companionship' marriage.

The next night she could not sleep. Usually when this happened she would wake Tom who would make her a glass of hot milk, or tell her a story; but on this occasion she crept into the sitting-room at three o'clock in the morning, leaving Tom sleeping soundly, to write in her notebook. She said she was tempted to kneel down and pray, but it would be false; until a belief in God returned, she must get strength only from herself. Her conclusion after two hours of writing was different from the one she had made in the café: 'I believe I do love Tom, but I think I must be brave and leave him.'

The next day, Sunday, she went to look at a room to let in a house in Oakley Street, near Albert Bridge, where Phyllis Jones, whom she had met that summer at Warblington, lived. Phyllis would become a friend for life. On returning to Cecil Court Antonia wrote only two sentences:

March 17th, 1935

> I have definitely decided to leave Tom, anyhow for the present, on Thursday. The room looks grim and bleak but I know I am right to.

On the Tuesday, Nurse took Susan and me to stay with Tom's parents in Cockermouth for the Easter holidays.

On the Wednesday, Antonia asked Tom to meet her for lunch.

'I'm tired of marriage,' she told him, 'I need a rest from it.' Then, with a toss of her head, she told him she was moving out.

Tom kept calm. 'If anyone wants to know where you are,' he said, 'I shall tell them you're taking a holiday from me.'

She looked at him with a little smile. 'Still afraid of the truth?'
'Why?' he asked. 'Surely that's true?'
'Darling,' she said very gently, 'I'm leaving you.'

CHAPTER 10

❦

Child of 'The Beast'

*I suppose the production of children is a very satisfying
thing to a real woman.*
Antonia White, 15 August 1937

Before starting to write this book, I had always felt as if a black cloud
spread over my life like a pall from the moment I was born, keeping
away the warmth and light of the sun. And because my mother and
elder sister often told me what a cry-baby I used to be as a child, the
feeling was enhanced and made me suppose that this had been my way
of protesting at being born of an unhappy mother into an unhappy
family. My feeling of inadequacy, which I had always thought was
life-long, seemed justified by having a mother who did not seem to
think much of me.

But now, after reading my father's notebooks and letters of the
period of my early childhood, and having talked to Mary, my nurse,
after having lost touch with her for nearly fifty years, a different
portrait of myself when very small emerges.

I discover that I started out funny and honest and bold. So when
did I become the melancholy, devious and uncertain human being I
had always assumed I was by nature? When did that 'sunrise in June',
as my father called me once in a letter to my mother, become
that autumn sunset I felt I had always been? What had turned
me by adolescence into such a pessimist that I was sure that
whatever I did was doomed to failure so that my mother added a
new noun, 'Lyndallism', and a new adjective to her vocabulary? 'I
wish you'd get over this awful Lyndallistic notion that anything you
write is bound to be a failure' she wrote to me when I was twenty-
three.

Most of my life I looked for happiness outside myself, in people,
places and things; and each time I realised I had not found it, after

thinking briefly that I had, I became more unhappy. Should I have been trying to re-discover it inside myself?

'You didn't cry any more than most babies,' Mary said. 'You did cry a lot during the first month or two of your life, but not after I found a baby milk that suited you.' But compared to Sue I was a cry-baby: I can never remember her crying as a child, not even when she walked into a lamp-post and cut her forehead.

'Apart from when you were tiny you didn't cry all that much,' my father confirmed, 'though when Mary first brought you home you yelled so much that a neighbour threatened to call the police. I told him if he thought they could do something, I should be extremely grateful!' Then Tom added, 'I do remember you making *me* cry once when you wept after I had told you that Tony had gone to live somewhere else. You'd have been about three then I suppose.'

I was incredulous. Why would I have cried when Mother left home, since, I thought, I had always been terrified of her?

But Tom assured me that in the beginning I was not afraid of her. Sometimes, when I was very small, he told me, if Nurse was away for her monthly weekend off, I used to come into their bedroom on Sunday morning, climb into their bed and snuggle up between them.

In bed by my own choice with my dragon of a mother? It was almost impossible to imagine.

But then, thinking things over, I realised that it was possible that before I reached the age of conscious memory my mother might have been a less frightening figure to me. After all she never handled me as a baby and I did not see much of her. For the first year after my birth she was happy with Tom: her mental illness only became really serious around my third birthday in 1934, when she spent most of the summer away with friends. Sue and I had already left to stay with Tom's parents in Cockermouth when he and Antonia set off for their disastrous holiday in Brittany; and by the time we came back she was away at Eric's in Shaldon. In the autumn, shortly after she returned, Tom made his mad gesture of renting the 'little house' in Godfrey Street and sent us back to his parents with Nurse.

So our co-habitation with Antonia during the worst period of her illness, when she was haunted by nightmares and headaches and trying to throw herself out of windows, was in fact for a few months only at the beginning of 1935. Then, while we were once again away staying with Tom's parents for Easter, she moved out to a room of her own.

Most of my first conscious memories start when our household at Cecil Court consisted of Nurse, Tom, Sue, the cats, and the daily cook Mrs Anning, though there are a few isolated glimpses in my mind of events which happened when Mother was still there.

What must be the earliest memory, for I was only two and a half, is of my mother coming to see Sue, Nurse and me where we lay ill in the same room with chicken-pox. She wore a dressing gown of pale blue silk with black squiggles on it. I also remember Nurse telling us to be quiet sometimes when we went through our parents' quarters on the way out for a walk because Mother was lying down with 'one of her headaches'. And I remember my mother making Sue and me do exercises with her some mornings, commanded by a brisk woman's voice on a scratchy record which kept running down on the wind-up gramophone. Those must have been the slimming exercises she started after going to Dr Carroll, when I was three and a half.

I see now that my very early childhood, unlike Sue's, was not unhappy. For the first five years the three most important people in my life were 'fixed', Nurse, Tom and Sue; and the two who mattered less, my mother and the current cook/housekeeper, were 'mutable'. Cecil Court was my only home until I was seven, whereas Sue had already been shifted three times to new places with new faces before coming to Cecil Court to become Tom's eldest daughter around her second birthday. No wonder she latched onto Tom who, even before she came to live under his roof, had been a thread in her life since he had started visiting her in the children's home. And no wonder she wished she did not have to share him with a younger sister.

Tom's very first mention of Sue in his notebook was in September 1932. She was just three years old and I was barely one.

> Susan is very jealous – like the rest of us. She is jealous particularly of Lyndall. If Lyndall cries people come running. Several times I have seen or heard Susan burst out crying out of an absolutely clear sky – to call attention to herself. The other morning when I went in to say 'Good morning' to her she lifted up her arms in a silly affected way and said 'I'm a little teeny baby, I'm a little teeny baby.'

And the second time Antonia mentions Sue in her notebook, it was to record that, aged four and a half, she had said to her, 'I suppose you had Lyndall and Tom had me.'

But if Sue was jealous of me I was not aware of it. She had just as important a place in my order of things as did Nurse, who was sternly affectionate and dependable, and Tom, who was warmly affectionate and told good stories. It seemed to me that Sue, whom I liked and admired, was tolerably fond of me: when I did what she wanted there were crumbs of praise which I lapped up, and when I didn't there was a risk of having 'rum-tum-tiddle-um' drummed out on my tummy with her fists which I appreciated less.

Whatever dramas were going on at our parents' end of the flat, life down our corridor was calm in those days. This was mainly due to Mary Hitchcock, our nurse, whom Tom described in his autobiography as 'young, warm-hearted and capable, but not so strong-minded as to make their life a burden'. For me, although she was strict, she was an excellent mother-substitute. For Sue, after the traumas she had been through, which had made it hard for her to trust women, there was a less easy relationship with Nurse, which sometimes ended in arguments and Sue getting more spankings than I did.

But Nurse and I had a daily battle over lunch. I hated just about everything that it was considered healthy for a child to eat: meat, green vegetables, fish, eggs. When she could no longer bear to see me pushing cold scraps around my plate, and her exhortations of 'Eat up Lyndall!' were having no further results, in despair, she would hold my nose and shovel the remaining food into my mouth until I nearly choked.

Though I may have wept on being told my mother was moving away early in 1935, I have no recollection of life being different at Cecil Court in her eighteen-month absence; particularly as she used to drop in occasionally. Nothing changed in our routine, for it had always been Tom or Nurse who took us to our nursery school in Glebe Place, or out for walks in the park at weekends. But the questions we, and particularly Sue, asked Tom after Antonia left show that we were trying to puzzle out whether they loved each other and why people got married.

A few months after our mother left home, Tom wrote in his notebook:

This evening one of them looked at my red fountain pen – I was drawing pictures for them on scraps of paper – & said 'Where did you get that?'
  'Tony gave it me.'
  'She gave it you because she loved you, didn't she?' This was Lyndall.
  'Yes.'

'And you love her, don't you? That's why you married her, isn't it, because you loved her?'

'Yes.'

Susan broke in then. 'You love her' she said 'and she loves you. You think you love her more than she loves you, and she thinks she loves you more than you love her. Really you both love each other as much?' she ended as a question.

'Yes' I said 'really we both love each other as much.'

'People get married' said Susan 'because they love each other, but it doesn't seem as if they do. They don't seem to stay like that. You and Tony love each other. You're married friends.'

CHAPTER 11

֍

Married Friends

*I want a man, whatever I mean by that, & I can't be a
woman or happy as a woman until I have a man, not
a boy, however amorous.*

Antonia White, 9 January 1935

I want a happy mistress.

Tom Hopkinson, 26 May 1935

Ten days before her thirty-sixth birthday, 31 March 1935, Antonia
moved to 105 Oakley Street.

The immediate effect on her of leaving Tom was relief; but this was
followed by two bad days during which she did not manage to write
a single word of her piece for the *Daily Mirror* – for she was still
commissioned by their woman's page to produce a weekly article and
had only failed to do so for a few weeks during the previous summer,
at the height of her illness. On the third day, she had such a crisis that
during analysis she wept convulsively, but this brought no relief, and
on getting home she lay on her bed, moaning. Then, unable to resist
the temptation to see Tom, she got up, forced herself to do her hair,
and went to see him: 'fatal: brought on a violent attack, a direct
personal assault on him followed by appalling depression, tears & the
revival of the suicide desire'.

After this verbal and physical attack on Tom, she returned to Oakley
Street and wrote to him saying she felt they could not even be 'good
friends'. Tom wrote back:

We have certain solid things to give each other . . . for which, if only they
came from any one else, we should be grateful enough, & that on those
we might have built a . . . friendship.

. . . When you are in an attacking mood I am in your presence like the
slugs I have seen gardeners put into bowls of salt. I dissolve away. And

then I hate you for dissolving me away – and you, as you see me dissolve, think I am withdrawing out of your reach . . .

It was hard to start this letter, & now it is hard to stop. So it is with us – hard to be together & always reluctant to leave each other.

Three weeks later Tom became Antonia's 'passionate lover'.

Antonia had seen Frances for the first time for nearly a year, at a party given by John Summerson. She thought her rival looked pale and heavy. For a moment they were alone together. On a 'genuine impulse' she said, 'I am very glad to see you again, Frances,' but saw an expression of such fear and shrinking on the other's face that she said no more.

Tom and Antonia's 'love affair' was interrupted by his coming to fetch us back from his parents at the end of the Easter holidays.

The Hopkinsons were very much against him taking us back to London. They argued that with Antonia not in her right mind and away from home, it would be 'a quite impossible household'. They also put pressure on Mary, saying she should not live alone in the flat with Tom now that his wife was not there and the new cook did not live in. Tom won the battle and went home with all three. Mary was severely criticised for having made this brave decision, not only by Tom's family but by her own as well.

On his return, he and Antonia did not resume their 'affair'. She was angry that in those forty-eight hours he had discussed her mental state with his parents, and insisted that, despite his protestations, he was still influenced by them.

They would never make love together again.

Two weeks later, having just reached the age of thirty, Tom began to have nightmares and was feeling lower than Antonia. He sat at his desk and wrote, 'What is it I want? Where do I want to come out? Who, if anyone, do I love?' He was worried that traits which had annoyed him in Antonia were insinuating themselves into his nature, such as putting things off and then feeling guilt about not having done them. And, like Antonia when she put off writing an article or making a phone call, he spent far more time worrying about it than the time needed to do the wretched job. He also realised that for the first time in his life he was bored. Up till then, though suspecting he must often have bored Antonia stiff when he chatted about his work or Oxford friends, so that she must have longed for 'the walls to gape or heads to sprout from the gas stove', he had never known boredom himself.

Tom had not resumed his affair with Frances, although she had thought that they would take up where they had left off before her pregnancy. This was not because he did not desire her physically any more, for he did, but because Antonia had so successfully undermined his trust in Frances over the past months by constantly repeating that Frances had only used him to get Geoffrey to come back to her and to agree to having the baby she had always wanted.

So that late spring of 1935 Tom was suffering in Kensington, Frances was suffering in Hampstead, and Antonia was suffering in Chelsea.

In May there was a crisis in Antonia's analysis when Carroll shook a bunch of keys, arousing such strong memories of childhood fear on hearing her father's keys jangling in the lock of the front door when he returned home from St Paul's, that she was in a state of 'convulsive horror' for days afterwards. The last Sunday in May she was not able to drag herself out of bed until tea-time. Then she forced herself to try to write something, as she sat in front of the high open window of her room at Oakley Street, where she had placed three little dahlia plants out on the sill 'to remind me to keep my head'. She took one of her notebooks in which she had not written for three weeks, and with great difficulty – 'Hand moves in a stiff way, very slowly: can only make letters very small' – wrote a description of her room, and of the man in the building opposite who, though they had never met, afflicted her because she felt that he ought to realise she was a lonely 'creature in distress' who might suddenly fling herself out of the window. She ended, 'Shall I ring up Tom? Yet it is by my own wish I am to-day cut off, alone. I refused to see people.'

Two days later she said that 'deadlock, crisis and hysteria' had followed the writing of those last words. So, the next day Eric had gone to see Carroll who had told him Antonia was really ill:

> There *is* a beast in the jungle . . . there is more than a possibility that though Carroll can give me some years of complete self-possession (the brain is not affected) it may pounce in the end permanently & even again (but not fatally) quite soon.

A problem, which only later would worry Tom, was beginning to develop at Cecil Court around this time. Now that our mother had been away for three months, Sue and I were developing an even stronger attachment for Tom. But at this stage he wrote of it humorously in a letter to Antonia when describing 'as healthy an evening's Oedipism as could be imagined'.

We had been very obstreperous one evening when he had come to say goodnight on Nurse's day off. Sue, aged five, had given him 'a good kick in the middle and laughed' when he tried to tuck her up; I had got out of bed again as soon as he had left the room, and opened the door, looking 'daring and defiant, like a swaggering boy'. Sue was still in bed looking 'demure' but he suspected it had been her plan. He made me go back to bed and tucked me in again.

When he was going out of the room for the second time, Sue called after him, 'Why mayn't I come and sleep in your bed like – ?'

'Like what?' he asked.

'Oh why mayn't I come and *sleep* in your bed?'

Not being able to think of a better reply he said, 'What d'you think your own bed's for?' and firmly shut the door behind him in such a way that we knew there was to be no more playing about.

It must have been around this time that Sue began to have fantasies of killing Antonia. She imagined us stabbing her with the cook's knife, again and again, then burying her body in the little garden at the back of Mr Brown's sweet shop in Hollywood Road, just round the corner.

Antonia's crisis had been averted for a while, although she continued to have nightmares and occasional 'glimmerings of a headache'. In fact, within a week, she was well enough to enjoy an outing to St James's Park with Tom, 'walking hand in hand, very gay, and elderly people looked at us kindly as if we were lovers'. She had even regained her sense of humour about herself, always a good sign, and told Tom on that walk that she had rung up Logan Pearsall Smith to fix a day to go to tea.

When she had asked how he was, Logan had replied, 'I'm going crazy.'

'So am I,' said Tony.

'Oh,' said Logan, 'don't you find it *too* delicious?'

The next day, Sunday 2 June 1935, Antonia called one of the most important days of her life: 'It was as if that day I came of age, was initiated into a rite, given, as in fairy tales, the sealed packet with the instructions for my journey.'

The reason was that she allowed Ronald, the Jamaican sculptor, to take the risk of making love to her. It was painful; she was 'cold and terrified' and afterwards her fears returned, 'anxiety, sense of sin, even the colour bar (but only academically I think)'. She feared she had cut herself off from Tom irrevocably, and she wept. Ronald put on a Monteverdi record and lay with her in his arms:

> I heard his breathing, so quiet and regular, like the rise and fall of the phrases. I grew calmer. I found I was bleeding, like a virgin. And then a curious peace and happiness came over me. I looked in the glass as I dressed and my face which had been pale, distorted, swollen with tears, looked young and contented and my eyes were bright and cool. We had dinner & I was exquisitely, radiantly happy.

The happiness did not last. Within a week Antonia was feeling 'doubt, fear, humiliation, physical desire and misery'.

Although she had not meant to, she told Tom about Ronald. She was half relieved, but half disappointed, that it had seemed to make no emotional impression on him at all.

Antonia would soon learn that Tom too had started a new affair with a married woman called Vesti. He had tried to convince himself it was important, but he knew in his heart that compared to Frances she meant 'nothing' to him. And when it was over, after only three months, he confessed he had 'grabbed at Vesti' because he could not bear to be alone.

The next time Tom saw Antonia and took her to dinner in a Chinese restaurant she was having one of her Jekyll-and-Hyde days. According to him, the evening had started with her being 'very warm and gay and gentle' as they talked easily over dinner, glad to be together. But then something had come up about Tom's family which made her change her tune, and soon she was making the usual old stabs at him about how he had never intended theirs to be a marriage when he entered into it. She even complained that life went on without her at Cecil Court, and said, 'I feel so shut off from your nice self-contained little household. I've just dropped out of it like a book gone from a shelf. Nobody notices even that I'm not there.'

Tom became 'gloomier and dumber' until it was time to leave.

On the way home she took his arm. 'Don't take any notice of me,' she told him, 'I only want to be somebody's adored pet. It's nonsense at my age.'

On the steps of 105 Oakley Street she kissed him, 'as sweet and warm and friendly' as when they had set out.

But three days later she wrote him a cruel and critical letter in which she said the thought of him in another woman's arms, however beautiful, did not give her 'the fearful sense of shock in the very source of my life' that the thought of him with Frances had done:

> There has been very little radiance or joy in our love; nearly always numbness and misery. I can only measure it in a negative way by what I have been prepared to give up for you & put up with from you.

As with the scene in the restaurant, the storm blew itself out and the letter ended:

> I have such a warm strong feeling for you that is quite unaccountable on ordinary grounds!! It is not mother-love, or sister-love, or even wife-love now, but just *love*. Tony

It was a relief for Tom to get away for his annual holiday. He spent all three weeks of it with Sue and me in Westmorland, where his father had been transferred to a parish called Winster. Besides walking with his sister, and sailing alone on nearby Lake Windermere, he reflected on what to do with his life.

The first thing he did on returning to London at the end of July was to take Antonia out to dinner because he knew she was going through another critical period. He found her 'very, very tired'. Analysis was wearing her down, and on top of it she had just come back from a weekend at Peggy's where Emily had 'kept her hard at it' going over the first chapters of a new book Antonia had started writing in June. Her writing block had suddenly lifted after buying a new pen just like Dr Carroll's, but after only a week she had jammed again on the book, which was to be about Tom and Frances, and soon she abandoned it after only four chapters.

Over dinner at the Blue Cockatoo, a little restaurant at the end of Oakley Street, Tom told her he had been reflecting on his future.

'You make me feel like a corpse in a coffin,' she said, 'hearing all the people saying what they'll be doing on Thursday week and knowing that by then he'll be under the ground.' Then she added, 'I don't want to go on living any more, Tom, really I don't.'

He took her home and put her to bed, then stayed for a while to read to her. On returning to Cecil Court he wrote that she had said 'things to break the heart' in a sad, but matter-of-fact way, such as:

> 'I'm like a person who's been left behind on an island. Everything goes on without me. I have no place. It isn't that I haven't had chances. I've had

lots of them, but I'm too old to start afresh. Even combing my hair seems absurd to me now.'

In August Dr Carroll left for his annual holiday, having tied up his patients' problems for long enough to see them over until he came back. For safety's sake, he gave Antonia a medicine called 'Dial', a tranquilliser, to take if she should feel a crisis coming on.

She went away to Summerhill, the progressive school so fashionable with the intellectuals of the 1930s, to attend the Group Theatre Summer School run by her friend Rupert Doone. She told Tom in a letter afterwards that those ten days were the nearest she had come to feeling free for five years. And a young actress friend of his, who was there at the same time, told him that she and the other girls used to love being with Antonia because 'She always came up with such terrific remarks: sometimes blowing people up, sometimes making everybody laugh.'

While there she did something very un-Antonia-ish: she tried sleeping out of doors. She also surprised herself by having 'moments of unexpected insight, even generosity of behaviour' despite still being 'mentally unstable and flighty'.

She was not very impressed by A. S. Neill, Summerhill's founder, but she was interested in a young Quaker, 'half prig and half poet', who sounds as contradictory a character as she was.

She saw much of J.G., as she called him, for a while after her return to London. She found him sexually attractive and would like to have had an affair with him – for Ronald and she had stopped being lovers after only a month, though she still admired him physically and mentally. But J.G. turned out to have a problem: 'We are two maimed creatures: one impotent in body, the other in mind.'

In less than a month she decided he stank of corruption and felt as if she 'had been covered with slime even by contact with such a creature'. But, even before casting him out of her life, there had been a difficult time at the end of August when she had not only had to resort to Dial, but wished she had had a God to pray to for strength. She had been upset because Tom had dropped the watch she had given him for a wedding present into the river from his boat, and she felt it symbolised that something was over between them. She recognised she needed Carroll again, much as she dreaded the strain of re-starting analysis.

But the resumption of analysis in September did not ease the situation. Though still on Dial, she had one of the worst sessions she had had since starting to be psychoanalysed six months before.

That autumn Sue, aged six, became a pupil at 'Miss Baxter's' school, where I would join her a year later. It was in Rosary Gardens, slightly north of Cecil Court, whereas the nursery school in Chelsea was due south. So, while I trotted off with Nurse to Glebe Place, Sue now had Tom to herself for the journey to school each morning. He tells of a conversation they had on the way there one day, when Sue had said, 'I like you, but I like grandfather Ho'kinson better,' and he felt she wanted to provoke an expression of love from him: 'I think she wanted me to say "I love you Susan better than Lyndall."'

In October, Antonia moved to a larger room in the same building in Oakley Street and decided the time had come to make living there seem less impermanent. Eric had given her a desk, and she bought a tallboy and a bookcase. After putting the room in order in an obsessively finicky way, she then felt guilty about having enjoyed being domestic for a while and not having spent the time on trying to write the Tom-Frances novel. As a compromise, she stopped fussing about her room and made herself sit down at her new desk to write in her notebook instead:

> I feel frightened sitting here writing alone in this pleasant, safe cream-coloured room with the clock ticking . . . Yet . . . though I sit with my back to it [the room] nothing looks over my shoulder. No mirror is behind me . . . Why do I fear so much? . . . Never in writing, except perhaps occasionally in the notebooks, have I felt out of my depth. In life, yes, over and over again.

Was she 'cheating' she wondered in going to Carroll in an attempt to avert insanity? Was it the 'will of God (do I speak literally or symbolically?)' that she should 'go mad again and again and perhaps, in the end, irretrievably'?

She was amazed at how comparatively painlessly she was managing to write. By the end of that evening of 6 October 1935 she had written over two thousand words in her notebook. The entry ended with a long prayer she would have said aloud if she dared to pray. Among the things she would have asked God were:

> Let me not be puffed up by my suffering nor ashamed to be happy . . .
> And let me not desire eternal life or happiness or the assurance of Thy love,

nor be concerned in any way what happens to me, whether madness or sanity, fulfilment or frustration, provided only Thou wilt show me my right place, however humble, and keep me in it.

One of the subjects that kept coming up in Antonia's analysis, besides writing and sex, was money. Although she protested that Carroll was attacking her 'unfairly' over it, she admitted she had a peculiar attitude to money and did feel guilt over her extravagant ways. Her earnings for the year April 1934 to 1935, declared on Tom's tax returns, were £418, most of it from her weekly payments of eight guineas from the *Daily Mirror*.

However, in November, she lost her job on the *Daily Mirror*. Apart from the money, she had no regrets: 'My distaste for woman's page journalism increases and with it my incompetence.' But because, according to her, she needed work, not rest, she decided to look for something that was more her *métier* than advertising or writing fashion articles, even if it paid less.

She knew that the French actor/director, Michel Saint-Denis, had recently opened a school for acting – the London Theatre Studio – and was looking for a lecturer on Greek drama. Antonia had admired Saint-Denis's work ever since seeing his 'Noé' in the *Compagnie des Quinze* once when she was on holiday near Aix, and thought everything he said about the theatre had 'the stamp of the real right thing', so she applied for the job. The interview went well: she heard from a mutual friend that Saint-Denis thought she was 'intelligent, sympathetic, had good judgement, was not "stiff"', but he was apprehensive about her mental instability. Before offering her a permanent job, he suggested she work unpaid till the end of the year as his 'literary adviser and research hack'.

In early December Antonia admitted in her notebook that she had had explosions of rage in letters to Frances and to Tom's new mistress, his third, whose name was Joan and whom she had thought was her friend. She had also had a 'terrific outburst' against Dr Carroll which Tom described in his notebook:

How Things Happen

Tony has been struggling with a passionate longing for revenge – revenge on me & revenge on Frances. I could see that she was wanting this because for weeks she said whenever she saw me that she must *not* have it, and 'Vengeance really *is* the Lord's.'

Describing her analysis to me, she said 'a very odd thing happened'. Carroll had asked her to demonstrate something to him: 'So I got up off the couch & turned round towards him and suddenly I heard a very deep voice, which seemed to burst right out of my chest. It didn't sound like my voice at all. It abused Carroll for about 20 minutes.'

Soon after that Tony said to me, a little defiantly, almost mischievously, like a doubtful child not quite sure if it's done wrong, 'I wrote a 12-page letter to Frances today.'

A few evenings later Antonia went round to Cecil Court and for three hours raged on and on and on about Frances, following a reply to her letter, until she had reduced Tom to 'absolute speechlessness'.

Finally he could bear no more. He took hold of her and forced her into her coat, steered her downstairs and into a taxi and accompanied her to Oakley Street, saying hardly a word. Then he walked back to Cecil Court, sat down at his desk and described what had just happened in his notebook, ending, 'When she is at her most vindictive I am suddenly filled with passion – not of hatred which is slow-smouldering – with a passion of pity.'

Sometimes that pity would flood over him so strongly when he read her letters that he wanted to cry. He felt like this a few days later on reading two letters he found lying on his desk when he came home from the office one Thursday evening.

Antonia had been round to Cecil Court to read his notebook again: 'I *had* to though I know by all "standards" it is not right to do.' Then she had sat at her old desk at Cecil Court to write to Tom. In the first letter she told him she felt like a ghost haunting its old places, and had an awful feeling that she had been driven away from Cecil Court because she was 'not fit to have children and a husband and a home like a normal woman'. Then she wrote several pages telling him how much he had made her suffer. The letter, which had begun with 'Dearest Tom', ended abruptly with 'I am wild & restless. Tony.'

Shortly afterwards, having smoked all his cigarettes and got 'perhaps a little drunk' on his sherry, she wrote him 'Note 2'. It began 'My darling Tom' and said she wished she could be kinder and more generous to him. The tone of this whole long letter was contrite and affectionate. She now claimed she loved him more after reading his private notebook, and recognised how difficult living with her must have been because her illness prevented her from creating any happiness for herself or others when sex was involved:

I have all a woman's natural inclinations to a man ... but it is in the *expression* of them that I am overwhelmed with fear, guilt, coldness or nausea. Physical love I have never been able to test with a good conscience.

She then apologised for being back at her 'old whining self-absorption' again:

But how can I get out of it since I have to drag this self about which I hate – every day make decisions for it, feed it, wash it, put it to bed alone? ... oh, if I could explode and blow away all the filth in me and wake up clear & refreshed. Don't bother to understand – just let me talk – for talk I must. Tony

These two letters of Antonia's, written to the same person within a couple of hours of each other, show the dichotomic state in which she continued to exist as Carroll, like a skilled exorcist, lured 'the beast' out of her.

That Christmas Tom and Antonia took us to Binesfield to stay with Granny Botting, who was on her own since Aunt Agnes's death at the beginning of the year. Before going, Antonia had felt 'fearful anxiety'. But, according to Tom, the visit went well: 'The weather was mostly fine, Tony was well, the children good, Mama less loopy than usual.'

One evening Tom felt 'terribly happy' when Sue and I sang, 'in little squeaky voices swerving off occasionally into a too-high key', and then danced while Mother played the piano: 'I felt all the good of family life which you feel, I think, only in rare moments . . . I felt full of bliss & looked & looked & listened & could no more have said a cross word to anybody than have bitten my hand.'

But there were some minor problems on that holiday. One was a clash of wills between Sue and me in the double bed we were sharing. Reading my father's account of it brought it back vividly to me.

On Christmas night as Tony & I were going to bed we heard shouts & crying from the children's room. Romeo, the huge tabby-and-white cat, had come home from hunting in the night and had snuggled inbetween the children; their three heads lay side-by-side upon the pillow.

Lyndall was crying 'I don't want a wet cat in my bed – besides he's pushed me all up and there isn't any room.'

Susan was very contemptuous. 'Poor Romeo' she said. 'Let him stay, he only wants to be warm like you do, Lyndall.' Then, looking at Lyndall with disdain, 'I can't have a crying child in my bed.'

Tony asked me to decide. I ruled that cats should be a matter of choice & noone could be forced to lie with a large wet cat against their will.

Another problem was one that had been worrying Tom for some time: Sue had started to steal unimportant things. It had begun when Antonia was still living at Cecil Court and Sue had brought some toy money home from nursery school, hidden in her knickers.

Over that Christmas of 1935 at Binesfield Tom wrote,

> Susan's stealing continues. I saw her steal a biscuit and a piece of sugar in a few minutes. Analysts say that children steal when they want love and assurance. I think it is partly that, partly she always avoids a direct clash of wills . . . So, if she wants something and is afraid of Tony's or my refusing, she tries to steal – and so both keeps our good will and gets the thing she wants.

Shortly after our return to Cecil Court after Christmas, Sue persuaded me to ask Tom something she wanted to know:

> Susan listens & asks questions with great interest, but I cannot get her to start any asking, she must always shelter behind Lyndall who is naturally very honest & fearless. The other day after a lot of whispering in the passage Lyndall came first into my room & asked what boys had that thing in front of their legs for. I started to tell them that it was what boys need to 'make water with', & was wondering how to go on when Susan – who is always natural & honest when she becomes interested, but false & artificial in ordinary life – said 'I asked Terence what he had one for & he said "That's how I bore my little people"' ', which seemed to me an excellent explanation.

When he had finished explaining, one of us asked, 'Did you and Mummy do that to have us?'

Tom was relieved that we took it in our stride when he said that of course they had.

On reading my father's account of this, and other stories about us in his notebook, I was astonished that we called Antonia 'Mummy'. In my mind she has always firmly been 'Mother', and my father 'Tom', for those are the names we called them by from the time my conscious memory stabilised itself. It also surprised me that I knew sexual facts at four and a half. I must have put them straight into my unconscious, for when I heard them much later from my mother, having asked her what the words 'bugger' and 'fuck' used by my classmates at a progressive school meant, they came as a baffling revelation.

Sue's reflective nature, which had impressed Tom on many occasions, was also making her more introverted and withdrawn. One misty Sunday afternoon in January, a few days before telling us the facts of life, Tom had taken her down to the end of the pier on the Chelsea Embankment for a walk. As they walked over the wet boards, with the brown water swirling below, Sue said, 'I'm one of those people that like coldness and wetness and loneliness and lostness.'

She was then six and a half. A month later Tom mentioned her in his notebook again to say her 'jealousy flaring up' over Antonia in an argument with him had been so painful he could not bring himself to write about it: 'Things that strike deep I cannot put down and don't want to.'

For Antonia 1936 began with an even worse financial crisis than usual. She still had not managed to extract any money from Michel Saint-Denis and, though she was enjoying the research, found the writing hard. Her own creative writing was blocked, for the decision to return to the book on her father and drop the one on Tom and Frances had made no difference to that state of stalemate. She was beginning to wonder if her desire to write – 'or rather to have written' – might not be pure vanity, 'the passion to give evidence of being a "remarkable person"'. It consoled yet astonished her that people in the literary world, such as Logan Pearsall Smith, Hugh Kingsmill and Cyril Connolly, continued to believe in her in spite of her having produced nothing for two years, except what she called a 'weak sketch of theatre life', 'The First Time I Went on Tour', in 1934.

Had analysis affected her writing, she wondered? Certainly it had not shifted the deadlock, except for that remarkable couple of weeks the past summer when she had written four chapters, but at least there were 'occasional moments' when she felt she saw things more clearly than before.

In despair over her finances, Antonia went to see the trustees of her father's estate. She had not inherited anything after his death, but wondered if she could borrow against whatever might be due to her after her mother's death. But she came away surly and depressed from her meeting with Eichholz – a solicitor who had replaced one of Cecil's ex-pupils as a trustee – on discovering that, even after her mother died, Binesfield would not be her property outright, but would be held in trust to be passed on to her descendants. All she would receive on her mother's death would be any royalties that might be coming in from his Greek and Latin textbooks, for what little savings her father had managed to accrue during his lifetime he had lost on hopeless investments and lapsed insurance policies.

She was even more grateful for an allowance of £15 a month which Eric now gave her to pay the analyst after she had lost her job with the *Daily Mirror*.

A week after seeing Eichholz, Antonia and Tom went to a play given by the Group Theatre. Also in the audience were the Grigsons. Tom noticed that Frances looked 'very beautiful, though moving to me no longer'. In the second interval Antonia went out on her own and Tom went over to speak to Geoffrey and Frances. The evening once again ended in an argument, with Antonia upbraiding Tom for having 'betrayed' her by greeting Frances in public.

Less than a month later, in February 1936, the Grigsons' floundering marriage broke up. Frances, who knew nothing of Tom's two affairs since the brief one with her, now hoped that if he could resolve his problems with Antonia, he would marry her. But Antonia was not alarmed: 'He says he will not marry anyone unless they are the bread of life to him and she is not that. So she does not want to go on seeing him.'

Frances felt she must get away from London and went to live in a damp little cottage in Cornwall with the baby who was now nearly a year old. But though she could not face seeing Tom, she still wrote to him. Her letters were flat and reserved, occasionally a little petulant, but they always affected Tom deeply because he knew they hid real feeling. Many years later he remembered with remorse having treated Frances 'with great unkindness after her child was weaned, when she wanted us to take up where we had left off and I could not'.

The affair Tom had been having with Joan since the previous August ended shortly after Frances left for Cornwall. Tom took Antonia out to dinner early in March, and told her the affair with her friend was over. She became extremely gay and 'a pleasure to be with'. She told him she had dreamt of a horse with false teeth biting her, and that Carroll, who had assured her horses were clearly female 'in her scheme of mythology', had said she was that horse attacking herself. But she insisted she had always thought of horses as male: 'So you see what sort of a tangle I'm in; I'm a hermaphrodite horse with false teeth.'

Although Antonia had shown no sympathy over his loss of Joan, she wrote in her notebook afterwards that she had realised he was unhappy and discontented, and mutely asking for comfort. She had withheld it partly because something in her seemed 'to want him to pay to the last farthing', and partly because when she was with him most of the time she was so conscious of her own suffering she could not get outside it. She concluded, 'I think nearly all his suffering has been of the barren kind.'

But Tom's suffering produced two of the best short stories he ever wrote. The first, 'I Have Been Drowned', he finished that spring. It was Antonia who had pointed out something of which he had not been aware while writing it: she, not *Scud*, was *Stella*, the boat which the first-person writer desired so overwhelmingly although she was almost everything a boat ought not to be. Sailing her had turned out to be such a nightmare that it caused him nearly to drown when she capsized and sank. Antonia told him that besides feeling she was that 'awful boat', she thought the story also showed his powers of endurance.

The other story was in a style Tom had never used before and never would again. In a surrealistic and poetical way, the writer, who is undergoing psychiatric treatment, tells of his strange experiences in letters to a woman he has loved. 'Over the Bridge' has echoes of the first story Antonia had written for him six years before, 'The House of Clouds': was it Tom's way of trying to make Antonia understand that he had suffered over having met and loved and lost Frances as she had over Robert?

By the spring Saint-Denis had promoted Antonia to lecturing on mythology at the Theatre Studio. She was pleased when someone told her that the students thought her lectures 'brilliant', and surprised to find she enjoyed giving them, in spite of being nervous and chain smoking throughout. But it alarmed her that lecturing bore a resemblance to being a schoolmistress and that she might after all be 'inexorably committed' to what her father had wanted her to be.

At the beginning of the year she had met a man who attracted her physically and mentally, but she made herself act cautiously for once while making up her mind whether to have an affair with him. At times he was cold and quarrelsome, drank too much and was self-destructive; at others he was tender, sensitive and penetrating. 'I never saw demon and angel so mixed in a face.' She decided he needed affection while driving it away.

His name was Eric Siepmann and he was a journalist and writer.

Still holding out against having an affair with him, in the spring she could not resist his offer to pay her fare to join him in Spain at Torremolinos, then an unspoilt little fishing village.

Before leaving she wrote Tom an attacking fourteen-page letter about his love life which ended, 'I think it is definitely better for us not to meet for a time. Feel quite free of me: soon I will go to Spain and it will be easier.' Even so, he sent her a birthday present of a box of cigarettes, though the note with it was signed 'Your loving but very angry Tom', and said: 'I hope this is a brand you particularly dislike and that the bottom layer has been left out of the packet.' The day before sailing she sent him a contrite note about her 'outburst of extreme bitchery'.

The holiday began badly. The voyage out was so rough that she was sea-sick, and the ship ran aground in sight of Torremolinos in the worst gale off that coast for years. (Eric Earnshaw-Smith, who read about it in the English papers, feared that she might have 'got separated from all those toilet appurtenances so familiar to me', but her luggage and all her make-up had been rescued, too.)

She had not had time to unpack when Siepmann had a wire from the *News Chronicle* asking him to cover a story in Gibraltar.

From there Antonia pencilled a letter to Tom, as she sat in bed in an uncomfortable hotel, drinking tea with goat's milk and feeling most apprehensive after an alarming experience with Siepmann the previous night.

He had started the evening being 'excellent company, sober, and as considerate as a whole family of doting brothers'. He quite understood when she had wanted to go to bed early to recover from her unpleasant journey, rather than accompany him to look at the night-life of Gibraltar. But at 3.30 in the morning he woke her out of the first good sleep she had had for nights by crashing into her room, very drunk, and hurling abuse at her for two hours. Antonia was terrified and told Tom she did not know what she would do if this went on, for escape was impossible since it might take some time to find a passage home.

Tom replied by return of post, sympathising over the terrible voyage and the bloodiness of Gibraltar, but made no mention of Siepmann. He did say, however, that if she felt 'landed', he would somehow find the money to fly her back.

In her next letter Antonia was desperate. It was no longer Siepmann's fault, he was behaving like an angel and had not drunk for a week, but she was feverishly ill with a very painful gastric infection, and it was her turn to disturb Siepmann's sleep: she asked him to keep his bedroom door open so that she could talk to him whenever she felt low or lonely in the night.

This letter was preceded by telegrams to Tom appealing for help.

She also sent an SOS to Eric who wrote back immediately to his 'dear Puss-Cat' saying 'of course one always gets ill in those foreign parts, I never risk them myself', and telling her Tom was 'ready to take wings' to fetch what remained of her home.

Despite their bitter exchange of letters before her departure, Tom took out a bank loan of £70, over a month's salary, in order to fly out to Spain to bring Antonia back with him.

On her return Antonia felt frustrated and lonely. Siepmann, who had remained at Torremolinos, was still uppermost in her thoughts: 'always straying into my desires from which I must exclude him'. She wrote pages about Siepmann in her notebook in early May, unable to decide whether she felt 'deep affection' for him, or whether she only wanted to thrust 'rape' on him in order to escape from herself.

The rest of that spring and early summer Antonia was very depressed. She had been under analysis now for over a year and most of her friends found her 'remarkably better'; but she was worried about herself. She had no sex life, except for masturbation which was 'accompanied always by fantasies of cruelty, whipping, humiliation'; she had become greedy again, devouring marshmallows and bars of chocolate. She was also devouring books and, as always, spending too much. She wrote that she was resentful that Tom 'salved his conscience' by giving her £1 a week, whereas he 'willingly' paid all the expenses connected with Sue and myself and, in her opinion, overpaid Nora, his new live-in housekeeper; but she made no mention of how many times he had bailed her out of crises, and that he was struggling to pay off the bank loan which had rescued her from Spain.

Summing up how she felt about herself in early June she said: 'for all my apparently sincere attempts at goodness, at bottom I am vile and disgusting. Sometimes I wallow in my own nastiness.'

On 1 June 1936 Tom wrote that he felt he was 'coming to pieces'. To be 'strong & happy' he needed someone to love 'with all the breath in my body & all the fibre of my mind'. Although he was now 'terribly fond' of a new woman, a young actress called Joan Geary who was still a virgin, she had refused to have an affair with him.

All Tom and Antonia could give each other at this time, when they were not the cause of each other's suffering, was consolation and advice.

At the end of June Antonia had to undergo minor surgery for an infection of the cervix. She dreaded the operation and Tom was particularly kind and understanding about it. A few days before she went into hospital he took her to her favourite restaurant in the King's Road, The Good Intent, where they carefully chose the cheapest items on the menu because Tom was still paying back the bank loan for her Spanish fiasco. To keep her mind off the operation, he told her he had dreamt he had bought a girl for five shillings.

'Oh,' said Tony, 'that wasn't much to pay.'

'No,' Tom said. 'And what's more, I never actually paid it because I remember when the dream ended I was still holding two half-crowns in my hand.'

'Did you enjoy the girl?' Tony asked.

'Yes I did.'

'Then,' said Tony, 'I think you should give the five shillings to charity.'

He was with her in the hospital when they wheeled her away for the operation, and waited until she regained consciousness afterwards.

Soon after she came out of hospital Antonia went into one of her worst mental states. She felt 'full of impotence and indecision, guilty about everything, even the things I enjoy'. When it reached suicidal pitch, Eric begged her to wait six months before doing anything rash; then, he said, if she still did not wish to exist it would be perfectly reasonable for her to kill herself.

According to Tom, Sue was also in a state of crisis that summer of 1936. On 6 July, he wrote to Antonia saying he had been to talk to Carroll who thought Sue should be analysed as soon as possible. He told Tom she would need about a year of treatment with four visits a week, which, if he could not find a place with a clinic, would cost 10s 6d a time with a private analyst. Before going to see Carroll, they had been considering Tom's adopting Sue, who did not yet know he was not her father, but Tom wanted Antonia to remain her legal guardian because he did not wish either of us to be brought up by his father and mother, 'with whose views on good and evil' he did not agree, if anything should happen to him. Adoption was never mentioned again, and Tom did not say what the 'temporary measures' Carroll suggested to him to keep Sue's jealousy at bay were to be while he tried to find someone to analyse her.

The next day Tom wrote in his notebook that he had been 'deeply obsessed with the need for a lover' for several days, and overwhelmed by thoughts of Frances: 'When I go to bed I feel the smooth lines of her body lying close beside me.' A few days later he had a letter from Frances that made him suspect she was not well, followed soon after by another confirming those suspicions.

In August Antonia went to stay in a hotel at Lyme Regis with Eric. Before leaving she jotted down a short cryptic entry in her notebook in the form of a list entitled *Joys and miseries of one day*. Two of the eight miseries – 'The horror of the thought of living in this one room *for ever*' and 'That I have no home, belong nowhere, that Tom will not make any decision' – make it sound as if she was beginning to get the idea that she might like to move back to Cecil Court and had been discussing it with Tom.

From two letters which my mother wrote to my father during her holiday, it also sounds as if things were strained again between them before she left. The first letter started 'Dear Tom', the stormiest reading on her barometer of goodwill, and was hostile; the second one, written five days later, predicted fairer weather with its 'Dearest Tom' opening – perhaps because in the meantime he had written her an affectionate 14-page letter reviewing the history of their effect on each other and greatly praising her writing, even calling her 'a niece of Dostoievsky'.

He wrote from Winster Vicarage where he had already taken us to stay with Granny and Grandfather. That summer holiday started particularly happily for us. For the first two weeks we had Tom and his younger brother, Paul, whom we had never met before. Paul was an army officer who lived in India and told us marvellously dreadful stories about tigers and snakes and having to shake his shoes out each morning in case there was a scorpion in one of them.

Paul and Tom took us for our first boat-trip on Lake Windermere; and there was a day when we all piled into Grandfather's very old car which took an unbearably long time to cover the twenty-odd miles to Morecambe Bay. I still remember the smell of its leather upholstery and peering anxiously out of the window for my first glimpse of the sea.

Tom described that 'perfect comic picture-postcard party' in a letter to Antonia. But something he said in that letter disturbed me when I read it fifty years after it had been written.

After much discussion he and Antonia had agreed that she would come back to Cecil Court in the autumn, and in the letter he told her what our reactions were when he broke this piece of news to us:

> They were delighted . . . Lyndall laughed & skipped along & Susan said 'How lovely to have Mummy back' and skipped along the road. But you know it is quite likely when you get there they will . . . ask why I'm not there, or say something that hurts your tender feelings, Tony dear . . . Assign no importance to it.

It did not seem possible to me that Sue and I would have been so joyful on learning that Mother would be in charge when we returned home with Nurse, who had now joined us at Winster. Perplexed, I asked Tom whether, when he had told us of our mother's return to Cecil Court, he had perhaps not revealed that he would be leaving?

He confessed we had in fact behaved very differently, and that the reason he had pretended to Antonia we were pleased was because he was worried about how we were going to react to her, and vice versa. He had tried to make it appear to her, particularly as she was always accusing him of having stolen our affections, that we were happy at her homecoming, but put in a warning that we might make some hurtful remarks because he knew how upset we were about his going.

What actually happened, he told me, was that on the last day of his holiday – he could not bring himself to do it before – he had taken us for a long walk on the fells above the vicarage and sat us down on a rock with the excuse that we probably needed a breather. There he explained that he was moving out and Mother was moving in. 'You were both crestfallen. You even more than Sue. You didn't cry, but all the time I was trying to explain things wouldn't be much different – that I would love you both as much as ever, and still come to take you to school, and do things with you at weekends, and so on – you never took your eyes off me, and said after every explanation, "I see Tom", "Yes Tom", "All right Tom", "I understand Tom", until I had to turn away because I couldn't bear to see your sad little face any more.'

I had joined my father and mother and sister in knowing what unhappiness meant. I was just five years old.

CHAPTER 12

֍

Much Suffering

I have lived with madness and watched death. Henceforth,
I must carry these things with me and they are a part of me.
Tom Hopkinson, 22 April 1939

On Monday 31 August 1936 Tom and Antonia both wrote in their notebooks, neither having written anything during their separate holidays. Antonia, the victor who had retaken possession of Cecil Court, sat at her old desk and began her entry: 'I have moved back into the flat and there is no ink.' Tom, the loser banished to Oakley Street while waiting for a room he had found nearer to Cecil Court to become vacant, described the pleasantness of the room with its 'high-up feeling, like being in a tree-top'. He then wrote gently about Antonia and the progress they had made since their separation: Antonia, on the other hand, raged against him.

The first thing she had done on returning to Cecil Court was to read Frances's letters to Tom and learn many 'not very agreeable things'. This brought on a ten-page outburst against him; but her next entry, ten days later, starts 'The last entry was written with a good deal of spleen and self pity. I would take back some of what I said about Tom but not all.'

In fact Tom was more unhappy than Antonia that autumn. While at Winster he had had a letter from Frances saying that her illness had been discovered to be TB and that she was coming to London to go into hospital.

As soon as Tom returned from Winster he went to see her. She was not allowed to talk because it aggravated her 'terrible loose cough', so she had to communicate by writing notes on a pad. He came away from their meeting deeply distressed; she had looked so pale and thin, and her hair was beginning to turn grey.

For the remainder of 1936 Frances alternated bouts in hospital with staying in the country with friends, for she was not allowed even to see her baby daughter lest she pass on her disease. The child was with Geoffrey Grigson, who knew of his wife's brief affair with Tom but had never mentioned it. He accepted that Tom visited her regularly: 'There aren't so many people who care about Frances that I should want to keep one of them away,' he told Tom.

Antonia, now that she had a place where she could entertain again, became very sociable that autumn. Besides continuing to see her close friends, like Phyllis Jones who had lived on the floor below at Oakley Street, and Emily who also now lived there, and Djuna whenever she was in London, she started to make new acquaintances in the literary world who were nearly all younger than she was: 'I feel much more at ease and stimulated among the young, Barker, Jennings, Gascoyne, than among the Connollys, Quennells, Mortimers. I seem in a way to have gone back seventeen years.'

In fact she had fallen in love with one of these young poets, David Gascoyne, and would become 'deeply attached' to another, George Barker. Humphrey Jennings was involved with Emily at the time.

One night in September Antonia sat up till 4.30 a.m. with Emily, Humphrey and David Gascoyne, and had the feeling she liked best, 'of flow and communication between people'. A few days later she sent David an invitation to visit her at Cecil Court.

David, then aged nineteen, wrote in his journal[1]:

> Antonia White, E[mily]'s friend, whom I met for the first time last week, and from whom I received an invitation this morning, interests me very much: an extraordinarily lively intelligence and at the same time completely feminine.[1]

After the encounter he wrote:

> It is so absurd that I can hardly bring myself to set it down on paper: a woman of 37, – a woman who has had three husbands and two children, has been in an asylum, is being psycho-analysed and, having been living alone for about a year, is starving not so much for sex as for simple, or rather an object of, affection – has fallen in love with *me* . . .
>
> My reactions to all this were chaotic and I am hardly proud of them. Terror, pity, self-mistrust, mistrust of her, etc . . . There is not the least possibility of my ever loving her, I am far too conscious of her age and she has no physical attraction for me . . . Why should the poor thing have chosen me?

[1] *Journal 1936–1937* by David Gascoyne. The Enitharmon Press, 1980

She wrote him a letter afterwards, telling him, 'You have already given me some increase of life – I hope I may have something for you but we cannot tell yet'; but there was no mention of that first evening with David in Antonia's notebook.

Her next entry was about Emily, with only a short pause to note 'I feel uneasy to-night alone in the flat except for the children: it is so quiet.'

There were some changes down our nursery end of the flat now that Mother was back.

Sue and I no longer shared a room. The night nursery had become her room, and the day nursery mine. How well I now came to know those curtains with the blue, pink and green children carrying blue, pink and green balloons, and would grow to detest even more the painting that hung over the mantelpiece of three girls with bright pink legs standing on their points and wearing daisy chains round their foreheads. Antonia had bought it for 2s 6d from Peggy Guggenheim's daughter, Pegeen. I had been secretly outraged. Sue, who was three years younger, drew far better than Pegeen, I thought, and what's more she drew horses, not soppy ballerinas. Why couldn't we have had one of Sue's paintings in the nursery and been given that equivalent of three months' pocket money to spend on sweets at Mr Brown's shop instead? (In fact, Pegeen grew up to be an artist: Herbert Read said of her paintings after her suicide in the 1960s that she always brought the same 'magical innocent touch to her work as she did at the age of eleven'.)

Having separate rooms did not make much difference. Sue had never been interested in playing childish games with me, and my blue rabbit, 'Nibby', continued to be better company than she often was; and I could give him orders instead of always having to take them. The cats now became 'ours': Mother allowed Sue to take Vanya into her room, and I was allowed Fury. He seemed to spend most of his time throwing up under my bed which made Nurse cross.

Nurse was still the most stable thing in my life, though I was beginning to feel I was not quite as important to her as I had been. She and Nora, the housekeeper, were both in love. They talked a lot about their boyfriends and listened to scratchy records of 'When I Grow Too Old To Dream' and 'It Was On The Isle Of Capri' and curled their hair with paper and hot irons.

Of course we missed Tom coming to say goodnight but, true to his word, he came every weekday to take us to school – I was now at the same one as Sue. We passed through pleasant streets behind The Boltons to get to Rosary Gardens, and on the way he told us stories. Nearly every weekend there was an outing with him, to a museum or to the zoo or to look at *Scud* at her moorings on the Embankment and then to eat sausages and mash at the Blue Cockatoo opposite.

Our relationship with Tom had remained easy and natural: we could let off steam with him which we could not do with any other adult. On one of the days he was late fetching us, so that we had to run most of the way to school, I called out as I panted after him and Sue, 'You're a disgraceful old man!' and Sue approved my words, telling him, 'It deserves you right!'

My relationship with my mother, if it had not been so before, was from now on dominated by fear. Because of the layout of the flat, anyone living in the front end had to make sallies down the passage to our part to get to the bathroom or kitchen. In the old days, whenever we heard Tom approaching, we rushed out of the nursery. Now, at the sound of my mother – she had an irritating two-beat smoker's cough which served as a warning – I would hide behind my door, hoping she would not see me if she looked into my room. On the rare occasions she came to say goodnight I would sometimes pretend to be asleep because she so often seemed to be cross about something.

The first thing I remember her being cross about was my not wearing a yellow dress she had given me for my birthday just before leaving for Lyme Regis. She had knitted it herself while she was in hospital for her operation.

At the time I had been delighted with it, partly because I liked it, but more because I was so pleased and surprised that she had made it with her own hands, for I thought only Granny Hopkinson knew how to knit. I had put it on and skipped off to show it to Nurse, Nora and Sue. 'You look like a scrambled egg!' was Sue's only comment as she gave me a quick 'rum-tum-tiddle-um' before Nurse intervened. I could not bring myself to wear it again. Sue's disapproval was more painful even than my mother's displeasure, for however cross my mother became, she never played 'rum-tum-tiddle-um' on my tummy. (When the first chapters of Antonia's autobiography, *As Once in May*, were published posthumously in 1983, what did I discover but that at the age of five – the very age I had become on the birthday she gave me the yellow frock – her beloved Gérard had refused to sit next to her at a party because she was wearing a yellow dress and a boy in his form had asked him whether she was in fancy dress and supposed to be a scrambled egg?)

Sue, aged seven, had started analysis that autumn. Carroll had not been able to find a cheap way out, so she was sent to a private therapist, Miss Searle.

Four afternoons a week I sat with Nurse in Miss Searle's waiting-room while my sister's mind was poked into. Of course I had no idea what 'analysis' meant and Sue was very mysterious about it and refused to discuss it on the bus home, though she implied that, since our mother did it too, it was something rather grown-up and important like writing books. But occasionally there were rewards for those excruciatingly long and boring vigils in the waiting-room.

One day there were bumps and thumps and yells outside the door. Before Nurse could stop me, I had rushed to see what was going on. Sue was astride Miss Searle on all fours, riding her up the stairs. 'Gee up! Come on you lazy brute!' she was shouting while beating her analyst on the rump with her fist. Nurse quickly pulled me back and shut the door, but not before I had noticed the desperate glance Miss Searle had cast her.

Another time Miss Searle came into the waiting-room not long after the session had begun. Her grey hair hung dankly and her soaked green dress clung to her body in the most revolting way as drops of water trickled down her nose onto the carpet. She had always been plain, now she was grotesque.

'I'm afraid I cannot continue with Susan today,' she told Nurse.

On the way home Sue told me triumphantly that she had poured 'buckets and buckets of water over the silly old cow!' I was full of admiration and wished she would shorten the sessions that way more often. It never happened again.

Soon after Sue started going to Miss Searle, Antonia told Tom that Sue and she had had a long discussion about analysis. Sue had said, 'I do hate having the private parts of my mind poked about in. It's so much nicer living inside my head than outside.' In answer to a question, Antonia had reassured her that it was quite natural for girls to prefer their fathers to their mothers. Sue had looked relieved and said, 'But I do like talking to you.'

Antonia only mentioned us once in her notebooks in the first few months after her return to Cecil Court: she had been back for two weeks and was describing how an evening had gone well until dinner-time, 'talking to Emily, practising the piano, playing with the children', and then had suddenly become a nightmare when she started trying to plan what clothes to buy with some money Eric had promised her as a gift.

But the fact that Antonia did not write about us, did not mean that she was not in contact with us. Tom's notebooks of that time record other talks which Antonia reported having had with Sue.

In fact Antonia only made six entries in her notebooks that autumn of 1936. This makes it hard to find out what role David Gascoyne had in her life then. But from welding together extracts from his published journal, and her mention of him in all but one of her entries – written a week before she met him – it is possible to piece together what was going on, or rather what was *not* going on, between them.

After David's consternation over Antonia's having fallen in love with him on their second meeting he avoided her. But fate decreed they should soon meet again. The first Sunday in October he took part in an Anti-Mosley demonstration with Emily and then went to her flat for tea and supper.

> Antonia came in the evening. I felt that she felt I was frightened of her eye; she was horribly nervous and made me feel the same. Presently she offered to put me up for the night, as it would be difficult to get back. I wanted to refuse but, fearing she would interpret this wrongly, said I should be very glad . . .
>
> . . . long and difficult conversation in front of a gas-fire. Entrails, entrails . . . At four in the morning she lay on the divan in my arms and could not bring herself to go to bed.
>
> Next morning I was awakened by her husband. He comes to the flat every morning to take the children to school. He put his head round the edge of the door and smiled in mild surprise. I very much wanted to laugh.

They spent the day together, and over lunch began to quarrel. It took Antonia most of the afternoon, as they wandered about the West End in a cold wind, ending up at the National Gallery, to get over it.

Except for an enigmatic sentence in David's journal a week later – in which he said he felt 'horribly insincere' after having written a note to Antonia assuring her of his 'wise tenderness' towards her when really he felt only numbness – they wrote nothing about each other for two weeks. Then, on 22 October, Antonia mentioned how fond of David she was and how worried about his safety, because he had just gone to Spain where the Civil War was being fought. 'I have some bond with him very real and very tangible.'

She did not mention that she had persuaded him, against his will, to spend the previous night at Cecil Court. As he had feared, she kept him up most of the night talking, although she knew he had a long journey ahead of him. In the morning they had 'a protracted and uncomfortable parting' at the end of which she insisted on giving him ten shillings, saying it was for his twentieth birthday which had been a few weeks before. Although he desperately needed the money, it somehow dropped out of his pocket in the Fulham Road. He noted sadly in his journal that this episode had revealed to him 'the disillusioning truth about my relationship with Antonia far more clearly than any conscientious self-examination could ever have done'.

For Antonia, who was still without a job, except for the Saint-Denis lectures for which, when he paid her at all, she received only two guineas a week, this had been an act of crazy generosity. Her own writing was still at a standstill, except for a poem she had suddenly produced and which Humphrey Jennings had persuaded *Contemporary Poetry* to print after the *New Statesman* had turned it down as being 'too violent and emotional'. She commented, 'It is amusing to be called too violent and to appear for the first time in poetry among the revolutionary young.'

During David's absence she saw much of another of the young poets, George Barker, who was twenty-three. Despite his moments of 'almost morbid melancholy and negativism', she discovered he had 'the sweetest, lightest, most birdlike gaiety'. Although he was married, to the first of his wives, he told Antonia he preferred boys to women, but he was being unnecessarily cautious because her love was still focused on David.

On the night David was due to return from Spain, less than a month after he had left, she tried to persuade herself that she was not hoping David would ring up on his arrival – which of course is exactly what she *was* hoping. To make the hours pass more quickly she wrote pages about Barker – his appearance, his nature and his resemblance to Keats. She was by now very tired, but hung on 'smoking endlessly, with itching eyes, feeling oppressed by my clothes', involuntarily raising her head every time she heard a taxi stop in Fawcett Street, in the hope it might be David turning up directly at the flat without first having stopped to telephone from Victoria Station.

Instead of going to bed, she changed to writing about religion. Three times lately, without knowing whether she believed in God or not, she had gone into a church and repeated the Our Father over and over again. She told herself she must not trust in future salvation by a merciful God: 'We are not strong enough to bear such violent happiness.'

From the way the writing in her notebook draws to a neat ending after three more pages, it seems unlikely that David appeared on Antonia's doorstep that night of 16 November 1936. But by early December David had become her lover and she was beginning to wonder whether she needed the sexual side of their relationship less than she thought she did. David, who wrote nothing in his journal between the day of his departure for Spain and Christmas, throws no further light on the affair.

Having a lover at last – a year and a half had gone by since her very brief affair with Ronald – made Antonia more indulgent towards Tom who was very distressed over Frances, who was not getting better.

Tom had had a sombre autumn. At the office he worked extremely long and hard hours, 'obsessed with the idea that I must somehow make extra money to pay all the bills, insurances, borrowings, over-drafts'. His new room in Gunter Grove was too noisy for writing, and at weekends he found he had to spend 'a prodigious amount of time on housework'. He admitted he was too concerned with neatness and could not sit down to write 'while the mantelpiece is dusty or there are dirty cups in the kitchen'. He was also still half in love with Joan Geary, who was turning out to be as complicated as she was pretty, 'a split and divided creature' who bore a resemblance to Antonia and made things much harder for someone who cared for her than he had foreseen.

Although Joan still would not have an affair with him, she was important to him, and he told Frances about her when he went to see her in a sanatorium in Sussex where she was convalescing. Frances said, 'While I am out of the world like this I am not worried about your life. It's nice for me to see you, but if you get bored, stop. The difficulty will be when I'm better, because in a busy life like yours there's only time for one important relationship.' This gave Tom relief from a sense of guilt that he was being heartless to pursue another woman.

Just before Christmas, Antonia asked Tom how he would feel if

Frances should die, bringing to the front of his mind something he had been trying to keep firmly at the back of it.

Very disturbed, he had answered: 'I'm not at all prepared for Frances to die.'

'I know you're not,' said Antonia. Then insisted, very gently, 'But if she were to die what would you feel?'

Tom thought for a long time. 'I should feel as if part of me had died too; and part of me had never come to life.'

Antonia was tender and understanding. She insisted Tom should visit Frances again in Sussex.

'You mustn't go empty-handed,' she told him, and said she would not feel hurt if he told Frances he would be waiting for her when she got well – a way of saying that, if he wanted, she would one day release him to marry Frances.

'It was strange,' Tom wrote afterwards, 'it was as if I had been waiting for a liberating word – as though having given Frances up for Tony's sake I could not go back to her without Tony's permission.' On hearing Antonia's words, suddenly she and Joan Geary had shrunk in importance: he wanted 'only to see and speak to Frances, and for us to be as we were before.'

He went down to see Frances in Sussex and gave her a ring. Before leaving on the Sunday afternoon he told her, 'You know that I love and adore you.'

'I should die if you didn't,' she said.

That autumn I had my first conscious encounter with loneliness. It remains one of the most vivid of my childhood memories.

One November day I woke up with a cold which quickly developed into a chesty cough. By the afternoon, when the time came for Sue to go to her analyst, I was hacking away. Nurse was in a quandary: the weather outside was cold and foggy and she did not want to take me out. On my assuring her that I did not mind being left behind – anything seemed preferable to Miss Searle's waiting-room – she had locked me into my room with my potty and many exhortations of what not to do. At first I had felt proud and grown-up, but that quickly wore off and I grew bored and lonely.

My room overlooked a dingy garden at the back of Cecil Court where nothing but a few sooty plane trees grew, mere outlines now because of the fog which had dimmed sights and muffled sounds so that the outside world seemed to have ceased almost to exist. I strained for the sound of the muffin man's bell or the scampering hooves of the milk ponies returning to the United Dairies' stables in Hollywood Road, but the humming of the gas-fire behind its wire cage was all I could hear, except for the telephone which sometimes rang and rang in the void at the other end of the flat.

It grew darker and darker until the room was lit only by the glow of the fire. I was getting hungry and thirsty. I battled with my conscience for a long time before climbing onto a chair to take down the bottle of Cherry Linctus cough mixture which Nurse had put out of reach on a high shelf. I drank it all; and then I no longer wanted her to come back because I thought she would be angry and spank me. I huddled in a corner with my rabbit, Nibby, in my arms and sobbed myself to silence.

When Nurse came back she picked me up and gave me the longest hug she had ever given me. I could not understand why she did not seem to mind at all about the cough mixture.

Late in December Antonia took us to Binesfield, where Tom joined us over Christmas.

In the twin-bedded room they shared above ours, Antonia had a nightmare about Tom on Christmas night. She dreamt he was lying on an operating table with surgeons standing over him. When she looked closely she saw he had no top to his head and his brains, which were made up of green bean-shaped objects, were spilling out. She wanted to put them back, and Silas appeared to help her, but she felt it might damage the green bits, which she now knew were the 'thinking parts', if she touched them. So she tried to lift Tom's head to stop him losing any more and he was sick all over her. She knew, when this happened, that his black vomit had stained her in such a way that she would never get clean, and that Silas, with whom she was about to have some happiness, would leave her.

When she woke Tom up afterwards he noticed that, not only was she much less frightened than she used to be after nightmares, but instead of seeking to be comforted, she tried to reassure him that he had probably represented her father in the nightmare, as he had often served as a substitute for him in dreams before.

He noted a few days later that Carroll had said that 'something very sweet and womanly' was emerging in Antonia, and Tom also had noticed that she had started showing consideration for others in the 'best way'.

At the beginning of the New Year, 1937, Antonia wrote her annual summing up in her notebook. She felt that 'something positive' had happened during the past year, in spite of very bad patches in the spring and summer, and seemed happy in her 'delicate and difficult' relationship with David.

In January she took a full-time job at the highest salary she would ever earn, £1000 a year, with J. Walter Thompson – an American advertising agency which had recently set up a London office. Although she had sworn she would never go back to advertising, she took it, hoping that within three months she would have paid off her debts and got straight.

In March David said in his journal that he and Antonia had been through 'the most difficult stages' of their relationship, and he had passed 'a frightful month of depression following a visit to Antonia's analyst'. Two days later he resolved, 'No more Antonias . . . The Marys are all very well, but give me the Marthas in the long run.'

In April he discovered that he loved a man: 'It is not a normal homosexual relationship, but it is more than friendship.' He was worried about Antonia and went to see her. Afterwards he wrote:

> It is hateful to have to say so, but I must remember that A. is a *schizophrenic*. It seems improbable that she will ever be entirely cured; her suicidal tendency is so marked that she can't take out an insurance policy on her life . . .
>
> She is really one of the most wonderful people I have ever known, or am likely to know, and has had more influence on me than any single person I can think of. But on the whole, I think her influence on the people she comes in contact with is bad: her husband, S–,[1] Emily, and now Norman Cameron – she gradually undermines everyone's self-confidence. There are very few who can stand the dazzling (but how depressing!) light of moral Truth she radiates. Exposed to their selves, her intimates begin to wilt, and with what ruthlessness she tears their illusions to shreds! very often, I believe, out of revenge for (imagined?) neglects or slights . . . A nice sort of influence for an unstable and impressionable young man!

David continued to see Antonia occasionally in the company of others. His last mention of her is in a description of a wild evening in May with a drunken Dylan Thomas, which had ended in 'a gruesome scene' at Cecil Court:

[1] Siepmann? or Silas?

... A. and Dylan pretending to play 'wolf-dogs' on the carpet and altogether getting on each other's nerves in a bad way, till I blunderingly tried to stop them and succeeded in putting Dylan's back up. 'Where are the halo and the wings,' he asked, 'of Tony's guardian angel?' ('He is *not*,' she remarked, of Dylan, 'a child of light.' We none of us felt like one. It was very miserable.)

In May, Antonia noted, 'I fall in love with a schoolgirl rapidity and grown-up intensity.' Not only did she say that David meant nothing to her now, but also that Norman Cameron, yet another young poet, with whom she had been on holiday to Germany at Easter and who had put her into 'a frenzy of physical disappointment' because he had not wanted to sleep with her, no longer mattered to her.

The suicide crisis she had been through in March had abated, but analysis was being particularly gruelling now. She had to admit 'with what apparent sincerity, one disguises from oneself that one wants money, love, and success in work. How cunningly one avoids having any of the three.' She also admitted she feared sanity as much as insanity, because she confused it with lack of originality and imagination:

> To be a person of mature understanding often seems frightening & dull. I find it hard to kill (probably don't want to kill) the young girl who still persists in me at the age of 38.

When she next wrote in her notebook, on 15 May 1937, there was a new man in her life whom she wanted to marry and by whom she wanted to have a child. His name was Basil Nicholson.

For Sue probably the most traumatic event of her life took place in that spring of 1937, when she was nearly eight. Silas was due back after several years in Africa, and Miss Searle thought Sue should be told that he was her father before he reappeared on the scene. Miss Searle later admitted to Antonia that her decision to tell Sue at that age had been a mistake.

I remember Antonia shooing me out of the room because she had something important to say to Susan. I feared for her that it was going to be a blowing-up but, after a very long time, she came out holding her head high. Before I could ask what had happened she burst out with, 'Tom's only your father. Mine's Silas Glossop.'

I was astounded. More so than Sue apparently, for in the book she wrote about Antonia, *Now to My Mother*, she says that when Mother asked her to guess who her father was, after some quick deduction she suggested Silas. This was because he used to send her presents: she had a yellow dog Dingo he had bought for her before he went to Africa; and he had once sent her a book apparently called *The Tale of Glossop* which had made me think he must be important. By the time I had learnt to read and discovered it was *The Tailor of Gloucester* by Beatrix Potter, the idea that Silas was very important was firmly fixed in my mind.

Outwardly she took it very well and I admired her. She says in her book that, although it meant 'surrendering Tom' to me, she was proud to have a private father. She does not say in that book how she felt on meeting him for the first time as her real father. And Antonia never mentions how father and daughter now reacted to one another. All I remember is that Silas gave Sue a tricycle on his return, of which I was most envious, and that she used to pedal it with great ferocity along the pavements of Hollywood Road with Nurse calling after her, 'Do be more careful, Susan!' each time she near-missed a passer-by.

Tom, who for the past few months had been going through a gruelling time too, treated us both exactly the same as before, for he was equally fond of Sue and me and has always continued to be so.

Not long after Tom had gone to Sussex to give Frances the ring, she had had a relapse and been brought to a nursing home in London. Geoffrey had telephoned Tom in his office to say that the doctors had said Frances would probably die. Although it was a terrible blow, Tom had somehow managed to go on working and not to break down in the office. But back in his room off the Fulham Road he had wept, and continued to have to fight back tears whenever someone talked about her.

If Frances knew the gravity of her situation, she hid it. She never talked of her illness and said she was content to be back in London where friends could see her more often. She always wore the ring Tom gave her. At times she was 'positively gay', Tom wrote, chatting and gossiping.

But it was not always like that. One evening when he went to visit her, he found Frances lying in darkness. When he turned on the light she looked as if she had been crying, her cheeks mottled and her hair dishevelled. That was the day the doctors had tried for the second time to collapse her right lung, and she knew they had failed. She sat up and talked of other things, and tried to smile. Tom told her what he had been doing that day, and fed her goldfish on the table opposite the bed. When he held her hand before leaving he felt how hot it was.

Tom realised then he could no longer hope that the doctors would be proved wrong and she would not die. If she died, he wished only two things: that she should die peacefully and that he would be able to face it.

Antonia, who was at her best when consoling, became his 'greatest stay and comfort' all through that spring. But after she began her affair with Basil Nicholson, Antonia's attitude towards Tom returned to its usual state of dichotomy.

Antonia had never liked Basil, who was nine years younger than she was, since first meeting him at the *Daily Mirror* where he worked as a journalist. He had always been 'rude and cold' to her, he was ugly, and she mistrusted him. He was renowned for being very brilliant, very unscrupulous, and for his habit of pursuing women violently and then suddenly dropping them. The only thing she had ever seen in his favour was that he could be extremely witty.

One night in May 1937 she ran into Basil at a party, and although they kept up their usual running fight, he offered to see her home afterwards. At Cecil Court 'he suddenly began to make love to me,' wrote Antonia, telling her that only 'a strong sense of self-preservation' had prevented him from doing so before, for he seemed to think she was a man-eater. She was completely taken aback by this turnabout of her 'old enemy', particularly as it came at a time when she was feeling 'finished as a woman' after her two recent débâcles with David and Norman.

Suddenly Antonia found herself drawn as if by a magnet to this ugly man who had never before interested her, in spite of all the danger signals. She knew he had a permanent mistress with whom he had been living for years, and that he had caused her closest friend much pain when her affair with him had ended in an abortion.

'Why should this man attract me?' she now asked herself. 'He looks like a boy prematurely stricken with old age ... He is short, not well-built, with irregular teeth and thinning hair.' Yet Antonia became the pursuer and spent the next three months unable to resist the temptation to get in touch with him whenever she felt she had waited too long for a sign from him. This pattern of behaviour started at once, for there was no word for some time after he first made love to her.

She grew more and more frustrated and anxious. She curtailed her social life in order not to be out if Basil should call, but invited friends to Cecil Court to distract her. Although she was usually most indiscreet about her personal life she told none of her friends about her new love, not even Emily with whom she always discussed men in detail.

At the end of May she gave a small party for Silas on his return from Africa. Her nervous anxiety before it about how Djuna and Emily would react to him had been entirely unnecessary, for by the end of the evening Djuna had fallen for him and they would soon start an affair. Everyone commented on how attractive Antonia was looking; but she was even more pleased that Djuna liked some prose poems she had been experimenting with.

After ten days Antonia wrote to Basil. He did not reply. Then she rang him, and left her name when told he was out. He did not call back and she grew angry. As the days passed and there was still no sign from Basil, Antonia, as so often happened when she could not express her rage directly to the cause of it, took a side-swipe at someone else. For the first time in months she had a row with Tom. She accused him of contempt for her work and a desire to destroy her confidence: 'I even accused him of having "stolen" my place as a writer.' She recovered her senses after a few minutes and admitted the accusations were 'purely fantastic'. She was also upset, as usual, about her writing. The whole idea of the father/daughter book had become 'abhorrent' to her and she felt 'hopelessly impotent' when faced with trying to write it. Yet she desperately wanted to write it for Carroll's sake as much as her own. Not only did she want to dedicate the book to him, but she also hoped it would earn enough to pay off her debt to him, for, although she had been at J. Walter Thompson's for six months, she had not cleared her debts, and was finding the job was 'not sufficiently interesting' to hold her attention.

Finally Basil reappeared. After they had made love for the second time, Antonia, who had started a new notebook to record her thoughts on him, noted he was 'entirely different' from any previous lover. Although he was aggressive in his approach to her, and 'deliberately ungracious', he was also 'tender and affectionate as well as physically very passionate'.

After their next encounter, Antonia wrote eight pages in French in her notebook about Basil. 'J'ai pour lui un attrait charnel qui m'éblouit,' she said, and spoke of his sexual ferocity. He saw her as a beast, sometimes a tigress, sometimes a fawn: his favourite term of endearment was 'Ma biche, ma biche à moi'. She suspected the sadistic streak in him was drawn out by her pudeur and frigidity, and yet he was the first man with whom she had not felt ashamed of her body.

Again several days went by without him telephoning. She kept the weekend free in the hope of seeing him. She frittered away Saturday afternoon at a cinema to pass the time. After coming home she felt 'both extreme languor and a nervous desire for action and company; the thought of reading or writing unbearable'. She rang up everyone she could think of, regardless of whether they were people she wanted to see or not, but no one was free. The 'real old rising hysteria' began, combined with impotence to decide on any action. In desperation, and out of a 'pure sense of duty', she went to say goodnight to Sue. She stayed half an hour: 'Susan hugged me which she very seldom does. We laughed and made plans to celebrate the end of [her] analysis. And somehow that lifted all the dead weight and relieved the tension.' Then she came to say goodnight to me.

This was the first time our mother wrote of having enjoyed our company, 'they were so fresh and sweet and alive'. After that she was able to pass a 'not discontented evening', reading old notebooks and writing about the evening in her current one.

On the Sunday, she went alone to Kew Gardens and found calm there, but in the evening, as she smoked endless cigarettes, and tried to work on the book about her father, she fell back into a state of languor and impotence again. She gave up on the novel and wrote about Basil in her notebook instead.

She described an evening when Basil and Norman Cameron had had a row over the fascist mentality which had ended with Norman throwing a glass of soda water in Basil's face before leaving. Basil had not moved. She had put her arm round him, but he had remained in his chair, rigid and wet, refusing, like a proud, sensitive child who has been hurt, to be comforted. She had sat on the floor by him and taken his hand: 'I want to cry,' she had said. He had stroked her hand and confessed, 'So do I.'

Her punishment for having caught him off his guard, and showing tenderness, was that Basil did not get in touch again for some time.

To distract herself, Antonia gave another party. Tom was among her guests. She was struck by his handsomeness and confidence and amused to see him make for the most striking woman in the room:

'He was such a fine young cock bird strutting.' But she preferred Basil, 'crabbed and harsh', who suppressed any charm he had.

When she next wrote in her notebook, on 1 July, something had happened which she had never dared to hope for. She had slept with Basil again and for the first time in her life had overcome her fear of sex: 'I feel so rich and yet so free.' But, though she did not know it at the time, she had made a bad psychological error that evening. On a sudden impulse she had told him, 'I love you.' He had taken her hand and held it fast against him, but said nothing.

More than a week passed without her hearing from him. She grew uneasy and depressed.

When he next saw her it was by chance. His first reaction had been to start with 'panicky nervousness'. When he had recovered his calm he told her he wanted to finish their sexual relationship. He said that she had more genius than he had supposed, but was less quick, hard and coherent than he had imagined; that she was very little aware of other people's existence; that she distorted and exaggerated her feeling for him.

Antonia managed with difficulty to fight down hysteria and even admitted there was truth in what he said. But she was bewildered: 'Having rushed the sexual side with great violence, he now renounces it with equal violence.'

Carroll explained to her that Basil was clearly a mass of complexes, which at least exonerated her from some of the blame for what had happened. As she licked her wounds she resolved she would not communicate with him again. She decided he was a mixture of Socrates and the Artful Dodger and she must get on with her life without him.

But the very next day she telephoned him, with the excuse of discussing a proposal Rupert Doone had put to her of starting a magazine for the Group Theatre. He was friendly and agreed to meet in a café to talk it over. After several cups of coffee, and staying an hour longer than he had meant to, Basil agreed to accompany her to a Group Theatre weekend the following Saturday.

There she felt they had made progress, but over that weekend she at last realised that every time they came closer, he recoiled and avoided meetings afterwards, so she determined never again to get in touch with him, but to wait until he felt the urge to see her.

Her wisdom was rewarded. Within a month of having said they must renounce sex, he made love to her again and they were 'in complete physical harmony'. But immediately afterwards she made another major tactical error: she talked of marriage.

The desire to marry Basil began to fill Antonia's thoughts. On 28 July she asked herself whether she would be prepared to get a divorce, without any hope of marrying Basil, and be committed to earning her own living for the rest of her life. In her notebook she continued:

> The children make everything very confused. I feel a duty to them, often love, but perhaps more often that they are rather hostile strangers . . . I MUST consider the children though often I feel I would like to walk right out & start a new life by myself.

By chance Antonia met Tom at a bus-stop that evening. After chatting a bit, she suddenly said she loved Basil and wanted a divorce. Tom was deeply disturbed. For the next few days he was so oppressed by the thought that a stage of his life was over that he cried while writing to her to explain why he had been so upset: 'The truth is I realised then how much I have been depending on you, how much I value being able to talk my life over with you . . .' He went on to talk of the practicalities of a divorce, saying that he should be cited as the guilty party, and he would tell his family that he had been the unfaithful one. He ended, 'You know you can rely on me in all matters to do with the children. I will try not to be *too much* of a father to them.'

Antonia's desire for a divorce suddenly turned another woman into a key figure in Tom's life.

A few weeks before, Gerti Deutsch, a young Viennese photographer, who hoped some of her pictures might be bought by Odhams Press, had been shown into Tom's office at *Weekly Illustrated*. She had come to England to look for work because her father was a Jewish businessman who was beginning to feel the effects of the Nazi persecutions in Austria. Although trained as a concert pianist, she had changed to photography, and her work had just been exhibited at the Austrian embassy in London. Tom was impressed by her pictures, and amused by her continental feminine wiles which contrasted with a tough determination to make a career in England. He invited her out, and found her gay and charming. She fell in love with him. By the time he saw Antonia at the bus-stop they had been having an affair for two weeks and he was planning to spend his summer holiday with her and his brother Paul in Austria.

When Antonia next saw Basil he wanted to give up their relationship because they did not have a single point of contact. 'It is rather like having an affair with a mermaid,' he said. Her old fear of being a monster returned, but she laughed it off, saying, 'I think the real trouble is that I am *not* a mermaid.'

Antonia took the separation – she could not bring herself to admit it was a final parting – bravely. She went away to stay with a friend, Gerald Reitlinger, in Sussex for the weekend and on her return to Cecil Court on Monday, instead of moping in the evening, tried to be positive by making a list of 'Pleasures Since Saturday.' These included, besides the smell of rosemary and sage, peaches and thyme in her host's garden,

Trying to learn to swim.
Making good shots at croquet.
Talking on a subject I know viz – Catholic Church.
Thinking out the Basil situation a bit more.

On the same date, 9 August, she wrote eleven pages in her 'Basil' notebook. Her disillusionment over how things were going turned her mind to religion:

... if, by sacrificing one's own inclinations, one could be rewarded by seeing a real increase of the true happiness of those one loved, it would make a difficult life seem worth while. I want so often to pray in gratitude, to worship, as well as to ask for strength for myself and comfort for others ... But in the cruel cat-and-mouse conception of the ordinary Christian God I cannot believe.

That evening she also wrote a letter to Tom, on holiday in Vienna, saying she had spoken to a divorce solicitor who said they should file a petition by October if they wanted their case to be heard in the Spring Session. She reported buying Sue a desk and chair for her birthday – '27/6d alas but she liked it so' – and a compensatory cricket bat for 3s 6d for me. We had just left for Winster and she was worried that the influence of Nurse and Nora was making us 'servanty', particularly Sue who was 'so impressionable'. She told Tom, 'It is a nuisance children have to be so looked after.'

Three days later Antonia accepted she had lost Basil, and told herself she must not grieve or hope. She went to Binesfield for the weekend so as not to be tempted to telephone him, but he was on her mind all the time.

She found the visit to her mother upsetting:

The house grows dirtier and dirtier. An open sore on her neck, drifts of powder, her cheap clothes crushed and soiled, her hair bright, soft and curly as a young girl's. Her nails half eaten away, patched with nail varnish. The terrible sense of sweet decay. I am sorry for her life, yet exasperated . . . She talks of nothing but sex. With a giggle she tells me, in veiled language, that she masturbates.

. . . She is completely divorced from reality. When she sits up in her shabby bed in a soiled flowered nightdress, with a velvet coat and a moth-eaten fur collar, she thinks she is the Pompadour . . . She simply does not see what she wants not to see whether it is another person or a lawn covered with weeds.

As thunder rumbles on in the distance when the eye of the storm has passed, Antonia continued to murmur about Basil in her notebook. Since she could no longer even dream of Basil marrying her, there was no point in insisting on getting a divorce from Tom. But now it was Tom who wanted the proceedings to go ahead so that he could marry Gerti to whom he had become secretly engaged in Austria.

Tom had told Gerti about Frances, but not Frances about Gerti.

One afternoon at the end of August, after his return from Vienna, he visited Frances in hospital. She said to him: 'I am so often disturbed in my mind and I get into a state and worry whether I can depend on you when I'm well.' Only then did he see, with horror, what he had done by asking Gerti to marry him: he had anticipated Frances's death.

Tom now lived in terror that some word about Gerti might reach Frances's ears.

He continued to visit Frances almost every evening after work and at weekends. On one visit he met Geoffrey coming out of the nursing home as he was going in, and turned back to walk with him to the underground station. Geoffrey said the doctors had just told him she had only a short time to live:

He went on to speak quite sharply about her, about how she was behaving & what should or should not be told her. His nose was rather red & his face lined. As he was going he was half holding his hand out, & I took it & shook it. He stepped back blindly away from me into a road full of traffic & I saw that his face had suddenly all crumpled up & he was crying.

Now that a divorce had become a reality, a part of Antonia kept saying, 'But this is all a mistake.' She suddenly realised she was 'going to be stripped of everything' and left to herself. She wrote to Carroll, who was on his annual holiday, and told him she was in a panic over a sense of terror of loss of something:

> It can't be a real thing because it appears now as loss of femininity, now of capacity to be an artist, now of money, now of security, now of independence. It makes me equally afraid of religion and atheism, success and failure, love and celibacy.

'The beast' came out of its lair and snarled at Tom for ever having married her, then, for the first time, at Eric: 'it was a kind of sin in him to ask me to marry him and heaven knows he has expiated it by trying to give me back to my own nature. But it is very late, probably too late for me to have a life as a woman.' She was 'sick of dreamy platonic friendships and rare civilised loves' and did not regret at all having been 'Basil's bitch'. Finally her thoughts turned to Silas, whom she feared she had damaged:

> But he was damaged already ... There is Susan and she must be saved from this legacy of our own devils. I wish I could have Susan and not Lyndall. I suppose it would be cruel to separate them?

In September Antonia went on holiday again in Germany with Norman Cameron.

The journey started badly with her getting drunk for the first and only time in her life. When the hangover headache finally wore off she went into 'a really black hopeless depression'. She took some Dial, and by the time they reached Cologne she felt peaceful, though ghost-like.

But Antonia's calm was short-lived. Travelling by train the next day, in a carriage where a doting mother was publicly acting out 'insane baby worship' over her small son – 'What the wretched child does not see is that it is not *itself* the mother loves at all, but *herself*' – threw her back into reflections about ways of giving and receiving love, which of course brought Basil into her mind again.

The holiday was not a success. The black swastikas on the red banners that adorned many buildings, and the groups of *Hitler Jugend* in their black shorts were constant overshadowing reminders that Germany was in the hands of the Nazis. As usually happened on holidays, Antonia's persuasive mood was depression and a feeling of futility. Norman proved to be a 'nerve-racking' companion and there were rows between them. She had made a terrible scene when, without asking her, he had given away some sweets Tom had given her before leaving, which she had not eaten because they represented a link to Tom whom she was feeling unhappy over because of the impending divorce.

But the real trouble was that Basil was back in her mind more strongly than ever and figuring in her dreams. On an impulse she wrote him a long letter; but, on her return to Cecil Court in mid-September, there was no sign from him and she felt her 'springs of love' dried up.

We, too, had returned from holiday to start going to a new school, King Arthur's. Antonia came to fetch us home in a taxi at the end of the first day and I remember telling her excitedly that something called the 'alphabet' had just been invented – I already knew how to read, but at Miss Baxter's they had not taught me that there was an order for letters. My mother's sarcastic comment, and my sister's superior look, made me vow never again to discuss what went on in my classroom. I began to keep many things to myself from then on.

In fact my school life started off well. We were awarded red stars for good work which were pasted in front of our names on a board. Soon my row was pulling ahead of the others in the class. Mental arithmetic was my best subject: my favourite game, which Sue refused to play, was to get someone to set mathematical problems and see how fast I could solve them in my head. Antonia sometimes did this for me in front of her friends, and I enjoyed the praise, but I sensed that being good at writing poems and drawing, like Sue, would have won respect as well as praise, and that my particular skill was admired in the way performing dogs I had seen when Tom took us to the circus were.

At King Arthur's, to be summoned to the principal's study was a double ordeal, for the school was run jointly by Miss Aldous who was squat and sombre and Miss Hacking who was tall and gaunt. It was in their presence that I had my first lesson on perfidy.

There was a fat girl, called Sybil, with fair stringy hair who struggled along red-starless at the bottom of my class. She decided she wanted me as her friend and quickly noticed my weakness for chocolate. In the cloakroom, when we were changing into our outdoor clothes to go to the playing fields in Kensington Gardens, Sybil used to bring out a small paper-bag full of chocolate drops which were hidden in her navy blue bloomers: they would all be for me if I would sit next to her on the bus. I accepted the first few times, but the taste of the chocolate drops, half-melted by the warmth of her thighs, was not enticing enough to lure me away from better friends, and I soon refused them and Sybil's company on the bus.

One afternoon when I had been at King Arthur's for about two months, I was summoned to the headmistresses' room. Miss Hacking was leaning on the mantelpiece, and Miss Aldous, who was seated behind a desk, spoke.

'You're a very nasty little girl,' she began. How had she discovered that, I wondered? 'Sybil tells us that you make her bring you presents.'

'That's not true. She—'

'And that you threaten to do nasty things if she doesn't.'

'I've never —'

'And that yesterday you said something so disgusting to her that she felt she had to come and tell us about it.'

I stood silent now as they exchanged looks of mutual indignation over my head. 'Sybil said you told her that if she didn't bring you some chocolate, you . . .' She hesitated as if the words were too dreadful to repeat.

Miss Hacking, looking down at me with cold disapproval, boldly finished the sentence, putting particular emphasis on the last five words, 'That you would wet – her – knickers – for – her.'

It must have been my look of horrified astonishment as much as my protestations of having been libelled, that convinced my two accusers I was perhaps innocent.

On the way back to the classroom, bearing a message for Sybil that Miss Aldous and Miss Hacking wanted to see her, I tried to puzzle out why someone who begged my friendship would denounce me to the highest authorities for threatening something I would not even have known *how* to go about doing. Yet in some way I felt tainted by the episode and there was no sense of victory when Sybil did not reappear in our classroom again.

The one person to whom I might have confided what had happened was no longer with us at Cecil Court: Nurse had left a few days before getting married, on 16 October 1937. She was now the wife of Gordon Palmer, the airman she had been in love with for some time. And two weeks prior to that, Nora also had left to marry her love.

I missed Nurse. Recently I asked her whether it had been difficult working for Antonia who had such an unreliable nature? She seemed almost surprised at my question. She had known our mother was going through a bad time and made allowances for it. She said Antonia had been generous to her both with pay and time off and often passed on to her lovely clothes she would never have been able to afford out of her salary. Her only criticism was that it had been difficult to get Antonia to take any interest in *our* clothes, and she had often made things for us, paying for the materials herself. For Tom she could not find a word of criticism.

Nurse and Nora were replaced by a German au pair Antonia had found on her holiday with Norman Cameron.

Our first meeting with Gerda was when Mother brought her to fetch us from King Arthur's. In the taxi home, while Sue chatted to Mother, Gerda tried to woo me with hugs. She wore a prickly suit and smelt of onions. Nurse had brought me up too well to show my dislike, but I could never stand her and was glad she stayed only a few months. According to Antonia she was despatched back to Cologne because the Foreign Office had had word that she was a Nazi spy.

Antonia was in a 'very bad and muddled state' all that autumn. In analysis she was trying to track down something that was still eluding her:

> I *know* the beast in my jungle . . . and yet, try as I will, cannot feel it fully and so escape from it. Obviously I am terrified and I know I am terrified, but of what?

One evening at the end of September, while talking to Emily and Djuna, some of the things they said made her wonder whether, if this 'terrible burden of fear' were lifted, she might become really dangerous.

> [Djuna] kept saying that I was marvellous, that the only trouble was that I hadn't the courage to be ruthless enough. She called me the last of the Borgias . . . She said 'You crash right into other people's lives and wreck them – look at Silas – you've done for him all right. Look at Tom – I saw him in his boat the other day and that engine kept right on stuttering "Tony – Tony – Tony – Tony".' Then she kept kissing me and pulling my hair, saying '. . . You're marvellous and I dote on you and I wouldn't have you any different but I would rather be dead for a row of pins than be in love with you . . . you've got a heart of leather and with that face & those little feminine ways, there's not a thing you can't get.'

Antonia confessed to them she had always had an 'idiotic desire' to be good. Now she wondered whether she was meant to be bad by nature: 'Perhaps to get to heaven I have got to have the courage to deserve hell.'

Emily agreed: 'You should have the courage to be the devil.'

As she reflected on what they had said, Antonia wondered whether

her 'painful efforts' towards recognising other people's existence were pure hypocrisy. Then, having said she did sometimes have warm and generous impulses towards other people, she wrote that she resented that she was to be left with us, tied and committed to making money:

And yet it is just possible that I care for those children more than I realise . . . I would find it very hard to part permanently with Susan in actual fact, I think. When I went in to say good-night to her, I did feel a wave of extreme affection for her. I have been selfish about Susan, shirked my responsibilities, & yet having her was one of the few genuine things in my life.

Her state of angst worsened. She had nightmares about being tortured by the Nazis and began to be afraid of being alone in the flat with us on Gerda's days off. She had grown listless again. In the evening she read or played the piano aimlessly, or asked Tom in for a meal and hung about waiting for him – for Gerti had remained in Austria to get all her things in order before moving to England permanently. Antonia felt 'utter and complete emptiness, uselessness, impotence . . . I CANNOT write.'

In October Antonia lost her job at J. Walter Thompson through laziness. She was upset; not just because the pay had been so good, though never enough to keep up with her extravagance and get her out of debt, but because she now had too much time on her hands to drive home the emptiness of her loveless life: 'It is like living in a country where the sun never shines.' Basil's flight had left her cold and disillusioned.

Basil Nicholson would appear in Antonia's dreams and be mentioned in her notebooks until his death at the age of forty-five. She heard news of him occasionally – such as that he had taken to drink and was living as a down-and-out in Dublin – through Cecil King, the *Daily Mirror*'s proprietor, who considered him one of the most brilliant journalists he had known.

Many years later, in February 1953, by which time Antonia was much changed, Cecil King telephoned to say that Basil was dying of cancer. He had been taken in by Catholic nuns who had found him in such a state of filth that they had had to burn his clothes. The nuns were praying for his conversion. Antonia did not think it 'humanly possible' that they would succeed. But when Cecil telephoned her a few days later to say Basil had died, he also told her he had been received into the Catholic Church at the end.

On Sunday, 17 October 1937, Tom wrote in his black notebook:

Frances died today.

I was rung up as I was sitting by the fire. I shaved & bathed & got dressed. I reached the nursing-home at quarter to one. They said 'I'm afraid you'll find her very much changed.' I had been finding her very much changed for a year & a quarter.

She was lying on her pillows, with her head bent up straight. Her knees were swerving away to one side under the bed-clothes. Her arms were on the bed-spread. One of her hands was clenched like a bird's claw, not closed into a fist, but gripped & cramped-looking. A nurse was holding the other. I took it. Her hands were very hot. She was breathing with a deep rasping gurgling noise, forcing the breath in & out with difficulty through all the stuff collecting in her throat. Occasionally the nurse would wipe her lips with a tissue of soft paper. Her face was yellowish-white. Her lips mauve. Her eyes closed.

. . . I said 'Frances, Frances' to her several times, but no sound entered through her ears. Gradually her breath came with more difficulty . . .

Soon Frances took one or two deeper breaths & there were long pauses in between. I thought perhaps she had died already & was praying 'Lord take her spirit'. But she recovered & took another gulping breath – three or four more, three or four more – in between each I thought 'she has not been breathing for so long she can't take another breath now'. But then she did. And then she took one & the pause went on & on & on & did not end. Her eyes had turned up a few minutes before. Her hands were still warm. I was holding them both. I said to her nurse 'Is that all?' She nodded & looked at Frances kindly. Then she took out her watch, noted the time & put it back.

She told me Frances had said yesterday, 'I hope I die in the day-time because then Tom can be here.'

CHAPTER 13

·δ·

Growing Up

I have not the patience and self control of my own children.
Antonia White, 15 August 1937

After the death of Frances, Tom could not bring himself to write in his notebook again for eighteen months. By that time many things had changed in his life: he was married to Gerti, with whom he had been living while waiting for his divorce; he had become assistant editor on a new weekly magazine, *Picture Post*, which had been started by a Hungarian journalist called Stefan Lorant and was owned by Hulton Press; and he had had his first novel, *The Man Below*, published by the Hogarth Press.

Antonia, on the other hand, wrote more prolifically, and with fewer gaps, in her notebooks of 1938–9 than ever before. She poured out about 50,000 words in those eighteen months while Tom was silent. 'All these notebooks,' she said, 'though they're not entirely worthless, are a substitute for more creative and public writing,' which she was still not managing to do.

The next year, 1938, was to be almost as important a year in her life as 1929 – when Sue had been born, her father had died, she had started her affair with Tom, and written her best short story, 'The House of Clouds'.

At the end of 1937 Antonia had taken a twenty-year-old lover from a need to have some 'human warmth' in her life again. He was Nigel Henderson, the younger son of her friend Wyn, whom she had known since he was a small boy. For a while, she was very happy 'within the limits' with him.

Carroll warned her that she had once again fallen for someone who would cause disappointment. And the affair did, in fact, follow the course of its predecessors, with a reluctance on one side and a fear of sexual intercourse on the other; followed by Antonia's compulsion to provoke disaster: disaster which brought 'acute humiliation, sadness, sense of loss and failure' yet which also contained 'elements of relief, excitement, almost triumph'.

By the end of 1937, still without work and having mismanaged her affair with this 'sensitive, intelligent, impressionable' boy, who was also 'sullen, hysterical, ambivalent and uncertain', Antonia was feeling low. She made a list of *Wants*, the last of which was a wish that she could put herself in contact with 'a supreme intelligence' which knew how best to use her, and so believe, however frustrated and meaningless her life might seem, it was part of 'the creator's design'. Yet she feared such feelings might only be a projection of her father.

Just before the new year she took another lover. He was Nigel's elder brother, Ian.

At first she did not tell Nigel she had fallen for Ian and started an affair with him, too. But soon after, while in the throes of a bad depression, she let out the truth.

Nigel felt knifed in the back and became bitter against Antonia. There was a strong tie between the brothers and this brought out undercurrents of hate and jealousy. Antonia feared she was corrupt all through and thought she ought to kill herself, but decided that was cowardly, and continued having an affair with both brothers.

The drawing to a close of analysis after four years was bringing out many things Antonia had always managed to conceal from herself. At times she felt it drove her beyond endurance as it broke down her defences and revealed how many of her wishes ran counter to the accepted ideas of what was considered desirable, such as 'love, gentleness, endurance, justice, forbearance' etc., whereas she loved 'goodness *and* badness' and 'manifestations of power, both violence *and* control'. Perhaps this is why she sometimes had two men in her life: one for each side of her nature.

The two Henderson brothers were very different. In Antonia's opinion Ian was more phlegmatic than his younger brother and did not have his 'brilliance of imagination'. But he had a clear, logical mind, and was patient, considerate and warm-hearted. Nigel, whom she preferred, though more selfish, violent and unreasonable than Ian, and often sullen and selfish, was an '*âme bien née*'.

One of the problems with Nigel was a homosexual streak that interfered with his relations with both sexes. She had sent him to Carroll (a habit she had with her friends: Djuna and David Gascoyne had preceded him, but neither had been psychoanalysed) and for a while he went to him, irregularly. Ian, on the other hand, did not have this problem, although he was attractive to men – Eric had confessed to Antonia that he had fallen for Ian a few years before, but had been rejected.

It is remarkable that twenty-one-year-old Ian was a match for so complex and unstable a woman of nearly forty, under great mental stress from psychoanalysis and a pending divorce, and would have with her the longest affair outside marriage she had ever had. Perhaps one of the reasons was that Antonia was more immature in many ways than he was. Only very recently, as a result of analysis, had 'the vain, greedy, rapacious' child inside her begun to grow up emotionally, though she admitted constant relapses into childish behaviour. She noted that she had reached the stage in her life emotionally just before the asylum, when she would have been Ian's contemporary: 'If things had gone straight for me then I would have been about to have my first satisfactory sexual relationship.'

In spite of Nigel's bitterness, 'this curious double thing' with him and Ian lasted for four months.

During this time Antonia was growing more desperate than usual about money. An idea she had had at the beginning of the year – to treat freelancing like a regular job by going every day to a room Eric had lent her in his house in Selwood Place, three bus-stops away from Cecil Court – was not yielding the results she had hoped for. She was still in debt to Carroll, and her overdraft was larger than ever.

The divorce hearing came at the end of March.

For some time Antonia had been resenting the fact that her allowance from Tom would be cut when the divorce was finalised. Tom felt she ought to get Silas to maintain Sue; she feared Silas would not be able to because he was still struggling to pay off Miss Searle for Sue's analysis.

Tom sent her a friendly letter with some cigarettes for her thirty-ninth birthday – they were not allowed to meet now until the decree nisi came through – begging her not to let 'the practical affairs of the divorce' destroy their 'real friendship'.

Two weeks later she wrote to him for his thirty-third birthday, admitting she still had some bitterness, though mainly sadness, at the feeling of waste over the breakdown of their marriage.

Another change that was coming over Antonia was her attitude towards her children. This was partly due to the fact that we were beginning to grow into human beings with whom she could communicate, particularly Sue, not just because she was older, but because Mother found her to be a 'born thinker' who every so often came out with some profound observation which aroused her awed respect. She was now 'perfectly willing' to spend on us the children's allowance Tom gave her, but admitted she still did not feel 'maternal and unselfish enough' to make any sacrifices for us out of her own pocket.

In our different ways Sue and I were both unhappy. We saw much less of Tom now that we could get to school on our own. And at weekends, if we did see him, it was usually to have tea with him and Gerti in their shared flat in Fernshaw Road.

I began to steal things too, but, unlike Sue, I did not get caught. There was a terrible rumpus at King Arthur's because Sue stole a watch; but my crime of stealing a sea-horse's skeleton from another child's locker went undetected. My guilt over this first theft weighed so heavily on me that before the end of term I put it back. But I did not put back a threepenny piece I took from Gerti's bag when she was preparing tea for us one Sunday, and helped myself to several more over the next few years.

In fact Sue and I had come closer because we had entered a sort of 'Babes in the Wood' phase of our childhood after Tom, and then Nurse, left: our only remaining security was each other. Gerda had been replaced by a nicer, but dimmer girl, who never tried to exercise any authority over us. We lingered on the way home from school and played in the streets till dusk.

Our favourite game was 'playing horses'. Sue had a passion for horses and so, naturally, I developed one, too. We alternated being the horse and the driver. It was more fun being the horse, with a piece of wire in one's mouth attached to two long pieces of string. The streets of Kensington seemed less dreary as we came home from King Arthur's at a spanking trot, the horse frisking and farting (making the sound through its mouth), and the driver calling 'Steady there, whoa there my beauty!' at every traffic light.

We also hung around the nearby United Dairies' stables, imbibing the exquisite smell of manure, and hoping some stableman would let us pat a milk pony and give it a lump of sugar. Sue took to following horses pulling carts: for a while I would try to keep up, but she always out-trotted me and would disappear into the distance, sometimes not to return for hours.

We were both avid readers of comics at this time. Antonia had given Sue a subscription to the *Dandy* and me one to the *Beano*. One week the *Beano* ran a short-story competition for under sevens with a prize of half a guinea. I wrote a story and copied it out neatly. I showed it to Sue who thought the story was not bad but the handwriting would not do at all: it was too neat, she said, no one would believe I was not yet seven and so I would be eliminated. Swollen with pride at so rare a compliment from my elder sister, I happily set to re-writing it with her help. We made the words slant in all directions, crossed things out and added others in, and, as a final gesture, she shook the inky pen over the page to make some splendid splotches. It was a masterpiece of fakery we thought.

A few weeks later I received a letter addressed to Master Lyndall Hopkinson. It was from the *Beano*. They said they liked my story but it had not won the competition because it was too untidily presented. My only consolation was the word 'Master' on the envelope, for I had always wanted to be a boy.

Shortly afterwards, Antonia gave us the best present she would ever give us: Rook. We had always longed for a dog, and could not believe it when she said she had bought us a black cocker spaniel who would be kept at her expense at Granny Botting's. '"Rook" is a great success,' Antonia wrote to Tom from Binesfield, 'I have never seen anyone in a state of such solemn ecstasy as Susan. She is really in love.'

On that Easter holiday, Sue confided to her that she had a nightly fantasy of being an ill-treated horse forced to drag heavy loads up a hill. 'She is beaten and the climax is that a spiked club is thrust up her bottom. I said "Isn't it rather frightening?" She said "Yes" and added "But it's *lovely*".' This shows that Sue was beginning to have confidence in Mother, for she had admitted a similar fantasy to Tom a year before, on the way to school.

On that visit to Binesfield Antonia decided it was far more strain to be with her mother than with us. Though she felt pity for her mother's condition, she was repulsed by it: 'I am so frightened of becoming like her.'

A few days later, having read what her mother, who now liked to be called by her second name, Julia, had written in a 'ludicrous, pathetic, nauseating' diary about a love affair with a man called

Oswald which had taken place shortly after Cecil's death (particularly the phrases 'Cleopatra had a famous wriggle last night. Julia ully-ully'), Antonia felt 'nothing can be so preposterous, so undignified as "love"'. She wrote: 'The sexual act is not indecent but almost any verbal description of it is.'

As always, when she was at Binesfield, her lovers seemed less important: 'Ian seems very remote: Nigel too for that matter.'

Nigel had recently taken his revenge on Antonia by starting an affair with the wife of one of her friends, which she had prophesied would quickly end because of his 'sadistic, contemptuous side'. At first she had been upset; but it had brought her closer to Ian, who, at his best, was 'like a wholesome climate in which someone can expand and feel calm and safe'.

On her return to London, she kept to her resolution to sleep only with Ian, with whom she was beginning to have a satisfactory sexual relationship for the first time in her life, but continued to see Nigel for a while. 'Obviously all three of us are working out something by means of each other.'

Now that analysis had helped clear up some of Antonia's problems over sex, she feared it had driven 'the demon' even more into money and writing. She still could not force herself to make more money or to live on less, and it was fortunate that Eric, whom she still considered 'the wisest, most delicate of human beings', continued to help towards paying Carroll. But over writing Antonia was becoming desperate. Carroll implied that one depended on the other, and she would not be able to concentrate on serious work until she had satisfied her 'passion for money'.

In May Antonia learned from a friend of Robert's that he had been killed in a flying accident three years before. With the 'peculiar clairvoyance' they had once had between them, she felt she should have known he had died. It was as if in some way he had cheated her. She lay on her bed, saying urgently, 'Robert, give me a sign – if dead people can communicate with us, give me a sign.' No sign came as she lay remembering that he had once promised that, even if he disappeared for a long time, he would eventually come back. She went over in her mind things they had done in the short time they were together. Just as she was getting drowsy she had a vivid hallucination of a man bending over her, 'a mocking, even a hostile presence', which was the way she saw Robert in dreams.

There followed a difficult patch in analysis. Only with Ian, 'in spite of setbacks', could she function properly. But he was now under pressure himself, studying hard to take exams to enter the Civil Service. Although she could not imagine him as a Civil Servant, she restrained herself from casting any doubts on Ian's choice of career since he had no income at all, and she was partly supporting him.

It was fortunate that Antonia was now offered a good job by Cecil King. He had not realised before that the Ann Jeffrey who had worked on the *Daily Mirror* was the same person as Antonia White who had written *Frost in May*, and he asked her to become fashion editor of the *Sunday Pictorial*. She decided this would be better than doing freelance work in advertising, which was like getting money from cheating.

Cecil King and his wife Margot would become important at this period of her life, but that did not mean they were above her criticism.

The quirks and queer economies of the rich had always intrigued and amused Antonia. The first time she was invited to spend a weekend in June with the Kings at Culham Court, their beautiful house near Henley-on-Thames, she noted that, although they had four gardeners and at least seven indoor servants, her hostess sold the surplus peaches from the greenhouse, which, Antonia reckoned, could not bring her more than £20 a season, and would not let Antonia eat them 'out of hours'. A 'peculiar gleam' would come into Margot's eye when she was thwarting someone's wishes: 'Her pleasure in cutting every single one of the sweetpeas – I almost feel *because* it distresses the old gardener so much.'

Her host, she said, 'seems to have amassed so much knowledge, talks very intelligently and yet one feels he cannot use it'. For their four children, who ranged from older to younger than us, she had only praise: 'The brilliance and vitality of the King children is remarkable.' Yet it was Margot, the member of the family she most criticised, and who she wished 'weren't quite so moral', who would remain a life-long friend.

Not only was the description of life at Culham one of the rare occasions when Antonia wrote of something outside herself in the notebooks, it was the first time her sense of humour appeared in them, a sure sign that her state of mind was improving.

By now Carroll had cut her analysis down to three times a week and she was finding this 'weaning process' a great strain.

Carroll drove her hard as they entered the last lap of analysis, confronting her with truths it would have been less painful to let lie, such as that she still often engaged in childish thinking by feeling that if she had a strong enough personal conviction about something it must *per forza* be true, and that she still had an idea somewhere that she was 'infallible'. She despaired of ever becoming humble, since humility was not in her nature.

A few days later she wrote that she had had a recurring sense since childhood of an inner life being the most important thing; and saw that her self-centredness had resulted in 'a curious poverty of life'. But she felt analysis cut at some of the things she held precious in poetry and religion:

> Can these all be explained away by anything so apparently boring and trivial as the desire to have a penis or the fear of losing one or the desire to appropriate and damage someone else's? . . . I come back and back to 'Suppose the Catholic religion *is* true after all, and I shall have no peace until I submit to God.'

When she picked up her pen again three days later, on 28 June, the handwriting in her notebook was strangely altered. However, the first paragraph, starting 'I suppose by this time Carroll knows what I really want but *I* don't,' does not lead the reader to suspect what lies ahead. Even the second paragraph, though the writing is now more chaotic, its usual roundness edged with spikes, does not prepare one for the outburst that is soon to come, though a mysterious 'THEY' in capital letters has a warning of paranoia in it: 'fundamentally I think I really feel that the mere FACT I want something and say so is enough to ensure that THEY won't at any price let me have it'. And then in the fourth paragraph it all comes pouring out. As if swept by a hurricane the words fall about in all directions, capitals have taken the place of the usual underlinings, letters sometimes slope backwards and forwards in the same word as they grow larger and more distanced from one another. Grammar has been swept away by the winds.

> Now if as it seems clear from several indications I want my father's penis or a child by him e.g. a work engendered with his loving approval what am I fussing about.
>
> I can't have his loving approval because he is DEAD.
>
> I couldn't have had intercourse with him anyway because presumably apart from morals

(a) he didn't want it

(b) I couldn't have endured it without mutilation . . .

   Even [if] I've not got a penis I've not got nothing. Feel no one wants me yet I undervalue them if they do want me . . . All the time I feel far more hate & contempt than love. Sometimes hate & contempt for myself: more for other people. Hate & envy . . . Yes I will write backhand in spite of my father I WILL WILL WILL. Couldn't even write – filthy dirty beastly old man – the way I WANTED TO. Well I will . . . You've ruined my life.

And so it continued for another page.

At this time, while Antonia was going through the most difficult part of analysis and getting a taste of what the final withdrawal symptoms would be like, Ian was trying to work for his exams. He often spent the night at Cecil Court, but she gave him little peace and kept giving in to the temptation to interrupt his studies. She kept him up late talking, or reading her notebooks to him; and if she could not sleep she used to wake him up in the night: 'I really am awful – I just can't bear to think of people existing when I'm not there.'

Just before his exams Ian received an unexpected cheque from an uncle. His temporary financial independence made him treat her differently: in public his manner became cold and offhand; 'in private he wants to call the tune.' But she continued to indulge him for fear of losing him, and decided their affair was 'at once a delight, a consolation and an ordeal for us both'.

They planned to go to France on holiday when his exams were over – each to pay their share. But Nigel wrecked the plan by insisting his brother should go with him if he went with anyone, which meant Ian would not have enough time and money left to travel with Antonia as well. Was Nigel carrying out an old threat he had made that he could break them up, she wondered, or was it that Ian was still under Nigel's thumb? In the end Ian compromised and rented a cottage at Turville Heath, near Henley, where a disastrous holiday was spent by all three, *plus* their mother, who soon became 'very much in possession' of the place.

Antonia had written about Wyn three weeks before going on that holiday:

First she helps me procure an abortion . . . Second she encourages me to write and publish a book . . . At a party of hers Tom meets Frances. Through her . . . I get on the way to being analysed. I have an affair with both her sons. The second affair with the eldest turns out to be the most satisfactory sexual relationship I have ever had . . . I produce a short poem as a result of my relation with Nigel.

The six-line poem, called 'The Crest', is published at the end of *The Hound and the Falcon*.

By the time the holiday was over Antonia could not find words vile enough to express what she thought of her lover's mother.

Antonia set off for that holiday, in early August, tired and battered from analysis and suffering from what she called 'after-September fear', for in September her analysis would finally end and the divorce would mean her income from Tom would be less. No wonder she went armed with Dial.

But on her third night at Turville Heath she had a 'crisis of panic' which even Dial could not calm; she made a tremendous scene with Ian, who luckily kept his head so that she managed to get back into focus again. The next day she was 'horrified at the extreme possessiveness and jealousy' of her nature, and in writing about it said that, although her pride hated to admit it, she doubted if she could behave as a decent human being without the support of a religion.

She only wrote twice in her notebook during that holiday. The second and last entry, written on the fourth day, was brief and described the physical difficulties that she was trying to cope with:

Food will not keep in this hot weather. Meat turns maggoty in 24 hours, the butter melts, the milk turns sour. Ian is laid up today with painful sunburn. The cottage is full of flies and wasps by day & moths by night: the window sills littered with dead ones. I seem always to be doing odd jobs in the house yet it never seems clean and orderly.

It was on her return to Cecil Court, late in August, that she inveighed against the Henderson tribe:

Wyn, I think at last, is really a *bad* woman – what Djuna would call 'unimportantly wicked'. There is something false even about her apparent generosity . . . She is a born procuress; she will procure you any drug or distraction you want – at a price . . . I would value most from Wyn half her dinner when she was really hungry!

It is interesting that one of the things for which she could not forgive Wyn was that she was a loving mother and had brought up both her sons 'as if they were little princes to inherit the earth'. She considered that Wyn had debauched her children. But she also said she was glad she had made the experiment of living with Ian, and that at Turville

Heath they had had some of their best moments as well as their worst. She was uncertain about her future as his mistress and friend. She was grateful to him and liked going to bed with him, sometimes even loved him: 'But I don't feel I would leave all and follow him, be with him against all the world as I felt about Basil.'

Ian had not come back to London with Antonia but had stayed on with his family in the country. Soon she became outraged because he had not written since her departure, and decided he had 'probably relapsed on the maternal bosom'.

In the middle of her long diatribe against all the Hendersons, Antonia paused to note that women had more potential for loving than men:

> This extra capacity to love is obviously meant for one's children. I cannot spend all mine on that owing to a radical defect in my nature as a woman so I must spend my love . . . on creating something.

And a few days earlier she had written:

> What I should be doing is making a home for my children and without the impulse of love I cannot see it as anything but a mutilated and dreary life to centre my life round them . . . I salved my conscience by thinking that Tom would never in any circumstances desert Susan & Lyndall and I was wrong.

Antonia was right, she was not suited to bringing up children. When we had been staying at Binesfield the previous holidays, she had given Sue *Frost in May* to read. Sue had been so terrified by a story recounted by one of the nuns about a child getting lost in a cellar that she had had nightmares. It was probably the only time she was pleased to have me beside her in the double bed for, according to Antonia, I had comforted her and Sue had told her afterwards, 'It's very nice to have a sister.' If Mother had had an ounce of understanding about children, she would not have given such a book to a highly strung child of eight; but such was the childishness of our mother's vanity that she craved admiration from those she admired, and could not resist showing off her greatest achievement to her precocious daughter.

I always far preferred holidays in the carefree chaos of Granny Botting's crumbling cottage to the ordered bleakness of Winster Vicarage. As I played in the garden at Binesfield, I did not notice the weeds on the croquet lawn, or that the asparagus bed had gone to seed, or the laurel hedge's straggling outline.

I enjoyed the cottage much more when we were there without

Mother or Nurse, not just because it meant we did not have to share a bed, but because we were free to play outdoors all day long. Our greatest pleasure was helping Mr Cox the next-door farmer clean out his cowsheds – he even taught us to milk – and, I am ashamed to say, another pleasure was to watch Granny's old gardener, Stepney, kill a chicken. I cannot understand why this held such a fascination, for we both loved animals and could not bear to see them badly treated. And after the arrival of our dog Rook, Binesfield became paradise on earth, even though he meant Sue and I had something new to squabble over.

Our material needs, like those of Granny Botting, were taken care of by faithful old Lucy Dumbrell. Despite her poor bandaged legs always being 'ever so bad today' – she must have had varicose veins – she never stopped fetching and carrying, kindling fires and cleaning grates, filling and lighting oil lamps, pumping the water, cooking and serving the meals, washing and mangling and ironing.

Once a week Lucy would change out of her faded pinafore and large, coarse apron into a black dress with a little white lace collar in order to act as Granny's (very unconvincing) French maid and take tea in for the bridge guests. That was the only time we had to put on dresses and indoor shoes, instead of our favourite attire of shorts and sweaters and muddy wellington boots, as we followed Lucy into Granny's study upstairs. She carried the tea-tray, the china and silver tinkling together as her gnarled old hands trembled under its weight, and we bore the sandwiches which we had to pass round once. Then we were allowed to be off again, but not before we had made a little bob curtsey to each guest.

We saw Granny only at meals, and since she talked to herself, and most of what she said made no sense anyway, there was no need to make conversation. Occasionally she descended into our world for long enough to notice I was eating too slowly, and said 'Mr Fuzzy Wuzzy', who lived in the chimney, would be 'vewy vewy cwoss' if I did not 'huwwy up'.

Whenever our mother came with us to Binesfield she was a slightly less alarming figure. And so had her father been when she was a child there. It was the place where she had been happiest with him because he had more time for her there, instead of being absorbed with his work and appearing only at mealtimes to assert his authority over her as he did in London. Only at Binesfield had she seen her parents in bed together when she went in to greet them every morning, and it had seemed the most natural thing in the world, whereas in London she felt a 'conspiracy of two' took place in their bedroom from which she was firmly excluded.

At Binesfield Mother had once let Sue and me, pretending to be two horses, pull her down the road all the way to the nearest village on Mr Cox's milk trolley, which must have been an alarming, undignified and uncomfortable experience for her, something we would never have dared to suggest to the dragoness who lived at the top end of Cecil Court.

By September 1938 Antonia was nervous. She had only a few sessions of analysis in front of her and her divorce had just come through entrusting us officially to her custody. She wrote in her notebook:

> My children certainly *are* a responsibility but one that I am becoming inured to gradually. I do *want* (faintly!) to do the best for them – and of course for myself too. I wish I knew what they need most . . . I want Susan to have every opportunity of *real* achievement; that is why I want her to go to a school where she will have rivals worthy of her.

Over the next months Antonia would be torn between her wanting to send Sue to a good school and our longing to go to a school in the country where we could ride – not that she could afford either, but she had the idea that when she no longer had to pay Carroll she would be well-off.

As analysis drew to a close Antonia was surprised to find herself less 'inclined to melancholy and depression' than she had been during the August break from it while staying at Turville Heath. She had begun to see that her father might sometimes have been justified in disciplining her, but that she could not bear anyone to criticise her or have power over her:

> I seem to look on myself as sub-human or super-human, never as just 'human', and I would prefer to be called a devil to an ordinary human being. I am like Susan, I can't bear not to be best at everything. While admiring Tom's book,[1] I have great pleasure in finding its weaknesses and though I cannot help admitting there are passages in it far beyond my own powers, I feel resentful of this and think in some way such passages must be due to my influence . . . I really hate anyone to have anything except

[1] *The Man Below*, which would soon be published by the Hogarth Press.

what I give them, that anyone should hurt them or comfort them except myself.

The last sessions with Carroll pressed very hard on the sorest spots. She got no quarter from him, was having very restless and nightmarish nights, but still managed to be in better spirits than she had hoped. The end of analysis coincided with a week of war suspense: 'Impossible, of course, for the megalomaniac unconscious not to think the two connected.'

At the very end of analysis Antonia broke the news to Carroll that she suspected she had become pregnant by Ian during the holiday at Turville Heath. Carroll warned her she might go out of her mind if she had another child; he advised her to have an abortion, and suggested that at the same time she should have her Fallopian tubes tied so that she could never conceive again.

Antonia told no one, apart from Carroll, when it was confirmed that she was pregnant. She told Ian only after the abortion.

As she and Ian had both been getting steadily fatter since starting their affair, when she went into the nursing home for the abortion, she told everyone she was going to lose weight. But she told a friend ten years later that she was sorry she had got rid of the child.

She stayed in the nursing home for two weeks, combining the operation with tests, a diet and a cure 'to stabilise her glands'. Her tendency to swell up when her life was dull and without stimulation and to lose weight when happy or in love, had been a problem since her twenties; but recently growing fat had become an obsession, judging from the many references to it in her notebooks in 1938. After staying with Wyn who was double her size, she said 'I wonder if being fat is taking up more room in the world than one is entitled to as a compensation for feeling deprived of power?'

In those two weeks of forced rest Antonia had hoped to study German and Italian and read some history, but she was too languid and depressed to do more than read 'Sherlock Holmes' stories or snatches of War and Peace, stitch a little patchwork, and make herself skim through a novel Emily had just written, which would never be published.

She wrote very little in her notebooks while at Devonshire Terrace. In the longest of four entries she decided she was both a 'prig and a scatterbrain', and thought that, although she was often solemn, she

Facing: 1 Cecil Botting as an undergraduate. 2 Antonia, aged seven, with her mother. 3 Antonia at fourteen. 4 Perham Road where the Bottings lived for 30 years.

1

3

2

4

5 *Antonia and Reggie Green-Wilkinson at their wedding in 1921.*

6 *Robert.*

7 *Eric in middle age.*

8 *Silas Glossop, Sue's father.*

9 *Antonia at the time of her marriage to Eric Earnshaw-Smith.*

5

6

7

8

9

10

11

12

13

14

10 *Tom (back right) with his brothers and sisters.*

11 *Tom soon after he met Antonia.*

12 *Tom and Antonia in the South of France, 1930.*

13 *Lyndall with 'Nurse', Mary Hitchcock.*

14 *Sue and Lyndall at Mr Cox's farm near Binesfield.*

15 *Tom on an outing with Sue and Lyndall shortly after he left Cecil Court.*

15

16 *Antonia with Sue and Lyndall at Binesfield in 1939.*

17 *Gerti at Summer Cottage with Jenny.*

18 *Lyndall and Jeremy at Summer Cottage.*

19 *Nicolette and Amanda at the time of Tom and Gerti's separation.*

17

18

19

21

22

20 *Lyndall in Rome just before her marriage to Bobby Birch.*

21 *Lyndall and Dickie Muir on holiday in Capri, 1951.*

22 *Bobby Birch.*

23 *At Cinecittà preparing for the haircutting scene in* The Nun's Story.

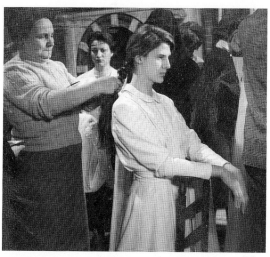

23

24

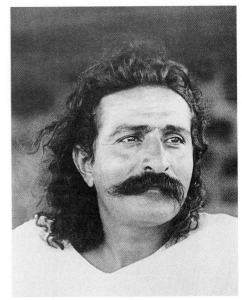

25

26

27

28

24 *Tom with his parents by St Mary's, Battersea, where his brother was vicar after the war.*

25 *Meher Baba.*

26 *Dorothy and Tom in Johannesburg at an exhibition in 1961.*

27 *Thomas Chitty, Sue's husband.* (photo by M. Etienne Pol)

28 *Wolfgang Reinhardt.*

29 *Lyndall and Sue on a riding holiday in 1968.*

29

would like to write something light and funny. This brought her back to an idea she had often had, that she would like to write a play, and she noted down some possible themes for one.

Besides work, her biggest problems were money and us:

> I begin to think it is best to try hard to send the children to a country school. Money is the great difficulty. Now I certainly do not love my children as much as I ought and natural strong affection is something one cannot counterfeit.

Yet, six weeks later, when she next wrote in her notebook, she was feeling guilty and frightened after spending 'quantities' of money in advance and frantically writing articles in the vain hope of making enough to catch up.

During that time Ian had returned. Wanting to make a fresh start with her lover, away from the haunting memories of Cecil Court, she had been caught up in a frenzy of furnishing both a maisonette in Cornwall Gardens, *and* a weekend cottage she had taken in Sussex. Hence her crazy spending spree to satisfy a 'tremendous lust' for furniture for both places.

Her attitude to Ian was still dualistic, and she was still questioning her motives for being with him. Her main problem in their relationship at the time was her being acutely conscious of their difference in age: 'I see myself either as a young girl or a hideous old woman bribing a young lover.'

In fact Ian was not now so financially dependent on her as before. He had a job, not in the Civil Service, but as a sub-editor, and no longer had an overdraft – unlike Antonia.

Although Cornwall Gardens was more pleasant than Cecil Court, and Mother was at a safer distance, having a floor above us to herself, I was not happy there. It was the same distance from King Arthur's in Bolton Gardens as Cecil Court had been; but instead of getting there through pretty little back streets, we now had to cross the wide and busy Cromwell Road to reach it. Even playing horses on the way to school had lost its appeal because I had started being sick a lot, and had to keep stopping to throw up in the gutter, of which I was very ashamed. Sue was sworn to secrecy, for I did not want Mother to know, nor the new housekeeper who was now in charge of us.

My ruling emotion for my mother was still fear; in fact it was growing worse. Wherever she lived afterwards, the smell of her face

Facing: 30 Antonia and Minka looking in the mirror.

powder mixed with stale cigarette smoke conjured up my terror of her at Cornwall Gardens. I began to tell any lie in order not to arouse her awesome temper. It was now that I discovered that if one could arouse her pity she was less fierce. When she sought me out to blow me up, if I could get in first with exaggerating some minor trouble, there was a good chance of the reproof I was about to receive being softened: 'Was it you who splashed water all over the bathroom? Remember to mop up after you next time, pet.' But if she caught me unprepared the attack could be fierce and wounding: 'How dare you leave the bathroom in such a disgusting state! Will you in future leave it as a place fit for decent human beings, even if you cannot manage to behave like one yourself, Lyndall.'

Sue and I shared a large L-shaped room. I was glad of her company again because Mother was less alarming when she came to say goodnight if one was not alone with her. Also Sue told me a 'Daffy' story every night which made up a bit for Tom never telling us stories any more.

Daffy, a girl of fourteen, twice my age, was a character Sue had once invented when we were sharing the bed at Binesfield. She possessed everything Sue and I thought worth having: a stable full of horses, a beautiful house in the country with a farm, a swimming pool, and a charge account at every sweet shop. She did not seem to have any relatives, only servants.

We despised her because she was hopeless and very vain. She fell off her horses – she only rode to show off her riding clothes anyway – and floundered around in her pool on a lilo because she could not swim. She never stuck it for long in the country but kept coming up to her grand flat in London to buy clothes and make-up and go to the hairdresser – for she was preoccupied with her looks. I see now that Daffy, if she had not been so rich, bore a strong resemblance to Antonia, particularly in her mania for hats and high-heeled shoes.

We were her henchmen. We calmed down the horses she was too afraid to ride, we saved her from drowning when she fell off her lilo, we rescued her from charging bulls and jeering louts. Without us Daffy could hardly function because she was so busy flapping around in her own fecklessness. But we also took pleasure in taunting her. We challenged her to do things we knew she would fail at but which she was too vain to refuse to try, such as jumping a stream or vaulting a stile. When she made a fool of herself falling into the stream, or getting impaled on the stile because her skirt was too tight, she used to get in a huff and speak in a peevish voice, using Antonia-like expressions, as she demanded we rescue her.

Some weekends we walked over for tea to Fernshaw Road where Tom and Gerti, now married, lived. Or Tom would come and fetch us from Cornwall Gardens to take us out. He was always late. Every time as we sat on the banisters by the front door waiting anxiously for him to arrive I was sure he had got run over in Cromwell Road.

Soon after we moved in, instead of taking us to the circus as he had in the past for our Christmas treat, Tom took us to see our first film: Bernard Shaw's *Pygmalion*.

I was still so wrapped up in Liza Doolittle's world on returning to Cornwall Gardens that I hardly bothered to ponder on why Mother was embracing Ian at the top of the stairs or why they quickly broke apart and disappeared on seeing us. It was the first time I saw her embracing a man, including Tom. We still had no idea that Ian was more or less living in the flat. It would not have worried me if I had known. Ian was one of her friends I liked; he, like Silas, was always prepared to set me a quick mental sum if I asked for one, whereas her woman friends, like Emily, clearly disdained arithmetic.

At the close of 1938 Antonia did not make her usual annual summing up in her notebook, although it had been one of the most important years of her life: her analysis had ended, her third and last divorce had come through, she had started her last love affair, had an abortion, and moved house.

Her opening words in a new notebook at the beginning of 1939 were: 'Chaos is come again so I must see where I've gone wrong.' Without self-scolding, she tried to see what she was up to. Not only was she piling up things she did not need, like books she would not read and cosmetics she would never use, but her pleasure in the arts was marred by envy: for example, she had hardly been able to enjoy a concert because she had felt such envy of the pianist's talent. She lamented, 'I just CAN'T be truly humble. Abject – yes.'

In twelve pages of self-analysis she recognised the heavy burden she was carrying round was not 'debts, responsibilities, frustrated ambition or lack of love': it was herself. She wished she could have a true belief in God as a strong 'spring of action and happiness'. This God would have to be 'immensely transcending, and yet something of which one feels a part'.

Her attempts at her own writing were more disastrous than ever. The book was proving 'painful and terrifying' because of her ambivalence when writing about her father:

> I feel I shall never be at peace with his ghost until I have shown the full force of my love & my hatred of him, neither of which I showed in his life. Yet I feel too that he would never forgive me if I wrote about him – that it is the unforgivable sin to expose his nakedness to the world ... I am afraid of punishment from outside if I do write, punishment from within if I don't.

She tried to turn Ian into her taskmaster now that she no longer had Tom, and discussed with him the possibility of making the book more autobiographical. Yet while seeking his advice, she often made discouraging remarks about his capability in his new job, and made it clear she did not have a very high regard for his powers as a sub-editor. After having read the first bit of her book to him, she was shocked by his lack of enthusiasm. He had said there were good things in it, but it was 'too short-circuited'. Angrily she threw the manuscript into the fire, hoping he would stop her. He did not.

> I wrote to please him and he wasn't pleased. No good pretending one doesn't want an audience for one's work – I do anyway. I want to delight and to be praised.

In the spring of 1939, although still in debt and spending more than she earned, Antonia felt the time had come when she could pay to send us to a school in the country. Besides the steady trickle of money coming in from the *Sunday Pictorial*, she was also earning from freelance fashion articles. Tom was giving her occasional commissions on the two magazines of which he was now assistant editor: *Picture Post* and *Lilliput*. They required quite different writing styles, for *Picture Post* was an illustrated weekly, similar to the American *Life*, dealing with anything from politics to sport, whereas *Lilliput* was a humorous pocket-sized monthly. She had just received a small cheque from Penguin who were going to bring out a paperback edition of *Frost in May*. Antonia's unearned income, since the divorce, consisted of £200 a year alimony from Tom plus £100 for me; £60 a year from Silas towards Sue's upkeep, and the contribution from Eric which continued, even though it was no longer needed to help her pay for analysis.

Sue and I were overjoyed at the wonderful news that the next term we would be going to a boarding school in the country and that our mother would pay for us to have riding lessons there.

Even the ordeal of buying clothes and sewing on name tapes could not dampen our excitement.

Shopping expeditions with Antonia, luckily rare, remain in my memory as one of the most unpleasant experiences of my childhood. I was only too glad to inherit Sue's outgrown clothes if it meant being spared from going shopping. Invariably Mother ended up losing her temper with the shop assistants and us while fellow customers looked on in astonishment.

'What do you *mean* you don't have her size?' she would rage at a salesgirl. 'My daughter is not a monster you know, she's a perfectly normal shape.' Then she would turn to me: 'Stand up properly, child! No wonder it doesn't fit if you stick your tummy out like that.'

Then it was Sue's turn. 'Stop day-dreaming and come over here at once and try on this coat.' Before she had even got her arm into a sleeve Sue was being asked, 'Well do you like it or not?' And before she had had time to make up her mind she was being told, 'I hope at least you're going to say "thank you", child.'

Everything went on account, even a hair-band. 'I can't stand here waiting all day,' Mother would say to the flustered assistant struggling to write out the bill as fast as she could, 'I've had an account here for ten years and I've never known it take so long. For goodness' sake, woman, can't you tell the difference between Hopkins and Hopkin*son*.'

And so it went on as we trudged miserably behind her from one department of Harrods or Peter Jones to another.

In the taxi home, where she was probably beginning to smart as it dawned on her how much she had just overspent on us, to be silent was taken as proof that you were not appreciative of what had just been bought for you: to speak meant risking getting your head snapped off.

Brickwall was a magnificent black-timbered Elizabethan manor house on the edge of the village of Northiam in Sussex. Here, in idyllic surroundings, a progressive girls' school with about thirty pupils had been created.

There was only one rule at Brickwall: everyone under the age of eleven had to swim naked unless they had a special dispensation from Mrs Heath, the founder and headmistress, to wear a bathing dress –

which it was almost impossible to get. Lessons and meals were not compulsory. Nowhere was out of bounds.

I had looked forward to going to Brickwall so much that it was bound to be an anti-climax. Only the riding lessons lived up to expectation.

My main problem was loneliness.

I was the youngest girl in the school by two years – the others ranged from nine to fifteen – and was put in a little attic room with the matron's son, Christopher, who was five and not part of the school because of his age and sex. His mother slept in the room next to us. All the other children slept in dormitories two floors below. Sue soon made friends with some of the older girls in her dormitory and barely acknowledged her younger sister when we met. Only on our weekly riding lesson, when she was in ecstasy too, was she well-disposed towards me.

The older children started to taunt me.

Once some of them, including Sue, lured me to an attic at the top of the west staircase that was said to be haunted by the ghost of Anna Maria, saying there were precious coins hidden under the floorboards which my smaller hands might be able to reach. No sooner had I bent down to see if I could spy any coins than they toppled me over, rushed out of the room and locked me in. After a while I heard scratchings and moanings and became terrified, battering at the heavy oak door to try and get out. It was only when a voice started chanting 'I'm the ghost of Anna Maria, oooooooooh! I'm the ghost of Anna Maria,' and I recognised it as my sister's, that my fear subsided. I yelled out staunchly, 'I'm not afraid, so there!', but afterwards wished I had kept quiet: my tormentors stopped their yowlings and departed, leaving me alone. It was some time before the French mistress, returning to her room nearby, heard my pleading to be let out.

Sue became obsessed by ghosts at Brickwall. In the dormitory she told such frightening ghost stories that some of the girls could not sleep, and eventually Sue was banished to a room of her own.

The exercise of free-will put too much onus on my embryonic conscience. Although I had always liked lessons at King Arthur's, at Brickwall, when offered the choice of attending a history class or hanging round the stable block, going to geography or brushing Bob, the school's sheepdog, I never chose the classroom. Most of my time was spent mooching around the beautiful grounds, wondering what to do next with my time. I took to stealing pennies from Matron's bag to buy sherbet fizzes in the village shop in Northiam. I even avoided swimming which I had been looking forward to almost as much as riding, because I so loathed having to be in the nude.

There were some pretty odd girls at Brickwall who tried bribing me with rides on their ponies to do far stranger things than Sybil would even have dreamt of. And there were some weird grown-ups, too.

One of these was a middle-aged Russian called Tamara, who they said was a princess. She was not a teacher but had as much authority as Mrs Heath – looking back I suspect she replaced Mr Heath, if he had ever existed. Whenever she found me wandering around on my own she would cross-question me about the matron's son Christopher and ask me whether I played games with his 'tail'. She took to tracking me down in recreation time and forcing me to go swimming. When we came out of the pool we were meant to get dry by playing leap-frog, but she let me off that and dried me herself with a towel. It made me uneasy that she always insisted on rubbing the towel between my legs long after I was dry and held onto me, laughing, when I tried to get away. Once she said to me 'Little girls have tails too' and, though I puzzled and puzzled, I could not work out what she meant, but felt it was another reason to avoid her.

Of course I did not confide my miseries to Antonia when she came to visit us. Nor to Tom when he and Gerti turned up in his new acquisition – an old two-seater car with a boot that opened into a dickey seat – to take us out to tea in Rye.

We stayed at Brickwall for only one term. It turned out that the 'no bathing dress' rule had been enforced so that Mrs Heath and her friends could enjoy peeping at nude nymphettes through the thick yew hedges surrounding the swimming pool. One of those friends had taken some photographs of the naked girls playing leapfrog which had appeared in a magazine called *Eves without Leaves*, causing several parents to remove their children, so that Mrs Heath doubted whether she would be able to keep the school going. This, and the fact that Mother had realised she could not afford the fees anyway, were the real reasons why we would not be returning to Brickwall in the autumn of 1939, not the threatened outbreak of war as we were told at the time.

The 'war menace' was now very real to Antonia as to many others:

'anxious to acquit myself well – if it can be done without trouble' she wrote.

In her last pre-war entry in her notebook, written on 22 July, she also wrote a twelve-page self-portrait of the person she had become since analysis had stopped nearly a year before, bringing up all the usual subjects – love, money, fashion journalism versus creative writing, her looks, her hopes and fears – but there was a new fear: loneliness. She was afraid that if she were quiet and alone, something she wanted, but feared, might make itself known. This was probably religion, since religion had been coming more into her notebooks in the past two years.

Antonia did not write again in her notebook in 1939 until three months after the war had started, by which time her mother had died. The former is only mentioned in passing, 'money has ceased to have the same meaning since the war', and the latter as one of the 'events' of that year in her annual summing-up on 31 December. But she did write about her mother's death eighteen months later, saying it had caused her a great deal more 'natural grief' than she had expected, and much more than her father's which had come as a relief.

Now that her mother was no longer alive, she saw she had had some remarkable qualities: 'real sweetness of disposition, an extraordinary capacity for forgiveness, a kind of independence in judging'. In the last months of her life, knowing that she was dying of cancer, Christine had shown amazing courage and unselfishness.

Many years later, remembering the period when war had started and 'cracked down on her', Antonia said that if it had not broken out she might have had another breakdown at the end of 1939. She had reached a state of constant anxiety because she could not get on with her book, and although she had been writing 'well-paid tripe' she had been finding it a strain to keep up the flat.

When war broke out Ian was called up to join the army; Antonia sub-let Cornwall Gardens and went to stay in the country with two of her oldest friends, Douglas and Kathleen McClean; and we stayed on with Tom's parents, where we had spent the summer holidays.

Life at Winster Vicarage was a complete contrast to Brickwall, but I was just as wretched for different reasons.

My main cause for unhappiness – apart from Granny's constant exhortations to goodness, and the lengthy dullness of Grandfather's sermons on Sundays – was Miss Limb.

Miss Limb ran the village school which we now attended and I was terrified of her. She had coarse grey hair scraped back tightly into a bun, and a grey moustache. Her eyes were cruel and cold, and the pleasure she took in meting out punishments horrified me. We had not been in the school for half an hour before she had reduced her first prey to tears by thrashing him over the knuckles with a ruler.

There were only two classes and about twenty-five pupils at the school. Although we were younger than the others in the upper form, the term without lessons at Brickwall did not hinder us from being top of the class, for the standard was dismally low. Miss Limb never attacked either of us physically, though there was a bad moment once in needlework class when blood from my pricked finger fell onto the piece of white calico on which I was practising chain stitch: the iron hand was raised, but Miss Limb must have remembered that I was one of the archdeacon's granddaughters and that he was chairman of the board of governors of the school, for the blow never fell.

Yet when Tom came to visit us in November, we assured him stoically that we were happy and enjoying the village school, he told Antonia in a letter.

Tom and Antonia were fighting about her alimony at the time. In a letter written just before he had been to see us at Winster, he pointed out that from the time he had left Cecil Court in 1936, until their divorce became final two years later, he had paid all the rent, the heating and lighting there, plus our school fees at King Arthur's, plus three insurances he had taken out for her and us, and the Income Tax on both their earnings:

> I had about £5 a week to live on for myself, to cover everything. When this arrangement came to an end, I was £500 in debt, & everything I had was worn out. I had furniture for one room . . . I still owe £320 and I have made no provision of any sort for Gerti by insurance or anything else.

He suggested she ought to take over the insurance he was paying for Sue out of Silas's allowance since Sue was costing her nothing at present – for Granny Hopkinson, unlike Granny Botting, never charged for having us to stay.

Tom thought we needed a break from Winster for the Christmas holidays, after five months of his parents' 'withering influence for good'. Grandfather had told Tom, to his consternation, that he hoped to baptise and confirm Sue, now aged ten, in a single ceremony in a year or two.

Tom proposed to Antonia that we should stay part of the time with him and Gerti in a cottage he had rented at Turville Heath, close to Wyn Henderson's, and the rest of the time somewhere with her. He offered to pay our fares and any hotel bills. His parents were against it: the reason they gave was that they were worried about us travelling alone on over-crowded trains carrying troops south, but Tom suspected it was because they feared contact with our mother might turn us from the path to becoming Protestants.

As we were costing Antonia nothing at the time, Tom's parents suggested that if it were possible she put aside something towards our education later on. When Antonia heard this from Tom, the 'money situation' stirred up a great deal of hostility in her: 'I feel I could do real violence to the whole Hopkinson family. I can't forgive them for not loving me . . . I'm sulking in my tent and don't want to pit myself against the world.'

The McCleans, with whom Antonia was still living, could not have us over Christmas, so she persuaded the Kings to invite us with her to Culham Court in the new year. But first we went to stay with Tom and Gerti at Summer Cottage, Turville Heath. Tom wrote in his notebook:

> Lyndall very sweet – though letting off a good deal of steam because of long repressions at the vicarage. She said 'damn' and 'bloody' and talked a lot about her bottom. Susan was strange, profound and curious as ever, but much more harmonious.

At the last moment Antonia suddenly decided she wanted to have us for longer than Tom. When he objected, she made such a scene over the telephone that he backed down, and sent us on our way to Culham a week early armed with a tactfully written letter suggesting some motherly things that needed doing:

> Hairs have been washed . . . Gerti has done what she can about their clothes, but except for the coats you gave them, their wardrobes are a bit patchy. If you have to fit them out a bit, ask me for a contribution. Their spare pairs of garters are too tight to wear. I would have thrown them in the fire, but we had no elastic to make new ones . . .
>
> Their tusks look a bit yellow. I don't know whether there's a good dentist in Henley you could take them to.

We had a good time at Culham playing with the Kings' four children, of whom only one of the three boys was younger than us. We seldom saw Antonia who was trying to write a play, hoping that if it were put on she would make enough money to put Binesfield, which she had inherited two weeks before, in order. Although she had not earned anything for three months, having left the *Sunday Pictorial* at the outbreak of war, at least she could now look forward to a small annual income from the royalties on her father's textbooks which would continue for the rest of her life.

The play, called *Three in a Room*, based on an idea she had had when in the nursing home in Devonshire Terrace in 1938, would be performed eventually in 1944 by the Oldham Repertory Company. It barely paid enough to cover the cost of our rail fares and hotel rooms, for she took Susan and me with her to see the first performance.

When we returned to Winster after that first Christmas of the war, the coldest winter I can ever remember set in. We trudged to school through deep snow; some of the children from the remote farms fell into drifts on the way and arrived soaked through. The wood stove could not raise the temperature in the classroom much above freezing, and there was a ceaseless symphony of coughing and sneezing. But Miss Limb's ruler continued to fall without mercy on cold hands swollen with chilblains.

Among Antonia's New Year resolutions for 1940 were 'To make something much stronger and more definite of my relation to the children'. It came penultimate in a list which included 'To master as much of Spinoza as I can grasp and to apply it'. And when she next wrote in her notebook, back with the McCleans at Rabley Willow again two weeks later, the entire entry said:

Things I must work towards now. Making enough to choose for the children instead of having my hands tied. This means I M U S T get the play finished & out of the way & get going on a book.

By 1 March she had finished the play and, despite lamenting her lack of money to Tom, had 'completely furnished, redecorated and repaired' Binesfield. But the strange thing is that during the Easter holidays we did not stay at the cottage, but were all paying-guests at a farm further down Bines Green. But at least Sue and I were reunited with Rook whom we had not seen for a year, although he had become

Lucy Dumbrell's dog by now, and we spent most of the time happily at our favourite occupation: mucking out at Mr Cox's farm.

Our mother always claimed that the Hopkinsons had 'kidnapped' us; but if she had wanted we could all now have lived permanently at Binesfield, instead she chose to return to her friends in the country with whom she was no longer happy. Their conjugal rows appalled her, though she confessed 'something in me delights in violence'. She had always thought Douglas McClean, a doctor and researcher, whom she admired and respected, a self-centred male chauvinist who ruled his wife, Kathleen Hale, a painter who illustrated and wrote the well-known 'Orlando the Marmalade Cat' books. Now, having lived with them at Rabley Willow, she saw that Kathleen had a will of her own, too, hence the frequent clashes.

Soon after we returned to Winster Vicarage, the strain of behaving well as the archdeacon's granddaughters became too much.

Our first crime was foolish. One Sunday morning I hid under a pile of bedclothes, and when Granny came back from Holy Communion, Sue told her I had got out of bed very early that morning and had not come back again. Being a good story-teller her tale must have been convincing, for soon Granny and Grandfather were searching for me everywhere. Every so often Sue sneaked up to give me bulletins of what was going on and to let me have a breather, for it was suffocating under the bedclothes. When she told me that the neighbours had been called in to help search the fells behind the vicarage, where bogs and loose stone walls and deep tarns were a hazard, I realised it was time to give myself up.

When Granny and Grandfather returned from the search and found me sitting in the kitchen, their pained looks were more distressing than any tirade. Grandfather quietly stuttered that after going to church we would be put in separate rooms for the rest of the day.

Lunch time came and went and no one appeared. By tea-time I feared the happiest time of the day at Winster would be denied us, too. I was right: that evening there was no reading aloud while we knitted for the troops after tea; and although Granny did appear at last at bedtime, bringing a larger supper than the usual chopped apple with brown sugar, there was no bed-time story, after we had said our prayers, about Tom and his brothers when they were little. Yet, on this particular evening, as she sat silently by my bed waiting for me to finish my supper, Granny suddenly started to stroke my head tenderly, but without her eyes acknowledging what her hand was doing, for she was staring firmly out of the window. Although I think in her way she was fond of us both – Tom often said in letters to Antonia that his parents loved us – Granny had never demonstrated affection, and certainly never petted me before. I fell asleep penitent and perplexed.

The next day life returned to normal and our prank was never mentioned.

But in May something far worse happened. At school two shillings disappeared from a child's coat in the cloakroom. It did not need a detective to trace the deed to us when the woman who ran the only shop in Winster reported that we had been on a spending spree and paid with a two-shilling piece. I had never even questioned where Sue had got the money, I suppose because I was so overjoyed at being told I could choose a shilling's worth of whatever sweets I wanted.

We were summoned to Grandfather's study. He wept when Sue confessed. Then he gave her two shillings and said we were to take it to Miss Limb and apologise. The dread in my heart as we descended the hill and knocked on the schoolmistress's door was worse than any I had ever felt.

Miss Limb led us into her dark cottage which had an unpleasant smell and was poorly furnished. Suddenly, in this humble setting she appeared less formidable; the cruel glint in her eyes had gone. Sue bravely made her speech, then I mumbled my apologies too. Miss Limb told us how disappointed she was in us, her star pupils, but did not beat us as I had feared she would. But there was further penance for Sue: she was told she must return the money in person to the child she had taken it from.

Tom and Mother were told what had happened. Tom suggested Antonia should talk to Carroll and Miss Searle and get their opinions on what might have caused Sue's return to stealing.

It was the most critical moment of the war when it looked as if England might be invaded. Just before hearing of our misdeeds, Antonia, who hardly wrote in her notebook throughout the war, made one of her rare entries. It was dated 13 May 1940 and said she felt calmer than she had done for a long time, despite worries over her mother's estate and the Hopkinson family. She had even given up the flat in Cornwall Gardens without sadness, although it was the 'pleasantest place' she had ever lived. She wrote:

All our futures look precarious . . . The war is in full swing now since the invasion of Norway, Holland & Belgium . . . Air raids are what we are all waiting for . . . I don't in the least want to die yet for I feel I've only just begun to get any control of myself or my life.

Both Carroll and Miss Searle felt that the best thing would be for us to leave Winster and come south, if the invasion and bombing scare calmed down. Miss Searle told Antonia she ought to live with us at Binesfield and send us to school in Horsham. She said, 'Many evacuated children have tended to slip back into their old troubles and being once more in a normal family life relieves the strain.' Miss Searle seems to have got it wrong again: to live at the cottage with Antonia would have been less like 'normal family life' than with Tom's parents, where we were not exactly evacuees. Carroll thought this a possible long-term solution, but felt it important that Sue and I should be separated for a while. He wanted me to spend the summer holidays alone at Summer Cottage with Tom and Gerti, while Sue was with Antonia. It should be 'put over' to us as 'a practical necessity', that, owing to expenses being heavy because of the war, it was fairest to divide the cost of our upkeep by each of them taking one child for the summer, to prevent either feeling the other was 'being favoured in any way'. Carroll also suggested that until the school term ended we should remain with Tom's parents, if they were willing to keep us. Our mother's letter to Tom expounding the two analysts' views on our future ended:

> If, in the situation, it is sensible to have the children back in July, I feel they are my war job . . . But if things get bad and we *have* to leave them at Winster, I feel I ought to do something and want to, though I have no idea where I'd be really useful . . . I just hate being inactive when they *must* need people and I'm healthy and capable.

Granny and Grandfather let us stay on at Winster. All of our shame was soon forgotten, partly because everyone was talking about the drought, and partly because there was now a drama involving me.

The drought at the end of the first spring of the war was an even rarer event in the north of England than the freezing winter that had preceded it. Some of the wells in Winster ran dry, but not the one at the vicarage. It became our job to distribute water, and we each set off for school carrying a heavy can to dispense a small ration to the neediest villagers on the way.

In one of the cottages without water there lived five sealyhams and two genteel old ladies, Miss Drew, who was very deaf, and Miss Packer. On this particular morning Miss Packer was in the garden picking strawberries, and only deaf Miss Drew was indoors. I knocked and knocked, but no one came. Afraid of being late for school, I went into the house to look for someone to give the water to. The pack of little dogs rushed at me, yapping and snapping at my ankles. Finally Miss Packer heard my yells and came in from the garden to call off her dogs.

Some of the bites were quite bad and I still have scars on my left leg where two fangs sank in, and a piece of flesh was torn away. During the time I was housebound and barely able to hobble around, I saw the tender side of Granny that Tom had sensed as a child. Twice a day she cleansed my suppurating wounds with a saline solution. It was very painful, but she tried to be gentle, and said soothing words whenever I winced with pain. Instead of making me finish the khaki scarf I had been knitting for months, she let me sit on the verandah playing patience and reading. Grandfather brought me one of his precious art books to look at, with reproductions of Paolo Uccello paintings. Every day Miss Packer visited me, bringing fresh strawberries from her garden.

One afternoon in the middle of June, when my wounds had healed enough for me to limp about but not to make the long walk to school, Miss Limb appeared. She was carrying two little parcels neatly wrapped. She kissed me on the cheek and her moustache was very bristly. In my parcel (the other one was for Sue) was Rudyard Kipling's *Kim* beautifully bound in leather. It was a farewell present. That was how I came to know we were leaving Winster and going to live with Mother in Gloucestershire.

After eight months of co-habitation with the McCleans, feeling always more crushed between 'the two egoisms of Rabley', Antonia had not taken the analysts' advice to set up house in her own cottage, Binesfield, which sat empty and furnished. Instead, when John Davenport, the writer and critic, and his beautiful wife Clement, a talented painter, invited her to join their ménage Antonia accepted with alacrity and set off for The Malting House at Marshfield:

> Just what I want. To be able to talk freely, read, hear music — I had forgotten what it was like. I feel like one of the shades in Homer who has just had a good draught of blood.

Among the inhabitants, besides the Davenports and their small daughter, were two musicians, Lennox Berkeley and William Glock, and Dylan and Caitlin Thomas with their baby son. To introduce two more children into this heterogeneous household would cause no problem, so Sue and I were summoned from Winster and put into the village school of Marshfield for the remainder of the summer term.

I had been so spoilt the last two weeks at Winster that I was sad to leave the vicarage and dreaded the thought of having to live under the same roof as my mother again. But as soon as we reached The Malting House I was less worried. There were so many people and children and cats and dogs roaming around the large house that the force of our mother was diluted.

Some of the grown-ups, like John Davenport who weighed eighteen stone and was always mopping the sweat from his brow, were very friendly to us; others, like his wife Clement who dressed in men's clothes, were off-hand; Dylan Thomas, whom Mother told us was a poet, barely noticed our existence. The other two children could not talk yet: Llewellyn Thomas was too small, and Nathalie Davenport, who was three, refused to utter a word, which worried her parents. The grown-ups were so busy painting or writing, practising the piano or playing squash, or going to the pub, that no one cared where we wandered or what we did.

Sometimes, when we were meant to be asleep, the sound of music would lure me out of my bed. I would creep downstairs and hide behind the open door of the large music room, decorated with Clement's surrealistic frescoes, to listen enraptured to John Davenport and William Glock playing duos on two grand pianos. I wondered why Clement turned over the pages of Mr Glock's music and not Mr Davenport's. This would be explained after we left, when the Davenports were divorced and Clement became Mrs Glock.

Antonia only wrote twice in her notebooks during the four months we stayed at Marshfield. The second entry, four days after the first, began:

Italy came into the war last night. The Germans are 30 miles from Paris. It looks inevitable. One goes on in a kind of trance, unable to believe it will happen or that it will not. In a few weeks perhaps everything one had been accustomed to live by and care for may have been destroyed and one will be a prisoner in an invaded country waiting to be destroyed oneself.

The remaining three pages are a description of the countryside.

But Tom noted in his notebook some of the things I told him afterwards about our stay there, under the heading:

Life at Marshfield as described by Lyndall

'Mr Glock was a very funny man. He used to drive his car at 74 miles an hour and when Mrs Davenport told him there were children in the back he took his hands off the wheel . . .

'One evening [when I was ill] Mr Davenport brought up a glass of port and put it by my bed. I didn't drink much of it because a wasp fell into it . . . He came back later and he drank it. I didn't tell him about the wasp till afterwards and he was rather angry.

'The Thomases who were there had a child. Its name was Llewellyn. Mr Thomas's trousers were always falling off. He was always in the pub with Mr Davenport and Mr Glock. They were there all day long. Llewellyn did nothing at all but wet. I never knew anyone do so much wetting. He just sat in his bed and wetted. Then they put him on the floor and he wetted. People said it was the dogs and cats.'

'Yes', chimed in Susan, 'they used to follow Llewellyn with a dishcloth.'

But my most vivid memory of Marshfield is not the mad geniuses who lived at The Malting House, but the village school. We arrived after the summer term had started, and the headmaster did not even bother to tell my form mistress she had a new pupil.

The first lesson was English. My form's homework the night before had been to learn a poem. The teacher checked to see if her pupils had done their homework by making the whole class chant the poem in unison. Anyone whose mouth was not moving in time with the others was called out in front of the class afterwards to say the poem through alone. I was summoned to come forward. I explained I was new and was told I was a liar. I flung an imploring look at the girl I had been put to share a desk with, hoping she would bear witness I was telling the truth. She grinned back at me and giggled.

My punishment for not knowing a poem I had never learnt was to stand in front of the class with my hands clasped behind my head: when they slipped the teacher prodded my back with her long cane. My shoulders ached; my neck ached; my leg still bandaged from the dog bite hurt; but worst of all for one who had always been top of the class, I felt humiliated being treated as a dunce and being sniggered at by a sea of unknown hostile faces. My only consolation was that in the break I could tell my woes to my big sister.

But for me there was no break that morning. The teacher made me stay in to learn 'The owl and the pussy cat went to sea in a beautiful pea-green boat . . .' And when at last I saw Sue as we walked back to The Malting House for lunch, she had such strange stories to tell about the goings-on in her class that my misadventure seemed less interesting.

The next day the teacher's unkindness shrank to nothing compared to that of my male classmates, a brutal bunch who resented outsiders. At break a group of them set on me. I fought back as hard as I could, but when one of them swung a skipping rope at me which slashed across my wounded leg, I let out such a yell that Sue heard and rushed to my rescue. Like a fierce dog she routed the enemy, using some of our best Brickwall swearwords that had never slipped out at the vicarage.

Coming home from school one afternoon we saw an advertisement for a bicycle for sale for five shillings. Since our birthdays were very near, we asked Mother whether it would be possible to have it as an advance birthday present. She agreed and we became the proud joint-owners of a very old sit-up-and-beg bicycle. One day its rusty brakes failed and I crashed. My dog bite still had not healed and here I was back at a doctor's having pieces of gravel extracted from my left elbow.

Everyone at The Malting House was very kind. They organised a birthday tea for me on 23 July, with a cake with nine candles and my name on it in the grown-ups' dining-room – we children normally ate in the kitchen. I sat at the head of the table with Mother, and the sight of everybody in their best clothes made me feel very shy, as if in the presence of strangers, particularly Dylan whom I had always seen grubby and dishevelled with a cigarette hanging out of the corner of his mouth and who now looked like a scrubbed cherub.

In the end I missed most of my party because I felt ill in the middle of tea. It was discovered I had a temperature of 102°F caused by the graze in my arm which had turned septic.

For two days I lay tossing and turning with fever. Years later, Antonia told me that the day after my birthday the doctor had said if my temperature continued to rise I might have to have my arm amputated.

When I recovered, Sue and I were sent to live on a farm near Marshfield: our presence during the school holidays must have become irksome to the grown-ups. Life was rough on the Hicks's farm.

Mr Hicks had been shell-shocked in the previous war and he was more unpredictable than Mother, and his rages were even more alarming. But the farm horses compensated for Mr Hicks's defects.

When term started there was no need to return to the town. We bicycled to school. Sue had had a brand new bicycle for her birthday and the old one, with new brakes, was all mine.

In the middle of that autumn term Mother summoned us to The Malting House. She told us we were to leave Marshfield. She would be going to London to work for the BBC; Sue would be going to a boarding school in Salisbury; and I would be going to live with Tom and Gerti at Summer Cottage. In trying to put this over in the way Carroll had suggested, she made my going there sound as if the Law Courts had decreed it in some way: 'But of course you won't mind, you've always preferred Tom to me,' she ended, to which there was no answer.

And so, after nine years of constant companionship with its squabbles and its moments of being very much united, Sue and I were separated and set off towards our different destinies.

CHAPTER 14

֍

Reconversion

Obviously the most important thing that has happened
to me is my reconciliation with the Catholic Church . . .
and my efforts to practise my religion again.
Antonia White, 12 May 1941

Antonia had accepted the 'extremely unsatisfactory' and badly paid
job with the BBC at the end of 1940, although air-raids on London
had just started, as a way to escape from the Davenports. Her ecstatic
first impressions of living at The Malting House apparently had been
short-lived.

An ex-lover from the Eric days who had remained a friend, Ian
Black, let her share his house in Linden Gardens off Notting Hill Gate.
While there she wrote almost nothing in her notebooks. But, a month
after her arrival in London, Antonia began the correspondence
with Peter Thorpe which was published fifteen years later as *The
Hound and the Falcon* and which gives some picture of her life at the
time.

The most important event was her return to the Catholic Church at
the end of 1940. It happened at Christmas in the Carmelite Church to
which she had gone so often as a child and for which she had a special
affection.

She had gone into the church to find out what time Midnight Mass
was to be on Christmas Eve – because of the blitz it would not be
celebrated precisely at midnight. Her intention to go to the Mass had
not been from real devotion or as an act of submission to the Church,
but as she put it 'from sentimental reasons'. On her way out she had
felt as if an invisible hand were pushing her into the queue of people
waiting to go to Confession, and in a few minutes she found herself
in the confessional without the least idea of what she was going to
say. She blurted out to the priest that for nearly fifteen years she had
not practised her religion and knew she had no right to be there

because, she had been told recently, her marriage to Tom in a Protestant Church automatically excommunicated her.

The priest, Fr Hugh, was a kindly man and undertook to ask his Vicar-General what her exact situation was, but in the meantime he gave her absolution from her sins and told her she could take Communion on Christmas Day, which she did: 'a very blind and doubting Communion'.

Although she then took to practising the religion of her youth again, and it would become 'the central point round which everything revolves, with the eternal conflict between love and hatred, fear and desire, acceptance or rejection', there remained a nucleus of real doubt.

When she wrote to tell Tom of this important happening she emphasised she had not returned to the Church at the 'most unhappy and bewildered' moment in her life, but when things were relatively calm, and she had not been 'in any state of fear or violent emotion'. Then she talked about us children, saying she hoped we would come to her Faith of our own accord; and now regretted they had not let Grandfather baptise us '(provided he did it properly!!)'[1]:

> Lyndall, I feel, would be much the same sort of person, humanly speaking, whether she is a Catholic or anything else. But simply for happiness & proper functioning I think Susan is likely to be more successful in a religion with definite rules & a rich field for speculation & imagination. Only she must approach it by attraction & love & not by fear & coercion.

When, after Christmas at Summer Cottage, Sue and I went to stay in the guest-house on Bines Green, where Antonia joined us at the weekend, she talked a lot about religion and made us go to Mass with her on Sunday at West Grinstead Catholic church. On the way in the taxi she gave long explanations about High Mass and Low Mass, and said there would be moments when we should cross ourselves and bow our heads when a bell rang. Sue seemed interested in it all, and to grasp the difference between consubstantiation and transubstantiation: I found it dull and confusing, and wished I had been allowed to stay behind and take Rook for a walk.

My mother must have suspected I had not understood much, for in the vestry she bought me a booklet with translations of the Latin Mass

---

[1] In the Roman Catholic Church, according to Antonia, the water had to trickle down the baby's forehead when it was baptised.

on one side of the page, and photographs of a priest performing various tasks, such as blessing the sacrament, on the other.

I had never been inside a church with my mother and started straight off on the wrong foot. I did not imitate her crossing herself with holy water when we entered, so she did it for me; and I was too embarrassed to genuflect to the altar until she pushed me to my knees. I kept losing my place in the booklet during Mass and her gloved hand would reach across to turn the pages forward. The smell of incense was overpowering, and it seemed the service would never end; the dullest of Grandfather's sermons would have been a light relief in the midst of so much Latin chanting.

Afterwards she insisted on buying us each a statuette. They were all vile, except St Francis and the wolf which Sue picked out first. I did not want any of them, but, as Mother was getting impatient at my dithering, I took the Madonna she suggested though I thought it was one of the most revolting sentimental objects I had ever seen.

This episode as recounted by Antonia in *The Hound and the Falcon* is what first made me sense something false about the letters she wrote to Peter Thorpe in 1941, or was she really so oblivious of what one, probably both, of her children felt?

> Already, of their own accord, they went to Mass ... and they were fascinated by the statues of the saints in a Catholic shop. Sue has gone back to school with St Francis (her own spontaneous choice not uninfluenced by the animals!) and Lyndall with Our Lady. They also have simple prayer books and like trying to follow Mass from pictures. God must want these children.

The reactions of Antonia's friends varied about her return to the church. Eric was pleased and considered it a sign that she was cured: he urged her to continue practising even if at times she was tempted to give it up. 'Wyn, of course, takes the attitude one would expect her to take, but only the most perverse vanity could be wounded by Wyn's opinion.'[1] Ian Henderson on the other hand was not unsympathetic, and loyally defended her to his mother.

But in the spring she had morbid fears and anxieties which prayer could not allay. She started to have headaches, and her father returned

---

[1] Wyn Henderson, like Basil Nicholson, Emily Coleman, Phyllis Jones and Eric Siepmann, was among many of Antonia's wilder friends from the twenties and thirties who became Catholics before they died.

to haunt her dreams, 'always connected with fear of his discovering me in the sexual act'. That was when her correspondence with Peter Thorpe started to turn sour, and changed from near love letters, beginning 'Darling Peter' and ending 'Very much love', to harsher missives with 'My dear' openings and 'Yours always' endings. The blitz was at its worst, and one night in April a bomb exploded about two hundred yards away from where she lay sleeping. But she always faced outside danger bravely; it was the inner conflagrations that unnerved her.

Antonia had corresponded with Ian in the eighteen months since they had been separated, but in the early summer of 1941, when he moved to an Officers' Training Camp not far from London, they resumed having a 'very intense' sexual life, in spite of the fact that she had in the past always had an 'either/or attitude about sex and the spiritual life'.

Even though she was less depressed after Ian became her lover again, she lamented: 'I want my children back. I want a home. But do I want them enough to make an effort?'

On 30 July Ian sailed for India with his regiment. He had only been gone ten days when Antonia suddenly felt she had reached firmer ground in her beliefs, after months of 'hesitation' since returning to the Church. She recorded what had happened so that when the inevitable doubts began again she would have proof that she had once had a period of real, deep conviction *in which I perceived the necessity of faith*:

> I can't explain it anyhow except by 'grace'. It is not as if I had had any miraculous revelation or had arrived by my own reason at a satisfactory reconciliation of all the problems. All that I know is that an eye seemed to open somewhere inside me; an eye very filmed and feeble, seeing nothing definite but yet knowing that there *was* something to see. This is the nearest to 'faith' I have ever come in my life.

She also described this '*coup du ciel*' to Peter Thorpe in a letter.

By then their correspondence was nearing its end. He had finally realised she was losing interest in him after they had met for the first time. Antonia had gone to stay for a weekend with Peter and his wife in Wales in June, and she had been 'snappish' as she usually was when staying in other people's houses. He wrote her a very sad letter afterwards, which, though it aroused her guilt about having hurt and disillusioned him, made her point out in her reply that she had warned him over and over again that she was 'tough, harsh and impatient'.

At the end of the letter describing her glimpse of what it meant to know faith, she tried to bring the correspondence to a close by saying she needed to conserve her energy for reading good Catholic books, not disperse it in writing letters. Two months later, in October, when he had sent Sue his engraving tools, although Antonia had begged him not to – 'She is hopelessly careless and too young to look after them' – and asked Antonia for proofs of the existence of God, she wrote her last letter to him. She thanked him for the tools and suggested he ask a priest for proof of God's existence. The farewell sentence said: 'Just at the moment, Peter dear, I think we must stop deafening each other with our own voices and listen quietly for our particular words of command.'

One consequence of Antonia's religion suddenly having acquired a new dimension was that she now took its commandments more seriously. Since sex outside marriage is forbidden by the Catholic Church, my mother could have no more lovers.

There is a note in one of her diaries, added many years after the event, where she confessed to having slept with Ian Henderson one more time when he came back on leave from India and pleaded with her to make love. She held out against his and her own desires; but later, the same evening, she gave in when he climbed in through her window at Linden Gardens.

Ian Henderson is still alive, a widower and a grandfather. He speaks of Antonia with great affection: about her humour and her generosity and a strange innocence that existed in her in spite of all she had experienced. And so her last love affair, the only one that had been sexually satisfying, was the only one that ended with no hard feelings on either side. For her remaining forty years Antonia never slept with a man again.

CHAPTER 15

ॐ

A Donkey and a New Half-Sister

*Lyndall is like me: she withers without stimulus. I need
incessant encouragement.*
Antonia White, 8 June 1955

Summer Cottage, Turville Heath, which became my home for two
years after leaving Marshfield, was one of a pair of small cottages set
back from the road on a stretch of bracken-covered common surrounded by beech woods. In the adjoining cottage lived a bodger[1],
Mr Rockell, and his family. About two hundred yards down the common
lived Wyn Henderson, in the cottage where Antonia had spent her
tumultuous summer with Ian two years before.

When I read John Mortimer's autobiography, *Clinging to the Wreckage*, I recognised Summer Cottage as the place where he had lived as
a child of my age. Tom and Gerti must have been the tenants after his
parents, by which time the tin bath and outside loo had been replaced
by a bathroom in a lean-to shed outside the back door, freezing in
winter, stifling in summer, and always smelling of creosote.

The cottage had four small rooms and a kitchen. Of the two
downstairs, one was taken up with Gerti's grand piano; and one of
the upstairs ones, my bedroom, was almost filled by a boarded-in
water tank that gurgled and hiccoughed whenever a tap was turned
on; yet, whenever Sue came to stay in the holidays, somehow a camp
bed was fitted in beside my bed.

Sue and I had already stayed at Summer Cottage the previous
Christmas, but now I was an 'only' child living with a stepmother, for
Tom, who had recently become editor of *Picture Post*, only came down
at weekends, and for an occasional night during the week when his
petrol ration and his busy job allowed.

[1] A maker of chair legs.

My feelings about Gerti at that time make me ashamed now. She was not yet thirty and living in an alien land having lost most of what she possessed at the hands of the Nazis. Her father was dead and she was worried about her mother. I disliked her for being 'different' and could not see the charm of those Viennese ways that had delighted my father. She had a brittleness in her voice, and a tactless manner, that made me think she disliked me: reading Tom's notebooks I see now that she did not.

When Sue and I had stayed there at Christmas she had made us both dresses of blue-and-white striped silk. Instead of being pleased, I avoided wearing mine because I thought it looked like a butcher's apron. Before long I had decided she was a witch because she always knew when I had stolen chocolates from the pink porcelain box where she kept them. I thought the only way she could have known I was the culprit was through Jenny, the dog, whose ears pricked hopefully when I unwrapped the silver paper, although I knew it was absurd to fear that Gerti could read a dog's thoughts.

I was very lonely at first at Summer Cottage, though grateful not to be sent to the village school while some suitable place of learning was sought. My only lessons for the remainder of 1940 consisted of Gerti's attempts to teach me French and the piano.

At Marshfield I had discovered the pleasure of listening to music. But as I lay in bed at Summer Cottage, the way Gerti played Schubert impromptus and Beethoven sonatas in the room below made me weep. There was a painful sweetness in the sound that awakened a nostalgia for something I had never known, as if some distant happiness connected with music were evading me. But although I longed for her playing, I never told Gerti what pleasure it gave me; as far as our musical relationship was concerned she only saw me sulking when she had reprimanded me for getting the fingering wrong in some simple scale. I sulked at Gerti over other things beside lessons, such as being made to lay the table, and eat brains from the sheep's head that was boiled up for Jenny once a week, for rationing was now severe.

If I was ever rude to Gerti in Tom's presence, he sent me to my room to learn some French verbs, where I sulked even more until I learned I could get out via the bathroom roof without being seen and could forget my bad mood by sneaking off to see Wyn Henderson who, I thought, was the wittiest person I had ever met. This was because she had once been overjoyed at my appearing when she was imprisoned in an arm-chair and needed hauling out. Panting from exhaustion, she had told me I was an answer to a prayer, which made me feel very important, and, as I tugged away at her colossal bulk, she said, more as a reminder to herself than to me, that she must never take a nap in that chair again when she was alone, because once in it she was as helpless 'as a beetle on its back'.

In fact all the friends I had at Turville Heath were grown-ups. Besides Wyn, there were Basil and Frances Creighton, old friends of Tom; they lived a bicycle ride away at North End. I appreciated the way they treated me as a grown-up and told me local tales like why the mechanic had a wooden leg and which houses were said to be haunted.

The grown-up I loved most, apart from Tom of course, was Charles Fenby, Tom's assistant editor on *Picture Post*, who came down most weekends and rented a room from Wyn. The more he pretended to be off-hand in his treatment of me, such as knocking his pipe out on my head, the more I worshipped him. I was fiendishly jealous when one weekend he came down with Cecil Day-Lewis and neither paid much attention to me. But I soon forgave him when he gave me the best present I had ever had: a bow and arrow.

Fenby, as I always called Charles, was allowed to take me away one weekend to stay with friends of his who had children of my age and horses. But I fell off one of the horses and hurt my right arm. Fenby was so upset that I had to console him.

An X-ray revealed that I had a green-stick fracture and I was an invalid again for the third time that year.

By the time Sue came for Christmas it was healed.

I had been counting the days to Sue's arrival, but when she appeared there was something different about her, her domineering air had been replaced by a superior detachment which implied she lived in a different world and knew things I was still too childish to understand. She spent a lot of time reading Dickens and was not a bit interested in my discovery of Sherlock Holmes and archery.

But when we went to stay at Bines Green in the New Year Sue became more like her old self as we mucked out Mr Cox's cowsheds and took Rook for long walks. It was then that our mother took us to Mass.

I was so ashamed of the Madonna statuette Mother had given me that, on my return to Summer Cottage, I hid it in the water tank in my room, before setting off to a new school as a weekly boarder.

The school was known by the name of its headmistress, Miss Clutton's, and had been evacuated from London to a handsome Queen Anne house in spacious grounds near Reading. Of the seven schools I went to, Miss Clutton's would be the only one I enjoyed wholeheartedly – except for the swede and artichoke soup we were given as a 'nightcap'.

Again Sue and I spent the school holidays together. When she came to Summer Cottage I plucked up the courage to commit a crime I had been planning since the end of the last holidays. I asked her to go into the garden and then call me urgently. While she was going downstairs I quickly fished the statuette out of the water tank and put it on the window sill. When Sue called, I leant out, knocking the Madonna down onto the garden path where she shattered into a hundred pieces. If Mother were ever to ask me about her, I could truthfully say she had met with an unfortunate accident, and there was a witness to prove it.

In my second term at Miss Clutton's Tom let me take riding lessons. Then, at half-term, I fell in love.

On the Saturday afternoon a large van drew up on the common outside Summer Cottage. 'Let's go and see why that monster's blocking our gate,' said Tom. After some confabulating, Tom and the driver lowered the back. Out stepped a shaggy little donkey, neatly crossing its front feet one after the other as it came warily down the ramp. Its halter rope was put into my hands: 'It's for you,' my father told me.

I called it Jeremy and loved it more than I have loved any animal since. In fact Jeremy turned out to be a 'she' we discovered when we clipped her in the summer holidays.

I cannot pretend that riding Jeremy was very exhilarating; going away from her field she would hardly move, and coming back she broke into such a fast trot that it was often impossible to stay on. It used to take most of a day to coax her the three miles to Stonor where the nearest blacksmith lived, but just to be with Jeremy was happiness. She tolerated the great love I bestowed on her with donkey-like resignation, standing patiently while I constantly brushed and groomed her, and even tried to clean her teeth, which I thought were too yellow. Very rarely she would return my affection by leaning her head on my shoulder and nibbling my hair.

My next surprise was that a hut had been built at the end of the garden where I would sleep when the summer holidays began.

My life had become idyllic compared to Sue's. I owned a donkey and took riding lessons; I had Tom at weekends, even though I had to share him with the Home Guard and with Gerti, of whom I was certainly jealous; I had a hut of my own, whereas Sue did not even have a room she could call her own, since Antonia was still living in Ian Black's house in London.

Antonia was trying to be a more concerned mother to Sue now, even if she did not live up to the portrait of maternity she was giving of herself in letters to Peter Thorpe. Sue admits she went several times a term to Salisbury to take her out from school, and managed to be remarkably good-tempered despite being tired from nights in the blitz and days at the BBC.

Silas too had begun to take more interest in Sue. He, like Tom, had not been called-up because he was working on a top-secret engineering project. That summer he took Sue to stay on a farm where horses were bred, and gave her an unbroken foal. Unfortunately, not long afterwards it broke its leg and had to be put down.

My tenth birthday fell while Sue was with Silas. Gerti asked whether she had sent me anything. Tom wrote down my answer: 'No. She didn't send me a present. She didn't send me a letter. She didn't even send me a piece of paper with nothing on it.'

In August Mother took us to stay at a hotel perched above the sea at St Ives in Cornwall. She had just had her revelation of faith which may explain why she was nicer on that holiday than I ever remembered her having been – less impatient, less critical, less quick to take offence – although, she told Peter Thorpe, 'the place, though lovely, didn't suit me and I felt tired the whole time'.

We loved it. It was our first seaside holiday and we were happy together as we braved high waves, raced on the sand and clambered over rocks, or played with Barbara Hepworth's children. Sue was kind to me when I got stung under my foot by a jellyfish, and piggy-backed me up the steep path to the hotel.

Sue spent the rest of her holidays at Summer Cottage where we inaugurated the new hut, but we bickered as we had not done in Cornwall. Sue still looked down on me; and I was insensitive to her suffering over not having some of the good things I was now lucky enough to have.

One Sunday in November Tom came to my hut while I was reading on my bed after lunch and told me that Gerti was going to have a baby.

According to Tom, who had been very apprehensive about how I would take this piece of news, I looked 'really delighted'.

I remember at tea-time, after he had told me, taking furtive looks at Gerti's tummy and wondering how on earth I had not noticed so sizeable a bulge there before, for she would have been in her seventh month by then. I also remember, which is confirmed in Tom's note-book, going out of my way to be nice to her and being more helpful than before.

It's odd that in our family, where there was plenty of envy about of which I gave and received my fair share, I never felt jealous about Tom's having another child. Even the possibility that it might be a boy – something I still wished desperately I had been – I seem to have taken in my stride, and told Gerti when she was driving me back to school that evening that it would be a good thing if she had a son, because otherwise 'Tom's name would not be carried on'.

Now I understood why the hut had been built: the baby needed my room. But I did not feel an outcast in the hut, though I was a little afraid sleeping there without Sue, specially when it rained at night making it sound as if little feet were pattering across the tin roof. I never admitted to Tom I was frightened, in fact I encouraged him to make me more so by insisting that he played a game he had invented called 'scratchy', which involved scratching at the door and rattling the knob when he came to say goodnight.

Gerti's first daughter, Nicolette, was born on 3 January 1942. I was not very impressed by my first glimpse of her at the nursing home in Beaconsfield, but when I next met her at Summer Cottage, and she was put into my arms where she lay trustingly, looking up at me with intense blue eyes, new feelings were aroused. I had always thought babies as repellent as dolls, which I had never been able to abide, but this baby, who did not howl when she looked me in the eye, seemed all right. And over the next two years, as she continued to acknowledge me as part of her world, first with a smile, then by crawling to greet me when I came back from school, then with a name, 'Linty', I became fonder and fonder of her.

Gerti's tactless streak came to the fore over Nicolette and at times I was made to feel like Cinderella. Being a professional photographer, she took thousands of pictures of her daughter from the moment she was born, many of which were used to illustrate articles in *Picture Post*. When I was playing with Nicolette, sometimes Gerti would call,

'Out of the way, Linty, quick, quick, I don't want you in the picture.'
Fortunately her behaviour, though it made me dislike her more, did
not alter my affection for Nicolette. But it increased my feeling that I
was only living with her and Tom because the Government had so
decreed, as Mother had implied at Marshfield.

It has always mystified me that, though Gerti treated Nicolette like
the most precious creature ever born, from the time she was about
eighteen months old she would sometimes entrust her to my care for
a whole day during the holidays so that she could go up to London. I
did not mind, in fact I preferred being alone with Nicolette, for I was
always self-conscious if Tom or Gerti were around when I told her
stories or played games with her.

Tom doted on Nicolette too, but not to my detriment. After she was
born, until I went to a new school as a full boarder, Tom usually did
one thing alone with me every weekend: a walk, a bicycle ride, a drive
into Henley to buy a book, or to Watlington where there were horses
for hire. My happiest memory of that time is charging along the
Icknield Way on Torphil, a failed racehorse, trying to rein her back
from overtaking Tom on a sturdy cob called Over.

After I went to Headington School, Oxford, being alone with Tom
became a rare treat, though he came once or twice a term to take me
out. I looked forward to his visits as much as I dreaded my mother's.
She wore pencil skirts that were too tight and hats that were too
conspicuous, so that I could sense my housemistress's disapproval as
she handed me over for the afternoon.

I started off well at Headington when I went there at the age of
eleven. Within a few weeks I had been moved up a class, to become
the youngest in the Lower Fourth. And, for a year or two, it needed
no effort to keep abreast of the top half of the class. Even though I
was not enthusiastic about games, I got into the Under-14 hockey team
for my house, and even won my colours.

But with adolescence things started to go wrong. Comments that
had never applied to me before appeared on my school reports:
'Disappointing', 'Has the ability but does not try'. The one that upset
me most said 'Lyndall's tendency to self-pity is distracting her efforts
from her work'. I was indignant until it slowly dawned on me that it
was true. Even mathematics had left me behind; geometry had become
one of my worst subjects.

A few months after starting at Headington I had the first symptoms of what would become the bane of my adolescence. It happened during the Christmas holidays of 1942 when I was staying with Mother in London.

Antonia had just moved into a place of her own, a rented maisonette in Thurloe Street, opposite South Kensington tube station, which she shared with Ronald Moody and his wife. The blitz was over and 'doodlebugs' had not yet started, so it was thought safe for Sue and me to stay with her in London over Christmas.

Christmas was one of Antonia's life-long obsessions, but this one was of special importance, not only because she was back in the Church, though assailed by doubts again, but because it was the first one she had spent with us for four years. She prepared a crib and Ronald Moody carved the figures for it out of wood. Sue and I were put to work decorating the tree and laying the table. With Hélène Moody's help Antonia cooked her first Christmas dinner – in her forties Antonia found herself having to learn to cook and be domestic and it cost her much effort. Even the most sumptuous feast could not have compensated for Antonia's neurotic fluster and frenzy of ill-humour beforehand. I could not have enjoyed the dinner anyway because Tom and Gerti and Silas were there and I was in a state of terror that Mother would create some scene in front of them, for it was a unique occasion for all six of us to be together.

After dinner Sue and I had to sing carols, among them Mother's favourite, the Bach setting of *In Dulci Jubilo*.

As we were helping with the washing-up, after what Antonia called '*les Papas*' had gone home, suddenly I could see only half my mother at the sink. I looked across to Sue and she too was partly blurred. Within a few minutes psychedelic lights were zig-zagging in front of my eyes. I began to feel nausea and rushed off to be sick. I went to lie down and soon my head felt as if it were being cracked open and then clanged shut again. When Mother came to see why I had abandoned drying-up, the glare as she turned on the light made me turn my face to the wall. I could not even answer her question of what was wrong because my tongue had gone numb. She gave me a Veganin, but I could not keep it down. Ahead of me lay the worst night of my life so far, in which the painful throbbing in my head, mingled with the nausea and numbness, which had spread to my hands and feet, were like some terrible initiation to an unknown realm of suffering. But the next day, except for feeling knocked out, I was well enough for everyone to assume it had been because I had eaten too much Christmas pudding with brandy butter.

Sue and I spent the rest of the holidays in 'Stayes', a new house Tom and Gerti had rented near Turville Heath.

At school the next term, in the middle of a lesson, half the teacher disappeared and the experience of Christmas night was repeated. This time the headache was worse and the aftermath dreadful; for two days my head still hurt if I bent down, my mind seemed somewhere just out of reach behind my brain, my eyes felt askew, and the whole world was remote and out of focus.

The school doctor was called and my malady had a name, but not a cure: migraine.

I had been having two or three migraines a month for over a year, when Gerti took me to see a Harley Street specialist who prescribed half a tablet of phenobarbitone to be taken night and morning. The headaches continued, though with slightly less frequency, so I was made to go on taking barbiturates until I left school.

Migraines, love and religion are all mixed up in my mind in my memories of Headington.

My housemistress, who was also the Classics mistress and was nicknamed Scottie, seeing how I suffered during a migraine, let me sleep in a room of my own instead of in a dormitory. During an attack, she would come in to see how I was getting on. Her visits were reassuring, because during a migraine my mind used to be assailed with strangely contradictory thoughts about death. Every time I got one I wished I were dead, and yet I feared that if I died during an attack, the headache would remain part of me for eternity: a perpetual hell.

My views on religion and death and a possible after-life were very confused at this time, and would remain so for another thirty-five years, though I spent a great deal of time trying to make sense of God.

At Headington religion was important. Part of me was attracted by it, though I suspect this attraction came more from a love of singing Bach anthems in the school choir than from a thirst for mysticism. I found the Bible poetical, the Old Testament God less so. The New Testament Christ worried me with his contradictions.

Mother was still trying to convert Sue and me to Catholicism. She took us to Brompton Oratory whenever we stayed with her, and had now given me *Frost in May* to read. Though I never dared to tell her, it was her description of the nuns' behaviour that made me vow I would never belong to her Church.

Yet all the time Antonia was trying to impose her religion on us in the early forties, she was alternating 'an almost steady rhythm of faith and doubt'. She wished she could practise with joy, instead of using religion only to curb her 'immense egotism'. She was living in 'terror of failure in the spiritual life'. Just before I started migraines, she wrote 'I keep saying "Thy will be done" but I really want mine.'

When I lay in a dark room, groaning under the agony of a migraine, I used to wish I could appeal to God for comfort and strength, but it seemed wrong to pray to someone you were not sure existed. As I came round from the attacks, I would question Scottie about God, in whom I knew her to be a firm believer. She would sit on my bed and talk, but it always came back to the same thing: to believe in him one needed faith, humility and love.

I fell in love not with God but with Scottie. To call it a schoolgirl 'crush' is to degrade what I felt for her into something too trivial. But to say I 'fell in love' gives a wrong connotation too, for there was no libido in my passion, yet even in my most desperate fallings in love with men later on I was never as obsessed with anyone as I was with Scottie. I used to listen for her footfall, try always to position myself where she might pass by, think up any excuse to go to her study, and, at the height of my infatuation, hide outside her room at night until the chink of light showing below her door went out.

I became moody and brooding: I read Rupert Brooke instead of doing homework and imagined Scottie and me flinging ourselves 'on the windy hill'; and instead of going to hockey practice in the hope of being picked for the team, lay on my bed reading Byron and wished I could with her go 'a-roving by the light of the moon'. But my love was innocent. Perhaps, after so long a gap, she had succeeded Nurse as a mother-substitute, for Gerti had never been one. At the height of my fervour over her, I did something to please Scottie which did not please my mother.

In the spring of 1945 I became a Protestant and Scottie became my godmother. I was baptised by Grandfather in St Mary's Church beside the Thames at Battersea, where Turner had once sketched and where Tom's youngest brother, Stephan, was vicar. In his old age, Grandfather had left his beloved Lake District to live with Granny in a dingy flat in Battersea and become his son's curate.

I too lived in London now just across the river. A few months before the war ended Tom and Gerti had rented a fine house in Chelsea, at the top of which I had an attic bedroom that looked out over Thomas Carlyle's fig tree in the next door garden. But, as Tom says in his autobiography, there was something 'chill' about 26 Cheyne Row. This chillness was not so much because it was on five floors and Gerti's tendency to stinginess meant it was underheated, but because of an atmosphere of hostility that pervaded the house. I was frightened whenever I was alone there, more than in the hut at Summer Cottage.

Tom described me at this time as 'just passing over the half-way line that leads to being grown-up, with enormous knees and a dirty neck'. He also said: 'With luck she can be much happier as a grown-up than she has been as a child.'

Tom changed, too, after we all came to live in London, maybe because Gerti's presence there curtailed his freedom.

Apart from the hazards of the blitz to which he had been exposed with some near escapes, Tom had had a happy life in London during the war. He had met interesting people – artists and politicians, philosophers and scientists – and the opinions he printed in *Picture Post* were often feared by those in power and respected by fellow journalists. Though his job left him little time for his own writing, he had had a story published in *Horizon*, Cyril Connolly's literary quarterly.

'The Third Secretary's Story' attempted 'to set down the magic of Frances'. Gerti guessed who it was about and thought it was 'a beautiful tribute'. Antonia told him after reading it, 'Now I see what was her real quality.'

Tom also had a mistress in London during the war: in other words, he had a complete 'other life' in London during the week from the weekend one at Turville Heath with his wife and children, his gardening and the Home Guard.

Antonia had also moved. She now shared a spacious unfurnished flat with the Moodys at 13 Ashburn Gardens, near Gloucester Road, so Sue and I were now a fifteen-minute walk away from each other in the school holidays.

Sue had become a Catholic before I became a Protestant. Then, on the day the Second World War ended, 15 August 1945, she made her First Communion in the Catholic Church in Cheyne Row where Antonia used to go to Mass when she lived in 'the sugar house'. Her reasons were as serious as mine were flippant; she told Mother, who was overjoyed, that 'she wanted to feel there was a centre in her life'. The priest who prepared her told Antonia, 'You have been given a very great grace,' and said she should go on asking God that I be converted too.

The following November, I was confirmed at school. At that time I came nearest to believing in Christianity. As the choir sang while we took Communion for the first time I prayed fervently that the Holy Ghost would my heart inspire, and that God would be in my head and in my understanding. But my faith cannot have been very profound, for within a year I had partly fulfilled Emily's prophecy to Antonia that I would soon react against the 'watery mixture' offered by the Protestant religion, but not, as she had predicted, to become a Catholic like them. I stopped taking Holy Communion after having rejected Scottie overnight.

It is a shameful story. She came to London, in her role of godmother, to take me to a theatre in the Christmas holidays. It was the first time I had not seen her wearing the dreary clothes suited to a house-mistress. Instead she wore a smart suit and a yellow hat, make-up and high-heeled shoes. I thought she looked ridiculous, and my heart turned to stone.

The next holidays I went to stay for the first time with Tom's second cousin, Alice Roughton, who had given my donkey a home when we left Turville Heath.

Alice was a doctor who lived in a rambling house on what was then the outskirts of Cambridge. At the end of her garden in Adams Road was a farm where Jeremy now grazed with Alice's cows and a pony. Through her ever-open kitchen door came guests of every age and nationality. In spite of a busy medical practice, and the house and farm to run, Alice had time for everyone and was interested in everything. She never seemed harassed and never lost her temper, and in the carefree atmosphere of her untidy house one could live without having to be on one's guard. I wished this amazing woman had been my mother. And Alice's only daughter, my third cousin Rosemary, was the nicest contemporary I had met.

While I was there an entire ballet company came to stay complete with its founder and choreographer, Kurt Jooss, who was a friend of Alice. When Rosemary took me to see them perform at the Arts Theatre, as the primo ballerino in *The Big City*, Hans Züllig, danced out the despair of a labourer whose girl had been abducted by a rich libertine, he filled not only the bare stage, but the space so recently left empty by Scottie in my fickle heart.

The theatre was already beginning to attract me. The only consolation for living in London – for I missed the country – was that Tom got press theatre tickets and took me to plays. Still in my mind's ear I can hear the terrible wail, piercing yet controlled, of Laurence Olivier as he staggered onto the stage of the Old Vic with blood-stained cheeks to bemoan his dreadful fate as Oedipus: 'Woe, woe is me!' It was that, and his villainous asides in *Richard III*, and the pathos of Alec Guinness as Richard II, and Ralph Richardson's Uncle Vanya and Cyrano, which had made me decide that when I left school I must find a way of working in the theatre.

When I discovered that the Ballet Jooss were to perform their most famous ballet, *The Green Table*, in Birmingham I resolved to go and see it. But how?

It was so unlikely that Tom would let me go to Birmingham alone and pay my fare that I did not even bother to ask him when I returned to London. Instead I borrowed ten shillings from the new German cook, knowing that in a few days I would be getting my term's pocket money, and told Gerti I was going to see a schoolfriend for the day.

Unfortunately I missed the last train back to London after the performance; but there was a late train to Oxford. In spite of my changed feelings, I telephoned Scottie, who was back at Headington, to ask if I could spend the night there. Then I called up Gerti and said my 'friend' wanted me to stay overnight.

I had an angry reception from Gerti the next morning. She had called my friend and learned I was not there; also the cook had informed her that I had borrowed money.

Although I told Tom the true story when he came back from the office, I was still in disgrace when I went back to school the next day. Much later I heard from Mother, with whom he had discussed the episode, that he had not believed my love for Hans Züllig was so innocent.

Now it was my turn to have my mind looked at. At half-term Mother took me to see a new friend of hers. She was called Dorothy, the wife of Hugh Kingsmill, and she was interested in psychology.

When my mother left me alone with Dorothy Kingsmill, I found her easy to talk to and answered her questions frankly. At the end of an hour's conversation she said, 'I know you're fifteen, not twenty-one, but I am going to ask your father to trust you with a front door key.' She also told me that I was good-looking and if I would do something about my hair, which I wore scraped back in two bunches at the time, and would wear a touch of make-up, I could be a 'stunner'. I had never thought about my looks much, and assumed from my mother's emphasis on Sue's beauty that I was plain. Though I would have liked to believe Dorothy, I feared she was talking nonsense, and nothing would have made me wear make-up which I despised.

Tom was so impressed by the suggestion that if I were given more responsibility I might behave less furtively (for I was very secretive and sullen in my teens), that he not only gave me a key to Cheyne Row, but took to consulting Dorothy Kingsmill himself. Unknown to me of course, he was beginning to have troubles in his work and his marriage.

One difference that not being obsessed with Scottie made was that in the sixth form I began to study again, ashamed at having got through School Certificate the previous summer with results that showed how mediocre a pupil I had become: no distinctions; no failures; just a row of credits in every single subject. All that can be said in my defence is that I was a year under the average age for candidates taking that exam and still had migraines.

Scottie left Headington and I did not get on with the new house-mistress who, I felt, disliked me.

Sue was in her first term at Somerville College in Oxford but she was too young to be allowed to take me out. One Saturday afternoon I skipped games to go to see her in town, which was strictly out of bounds. But Matron saw me getting off the bus and reported me. There was a great hullabaloo with the dreaded Miss Moller, Headington's headmistress.

Tom came down to see what the fuss was about. We had a long talk in Christ Church meadows during which I confessed my dream of working in the theatre, and told him about the school Saint-Denis had just started at the Old Vic, which included a Stage Production Course. He agreed I could try for a place there, and that there was not much point in staying on at an expensive school where I was not particularly happy. But he also said I could not live at Cheyne Row where Gerti was not particularly happy with me. If I could find somewhere to live, and someone to tutor me in the subjects that might help me get into the Old Vic, I could use the equivalent of my present school fees for upkeep and tuition.

I was delighted. I had not taken in from the way he had presented things to me in Christ Church meadows that I was being banished from my father's house.

Into my mind came one thought: Alice Roughton. I wrote to her asking if I could live at Adams Road as a paying guest. She wrote back at once saying I was welcome to come whenever I wanted for as long as I wanted.

And so at the end of the Autumn term of 1947, aged sixteen, I left school. My final report, except for my housemistress's comments, was better than I had expected, but one theme ran through it: lack of confidence. It ended with Miss Moller's surprisingly kindly summing up of a pupil who had been at her school for over five years:

> Lyndall underestimates her ability and gives up too easily. I hope she will grow more confident and be ready to face the discipline needed to develop her gifts. She takes with her our affectionate interest and good wishes.

CHAPTER 16

🖎

Dominating Women

Dominating people can usually be dominated by someone.
Antonia White, 12 September 1951

Antonia was lonely. Her return to the Church had cut her off from many of her friends of the thirties, but she found it difficult to be really intimate with Catholics. She even had trouble with Eric: 'He knocks down every statement I make yet he likes me to be a Catholic, though at times he seems to hate Catholicism.'

In the middle of 1943 she lost her job with the BBC and went into one of her old familiar states of angst, apathy and depression. She felt 'broken, full of corruption' and was having religious doubts and finding it hard to believe in the Church: 'odi et amo as much as ever.'

She did not write in her notebook for over a year.

By August 1944, her state had worsened. She was even having weeping fits in the office at her new job, working for a secret wartime department known as SOE – Special Operations Executive. By then she had made some Catholic friends, such as Barbara Ward and the actor Robert Speaight, as well as Graham Greene and the poet Kathleen Raine, who both worked in SOE.

Kathleen, who only became a Catholic after she had known Antonia for a while, says in her autobiography[1] that she was horrified at this 'cage of the soul' into which Antonia had put herself. And after joining the Church she so shocked Antonia by continuing to insist that stories such as Adam and Eve were clearly 'symbolic allegories' that for a time their friendship floundered.

It was during this period of her low and lonely state that Antonia moved to Ashburn Gardens. In the school holidays, now that we went no more to the country, Sue, aged fifteen, began to be much more alone with Mother. Antonia enjoyed conversing with her: after dinner,

[1] *The Land Unknown*, published by Hamish Hamilton, 1975.

until late into the night, she would tell Sue about her present problems, her startling past and her uncertain future; and of course she talked about religion.

It was then that Sue became a Catholic, which seems to have helped Antonia feel firmer about her own beliefs for a while.

Although Sue was exposed to Antonia's moods and often had to take the brunt of her confusion and unhappiness, she had some antidotes to Mother's neuroses. Apart from sometimes going away with me – I remember us cycling round Exmoor, happy despite pouring rain and cold youth hostels – she also had an admirer: the middle son of Cecil and Margot King. But more important than him or me was Silas's wife, Sheila, whom he had married before the end of the war.

Sheila was a war widow, lively, petite, attractive and efficient. In no time she had turned her husband's chaotic bachelor crow's nest looking out over Sloane Square into a civilised and friendly apartment where Sue was always welcome to drop in – as I was too. Even before Sheila came into his life Silas had already been taking an interest in Sue for some time, both personally and financially. Now, at Sheila's instigation, he gave her a dress allowance, and to eke it out Sheila made clothes for her.

Besides being kind and welcoming to both of us, Sheila also tried to keep on good terms with Antonia. It was not easy. Once she invited all three of us to a party. It was a rainy day and Mother was in a bad mood when we arrived because we had not been able to find a taxi. After Silas opened the door, she went straight to the bathroom to rearrange herself. Then she stormed into the sitting-room, went up to Sheila who was surrounded by guests, and said in a ringing tone that rose above all other voices in the small room, 'Sheila, someone has peed all over your bathroom floor.' It shows Sheila's good nature that she reassured Antonia it was the fault of the leaky skylight and coaxed her back into better spirits with good food and drink. Soon Antonia was being her most entertaining party self; but, as always happened after my mother had made a scene in public, I had withered into a state of misery and could not enjoy the party.

Sheila tolerated Antonia's erratic behaviour on more than one occasion because she did not want to do anything that might make it difficult for Sue to have access to Silas. But both Silas and Sheila became less willing to be well-disposed towards her after the 'Benedicta affair'.

In the spring of 1947 Sue came home from her last term at school, having won an Exhibition to Somerville College, to discover Mother was in love. The object of her passion was a tertiary of the Dominican Order, Benedicta de Bezer, a penniless painter and pianist who wrote religious articles and wore men's clothing. Although she was younger than Antonia, she became the first of what Antonia later called her 'dominating women'. Benedicta dominated Antonia through 'sex, religion mainly', and had a 'psychic effect' on her as well.

Since Benedicta persuaded Antonia to burn her current notebook, together with the first two she had ever kept, it is difficult to piece together what went on between them from the only contemporary chronicle, a small agenda with cryptic notes in Antonia's handwriting. But despite a strange phrase in that agenda, 'Sex and the fingernail', and Antonia's never denying she loved Benedicta, it is improbable they had a full lesbian affair, since seven years later Antonia wrote that she had had no sexual life at all for fourteen years, which would have taken her back to the affair with Ian Henderson.

In the privacy of her flat in Belsize Park, or at Ashburn Gardens, Benedicta would don a monk's black habit and say Office. They also rushed from church to church in a frenzy of religious fervour, seeking benedictions and answering Masses, making confessions and lighting candles, saying rosaries and chanting litanies, crying under crucifixes and having masses said for each other.

But by the time they had known each other less than two months there was a crisis. Antonia had had a disturbing dream in which she saw Benedicta as evil, and estranged from Our Lady. She began to feel uneasy about Benedicta's religiosity and consulted with priests, in particular with her friend Father Victor White, a Dominican who was the rare combination of priest and Jungian. But she let Benedicta intervene with the Prior at the Dominican Priory to have her received as a tertiary too, and continued to let her say Office at Ashburn Gardens.

In the month preceding Sue's return home from school the agenda sketches a kind of spiritual danse macabre, in which the two protagonists alternate 'terrible' days after Antonia has told Benedicta about the dream of her being evil, with moments of being 'deliriously happy' when Antonia is received as a postulant to become a tertiary. The climax came just before Holy Week when she burnt her notebooks.

Sue came home a few days later, on the day of the Seven Dolours, just in time to share a Holy Week of frenetic church-going with Mother and Benedicta, whom she met for the first time on Palm Sunday at Westminster Cathedral.

The next day was Antonia's forty-eighth birthday. I came over from Cheyne Row and heard only of this mysterious and wonderful creature called Benedicta who had sent Mother a holy medal and a rosary as presents.

It was at the second meeting with Benedicta, when she donned the black habit she kept at Ashburn Gardens and said Office, that, according to Antonia, Sue also came under her spell. On Maundy Thursday, during High Mass at Westminster Cathedral, Sue fell in love with Benedicta as she watched her at prayer. But in the evening, when they all went to *Tenebrae*, Sue wept. As the candles were put out, and the altars stripped, in commemoration of Christ's crucifixion, Sue had a terrible sensation that Benedicta, kneeling beside her in the pre-Pasqual gloom, was doomed to eternal damnation.

On Good Friday all three went to Westminster Cathedral. Antonia noted, 'Sue is profoundly unhappy.'

On Holy Saturday the trio again went to Mass together. This time Antonia was unhappy because Benedicta vanished after Communion. However, she reappeared in the afternoon with a present of a bunch of primroses 'from Our Lady of Sorrows'.

On Easter Sunday I met Benedicta for the first time. It was impossible not to be attracted to this lean and dark hermaphrodite, chain-smoking in her monk's robe. She had a handsome, tormented face, and spoke in a husky voice, frequently interspersing her words with 'darling'. She had fine hands with long, bony fingers that could summon out sweet music from Mother's old piano. Dorothy Kingsmill and her daughter Edmée – a pretty girl of Sue's age – came to tea, and Benedicta accompanied Dorothy as she sang. Then we all joined in and spent the rest of the afternoon making music.

Gladly I went round to Ashburn Gardens the next day, knowing Benedicta would be there. Again there was singing after lunch, but suddenly the atmosphere became threatening and I sensed Mother wanted me out of the way. I asked Sue to walk part of the way back to Cheyne Row with me so that we could chat alone.

As we were going down Onslow Gardens we came across a little white dog lying in the road, so freshly run-over that blood was trickling from its mouth. It was the first time I had seen a dead dog, and it upset me. Sue seemed as dismayed as me; she refused to come any further and went home. I felt abandoned and melancholy; the dead dog seemed in some way connected with Benedicta.

What happened over the next few days, from which I was excluded as a non-Catholic, is outlined in Antonia's agenda, which says Sue became aware of a sense of evil and 'lost Our Lady'. A few days after Easter Benedicta came to spend the day at Ashburn Gardens and, according to Antonia, Sue was in a 'fearful state': 'Religion obscured by this dark cloud. She could not pray: could not even hold her rosary.' She lay down and Mother gave her a crucifix which she managed to hold on to. Apparently Benedicta was at a loss to understand what was going on, and said Office. When Fr Victor White, who had been invited to dinner, arrived, they asked him to bless the flat: Sue was 'very insistent that he should bless the bathroom'. Antonia told Fr Victor Sue's experiences and he suggested they should keep apart from Benedicta for a while.

Antonia noted that Sue was still afraid that night and, as she lay awake praying for help, thought she heard Mother calling. She went up to her room, but Mother was sleeping soundly, so she was then 'convinced it was Our Lady' who had called her.

Antonia decided they should see Fr Pius, the priest who had prepared Sue for Confirmation. Sue told him she had experienced love and evil together. Afterwards, when he was alone with Antonia, he warned of the dangers of spiritual friendships. His last words to her were, 'Do not be dominated.'

Sue felt she ought to explain to Benedicta why she could not go on seeing her. Benedicta seemed bewildered rather than upset that Sue and Antonia felt her to be evil, and said that Antonia always distorted things with her dramatic sense. But she became very unfriendly when Sue tried to defend Antonia.

However the next day Antonia received a note from Benedicta beginning 'Pax Vobiscum'.

Antonia wrote to Benedicta that she had changed her plans: instead of becoming a tertiary at the Priory, she would have the ceremony in Paris, where she would soon be going on her way to Alsace with Sue. Benedicta, who had already prepared a pair of scapulars[1], said it was

---

[1] A scapular is a wide band of cloth, with an opening for the head, worn over the shoulders next to the skin to represent a monastic habit.

a monstrous way to be treated after having put up for three months with Antonia's 'impossible temperament'. Antonia was so miserable she went to church to implore help for both of them. When she telephoned Benedicta to say she had done so, Benedicta was friendly, and they agreed to meet at Brompton Oratory the next day to ask forgiveness for each other. While they waited for confession Benedicta said she had been feeling bewitched and under a curse. After confession they knelt in separate pews to say their penitential rosaries.

Afterwards Benedicta seemed so shaken that, in the taxi home, Antonia took her hand. Then she noticed that Benedicta was crying and felt more love for her than ever before.

They spent an awkward evening at Ashburn Gardens. When Benedicta left she took away the monk's habit she kept there.

A few days before leaving for France, Antonia dreamt of Benedicta. She told Fr Victor White who said he hoped that from now on she would keep Benedicta for her prayers and dreams only.

On 24 April 1947 Antonia's reception as a tertiary took place in 'a wonderful ceremony' in Paris with Sue present. The scapulars Benedicta had made were on the altar; and during the service Antonia prayed for Benedicta, for my conversion 'and for the gift of charity'.

In May Antonia came back to a lonely flat after having left Sue with a French family at Kolbsheim in Alsace for six months. The Moodys had moved out just before the 'Benedicta affair' leaving her glad of the extra space but burdened by the higher rent. She did three things to assuage her loneliness: she acquired a black and white kitten and called it Domina; she found a lodger called Pat; and she got in touch with Dorothy Kingsmill.

Dorothy told her that not long before she had seen Benedicta looking very unhappy in a café. On questioning her, she had discovered that Benedicta was upset because someone had dreamt of her 'as a devil'. Dorothy thought this person might have contacted Benedicta's 'shadow side', or was projecting their own on to her. Antonia confessed she was that person. Dorothy then said she might be able to help them both, but emphasised it meant taking risks because Antonia had been in Bedlam and she herself was not qualified. Antonia decided to take the risk, not just to help Benedicta, but also because Dorothy said she might be able to help break her writing block: it had persisted now for fourteen years, except for the short story about Tom and Frances which Antonia had managed to write six years before, 'The Moment of Truth'.

Within a short time of going to Dorothy Kingsmill, Antonia had written two religious poems, 'The Key' and 'Sed Tantum Dic Verbo'[1]. She sent them to Tom to read, and also told him she was writing up to thirty pages a week for Dorothy in a special notebook which recorded dreams and 'queer reveries about the fourth dimension', as well as drawings she felt impelled to do and could not understand, 'though D. finds all sorts of clues in them'.

Only later did Antonia say she suspected that Dorothy had taken over from Benedicta the role of 'dominating woman' in her life.

For a while both Benedicta and Antonia were seeing Dorothy, but not each other. Then one afternoon Benedicta telephoned to say she must see Antonia. When they met she talked wildly and warned Antonia to beware of Dorothy because she was more Buddhist than Christian in her beliefs. Antonia assured Benedicta she was not worried because Dorothy had promised to get in touch with a priest all three respected, Fr Kehoe, in case Antonia ran into any religious troubles during 'analysis'. The next time Antonia went to Dorothy she heard that Benedicta had broken off her 'analysis' in such a cruel way that Dorothy had been reduced to tears.

Dorothy was not a Buddhist, but she did believe in reincarnation. She was a follower of Meher Baba, an Indian who claimed to be the 'Ancient One, come again to redeem man from his bondage of ignorance'. Dorothy was one of those who believed him to be the Avatar. Soon his photograph would stand next to that of Padre Pio, the Italian monk with the stigmata, on Antonia's bedside table.

When Antonia wrote down her dreams for Dorothy, she often commented on the characters who appeared in them; among these were Benedicta and Sue who both figured frequently. By the time Sue returned from France to go up to Oxford, the dreams had become nightmares in which Benedicta appeared as malevolent.

Antonia attempted an analysis of her and Sue's relationship with Benedicta: 'Sue was jealous of Benedicta and jealous of me *with* Benedicta, I of Benedicta and Sue, Benedicta of the two of us.' She decided neither of them had fallen in love with Benedicta in a lesbian way, but had seen her 'as the romantic prince on the white horse' who, for Sue, had also been a father-figure. Benedicta, on the other hand,

[1] Published in *Strangers* : Virago, 1981.

had seen Antonia as a mother-figure but had wanted to be her son not her daughter. She also thought that Benedicta had been trying to drive her mad again.

For a friendship which had lasted three months, and only two weeks for Sue, Antonia had managed to extort many odd conclusions from her first rapport with a 'dominating woman'.

Over thirty years later, shortly after Antonia's death, Benedicta died in an asylum for the insane.

༚

CHAPTER 17

Crises

How much do I really know even about my feelings for
Sue -- that great 'interruption' and turning point in my life.
Antonia White, 14 May 1951

When Sue came back from her first term at Somerville, Antonia was worried that she seemed 'in rather a state about herself'. She told Mother 'that she had no central interest in her life, nothing she felt was worth living for', which made Antonia fear religion had become less important to her.

As always happened when someone was on her mind, Antonia's notebooks began to be filled with conflicting opinions about Sue, who was rapidly becoming one of her obsessions. She was beginning to feel uneasy about having been 'a rotten mother' because of having seen her children as enemies out to take away everything, and had a morbid terror of their 'annihilating' her. She felt this particularly about Sue whom she had 'failed badly' as a baby; and although she had tried in recent years to make up for it, she knew she had not done enough: 'I've got to "earn" Sue. I've had her "on account" as you might say.'

As Antonia entered deeper into an analyst–patient rapport with Dorothy, dreams about her elder daughter began to disturb Antonia's nights after Sue had returned to Oxford for her second term. Then, in February 1948, after a 'sinister dream' about her, Dorothy warned that there might be 'trouble with Sue' ahead.

Dorothy's prophesy came true: Sue turned up from Oxford unexpectedly in the middle of term with what Mother felt to be a kind of nervous breakdown. The 'account' was being called in, but, as usually happened when Antonia acquired something on credit, she was caught without the resources with which to pay for it.

Antonia was in a shaky state herself at the beginning of 1948. In January, she had had an extraordinary session with Dorothy at Binesfield, which the Kingsmills now rented from her, 'in which we went so deep that I was babbling in a kind of trance'. It was followed by a 'straight analytical crisis' which had made her terribly depressed for some weeks afterwards. Though she was over the worst of what Dorothy had feared might be a long crisis by the time Sue appeared in a bad state, she was still exhausted from it. Besides sleeping a great deal more than usual, she often lay in a peculiar state between sleeping and waking in the daytime. She was also starting the menopause.

At the same time, Antonia had started working on what would become *The Lost Traveller*, and she was a dangerous beast when writing about her father. She had decided, with Dorothy's help, that her creative side was her feminine side, not the masculine as she had always imagined, which was instead the side trying to block her writing. 'The key problem,' she told Tom in a letter, 'is to "marry" the male and female in one.'

During a second crisis Dorothy had told her she had handed her over to Meher Baba, her Indian guru; and early in February, when Antonia had been in a low physical state as well—headaches, sore mouth, stomach upsets, and night fevers — she had become very conscious of Baba's presence. Over the next months he often appeared in her dreams or had 'mental conversations' with her as she lay in one of her drowsy states. In one of these 'conversations' he told her to be less fidgety and to cut down on smoking. The next day she had managed to smoke only five or six cigarettes, as opposed to her usual twenty.

Though her mental crisis had suddenly resolved itself, much to Dorothy's satisfaction, Antonia was still feeling low when Sue turned up unexpectedly from Oxford, 'in tears, very pale and all to pieces' unable to face an exam she was due to take.

The day after coming home Sue went to see Silas and Sheila. While she was there Antonia had a recurrence of her familiar 'lost, panicky sensation'. She fought to control her jitters after Sheila telephoned to say she was coming to fetch her for a family consultation, fearing something she said might make the Glossops think she was as neurotic as ever and quite unfit to handle the Sue situation.

They all agreed that Sue should see Dr Carroll since she was so depressed by her quandary about whether to go back to Oxford or leave it for good.

Three days after Sue saw Carroll, Antonia lost her temper with her over something trivial. It had not been the thing in itself that had maddened her, but Sue's 'cold, complacent contemptuous' expression, though Antonia knew she should not blame Sue for being hardly aware of other people's existence at the time: 'she talks and behaves like an automaton'.

'The battle is definitely on' Antonia wrote the next day, reflecting that the real battle was not so much with Sue as once again with herself. The worst thing she had to face was that her preferred child harboured 'profound hostility' against her of which she was 'hardly conscious'. However much that hurt, Antonia reminded herself it would be unjust to feel resentment over this since her daughter had plenty of grounds for hating her.

But Antonia's mind could not control her heart, and she felt not only resentment, but jealousy too.

Antonia admitted with shame to two types of jealousy of her elder daughter: envy when Sue was loved or admired by others; and jealousy whenever Sue had a happy relationship with someone. She knew it was unreasonable to be jealous of the new rapport between Sue and Carroll, but her 'beastly' side protested: 'Why can't she come to me for advice and understanding?'

Antonia also felt guilty that she would have liked her eldest daughter out of the nest. Although she was 'genuinely fond of Sue as a person' and at moments there was hardly anyone whose company she enjoyed more, she had to admit to herself that life was much easier when Sue was not at home.

One evening, after she had been home for about a month, Sue became really angry with Mother during a row over whether she should visit me at Cambridge where I had been living since leaving Headington before Christmas. Although Mother's knees were 'fairly trembling', she managed to keep calm, and told Sue she had two daughters, not one, whose interests she had to consider. Sue accused Mother of keeping her away from me. Then, according to Mother, Sue put on an air of being cool and detached 'but actually she was behaving exactly as in the nursery'. They finally agreed Tom and Carroll should be asked their opinions.

Once again my situation must have seemed idyllic to Sue. Living at Alice Roughton's in Adams Road I was away from home rule and not under the jurisdiction of any other authority. At Ashburn Gardens Sue could live free but under the emotional strain of close contact with a neurotic mother who was constantly nagging her about untidiness, extravagance and thoughtlessness. (Antonia, who was all these things, lived up to something she had written once about her father: 'Do we try to root out of our children our own faults while not appreciating their virtues?') Whereas at Oxford, although she was supported by a generous grant, every so often there was a heavy toll to pay: examinations.

Tom, who was much concerned about Sue, invited her out to dinner. He must have persuaded her tactfully not to visit me, for things calmed down between mother and daughter, and Antonia told Dorothy how sweet and helpful Sue had been to her over a painful eye.

About this time I came to London to be interviewed for a place on the Stage Production Course at the Old Vic Theatre School. I stayed at Ashburn Gardens. I had stayed there before, over Christmas, and it had not been a great success. Antonia had written afterwards that Sue had complained to her that they always quarrelled when I was there. Mother noted that if the three of us did something together Sue was 'apt to behave rather childishly and "spoil the party". I think she likes to keep me and Lyndall in separate compartments.'

Before my arrival Sue and Antonia had been close over the Christmas holidays. During the six months they had been apart while Sue was at Kolbsheim in Alsace, they had exchanged intense spiritual letters. And after Sue's return Antonia had felt Sue had a 'real love' for her, 'very anxious, almost protective'. Also there was strong sympathy between them, enhanced by an identical sense of humour. This meant that a new presence in their midst was like the arrival of a first baby in a marriage: the third who is thought to be welcome until it starts encroaching on territorial rights.

After my first visit Antonia had a dream about Tom which made her think about the relationship of another trio: Tom/herself/me. She felt Tom and she were afraid of each other because each knew the other's guilty secret: 'neither of us really love the child enough'. Any 'peculiar bond' they still had was not because of me, since, she maintained, he did not treat her as my mother, which made it harder for her to *feel* she was my mother in the way she felt she was Sue's: 'He treats my relation to Lyndall in the most *academic* way . . . no one, hearing him, could guess that he was the child's father talking to the child's mother.'

Things had gone a little better at Ashburn Gardens when I came for the Old Vic interview. Aged nearly seventeen, I was trying to communicate with my mother who was 'delighted' to find me more grown up and 'a real and attractive person'. She was also touched by my 'concern and perception' about Sue, whom I saw as someone being eaten up from inside. She wrote: 'I think she really is strong enough now not to be dominated by her & can help Sue a great deal.'

Antonia feared that Sue was going to hate her for the rest of her life. Both Dorothy and Dr Carroll told her that she must try to ignore any contempt Sue showed towards her and accept that her daughter was testing her to find out if she could trust her. But Antonia feared she might fail the test: 'After all, why *should* she trust me? How many times, consciously and unconsciously I have let her down, exploited her, hurt her.'

Carroll suggested Sue should leave home for a while so that she could decide on her own whether she wanted to return to Oxford. She went to stay in another part of London with a schoolfriend. Antonia imagined people secretly rejoicing and saying 'High time Sue got away from that dominating, possessive mother of hers.' Carroll told Antonia that if she felt she could treat Sue in a light, friendly way, he saw nothing against them seeing each other; so after a few days Antonia telephoned and invited her daughter for a drink. Sue accepted. They had a long talk in which Sue said that she had decided to write to Somerville to ask if they would take her back.

Thirty-six hours later, on Maundy Thursday, Sue turned up at Ashburn Gardens looking ill and all to pieces again. She said she could not bear the thought of returning to Oxford. She also asked if she could stay at Ashburn Gardens because her friend had gone away for Easter. Mother took her temperature, which was 101°F, and put her to bed. Dr Symes came to see Sue: according to Antonia, she wanted him to let her have her tonsils out, which he would not agree to. After a few days Antonia noted that 'the tearful child running home to its mother' was changing back to the 'icy, critical, patronising and superior young person'.

Lying awake in bed a few mornings later, Antonia had what she decided was an illumination about why Sue was 'only half-alive'. She had been ruminating over the fact that, despite two births and two abortions, she had never conceived a child in wedlock though she had had three husbands, and had been frightened of having children: 'But I did want Sue & went to considerable trouble to have her. But I wanted MY child – or Silas' child – not *the child God sent* . . . NOW I see . . . I have got to *have* Sue – the *real* Sue, not my "dream child".'

That evening she went to talk to Sue in bed, and managed with difficulty to refrain from revealing her flash of insight about her birth. Suddenly Mother said: 'I want you to choose whatever I possess that you like best and you shall have it.' After some hesitation Sue, to Mother's surprise, chose her Russian crucifix. When Mother handed it over, Sue said, 'I don't deserve it.' Mother kissed her and said, 'Nonsense.'

The next day Sue got up for the first time after her illness. She had a cup of tea waiting for Antonia when she got back from a Tertiary meeting.

But the evening of the following day things went wrong again, in the foyer of a theatre, when Mother took offence at something Sue said and lost her temper in public. When they got home she apologised for having behaved disgracefully; Sue told her, 'You are so inconsistent.'

A long conversation ensued, at the end of which Mother told Sue, 'I have to give up the two notions of you – the dream daughter who loves me, appreciates my work, tries to make my life easy, etc. and the burden daughter who's an expense, a nuisance, maddeningly uncooperative in the home and whom I wish would get herself a husband and get off my hands. But there is a real Susan who is a marvellous creature.'

Sue laughed. 'That's just maternal nonsense.'

My first reaction on reading in Antonia's notebooks about all these emotional exchanges between mother and daughter was of astonishment. Why did Mother, who realised it was a time when she must be tolerant and supportive of Sue, keep making scenes, sometimes merely because her vanity had been wounded? And why was Sue so rash as to keep provoking Antonia, for she must have known how easy it was to cause a storm of wrath, and I cannot believe she was impervious to the effects of our mother's flare-ups?

The principal of Somerville not only agreed to take Sue back, but to allow her an extra year to do the three-year degree course in Mediaeval History, deferring her first-year exams until the following spring. The two months Sue had been at home had proved what Antonia had already felt after the Christmas vacation: that prolonged periods together were a great strain on both of them, though she missed her after she left.

Antonia settled down to trying to write again. But after a while she realised she always seemed to have to have some human being round whom her thoughts hovered, uneasily; and now that Sue, like her predecessors, Tom, Frances, Basil, Benedicta etc., had fallen back into her right perspective, Antonia's obsessional thoughts began to hover round Dorothy, though she warned herself 'I must not take Dorothy into myself as a conscience or a censor.'

Since January, Antonia had had an arrangement with Dorothy that she could stay at Ashburn Gardens two nights a week to see her 'patients' in London. It had started off well with them being on the most affectionate terms, but at Whitsun there was a crisis when Antonia, who was staying with the Kingsmills at Binesfield, had a sinister dream about Dorothy: 'Dorothy's manner changed when I told it her.' Several weeks later she had a dream about Dorothy falling down the stairs. Shortly after that, she noted, the cat fell out of the window: it survived although her flat was on the fourth floor.

Antonia was also going through a religious crisis. This was caused mainly by the fact that working on *The Lost Traveller* brought to the surface all her resentment against her father for having complicated her life when he imposed Catholicism on her.

Her belief in some of the teachings of Meher Baba did not clash with her Catholicism; in fact many of the things he wrote about the tyranny of the ego impressed her.

One evening in July, puzzling over her faith in the kitchen while cooking dinner, Antonia found herself imploring Baba: 'Help me!' She wanted to know what was obstructing her from discovering, and doing, God's will. Suddenly into her head came the clear message: 'Give up smoking for twenty-four hours and you'll know the answer.'

So for the second time at Baba's instigation – 'But I asked Christ to help me' – Antonia gave up smoking for a while.

The next afternoon, at a tea party given by a couple she had met on a pilgrimage, Antonia was reminded how hard she found it to get on with bigoted Catholics. Suddenly she realised that they perceived things differently, and that perhaps her responsibility as an artist was to use her different 'consciousness' to write in a way that would help people to see things they had not seen before. Was this, she wondered, the answer Baba had promised for renouncing cigarettes for twenty-four hours?

But now Antonia was in a quandary over whether Baba represented God or was some figment of her imagination. She was also beginning to have some doubts about Dorothy. In the past she had been shocked when any of Hugh Kingsmill's friends had decried his wife. Now two of Antonia's Catholic acquaintances made a fierce verbal attack on Dorothy. She felt 'they would have burned her at the stake as a witch' and shut them up by telling them their accusations were wildly untrue and that she was not 'bewitched'.

But Antonia *was* uneasy about one aspect of Dorothy: at intervals Dorothy said she had unsolved problems of her own and thought she ought to have some more analysis herself, yet she never followed this up.

Money was a problem, too. Antonia had had no regular job since the war, and was living on her father's royalties, Tom's alimony and occasional freelancing, while trying to finish her novel. She was still always falling behind in paying bills, and getting into debt.

And another of her old faithfuls, sex, also came up often in her notes to Dorothy: 'I have forgotten what it feels like to be kissed. I think I miss it more than I realise: much more than the sex act.' And after an almost mystical dream, in which there were moments of 'bliss and burning desire', she confessed she had never realised just how strong a sexual nature she possessed. She felt if she were to be aware of it all the time as strongly as in the dream she would 'go mad if the desire weren't satisfied'.

On a hot afternoon in that summer of 1948, as Antonia lay on her bed, she suddenly perceived that an enormous part of the 'formidable array' of suffering in her life had been self-inflicted, and had even given her an excuse for not getting on with what she ought to have been doing: 'Pursuing suffering can be just as self-willed as pursuing joy.' She also decided that she had *lost* her faith when she became a Catholic; before that she had had a 'natural trust, cheerfulness and courage' which she had never regained: 'it was exactly like eating the tree of knowledge: the world was never the same again.'

She began to get into a state about what faith meant until she felt her head would burst and frantically implored light and help: 'I beseeched Baba, I beseeched Jesus, I beseeched St Paul.' She started having nightmares and headaches; insomnia at night, drowsiness by day.

One night she had a nightmare in which a young girl was murdered and her corpse mutilated with the genitals sewn up. She woke in a state of real horror as in the old days at Cecil Court. In the morning she telephoned Dorothy at Binesfield. Dorothy seemed offhand and asked her to write the dream down and send it to her rather than talk about it over the telephone. At the end of recording the nightmare, she made other notes for Dorothy which show that storm clouds were gathering. Antonia had begun to feel unsure of Dorothy's role: one moment she appeared to be on a pedestal, 'assuming the right to dictate', and the next she seemed a friend whose company Antonia greatly enjoyed and who talked 'very frankly and freely' of her own problems. It was an uncomfortable situation; she feared that if she broke off the analytical relation, as she was tempted to do, she would lose a friend.

The next day she wrote a diatribe against Dorothy. When she had calmed down, and knew her 'bursts of hatred' were largely unjustified, Antonia decided she loved Dorothy much more than she hated her.

In August Antonia had her severest crisis. Looking back she felt she had been in danger, because she had been in semi-cataleptic states and doing very 'peculiar' things under the influence of Baba: 'I think what saved my sanity was Lyndall's coming here and my having to nurse her through tonsillitis.'

I had just arrived to live under my mother's roof when this happened, having got a place at the Old Vic Theatre School, where I was to start in September. It was then I realised that I had been banished from my father's house, for Tom said I could not live at Cheyne Row while I was a student in London.

While unpacking my belongings in the tiny room which would become mine at Ashburn Gardens, I suddenly felt so ill that I knocked on my mother's bedroom door and, when she did not answer, walked in to her room – something I would never have dared to do if I had not been running a fever.

Mother looked very odd: she was lying on her back with her eyes open, staring at the ceiling. Later she told me why: she had been in a semi-trance having a mental colloquy with Baba. He had been 'telling' her that he was going to test her obedience to him: she was to go into the corridor outside her bedroom door, where the cat's tray lived, and eat a turd from it. After a battle in her mind – was it the will of God or of the devil that she should do this? – she had just decided she must fight down disgust and force herself to get up and perform this act, when I had burst into the room and flung myself on her mercy.

She put me to bed and called a doctor. My temperature was so high and my throat so inflamed that he feared I might have diphtheria. That night I was delirious and Mother came in to find me sitting on the edge of the bed weeping: my room had become a main thoroughfare with ceaseless traffic flowing through it so that I could not cross it to reach the door and go downstairs to the lavatory. She came with me: then she put me back to bed and sat with me, putting cold compresses on my fevered brow, holding my hand when my delirium set me off into those realms of terror she knew so well without needing a high temperature to send her there.

It turned out I had tonsillitis. For two weeks Antonia was so busy 'mothering' me that her dilemmas as to whether Dorothy represented good or evil, and whether Baba was God or the devil, faded into the background as she attended to my needs.

My illness seems to have been godsent for it broke down some of our awkwardness at being strangers in each other's lives, and set us off on the right foot now that we had to share a roof again. She said that, though she was especially tired and worried, she found she enjoyed looking after me, particularly as she felt I appreciated it: 'She needs a bit more "spoiling" & Sue considerably less.'

Sue had wisely taken to spending as little time as possible at Ashburn Gardens during the vacations and was abroad taking a summer course at Perugia. While she was there Mother dreamt that Sue turned up penniless from abroad expecting to be kept.

In fact a letter soon arrived from Sue in Italy, saying that she was running out of money but intended to stay on longer. Since there were currency restrictions, she had sold her return ticket home – 'vaguely hoping that a grant to study the art of the *Quattrocento* would arrive' – and asked Mother to send her a new one: but she forgot to enclose a cheque. So while Sue, unknown to Mother, was spending her ticket money on moving to Florence, Mother, who was in debt and over-drawn, was trying to scrape together enough to pay for a new ticket.

When Antonia received another letter a few days later, with a long 'essay' on the beauties of Florence, and a mere mention of the fact she had forgotten to enclose the cheque for the ticket she hoped was on its way, but still not enclosing it, Antonia was as amused as she was annoyed. She had to laugh that her daughter was behaving exactly as she did herself: enjoying something before knowing where the money to pay for it would come from.

Tom paid for Antonia to take me to Aldeburgh to convalesce after tonsillitis. Though I had appreciated her company and attention when I was ill, I felt apprehensive at the prospect of having to share a hotel room with her.

But our holiday went very well. Antonia came near to losing her temper only once – in the hotel restaurant when something she ordered had run out. We walked a lot, talked a lot, browsed in bookshops, had afternoon teas in quaint cafés, read and played dominoes. And when I discovered that she was as timid as I about following up an introduction Alice Roughton had given me to a close friend who lived in Aldeburgh, Benjamin Britten, I was amazed that my mother also suffered from shyness, and began to realise this person I had always feared as a monster was also a human being.

As our confidence in each other grew, though I was still unsure about revealing my innermost feelings to my mother, she told me what had been going on in the past months. She said she felt I had saved her sanity by turning up in need of nursing. Though I knew it had been mere chance, it pleased me to feel in some way important in my mother's life for the first time. I was surprised that Dorothy Kingsmill should be involved with an Indian guru who my mother thought had instructed her to eat cat shit. But Mother recounted the dramas of her life with such humour, that they always sounded absurd rather than sinister or tragic.

It is apparent from my mother's notebooks that after Aldeburgh she began to see herself as my mainstay, particularly as Sue now had Sheila as hers – for when she was not abroad in the vacations Sue spent much time at the Glossops, which soon aroused Mother's jealousy. And in some ways I was taking Sue's place, though I had no desire to fill the exclusive position my elder sister had always held with our mother, because I sensed it was not a warm place in the heart, but a cold area in the mind.

But perhaps what made my mother most well-disposed towards me in 1948 was that she suspected a crisis in my relationship with my father. When Tom had told me a year before that I could leave school if I could find somewhere to live other than Cheyne Row, because my moroseness upset Gerti, it had not altered my feelings for Tom; but Antonia had seen it as the beginnings of a breach between him and me, and told Dorothy shortly afterwards, 'No one's ever loved Tom as Lyndall loves him. Yet, *in effect,* he turned her out to please Gerti.'

Now that I had found favour with her, she wanted to be a champion for my rights with my father. She felt Tom gave me too small an allowance, particularly as it was half what he had originally promised me. Out of it I paid my mother rent for my board and lodging. My room was so tiny that there was only space for a bed and a desk. My clothes lived in a wardrobe in the corridor – next to the cat's tray. Any spending money I had left over, after paying my fares and tuition fees at the Old Vic School, was less than Sue had from Silas. I must admit I felt a certain envy for Sue's greater wealth, but more for her much larger room for which she paid no rent, particularly as it lay empty for so many months when she was at Oxford and away during the holidays. But I would never have dared to mention this, nor to ask Tom for a raise, and begged Mother not to do so on my behalf. She managed to refrain because she saw I did not want revenge on Tom for refusing me a home, and she felt that to attack him would hurt me: '& thank God there's one human creature I love without wanting to hurt'. She had noticed I was growing more confident and wondered whether this was because she now took me seriously.

Her only reference to Sue in those last months of 1948, other than a dream about her recorded on All Saints' day, was that it was the 'Silas part' of Sue, outwardly 'callous', but 'hypersensitive' underneath, which she found hard to understand: 'You play the drama with the father all over again with the child.'

But she did mention me again in connection with Gerti.

Antonia had always admitted envying Gerti some things, though having Tom as a husband was not one of them, for she thought him less interesting as a husband than as a lover. In fact, on the whole she felt sorry for her rather than envious, particularly as Gerti had been looking melancholy and 'muffled' for the past year or so, and seemed 'rather anxious, rather on edge'.

But now, in the autumn of 1948, there was a serious cause for envy beyond the old reasons – 'jewels, beautiful clothes, a nice house, etc. etc., whereas any old thing has been good enough for me and Lyndall' – which was that Gerti was expecting a second baby.

Antonia's and my feelings about this child reinforced what would become our strongest bond: mutual consolation. We both admitted we dreaded it being a boy: I because I feared a son would be more important to Tom than any daughter; Antonia because she had always wanted a son herself. It was then she told me – prefixing it with 'I shouldn't be telling you this, darling' – she had once aborted a male child before producing only daughters, and always regretted not having a son afterwards.

Gerti's second baby was born at the end of October, a girl called Amanda. Both mother and baby nearly died – Gerti from kidney trouble and Amanda from a blockage in her digestive system. During the days Gerti was on the danger list I could think of nothing else, and remembered with remorse how much I had detested her at times.

As the rush-hour tube train rattled me towards the Old Vic, I fought back tears as I recalled the pleasanter memories of her at Summer Cottage. I remembered with shame how unsympathetic I had been when, after Gerti had managed to get her mother out of Austria, Mrs Deutsch had committed suicide when living in a bed-sit in Oxford while I was not far away at Headington.

Gerti was too ill to be visited, so I could not go and throw myself down by her hospital bed to beg forgiveness for having been such a surly stepdaughter. It seemed she would die without knowing that I was in a strange way quite fond of her.

Gerti recovered, and Amanda grew into a pretty baby with blonde curls, but a light in Gerti's eyes that had been flickering before the child was even conceived, had now gone out. I would only know why much later.

Tom, who was worried about Gerti – although it turned out he was the cause of her melancholia – had sent her to see Dorothy Kingsmill some time before. But Gerti had not got on with her, and was now consulting a professional psychoanalyst.

After three months of co-habitation with my mother I was looking forward to Sue's return from Oxford at Christmas.

Antonia was a complicator of life who could not improvise. Her attempts to keep on an even keel meant she had to plan everything ahead and make lists. Every day the problem of the evening meal had to be discussed at breakfast so that she could make a list of what would be needed when she set off for the ritual of her daily shopping-round in the middle of every morning. Many a time I was late for the first lecture because Mother was still going on about our dinner menu – which was complicated still further by the fact that rationing had not yet ended completely – when I should already have been on my way to the Waterloo Road where the School was housed in the bomb-damaged Old Vic Theatre.

I never found a tactful way to make my mother understand that not only did I not expect an evening meal to be cooked for me, but would far rather have prepared something for myself when I came home. However I phrased it, any such suggestion was taken as an affront. She had got it into her head she had to cook me an evening meal and nothing would change her mind, although she often complained bitterly about the chore. Was it her way of expiating past neglect? Or was it that her self-pitying side wallowed in seeing herself as a martyred mother who every evening had to abandon her role of being an author and leave her desk in order to cook a meal for a daughter?

The sad thing was I could never enjoy a meal cooked by my mother because most of it was spent in calming down her fraught nerves after the tension of cooking. The best way was to repeat endlessly how good the food was, which was often true, and then listen attentively to exactly how each dish had been prepared. Not to have praised it would have been taken as a criticism. If something had gone wrong in the kitchen, like the collapse of a soufflé, or lumps in the gravy, the whole of dinner time could be a thoroughly wretched experience.

Then came the washing-up. Like laying the table before dinner, it was my job. When it was done, I prepared a tray of tea the way my mother wanted it done: *not* too much water in the kettle, *not* too much tea in the pot (which had to be warmed *not* by pouring in boiling water, but by putting it into the plate warmer); half, *not* a full jug of milk; the pink cups, *not* the green ones, taking care that one was *not* chipped. How I missed the carefree atmosphere of Adams Road.

Then I would carry the tea-tray up to Antonia's work-room. There she either talked about her life or mine, or read aloud what she had written that day of *The Lost Traveller*, on which she had started working again that autumn. When she read her work I was very aware that I was not the audience she wanted; in the way Ian Henderson had not been able to fill Tom's role, I could not fill Sue's. As with her cooking, not to praise was taken as criticism; but to criticise was impertinent. So I preferred the evenings when there was conversation. We would talk about her past and my future, or puzzle over why Tom had changed and why Gerti seemed so depressed, or her perplexities over something Sue or Dorothy had done, or just moan over our hopeless financial situations. On and on went the endless chewing of cud, as Mother lit-up one cigarette after another until I felt I could bear no more. By ten o'clock I was exhausted. 'Just one more ciggie, then you *must* go to bed, pet,' she would say; but I would have to watch at least five more cigarettes turn into stubs before we actually parted around midnight.

As a student of stage production, it was a pleasant duty to have to see as many plays as possible. We were often given unsold tickets very cheaply at the last minute at many theatres, but we never knew ahead of time whether we would get them or not. This made it difficult when I set off in the morning to plan whether I would be back in the evening and at what time. After having had to telephone a couple of times to say I would not be in for dinner after all, when Mother had already done the shopping, and having received such a blast of indignant rage about my inconsiderateness that I would continue to shake long after I had put down the receiver, I often said at breakfast that I would not be coming home for dinner, even if I did not yet know whether I would be going to a theatre or not.

The result was that I would sometimes find myself at a loose end in the evening, and ready to come home around dinner time after all. This created such a drama about there not being anything cooked for me to eat that I learned the easiest way for a quiet life was not to make an early appearance on those occasions. Rather than roam the streets or linger in some sordid café, I came home and sat on the stairs outside the flat door, doing my homework and eating a sandwich and an apple, until I heard no more bustling around and knew it was safe to creep up to my room.

Although I got on with most of my twenty fellow students, one of whom was Sandy Wilson who later wrote *The Boy Friend*, I did not have nearly as much social life with them in the evenings as I pretended to my mother. I would never have dared to invite a fellow student back to Ashburn Gardens even for a cup of coffee, and could not afford to eat out with them in the evening, so I was lonely during my first term as a student, which made me look forward even more anxiously to Sue's return from Oxford.

But in fact I did not see much of her during the Christmas vacation because we had both taken our first holiday jobs: hers was in the evenings as a dresser for a leading lady in a sort of pantomime on ice; mine in the mornings, charring at 1s 9d an hour for the family of the actor Dennis Price.

After Sue returned to Oxford for the spring term of 1949 Mother twice dreamt that I was unhappy. Then, just before waking one morning she had such a vivid image of me lying back across my bed looking very ill that she woke up almost sure it had happened in real life and began to worry about me. She decided my troubles must be connected with Tom: 'Thank goodness he has raised her pocket money. But it is ages since he has taken her out alone which is her greatest treat.'

Mother noted that a few nights before she had heard me lock my bedroom door after returning from having dinner with Tom and Gerti. When she had asked me in the morning, 'Do you always lock your door at night?' I had answered: 'No. I don't remember doing it.'

Of course I knew I had locked my door that evening. Lies, lies. I had not wanted Mother to peep round the door before going to bed to enquire how the evening at Cheyne Row had gone. There were some things I just did not want to discuss with my mother: a student from the acting course, with whom I thought I was in love, was one of them; Gerti was another.

Over dinner at Cheyne Row I had sensed again how deeply unhappy and discontented Gerti had become, and was beginning to suspect my father was partly to blame, for there was a terribly strained atmosphere between them. Since living with Mother, I had learnt a lot about my father's past, and had been shocked to hear that he had been unfaithful to both his wives on several occasions, which made me see him in a new light. It also made me see Gerti differently: she was no longer the possessive outsider who had captured Tom's love and taken some away from me, but the wronged woman, a stranger in a foreign land, who was suffering from a far greater loss of love than I had ever had to bear.

I did not want to confess my sudden fondness and concern for my stepmother because, if one confided anything to Antonia in a moment of easy intimacy, there was often a penalty to pay later: in this case I feared she would build up jealousy in the way she had over Sheila and Sue. The more I lived at Ashburn Gardens, the more I nurtured a secret part of me, and I would tell any lie and act out any deception to protect it.

Antonia finished The Lost Traveller early in 1949, but the completion of her second novel seventeen years after Frost in May had not brought the relief and release she had hoped for. There had been no 'immediate response' from anyone; neither Tom nor Eric had even asked to read it; and, although she told herself it was silly and childish, she minded: 'If I'm so bloody except for my work & people don't even care enough to want to see the work, it makes me feel awful.'

Since it would be a year before the novel was published, Antonia needed work while contemplating a third novel. She agreed to do some reviewing for the *New Statesman*, and undertook to translate Maupassant's *Une Vie*. (She later won the Prix Clairouin for this translation, and it was the beginning of a profession as a translator from French that would mainly support Antonia for the last third of her life.)

At this time relations were strained between Antonia and Dorothy, who, in December, had told Antonia that on her side the analysis was over and the 'third part' was for Antonia to deal with alone. This meant that Dorothy's turn as one of Antonia's 'obsessional' figures – 'by this I mean the people who "haunt" me' – was over.

The vacancy was soon filled: by the end of March 1949 Antonia admitted that Sue had become the haunter of her mind again and that she was envious of her, not just for her height and slenderness – 'I even feel it's unfair she should be so slim, for she eats more than I do' – but because she had everything paid for her, 'clothes and holidays and a very decent allowance just for pocket money'. When people told Antonia how beautiful and distinguished Sue looked, she felt it implied that she herself was common. She criticised Sue for treating Oxford as 'a playground' and thought she had become vain and snobbish since going there.

Just after writing the above Antonia became fifty. She admitted to being 'awfully childish' in thinking people ought to make a feast of her birthday, which of course they did not: 'It is silly to mind it but oh, I do, I do.'

She and I celebrated it alone, taking each other out to dinner because we were both too broke to pay for two.

Sue was away. She was spending part of her Easter vacation working backstage on an OUDS production of *Richard II* which was touring France. On the tour she fell in love with the person who would revolutionise her life, a fellow undergraduate a couple of years older than she, and who wanted to be a novelist: Thomas Chitty.

When she returned, Mother found her 'sweet and human and delightful' and easy to live with.

But a week later Mother changed her tune, and said Sue was as 'inconsiderate, difficult, rude and completely self-centred' as before, and complained she left all the housework to us and that Sue's room was 'more wildly untidy' than ever. Mother also noted that Sue had developed a mania for buying clothes and thought she was luring me into spending more than I could afford.

My new role of good daughter was an uncomfortable one, particularly as I felt much closer to Sue than to Mother. If Sue's presence meant a bit of extra washing up it was a price I paid willingly for the pleasure of having her around. I did not need my elder sister to lure me into spending more than I could afford, for I too had inherited extravagance from our mother. I used to feel excluded on those occasions when Mother and I sat eating *à deux* in the dining-room, unable to ignore the laughter of Sue and her friends in the adjoining room. Even when Sue invited me to join them, I dared not stay long, for I sensed that Antonia was jealous of the affection between us – as she was of our attachment to Sheila, who was becomingly increasingly important in both our lives as things became stormier at Ashburn Gardens.

On 15 May 1949 Hugh Kingsmill died, leaving Dorothy with no money to bring up their three children. Before dying, rather surprisingly, he had asked Tom to help his wife and, unknown to Gerti or Antonia, Tom now began partly to support Dorothy. Antonia and Dorothy's relationship changed to that of tenant/landlady: Antonia feared Dorothy might resent this unconsciously, since she had never asked to be paid for 'analysis'. Soon there was open hostility between them over Binesfield.

There had been times recently when Antonia wished she could get rid of Binesfield. A month before Hugh's death she had felt pangs at seeing it go downhill in other people's hands, but she did not have the money to restore it, nor to pay the labour to keep up the garden: 'Yet if I just cut loose and sold it, I would feel guilty.' And anyway, she noted, her father by leaving Binesfield in trust had virtually forced the house on her by making it difficult to dispose of freely. Suddenly it struck her that the cottage represented herself, 'forcibly converted' by her father and not altogether suiting her nature.

After Hugh's death Antonia thought Dorothy was becoming proprietary about the cottage, although she soon gave it up. Having told Antonia how much she loved Binesfield, and how sorry 'little Dorothy' – her youngest child who was around Nicolette's age of seven – was that they were leaving, she said Antonia ought to move there. And when Antonia explained she would be too lonely living at the cottage, Dorothy said she was prepared to come down at weekends.

As Antonia was writing about Dorothy and Binesfield, her handwriting began to go haywire, changing to a spiky and erratic calligraphy sprawling over the page, a sure sign that 'the beast' was lurking:

> Poor Dorothy has no husband and a *very* insecure position. I have no husband & also an insecure position. BUT . . . I own the cottage. To Dorothy, therefore, *my* position must seem very enviable. And she may well feel that morally I owe her money which I certainly feel myself.

Here she paused to ring up Dorothy and tell her she would let her off the rent until she left Binesfield in a few weeks' time, having decided that morally and psychologically it was the best thing to do. Then she picked up her pen again and continued in a more recognisable hand:

> We must try & live in some sort of reasonable harmony & be decent to each other and patient with our own & each other's faults. I'm so terribly lucky to be a Catholic. I've no EXCUSE for making such a lot of fuss.

Antonia now questioned her motives for ever having become involved with Dorothy. She decided they were all offshoots of her morbid preoccupation with self: 'VANITY!' ranked highest because she had been flattered when Dorothy showed an interest in her; then the need for a friend because of being 'too weak' to put up with loneliness.

Dorothy, who was not a trained analyst, should perhaps not have taken on someone with a case history like Antonia's. Yet, however unorthodox her methods, she had fulfilled her promise of getting Antonia writing again. Nonetheless, *The Lost Traveller* was dedicated to Hugh, not Dorothy, Kingsmill.

Although Antonia's relationship with Dorothy was deteriorating, Meher Baba still came into her thoughts and dreams. By July 1949, however, by which time she had seen Dorothy for almost the last time, she had decided to 'honour him as a holy man' but to have 'no master but Jesus Christ'.

Baba's photograph disappeared from the bedside table, leaving Padre Pio alone to keep watch over my mother's sleeping hours; but Baba is occasionally mentioned in later notebooks, always with respect. If Antonia had put into practice just one sentence of his – 'God cannot be explained, God can only be lived' – she would have spared herself thirty more years of mental wranglings over such problems as whether the story of Adam and Eve was literal or mythical – dilemmas which at times stirred up such a climax of confusion in her mind that they nearly drove her out of it again.

While Sue was away for the summer term at Oxford, Antonia's attitude to her calmed down. With Dorothy less on her mind, she decided her attitude to Sue was her next problem to work out, particularly her jealousy of Sue with Sheila. Although Sheila had 'interposed herself and made Silas perform his obligations to Sue', Antonia felt she had not managed to create 'a real father-daughter thing' between Silas and Sue, but instead had become a kind of 'rival mother'. However, Antonia admitted she was possessive, and had traits she deplored in Benedicta and Dorothy: 'I like "casting a spell" on people, am very ready to advise them, & also like to isolate people in a special relation with me.' She wanted to come first with everyone without obligations, and acknowledged that, though she was at times kind and generous, she could be 'exceedingly cruel' if someone tried to escape from her clutches. She also admitted her children had always had only the 'pickings and leavings': 'The love that should have been *first* for my children has by-passed them, or come through only in a thin, intermittent trickle and flowed freely on to others who had no claim on me.' Antonia resolved to be 'more of a *father*' to Sue and 'a *mother*' to me.

But however many times Antonia gave herself sound advice, she never seemed able to take it. She was continuously dynamiting her good intentions, as if there were a mad terrorist hidden inside her who did not want her, or anyone near her, to have a peaceful existence.

At the beginning of the summer vacation, Sue suggested we spend a few days in Paris. As Tom had just given me £5 for my eighteenth birthday, I was overjoyed at the suggestion and did some charring to earn the rest of the money needed.

It turned out we were a foursome, Thomas Chitty and his younger brother, Michael, came too. We found a small hotel off the Boulevard St Germain and took the two cheapest double rooms. After the first night, our thoughtful elders arranged for Michael and me to move into the quieter room, which had been Sue's and mine, because Michael had always been frail since a serious illness in childhood, and I still suffered from occasional migraines. For the rest of our nights in Paris, Michael and I lay primly in bed sniggering about our older siblings thinking us so stupid that we did not know exactly what they were up to in theirs. (Except, it turned out later, they hadn't been!)

Antonia was envious that Sue and I had been to Paris together, and that our fathers, '*les Papas*', gave us allowances that contributed towards such treats. As always happened when Sue and I were together at Ashburn Gardens, she found more fault with us. From what Mother wrote on 8 August, shortly after our return, we sound like three harpies playing two off against the third:

> [Sue] is jealous of me with Lyndall & of Lyndall with me: she likes to keep us apart & separately 'allied' to her . . . she admitted that Lyndall complains of me to her but was obviously surprised to hear that L. complains of her to me, though she knows Lyndall is a chronic complainer. Lyndall is affectionate and treacherous; she is more subtly selfish than Sue.

I wanted to get away from the oppressive atmosphere at Ashburn Gardens. I had finished my one-year course at the Old Vic and knew it was going to be hard to find a job in the theatre, and that my secret dream of being a playwright or scriptwriter might never be realised. It occurred to me that the best way of getting work in that world might be to become a director's secretary/assistant, although I had always detested the idea of being a secretary. To make the pill less bitter to swallow, I went to Cambridge to take a cheap secretarial course at the Polytechnic, thus finding a way of living under Alice's roof again.

While living at Adams Road, a very distant cousin who was studying engineering at Trinity College, started to taunt me ceaselessly: a virgin at eighteen, what was wrong with me? He was the product of a co-ed boarding school and assured me that no girl over fifteen, unless she was abnormal, had not had an affair. His teasing, off-hand manner began to intrigue me and I found myself noticing if he was not one of the many people round the kitchen table at meal-times, and feeling twinges of jealousy when he flirted with a pretty French girl who had come for a visit. After some weeks, by which time I was suffering from his disdain and mistook it for love, I did not put up much resistance when he felt the time was ripe to do me the favour of putting an end to what he considered my contemptible state of maidenhood.

I had always imagined this would be a cataclysmic moment, and that afterwards everything would be changed. But of course neither of us changed overnight. He continued to treat me with disdain, which hurt more now because I felt we ought to be close; I continued to be unsure of myself and also lived in terror of getting pregnant. After a short while I wanted to put an end to our love-making which I was not enjoying.

The outcome had a grotesque poetic justice. He fell in love with me. Weeping, he begged me not break off the affair. He decided the reason I did not love him was because he was not interested in the arts as I was, and he took to reading Donne and the metaphysical poets instead of spending his spare time rebuilding his old car. But the more he tried to please me, the less I responded.

About the time I lost my virginity in the late autumn of 1949, Antonia received an unexpected £500 grant from the Royal Literary Fund. She was overjoyed and grateful because this not only enabled her to get back to her own writing, and to pay off her most pressing debts, but, she felt, 'symbolised a pardon of some kind: an official permission from Society to go on writing'.

She started work on a novel which was to be about 'Tom-Eric', but by February 1950 had given up because she felt it was 'rather indecent' to write about ex-husbands who had remarried.

Eric had recently married a young journalist, Georgina Horley, with whom Tom had been in love during the war. Their marriage was a considerable blow to Antonia because she lost the undivided support of the one person who had always been behind her, although she liked Georgie and it had been she who had introduced them. The blow was made crueller by the knowledge that it was her own fault she had lost Eric: at the beginning of the war, before her return to the Church, Eric had proposed they should get married again, and she had turned him down, not because of Ian Henderson, but because she had still hoped for a normal marriage one day.

Antonia decided instead to write a continuation of *The Lost Traveller* which would be appearing very shortly. After it came out she noted: 'My talent both attracts and repels people: this is astonishingly clear from the notices of *The Lost Traveller*.' But Antonia was more perplexed than distressed by the contradictions of the critics in their reception of *The Lost Traveller*, and felt that, in spite of some bad reviews, it might establish her as a writer. She even dared to hope it might bring her money and success.

Although no money had yet come in from the book, by July she had spent £110 redecorating her room and Sue's and buying a new stair carpet; hoping royalties from the book would pay for it. And, counting more chickens before they hatched, she also gave up her only source of earned income by resigning from writing book reviews for the *New Statesman*.

There were more reviews of *The Lost Traveller* but she was proud of having stood up quite well to many very 'misunderstanding and even insulting' ones. Over twenty years later, after re-reading bits of it, Antonia decided that some of her second novel was quite good, and some dreadfully bad.

That summer Sue came of age. I was amazed at her daring to ask Mother to give a twenty-first birthday party for her. It took place at Binesfield, which was rented again, but there was a clause in the new tenant's lease that Antonia could have the use of the cottage every August. Thomas and some other Oxford friends of Sue's stayed overnight at the cottage; Silas and Sheila drove down from London. The party went surprisingly well; though the next day there were the inevitable recriminations over the clearing up. But not long after Mother wrote that Sue was the person with the most power to make her unhappy because of a 'ruthless determination to have her own way'.

Sue came into £400 on her birthday – money from an insurance policy for which first Tom, then Silas and Antonia, had paid annual premiums since she was small. (I would receive the same amount when I reached twenty-one.) Antonia must have felt twinges of envy, particularly as her finances were heading towards disaster because she had spent far more than *The Lost Traveller* had brought in.

Just before Sue returned to Oxford to start her fourth and last year, I came back to live at Ashburn Gardens to look for a job. The secretarial course had ended and I wanted to get away from my lover in Cambridge. Of course I did not tell Mother about my affair, but I wanted to confide in Sue. I assumed she was having an affair with Thomas, but when I asked her what she did about birth control, I was firmly told that she and Thomas did not make love. This piece of news astounded me, and I decided I had better not divulge my secret to her after all.

Through Tom's good offices, a friend of his from Pembroke days, with whom he had once shared lodgings, gave me my first job as his secretary. To celebrate the Festival of Britain which would take place the following year, Bernard Miles was building a theatre in his garden in St John's Wood, to be called 'The Mermaid Theatre' in memory of Shakespearian times. It was to be inaugurated with a production of

Dido and Aeneas with Kirsten Flagstad in the leading role. My main task was to type hundreds of personal letters, each one different, he was writing to ask for funds to finance his project. But although I met many interesting people who came to the Miles's house, I did not enjoy the job, partly because of my shyness and partly because I felt being a secretary was humiliating. The salary was minimal, but luckily Tom continued to give me a reduced allowance.

Antonia felt very low that autumn and winter and in a very touchy state because her writing was going badly. She gave an example of how 'absurdly touchy' she could be in her notebook. She had gone to a stationer's to buy a ruled block and been told by the assistant, 'You don't get good quality paper in lined blocks.' She had taken this as an insult and retorted, 'So you don't condescend to supply paper for professional writers.' Afterwards she had wondered why she had been 'so childishly furious'.

What was really worrying her was not whether the texture of the paper was suitable for a professional writer, but whether she *was* a professional writer. She had begun to fear that her own writing was unprofessional and that she was perhaps more suited to translating.

Besides writing, the problem of money was getting even more desperate. In November she wrote: 'Here I am not knowing how to get to the end of the year and pay the rent, let alone my debts.'

Antonia's anxiety came out in her dreams. It was at this time she started having what would become a recurring one over the next few years: her 'packing dream'. In it she would be packing against time and trying to find the things she needed for the journey. There were variations on the theme, but it nearly always had a sexual accompaniment which added a further difficulty by distracting her from the packing as she fought off having an orgasm. After several pages mulling over her first packing dream in the hope of finding a clue to solving her real-life problems ('What does "packing" mean? A choice between essentials and inessentials') she wrote, 'Oh, dear Lord, please help me out. I just don't seem able to manage.'

Although I was living again as a paying lodger under my mother's roof, I was beginning to have a life of my own in London. On New Year's Eve I had gone to a party given by a Cambridge acquaintance, Christopher Layton, the youngest son of the proprietor of the *News Chronicle*, and had dined afterwards with a group of people I would now see often. Among them were Hugo Philipps, the son of Rosamond

Lehmann; Francis Haskell, now an eminent art historian; Mark Boxer, the future cartoonist; Ian Murray, considered by his tutor Noel Annan to be either a genius or mad; Peter Dixon, a handsome hedonist whose life would be happier than any of ours because he could take work lightly and pleasure seriously; and Simon Raven, who would later put us all, barely disguised, into his novels. The only other girl was Margaret Heathcote, with whom several men were in love, for not only was she brainy enough to have been at Cambridge, but so beautiful that she would shortly win the *Vogue* contest to become a top model.

But the one who interested me most was called Richard Horsfall Temple Muir. He was nearly thirty and had just come down from King's College, where he had been an ex-service student reading languages, and was now setting up a magazine publishing business. Soon I had fallen in love with him.

Antonia, too, had a new acquaintance in her life at the beginning of 1951. This was Edward Thornton, a psychologist. She found him easy to talk to and poured out the story of her life, including the recent Benedicta and Kingsmill 'business'. He talked about the unconscious male side of women which could become 'diabolical' when a woman is too animus-ridden; and suggested Dorothy's having broken off with Antonia so abruptly might be explained by Jung's theory that no one can take a person further in analysis than they have gone themselves. Reflecting on her own animus and anima – 'I obviously represented both son and daughter to my father' – Antonia wondered whether much of her trouble was not connected with her animus which, she suspected, was 'the sort of chap' her father would have disliked.

Not long afterwards she saw Tom whose animus/anima had for so many years been entangled with her own. They met by chance at a friend's house. When she told him about some of the things that had happened between Dorothy and her, he listened with a 'reserved smile', and soon found an excuse to leave. It suddenly dawned on her he was not just still seeing Dorothy, but must be considerably involved with her.

Even now, twelve years after their divorce, her unconscious would not let go of Tom: that evening she dreamt she was to remarry him, but he kept putting it off. A few nights before she had dreamt she was going to have his baby.

Antonia was still struggling to finish her third novel, and turning down offers of translations although she badly needed the money. At this stage, to judge from the sporadic jottings in her notebook early in 1951, the novel which would become *The Sugar House* was to recount far more of her life-story than it eventually did, including something she would never in fact put into any book: the abortion she had had soon after coming out of the asylum.

In the middle of February she had such a bad attack of conjunctivitis that it stopped her working on the book for more than a week. When her eyes were a little better she wrote in her notebook that she thought the first abortion was worrying her, not just because she had committed a grave sin, but also because it brought up all the other times she had hurt and disappointed her father, and the times he had injured her.

Two weeks later she was in severe trouble with the book. She had even tried sitting in her father's chair at her desk, which had been his, but that caused a new dilemma: while telling herself she must not feel guilt over being different from her father, was she now trying to be too like him? 'My poor father,' she wrote, 'I am sure he never meant to become such a terrible imago in my mind.'

'The beast' was coming out of its lair, and the danger of breaking down she always ran into when writing about her father was looming again, but she struggled on with *The Sugar House*. In March she wrote: 'It is important I do not break down for Sue's sake as well.'

It was Sue who broke down. Her final examinations were approaching. She took an overdose of compound codeine tablets one morning and was found, semi-conscious, by Thomas Chitty when he called to collect her from her digs. While her stomach was being pumped out in hospital, Antonia and Silas rushed to Oxford to be at her bedside.

Family Ruptures

*However unsatisfactory a mother, I am a mother – and
a mother of two daughters, not just one.*
Antonia White, 27 July 1954

Sue had come home from the hospital in a strangely zombie-like state. After she had been at Ashburn Gardens about a week, I went into her room one evening, because she had not answered Mother's call to dinner, and found her sitting on the bed, staring blankly out of the window. She did not even turn her head when I came in. Beside her was a pair of scissors and on the floor next to the bed lay two lacerated ends of the cord of her electric fire. Luckily it was not plugged in.

Antonia at once telephoned Carroll who said Sue must go into the Maudsley Hospital immediately.

In May Antonia wrote that, though she had managed to behave with unnatural calm and efficiency since Sue's breakdown, she was developing as disturbed a state of mind as her daughter:

> The two of us obviously terribly tied together in this. She has this breakdown at the time most critical for her & for me: her finals: my book. She attempts to destroy herself and, in a sense, me too. Yet neither time does she succeed.

It was a tough time for Antonia. Besides Sue's breakdown, two other things had given her severe shocks. Eric, to whom she owed money, had used 'almost blackmailing' methods to get her to give him the £50 she had put aside for the rent: 'The old Eric would never have behaved like that. He has repudiated me all right.' And on the day she learnt that Tom and Dorothy were lovers she had the 'worst bad turn' she had suffered for a very long time.

A few months before Tom had been sacked from *Picture Post* over a question of principle. He had refused to withdraw a controversial article by James Cameron which exposed the brutal treatment of prisoners by both sides in the Korean War. Being at home all day had put an even greater strain on his marriage to Gerti, who now discovered how seriously involved he was with Dorothy Kingsmill. He rented a small flat to write in, but after a short while moved out of Cheyne Row completely. He then exchanged the small flat for a larger one, and Dorothy Kingsmill moved in with him.

Sue was still in the Maudsley, but Mother no longer crossed London almost daily to see her because the doctors had decided it would be better if she stopped visiting her for a while. It was an alarming time: Sue's psychiatrist was considering the use of shock treatment if they could not haul her out of her depression by other means. Mercifully it never came to that.

As always in times of crisis, Antonia was thrown into a frenzy of self-examination and producing a fine array of dreams, in which marriage and partnership were the prevalent theme. Was her unconscious telling her there was a danger of trying to make Sue this partner, she asked herself?

Antonia began to feel that Silas and Sheila were her 'worst nag' over Sue; partly because they did not acknowledge the importance of Sue's spiritual side, but mainly because she was jealous of them: 'I know I am wrong in wanting Sue's affection to be too much focused on me,' she wrote, but it did not alter the fact that this was exactly what she still wanted.

She decided she must see Silas alone, and succeeded, though it meant asserting herself against Sheila: 'I am so conscious that she has done a great deal for Sue and means very well.' Although Silas was much changed since she had first known him, and was now an executive of Mowlems, the engineering firm, wearing a bowler-hat to work, they managed to talk in a very natural and friendly way, and she was relieved to find how much he loved and appreciated Sue.

Antonia's state worsened as the incessant pressure in her head increased. On 5 June she wrote: 'This morning cried uncontrollably in the street. First time. I can see no way out of the impasse. I cannot work: the book is due on June 30th: I have nothing for rent or the quarterly bills.'

In mid-June Sue came back from the Maudsley, although she was still in an apathetic and melancholy state.

It was oppressive living with two such depressed people, even though I was not around much. Apart from my job by day, I was out several evenings a week, for I had by now started an affair with Dicky Muir, though Mother and Sue did not know of course. When I was in the flat I did my best to cheer them up, but with little success.

One night I invited them to come to the theatre with me. An opera by Gian Carlo Menotti, *The Consul*, was the talk of London, and with difficulty I had managed to get cheap tickets. But, although the story and music were very moving and left a deep impression on me, it was not an opera to quicken the down-hearted. Every time I glanced to see if Sue was all right, her pale, expressionless face made me realise what an unhappy choice of entertainment I had made.

But not long after our outing, I came home from work to find Sue had risen from the world of the half-dead and had suddenly become communicative. After a few days she was positively cheerful. Mother seemed as pleased as I was and the atmosphere at Ashburn Gardens was bearable again.

The following Saturday Mother set off for a Children of Mary meeting at Roehampton – she had been going to them since becoming a tertiary – knowing that when she came back Sue and I would have gone to the Glossops, where we had been invited for dinner.

If ever Mother was out when I was at home, I used to take the opportunity to play the piano, since there was no fear of disturbing her. I had not been able to resist buying a piano score of *The Consul* and was dying to see if any of the arias that had been haunting me had easy accompaniments. I had found one I could sight-read, and was beginning to learn it, when Sue came in and sat beside me. We were in full throat in the middle of Magda's lilting aria 'Yes, yes, yesterday' when Mother burst into the room. She had mistaken the date of the meeting and made the journey to Roehampton in vain. Seeing us two sisters happily singing together was apparently more than she could bear.

She grabbed Domina, the over-fed cat who had never been out of doors – except for the time she fell out of the window – and set off down the stairs with Domina under her arm, murmuring, 'No one cares about me except the poor puss-cat.'

The flat door slammed behind her. We were sure she would come straight back, but she didn't. We went to look out of the window, just in time to see her small figure disappearing down Harrington Gardens with the fur bundle struggling in her arms. We looked at each other aghast: Was this serious? Might she be heading for the river as in the Tom days?

We telephoned the Glossops. 'Now don't you worry, Lynnie!' Silas reassured me. 'Tony isn't going to harm herself. She'll come home as soon as she realises what a damn fool she's being. The best thing is for you and Sue to come straight over and we'll have dinner as planned.'

Relieved that we need not worry, Sue went to run herself a bath and get changed, and I went back to playing the piano. Suddenly I heard footsteps on the stairs and called Sue. Mother walked past us looking demented. Her arms were bloody from scratches but she was reassuring the petrified cat she loved only it in the world. I plucked up all my courage to ask, 'But Mother, what's the matter?' She seemed not to hear and went over to a cupboard and began ferreting around until she found a cat-basket. She shoved the protesting Domina into it and set off downstairs again, ignoring my second question, 'Where are you going, Mother?'

As she was about to go out of the flat door something made Mother look up suddenly. She turned round, and rushed back upstairs. She went straight to the bathroom which was above the stairs. We followed. The room was flooded and water was pouring over the edge of the bath-tub. As she turned off the taps, she bellowed, 'Susan, *your* doing I presume!'

The old Antonia was back in full force. The three of us spent the next ten minutes mopping up the bathroom floor while Domina yowled furiously from inside the basket. Then Antonia liberated her ally, made herself a cup of tea and went up to her work-room and shut the door without addressing a further word to us.

Sue and I left for the Glossops, walking all the way to Sloane Square, for it was a balmy summer evening.

Silas gave us each a glass of wine and put on a record of a Mozart horn concerto. From the kitchen came the smell of the excellent dinner Sheila was preparing for us. The flat was flooded with sunlight and through the open window we could see the sun setting. With the Glossops everything seemed so pleasant and easy. Why, I pondered sadly, did our mother, now locked in angry solitude, resent Sue and me enjoying ourselves with people who were prepared to take trouble that we should? It was her difficult nature, I told myself, not other people's animosity, that excluded her from such pleasures.

I feared that when we got back into Mother's firing range, Sue's new-found equilibrium might get a direct hit which would send her spiralling downwards again. But by the next morning Antonia had snapped out of her ill-humour; and Sue's spirits continued to rise until she reached a state of euphoria. I did not yet know about the behaviour of manic depressives, but was soon to learn.

Thomas Chitty, after getting his degree, had come to live in London, set on being a writer. To exist, he took a job working the big dipper at the Battersea Fun Fair, part of the Festival of Britain which had just begun. He had found a room in, of all places, Cecil Court, which had become a vast lodging house with rooms of all sizes and prices for rent. On the ground floor, a teak panel where the names of the tenants had been written in gold lettering, still bore the words 'Mr and Mrs H. T. Hopkinson' alongside Flat 18; and anyone passing the landing of the fifth floor could not ignore the life-sized fresco painted by Joan Soutar-Robertson in the 1930s, for the front door of No. 18 was always open now, exposing a naked Antonia and Tom wearing only a fig-leaf.

Now she was better, Sue also found a job in Battersea Park, looking after the animals at the little zoo attached to the Fair. When she was not at work she went on wild spending benders with what was left of her birthday £400, and her already untidy room was soon overflowing with new clothes and accessories.

It never occurred to me at the time, but looking back I find it odd, that, although Sue was now earning the same as I was, and had the same allowance from Silas that I had from Tom, Mother never expected her to contribute to the household expenses as I had to. This seems particularly incongruous, since Mother never ceased telling us her finances were in disarray and begging us not to leave on unnecessary lights, and not to talk too long on the telephone because she did not know how she was going to meet the next quarter's bills.

The last Saturday in July Sue moved out of Ashburn Gardens. A week after she left Antonia wrote over a thousand words in her notebook about Sue, describing how she had gone from apathy to wild high spirits: 'a crescendo of insolence, extravagance, endless demands . . . until I said if she could not behave reasonably she had better go off on her own.'

Sue had found a room to rent. History was repeating itself: she was living in Cecil Court, near an aspiring writer whom she loved called Thomas. She still made quick visits to Ashburn Gardens to pick up things she needed for her bed-sit, telephoning first in the hope Mother might be out; and if she was not, trying to sound 'grown-up and off-hand'.

Antonia's long dissertation about Sue that 3 August 1951 included some reflections about Thomas Chitty:

> Thomas is mild and gentle but he is, I think, every bit as selfish as she is ... he seems absolutely hypnotised by her & looks fathoms in love. But I think she is more dependent on him than he is on her.

Near the end of this essay on Sue, Antonia admitted to being afraid of how much of Sue was like her: 'I suppose I oughtn't to try and judge her.'

But Antonia would continue to judge her elder daughter for many years to come. And three days later she took up the subject of Sue again at even greater length, complaining about Sue's financial dependence on her until then, though conceding both Tom and Silas had helped. She came to the conclusion she could have a clear conscience about Sue now: 'She has made her own choice, she has enough to live on.' Then she added:

> I must realise and she must realise too that she has no more claims on me than Lyndall has. Both are my daughters & Lyndall too should not be costing me anything extra though I am very willing she should live here paying only what it costs me to keep her ... My attitude to money is too tense and nervous at the moment & with Sue here it was like a hole in one's bag. One could never reckon how much all her small nibblings and wastings would cost.

But Antonia continued to overspend, and would find that, even without Sue costing her a further penny, she would never manage to live within her means. Instead of settling down to write now that this whirlwind daughter had left Ashburn Gardens a calmer place, Antonia 'completely reorganised' the flat, and for days she and the charlady cleaned and tidied and rearranged.

August was the time Antonia went on her annual holiday to Binesfield. Before leaving, as Sue was still visiting the flat to collect more of her possessions, and sometimes removed things which Antonia felt belonged to the household, she changed the locks.

At Binesfield Antonia tried to get down to writing with the same fervour she had spent on the clean-out and reorganisation of Ashburn Gardens, but Sue was always on her mind. Although she acknowledged the separation had been necessary for them both, she kept 'coming guiltily back' to her confused feelings for her daughter.

Antonia managed to detach her mind from Sue to make some notes for what would become *The Sugar House*. But when she tried to visualise an ideal reader, in the hope that it might help her to find the right approach to writing the book, her thoughts were led straight back to Sue because she had once promised to dedicate the book to her. She decided she would still do so since she felt Sue probably continued to take some sort of interest in her work: 'Lyn of course takes none, though she is sweet about it as a job I have to do.'

As Antonia wrote about Sue, she had no idea that she was on her honeymoon in Spain. Within a month of leaving Ashburn Gardens, she married Thomas in Chelsea Register Office a few days after her twenty-second birthday. I was a witness, but sworn to secrecy, and Silas and Sheila were there too, of course. Afterwards Silas hosted a very gay lunch party at the Café Royal. After much excellent champagne had been drunk, he wanted to telephone Antonia and tell her the good news, because he felt bad about her being in the dark, but he was firmly dissuaded by Sheila and Thomas. It was agreed the Chittys would write to Antonia to tell her they were married, sending the letters to arrive after they left for Spain.

The letters reached Binesfield on 30 August. Sue included 'one sweet sentence' in hers: 'We both want our Mother back again.' Antonia was puzzled: 'I am not Thomas's mother and he has never shown any particular affection for me.' Thomas's explained why they had married in a register office: 'We neither of us have any religion.'

Antonia was shocked that Sue had repudiated her religion: shortly before her breakdown they had gone to all the Holy Week ceremonies together, and Sue had taken Communion. Here again it was history repeating itself: as Antonia had thrown up her religion to flout her father, Sue seemed to be doing the same: 'Obviously the Church and I are connected in Sue's mind. In throwing over one she throws over the other.' Was she perhaps envious that Sue could shuffle off Catholicism so lightly to marry someone she loved, while she was suffering the usual qualms over her beliefs?

Mother rang me up at work to ask if I knew about Sue's marriage. I denied any knowledge of it. Then she telephoned Sheila who also denied that she and Silas had been to the wedding; but admitted they knew about the marriage and were 'absolutely delighted'.

Antonia suspected that Thomas's and the Glossops' 'distrust' of her in connection with Sue was based on their suspicion of Catholicism. The Sheilas of this world, who behaved well, saw Catholics like Antonia as hypocrites when they behaved badly – as Mother was the first to admit she often did. If Sue was happier not practising her religion, then, to someone with a pragmatic approach, this proved she must be better off without it. And if Antonia was not a hundred per cent delighted over her daughter's happiness, it followed, in their eyes, that she must want her to be miserable.

In fact Antonia thought that in many ways the marriage might be very good for Sue, but it worried her that Sue had had to suppress the spiritual side of her nature which, she felt, would sooner or later need to assert itself.

What my mother wrote next makes me shudder with shame:

I like Lyn more and more. I don't suppose she can ever cause me as much agony or as much exquisite delight as Sue. But she is immensely lovable and attractive and there is something terribly sweet in her dogged little way of paying her way. My father once said to me 'You always foot the bill' and this is much truer of Lyndall. She pays: she doesn't steal . . . Well, Lyn and I will probably get on like two pussy cats, knowing each other well enough to avoid upsetting each other.

Little did my Mother suspect what a traitor she was harbouring.

After Mother returned from Binesfield, I went on holiday to Italy with Dicky Muir, and told her the first of what would be a chain of lies. Since I was still firmly denying that I was having an affair with him, I pretended Simon Raven was coming too, though of all the people in our group to have picked as a chaperone, he would have been the least suitable. It was lucky my mother did not ask how he was going to fit into Dicky's two-seater Triumph.

I had never seen Italy before, but my first impression was not very favourable, for it turned out to be a holiday of misfortunes.

On the way out Dicky's car blew a tyre as he was overtaking a Topolino between Pisa and Livorno. Our car went into a spin and turned round on itself several times before coming to a halt between two trees, its back wheels hovering on the edge of a two-metre drop. The driver of the other car had been so horrified at the sight of our convertible careening off the road that he had thrown up his hands and ended up against a tree. Luckily he was not hurt, but his Topolino was a write-off. We stood for hours in the boiling sun, a spectacle for every passing motorist and donkey-cart driver, waiting for the police to arrive and sort out who was responsible.

Dicky and I spent a few days on Capri, quarrelling most of the time, before heading for home again.

The disaster we had escaped so narrowly on the outward journey was waiting for us on the way back. After a couple of nights in Monte Carlo (where I changed the date on my passport by rounding the 1 of 1931 into a 0 in order to appear to be over 21 and be allowed in the Casino), we set off across the Alpes Maritimes. Shortly after Sisteron we paused at a crossroad to decide which of two routes to take; and since it was turning cold, we put up the hood of the car – an action which would save our lives.

On an almost deserted mountain road, a car suddenly overtook a lorry which was coming towards us. Dicky had to swerve violently to the right to avoid being hit. The Triumph hit a milestone on the side of the road with such force that it was catapulted across to the other side and shot over the edge of a precipice.

Down we fell, through trees and bushes that sometimes held the somersaulting car in their branches for a fraction of a second before letting it roll on downwards. It all seemed to happen in slow motion, but instead of seeing my life's picture in front of my eyes like a drowning man, I could only think 'If we're killed Mother will find out Simon wasn't with us and I shall end on a lie.' There were no seatbelts in those days and Dicky and I were thrown on top of each other, first one way, then the other, as the car rolled over and over. At last it came to a halt, but in trying to free ourselves our movements set the car falling again. This time the car came to a rest on its side. Dicky ordered me not to stir, though his whole weight was crushing me against the door handle, reassuring me that someone would surely soon come and get us out.

Eventually rescuers with a crow-bar managed to reach us and prised open the car's battered door to haul us out.

We returned to England by train, both badly bruised; Dicky limping, and I with a couple of cracked ribs.

'And what happened to Simon?' asked my mother when I had finished recounting the story of my dramatic holiday.

'Oh, we'd left him in Monte Carlo. We couldn't drag him away from the casino' I said, falling straight back into my cowardly habit of lying to my mother now that death no longer threatened.

Two things now revolutionised life at Ashburn Gardens.

Since Sue no longer needed her room, Antonia decided to take a lodger to bring in some much needed money. As a friend of mine from Cambridge, Daphne Borrett, who had been on the same secretarial course, was looking for somewhere to live in London, it was agreed she should rent the small spare bedroom upstairs and she and I could share Sue's large room downstairs as our sitting-room, and cook for ourselves.

More important, from Antonia's point of view, was that the daughter of a Catholic friend came to work for her for a token salary. Her name was Elaine Lingham and she had just come out of a nunnery shortly before taking her final vows. She became much more than a secretary to Antonia: as confidante, consoler and adviser she partly made up for the recent loss of Sue. Eventually Elaine would become Antonia's '"good" daughter: Heaven knows I don't mean Lyndall is a bad one. But she is too unaware yet of the "spirit" to understand many things.'

Elaine's good influence on my mother, and having more space, made my life at Ashburn Gardens much more bearable.

Things went well for Antonia, too. By 16 November, less than four months after Sue's departure, she had finished *The Sugar House*. The 'two-flat arrangement' was working admirably and Antonia was feeling better than she had done for years. She wrote that there was only one sore place: 'Sue'.

By December Antonia said she felt oppressed by the Sue/Thomas situation. Not only were they coming into her dreams as 'hostile' and 'mocking' presences, which distressed her, but she had been told by Thomas that they did not want to see her. Three letters she had written to Sue had not been answered, although, according to Antonia, Sue used to ring up under false names to speak to me, or if she did speak to Mother was 'obviously hostile', refusing to bring back things Mother suspected she had 'annexed'.

But there would be one bright spot in Mother's otherwise '*triste*' Christmas of 1951: a card arrived from Sue thanking her for a gift of a pair of nylon stockings, followed later by a present and a note from Sue and Thomas 'not refusing' to see her after Christmas.

At the end of 1951 I was in disgrace with my mother for two reasons. The first, which I shared with Eric and with Tom, was that, in her view, I had done nothing to bridge the widening gulf between Sue and herself. The other was that I did not spend Christmas with her, but went away with Dicky and my other friends. She wrote crossly about both us daughters just before New Year's Eve, saying we both wanted our own way too much:

> Sue rides roughshod over people's feelings . . . whereas Lyn is acutely sensitive to them & suffers quite a lot when having her own way involves hurting people. Nothing however stops her from doing what she wants even if she feels sorry or guilty about it. She is very like Tom in this way. Sue has Si's capacity for simply not noticing – or ignoring – what other people feel.

And yet, pathetically, our mother wanted to impress us, although she was not impressed by us.

Antonia had just heard the results of the *Observer*'s short-story competition which she had entered that autumn. Muriel Spark, then unknown, had won the prize; Antonia's story was not even among the runners-up. But there had been a field of several thousand entries, so Antonia decided that to win would have been as unlikely as winning a lottery. She minded only because she felt that something like winning a competition might impress us.

The promised meeting with Sue took place on 17 January 1952. Mother said about it that Sue had been 'perfectly agreeable – as any charming young woman one knew slightly might be'. The result was that Mother felt 'less pain but more finality' in the separation. But her ceaseless preoccupation with Sue until they next met, over five years later, would continue to fill her notebooks, her letters and her conversation.

With Sue so definitely gone from her life, Mother now attacked me. She felt I preferred any company to hers, and that I hid her from my friends because I was ashamed of her. But she told herself firmly to get on with her work and not bother about whether her children were proud of her. However, she admitted that when she saw daughters who seemed to care about their mothers she felt lonely and deprived, and 'silly' tears came into her eyes.

It is true that I now avoided my mother. Whenever we were alone she cross-questioned me about Sue, searching for clues I could not give her as she puzzled over and over why it was that Sue did not wish to have anything more to do with her. She knew I was still seeing Sue, but she did not know how often, nor how much more at ease I was in my sister's company than in hers. And another thing she had no idea about was that I was still seeing a great deal of Silas and Sheila, while denying this was so.

I was going out almost nightly with Dicky. Our 'group' had brought some pleasure and glamour into my drab life at home and at my new job – Bernard Miles had sacked me and I was working for a music publisher. With its members I could be carefree and spontaneous and was flattered when my caustic asides seemed to amuse them. I enjoyed the dinners in Soho which were often followed by a visit to the Gargoyle nightclub, where Dylan Thomas and his friends were drinking more than we were; or to the Cavendish Hotel in Jermyn Street, in the hope of hearing Rosa Lewis, well into her eighties, reminiscing about Edwardian times. Even when we did conventional things that I despised – like rushing off to the Fourth of June at Eton, or to Eights Week in Henley – I tried to express my defiance of the Establishment in the way I dressed: black was my basic colour.

But we were not only in pursuit of the trivial. Sometimes after dinner we listened to classical records at Peter Dixon's mews house in Archery Close; or philosophised late into the night in the flat in Belgravia where Hugo Philipps lived with his mother and younger sister.

It amazed me that Rosamond Lehmann did not mind her son turning up unexpectedly with friends: I would never have dared upset the equilibrium of Ashburn Gardens in such a way. Being with Rosamond made me see that being a good writer (I preferred her novels to Antonia's) did not exclude being a good mother, two things which had always seemed incompatible. Rosamond gave us wine and listened patiently to our youthful talk, never dismissing our ideas as immature or outrageous. Although I was the youngest of the group, I never felt I had to keep my mouth shut. I remember confiding to Rosamond that I was ashamed of being a secretary and wanted to be a writer. Without sounding patronising, she pointed out that every experience, whether painful or pleasurable, was important if one wanted to write, and that to feel humiliated over a job that was not in itself mortifying, unless I chose to make it so, was a narrowing down of life. Whereas, when I confided such things to my mother, depending on her mood, she either commiserated with me for being a mere secretary, increasing my already swollen sense of self-pity, or over-analysed what being a writer involved until my aspirations seemed ridiculous.

By the time Dicky and I went on holiday to Capri, the group had already begun to disperse. But I missed it, and was beginning to suspect I had been in love with the group rather than with Dicky, though I was still extremely fond of him. It disturbed me that since our holiday he had been trying to persuade me to marry him and that my refusal was the cause of frequent rows between us.

Dicky was the only child of a widowed mother with whom he lived in a grand and gloomy apartment in Hallam Street, W1, known to the group as 'Hallam Castle'. Strangely, his mother, whose main interest in life was playing bridge, liked me, though she tried to smarten me up a bit with presents like a pair of high-heeled shoes and a string of Ciro pearls. And I liked her, though I was a bit awed by her and always tried to fight against Dicky's smuggling me into her flat to spend the night with him, terrified that she would discover us in bed.

I also lived in terror of my mother discovering my dawn re-entry at Ashburn Gardens. There was an airing cupboard on the landing between the first and second flight of stairs inside the flat. Creeping back at daybreak, I would pause outside it to listen for the signal to proceed upstairs. If there was snoring, it meant there was a good chance of reaching my bedroom across from Mother's undetected. She left her door ajar at night in order that the cat, which slept on her bed, could get to its famous tray, so when she was awake she heard every sound in the corridor. Sometimes the snoring would stop and, with pounding heart, I would freeze, a foot on each stair, until it restarted. Worse still were the times when she was already up and getting ready to go to early Mass. I would get into the airing cupboard and hide there until she left the house. Once she opened the door, reached out to take some underwear which was on a drier in front of me, and shut the door again without having noticed me. Expert liar that I was becoming, I cannot imagine what excuse I could have concocted to explain my presence fully dressed in an airing cupboard at five in the morning. I took to coming home earlier.

Antonia developed a soft spot for Dicky, comparing him favourably to Thomas in a notebook: 'Thomas sneers at everything he does not understand. I find him shallower than Dicky though more intelligent – less human altogether.' And Dicky liked Antonia. If she was petulant over the telephone when he rang me at a time that interrupted her work, her bad temper did not perturb him at all.

Three months after finishing her third novel, Antonia was getting nowhere on its sequel. She decided that I was a contributory cause (Thomas was another) of a writing jam that had set in. She tackled me outright over my lack of appreciation.

Walking the tight-rope of truth, as I tried to explain what I felt in such a way as not to hurt her feelings, I had avoided falling off into the lie of telling her I was proud of her by saying, 'I'm not proud of Tom either.' This hedging seems to have been some consolation to her, for after recording this remark, my mother commented that I had been 'rather sweet and trying to be honest and tactful'. She then reproached me for not having asked to read the proofs of The Sugar House which had arrived a few days before. I told her that the 'Catholic thing' embarrassed me, quickly adding that I had the same trouble when reading Graham Greene.

A 'distressing scene' was avoided and the 'internal cloud lifted', Mother said, after she and I managed to have things out. She told herself she must accept her children for what they were, and put up with their disapproval, 'just as they have long ago learnt to put up with yours'.

In recording our conversation Antonia noted:

> It certainly is strange that, in modern 'intellectual' and 'near intellectual' society, no one is in the least disconcerted by homosexuality, but to be a Catholic or to be at all seriously religious is quite definitely a social handicap.

When Antonia next wrote in her notebook, just before her fifty-second birthday in March, it was to record a dream in which Tom had swum away from her, leaving her alone and frightened in a boat without rudder or oars to control it. Then she had written of Sue, saying that if she took no notice of her birthday she would be very tempted to write to her.

'She took none' is the opening sentence of the next entry; but as I had passed on to her that Sue had wanted to send a telegram but said she did not have the money to do so, Mother restrained herself from writing to Sue, though she noted: 'Sue could have made some sign if she had really wanted to. A postcard stamp is only 2d.'

Apart from my attitude to her writing, I was back in my mother's favour. Not only did she admit I was the only person who occasionally put in a good word for her with Sue, not that it did much good –

'Lyn says Sue looks embarrassed when I'm mentioned and Thomas be-comes silent and sullen' – I was also being 'very sweet' and confiding in her during a crisis with Dicky. 'I suppose one's children only want one around when they're worried or unhappy' Mother noted.

Dicky and I broke up after he issued an ultimatum: marriage or nothing. Although I was tempted to accept the former, I feared this might be prompted by my desire to get away from Ashburn Gardens, for since living there I had not ceased to look in every estate agent's window to see if there were even a bed-sit I could afford on my meagre salary. There never was. I explained to Dicky that in a couple of months, on my twenty-first birthday, I would be getting £400. Then I wanted to go abroad for a year and try to become a writer (whatever I thought that meant); then, when I had had a taste of freedom, I would know what my true feelings for him were.

But Dicky could not understand my dilemma. He was rich. He lived peacefully with his mother and did whatever he pleased without fear of her wrath or disapproval. He didn't question his love for me, so why must I test mine for him? His refusal to see my point of view only increased my doubts over marrying him. And so we split up. But of course I missed him, and life seemed empty and dull without him and our friends.

My friend Daphne, Mother's lodger, was deeply involved with her fiancé Harry, a Cambridge rowing blue, so I saw little of her.

But I saw more of Sue and Thomas who lived in a flat not far away in the Little Boltons; I kept quiet about it, dreading Mother's merciless curiosity and her begging for crumbs of hope whenever she knew I had seen them. Sue had entered a *Vogue* talent contest and was told that even if she did not win it they would probably give her a job. Thomas had finished a first novel, *Mr Nicholas*, and it was accepted by a publisher. Their life seemed enviably exciting and interesting. I decided Sue had been right to marry Thomas, even if he did sometimes sulk and put on what I called his 'maiden auntie look'. This look, when he puckered up his handsome face so that his brown eyes could scarcely find a crease to glare through, and pursed his lips so taut with disapproval that they too almost disappeared, was usually the result of Sue having committed some extravagance they could not afford, or my having made some remark about Mother. But most of the time he was loving to Sue and friendly to me; and with the Chittys I could let my hair down and laugh, finding that joy in life which always eluded me at Ashburn Gardens.

I often sneaked round to see Silas and Sheila, too. They were always warm and welcoming, and Sheila taught me to make dresses. If they sometimes implied that a girl without a dowry ought perhaps to have been less hasty before rejecting a rich and eligible husband, their main reason for being sad about my split-up with Dicky was that they liked him.

Sometimes I went round to Cheyne Row to see Gerti and play with my younger half-sisters, Nicolette and Amanda. Like everyone else, I sympathised with Gerti over Tom's defection. For the rest of her unhappy life she would try to make Tom pay, not only financially but morally, for having fallen in love with Dorothy Kingsmill, ruining her own chances of making a fresh start, although she was still an attractive and talented woman of forty when he left her. This desire for vengeance turned her into an embittered outsider who, as soon as her children were grown up, returned to live in her native Austria.

But at the time I think Nicolette, aged ten, was suffering even more than Gerti. Having known nothing of the deteriorating relations of her parents beforehand, she was shocked when her adoring father suddenly moved out. Strongly loyal by nature, and with almost tribal instincts (Nicolette corresponds regularly with a host of distant Hopkinson relatives I have never even met), Tom's betrayal made her become pathetically protective of Gerti and her younger sister. She must have been doubly hurt by the fact that living in the same house as her father was a girl of her own age, Dorothy's youngest child, 'little' Dorothy.

Since Tom had at last found that person he had been seeking since adolescence, whom he had described in a notebook in 1936 while still married to Antonia – 'somebody to relate my existence to, a secret confider and approver' who would be 'the breath of life' to him – there was little room for anybody else in his life. He and Dorothy had become like one person, and it was impossible ever to be alone with him. Because I had come to see Dorothy more through Antonia's eyes than through his, I found it difficult to get on with her, so I very rarely visited them. And when I did, I found their assumption that they were Nelson and Lady Hamilton reincarnated and reunited, hard to swallow.

It is not surprising that when Dicky wrote asking if we could meet,

I relented and after a while agreed to marry him, since he now accepted my terms: our engagement should be unofficial and I would be allowed to go abroad for a year.

But within a month he had persuaded me to let him announce our engagement in *The Times* for his mother's sake, because her conventional family had for some time been making unkind insinuations (not all unfounded!) about Dicky's still being a bachelor at the age of thirty-two. How getting engaged to a girl from such a mixed-up family background, who had never been presented at Court and walked around dressed like Hamlet, could have improved Dicky's image with his family was a mystery to me. But his mother had always been kind to me, so I gave in. If I had known what hell it would make my mother's life as well as mine, I would have held out against Dicky's insistence.

For days after the announcement, the telephone never stopped ringing. Since I was at work, Antonia's attempts at writing were constantly disturbed as photographers and florists, catering firms and hirers of marquees, rang up to offer their help in organising a sumptuous wedding. If they had known the bride's mother did not have the next quarter's rent in the bank, and was already worrying whether she would have saved enough money to buy herself a new hat for the wedding in a year's time, they would have spared her a lot of annoyance.

Dicky was winning every argument. I did not want an engagement ring, partly as a rebellion against convention and partly because I disliked most jewellery, yet I let him slip onto my finger an antique ring which everyone else admired. Luckily it was too large. I begged not to have an engagement party, but Dicky's mother gave a huge cocktail party for us at 'Hallam Castle'; and her brother, Sir Donald Horsfall, gave a dinner for us at the Savoy where I was inspected by the Horsfall clan.

Finally Dicky argued me out of taking my year of freedom. I should have stayed my ground, but a life-long terror of scenes as a result of my mother's propensity for them, made me agree even to his request for an autumn wedding in a few months' time.

Shortly before my twenty-first birthday I lost my job – too much social life was making me turn up late for work each morning. I did not look for another as I was busy furnishing a house Dicky and I had found in Molyneux Street off the Edgware Road. And, spending more of my birthday money in advance, I was taking driving lessons since Dicky had promised me a car for my birthday if I passed my test.

Dicky was very busy at that time. Besides running his magazine on motor racing, he and a partner had just started a restaurant called La Popote in Walton Street.

Antonia felt she ought to give me a party for my twenty-first birthday, which was the last thing I wanted her to do. Since she insisted we must celebrate it in some way, I made an odd request: to have lunch on 23 July with my two parents, with whom I had not been alone since being ill with tonsillitis four years before. Odder still, perhaps, was that Tom agreed, and took us to the Brompton Grill where we all three drank too much champagne which put my mother into her best and wittiest mood, but also made her indiscreet in reminiscing about the past. To my surprise, instead of clamping down to silence as he often did if a conversation became too emotional, Tom was relaxed and even reminisced amusingly too, so that we had a very merry lunch. He was affectionate, even loving, to both of us, which he had not been for a long time, but in his pocket he carried a time-bomb. Before parting, he handed me a letter to open when I got home.

It said that now I was grown-up and was about to get the £400 my allowance would end. But what distressed me was that there were some severe criticisms of my nature and attitude to life which made me suspect I was being cut off by my father in more than just a financial way. This was the last time for twenty years that my mother and father were to see each other.

Shortly afterwards Antonia went on her annual holiday to Binesfield. There her usual 'malaise and depression' were made worse by thoughts of Sue which were more constantly oppressive even than in London.

That summer Sue won the 'Vogue Talent Contest', and two books dedicated to her came out: Thomas's Mr Nicholas and Antonia's The Sugar House. Once again Antonia had not dedicated her book to the person who deserved it, and about whom she had said on finishing the book, 'I shall never be able to say how much I owe to Elaine. She has such a feel of the right order and where one is going right or wrong.'

But even if the author's dedicated copy of The Sugar House was not acknowledged, it had been read. I passed on to Mother that Sue preferred it to The Lost Traveller. And most of Antonia's friends – such as Eric, Barbara Ward, John Raymond – were enthusiastic over it, yet there were only four good reviews; some were 'downright sneering' and showed real hatred of her work. Antonia comforted herself that the contradictions were almost 'farcical': one review said it was 'sordid and squalid', another called it 'witty and gay'. But all agreed it was not nearly as good as *Frost in May*. Antonia felt 'crushed and depressed'. There was such a 'cruel' notice by Robert Kee in the *Observer*, and an even more 'subtly poisonous' one elsewhere, that Antonia began to question whether she ought not to stop all attempts at serious writing. She wondered whether it had been 'an extra blow' because of the excellent reviews Thomas's book was getting: 'I have seldom seen such public acclaim for any first novel.'

Thomas used the pen-name of Thomas Hinde for his autobiographical novel, *Mr Nicholas*, in order that his father would never discover what his eldest son had written about him. Antonia read the book twice with the utmost care, and though feeling 'occasional admiration' was left with 'profound "unease" and even a kind of horror' because of what she saw as the 'profundity of his hatred'. She said the author appeared to have no compassion for anyone but himself.

> Out to give others away, to bring out all their pettiness, unreasonableness, hypocrisy etc, he makes his young man a kind of touchstone of truth & never puts him in the same perspective as the rest. By doing this, he ironically and presumably unconsciously draws the portrait of a quite remarkably self-centred and self-satisfied young prig. He's good about himself as an artist – there he is honest and touching.

While regretting they were fundamentally antipathetic as writers, she conceded he might 'turn out a good writer in the end'.

Antonia had gone through Thomas's novel with such an eagle eye more in her role of mother, than of literary critic, searching for some clue to her son-in-law's nature which would justify her theory that he was behind her daughter's refusal to communicate with her any more. She thought she had found the answer in what she saw as Thomas's terrible capacity for hatred, which made her fear she had 'a formidable adversary' in Thomas, though she could not understand why he saw her as his enemy, since she was not against Sue's marriage to him.

While Mother was at Binesfield that August, I did something that would outrage her.

Dicky wanted to meet his future father-in-law and, still winning every argument, persuaded me to invite him and Tom for dinner at Ashburn Gardens in Mother's absence. Tom brought Dorothy, too. Afterwards Dorothy wrote me a very friendly letter, explaining that she and Tom would soon be getting married, and offering to play a maternal role in my life which she felt was sadly missing. I was so unnerved by this letter that I did not answer it. Not surprisingly, this was taken by Tom as a sign of my hostility to his projected third marriage.

Antonia later found this letter, another proof of my duplicity.

As the autumn approached, Dicky pressed me to fix our wedding date. I was hedging because I could not face a church wedding followed by a large reception, which his mother wanted to pay for, instead of what we had agreed on: a register-office wedding and lunch with a few friends afterwards. We seemed to argue constantly, particularly as I was suppressing resentment about my lost year abroad, and his not having given me a car for my birthday, although I had passed my driving test.

Finally I plotted to take my year abroad without his permission.

But where could I flee to? France was too near, I might be tempted to come home if things went badly; America too far and expensive, for I had already spent half my birthday money and was rapidly getting through the rest. In the end I picked on a place to which I could afford a single ticket and still have something left to live on until finding a job: Italy.

I had already secretly booked a ticket to Rome when something happened which put an end to any idea of ever marrying Dicky.

Near the end of August I had received a letter from a young art historian I knew very slightly, confirming an invitation to stay in Scotland he had flung out a few nights before at a drunken party. It promised there would be 'No shooters in knickerbockers or fishers in fisherknickers' in the house-party, and ended with the postscript: 'Your black trousers essential.'

Dicky made a monumental scene when I told him I had accepted Willy Mostyn-Owen's invitation. I argued that he had recently come back from sailing round the Greek Islands in mixed company. But I knew in my heart that I ought not to go, and went.

Aberuchill Castle stood in handsome isolation in magnificent countryside. The rooms were lit with candles and oil lamps, since there was no electricity there in those days; wood fires burned in the bedrooms at night, for the late summer evenings were cold in Scotland. The company was excellent – a mixture of old friends and people who would become new friends, like Quentin Crewe and Willy's sister, Liz. Even the presence of their mother, the Thurberesque Mrs Mostyn-Owen, did not dampen the zest of our youthful house-party; indeed she contributed to it by singing music hall songs of her youth after a few drinks in the evening.

But my guilt over Dicky, who telephoned every day, was a dampener on an otherwise perfect holiday. To make matters worse, by the end of the first week I had fallen in love with my host.

By the end of the second week Willy and I were having an affair. I entrusted him with my secret that I was off to Italy when I discovered that he was soon going to Florence to be Bernard Berenson's assistant at I Tatti.

When I got back to London early in September there were only a few days left until my flight to Rome, during which time I contrived to see Dicky only once. The more he said how much he had missed me and how radiant I looked, the more nails he hammered into my coffin of self-loathing. I knew I ought to confess my treachery and break off the engagement, but coward and liar that I was I did not; and with the excuse that my engagement ring was too large gave it back to him to have it altered.

As I watched Dicky's car disappearing round the corner of Ashburn Gardens, after we had kissed each other goodnight for what I knew would be the last time, I was overcome with ineffable sadness, and deep shame that my imminent departure would soon be hurting someone who had never intentionally harmed me.

I had told Mother I was planning to go abroad for a while. She was horrified and begged me to tell Dicky before leaving. I said I knew he would make such a desperate scene that in the end he would manage to dissuade me from going. I still denied that I was having an affair with Dicky, so could not tell her that one of the reasons I did not want to marry him was that I did not enjoy sleeping with him; and of course said nothing about Willy. In order not to seem an accomplice in my plot, she asked me not to tell her the date of my departure.

On the morning of 16 September 1952, I posted two letters timed to arrive with the afternoon post, by which time I would be on my way to Italy. One was to Dicky explaining why I was leaving, though not breaking off the engagement or saying I was in love with Willy (that would come later); and one to his mother, apologising for the abrupt manner of my departure and thanking her for all her kindness which I had not deserved.

While Antonia was having her daily lie-down after lunch, I walked out of Ashburn Gardens with my luggage, having first put a note on her desk to say I had left.

As I stepped out of the aeroplane into the glare of the Roman sunshine, to be greeted by a blanket of heat such as I had never imagined existed even in Africa, I was quite unaware of the extent of the confusion and drama I had left behind me in London.

CHAPTER 19

ॐ

A Fresh Start

Like you, I'm really starting on my own again: you and
Sue gone, and Eric, Tom and Silas all out now.
Antonia White, 9 October 1952

When the doorbell rang around seven o'clock on the evening I fled to
Rome, Antonia was horrified to find herself face to face with Dicky
on the doorstep of 13 Ashburn Gardens.

Something had gone wrong with my plan. Dicky always went home
from the office to have a bath and change before going out. As we
were to dine that evening, my letter should have been waiting for him
at Hallam Street in time to stop him coming to fetch me. But Dicky
wavered from his normal behaviour that September evening, and,
having worked later than usual, decided to come straight to Ashburn
Gardens. On the way he stopped to buy a bunch of flowers for me,
something he had never done before, and in his pocket he carried the
engagement ring he had picked up in the lunch hour from the jeweller
who had altered it to fit my finger.

What happened is best described in Antonia's own words:

I let him in & saw at once that he knew nothing: he arrived with flowers
for you. I had to make pretence of looking for you & I had to 'find' the
note and read it in his presence. It was not difficult to act shock for I was
actually shaking at the ordeal of having to read it with him standing over
me. I said it was dreadful news & he asked to read it. Luckily I had some
gin by me. He looked frighteningly bad for a moment; then pulled himself
together & behaved extremely well. He said he had had a presentiment all
day that something was wrong & it came on very violently about 3 p.m.
[Exactly the time my plane had left for Rome.]

Then they telephoned Dicky's mother who came straight over to
Ashburn Gardens: 'Poor Mrs Muir really was half-stunned: there were
times when she couldn't take in things we were saying.' My mother was

soon feeling such remorse over her part in my deception, particularly as both Muirs were 'being so sweet & sorry' about the shock to *her*, that she confessed she had known I was planning to go away, but not where or when. Mother told me Dicky was admirably 'good & sensible', though he needed 'a good deal of drink to get him through', and kept admitting he should have listened to her advice to him all along, not to rush me.

This letter from Antonia also contained some tough home truths which I deserved to hear, for Dicky had revealed, among other things, that we had been having an affair *and* that it had not been my first:

> Well, my dear Lyndall . . . I am afraid it would be easy for me to wonder whether you have ever been truthful or genuine with me at all, but I still believe that there is much that is sweet and good in you. But your habit of treachery and double-dealing and lying has grown to quite dangerous proportions.

Although I had sent Mother a night cable to say I had arrived safely, and giving the American Express as a mailing address, she promised not to pass this information on to Dicky yet because she was afraid he would fly to Rome to try and persuade me to come back, whereas she felt I ought to stay there if I could find a job in order to make 'a real new beginning and discovery and sorting-out'.

Her angry letter relented in the postscript: 'PS I do understand things have been awfully hard for you & often you've been forced into deceit & false positions.'

By the time my mother's second letter arrived, after having received a penitent one from me in which I made an almost clean breast of everything, I had had a full taste of loneliness and despair: only pride kept me from scuttling back to England while I still had enough money to buy a third-class ticket.

On arrival I had found a cheap room in the Pensione Svizzera near the Spanish Steps for less than the price of a coffee in Italy today. Instead of a window, it had a divided door like a stable: by leaving the top half open, some light could enter; so could flies and mosquitoes. It was the last 'loose-box' in a row of four that were reached by walking along a narrow balcony perched high above an internal courtyard. When it rained, which it soon did torrentially, every expedition to the bathroom meant getting a soaking. It was not a place in which to spend much time, for it was stuffy and dark even with the full door open, and the bedside lamp gave no more light than a candle to read by.

When I was not sight-seeing, or searching for a job at some embassy or language school, my refuge became the old-fashioned Caffè Greco which I could ill afford. Sometimes, when it rained, I would linger there all day over one *cappuccino* as I poured out my loneliness into an exercise book, long since lost, or wrote letters to England describing my wretchedness.

Never had time gone so slowly, and never had I felt so strange and solitary. The solitude I felt in my little room, or in the churches and museums, became an almost unbearable loneliness in the busy streets and overcrowded buses. Any inner calm I managed to find in havens like the romanesque cloister of SS Quattro Coronati, where I went almost every day to read while enjoying the scent of flowers and the soft gurgling of the fountain, was destroyed on the journey back to the *pensione*. In the tightly-packed buses, wedged between fleshy matrons sticky with sweat who stared at me, and men with wandering hands, my lonely state became more disquieting and self-pity overwhelmed me. Soon I took to walking everywhere, in spite of sweltering heat or drenching rains, and my blistered feet covered such long distances that for the only time in my life I wore out a pair of shoes in a couple of weeks.

During my second week in Rome I became suicidal. My mother's stern letter had poured salt into my already painful wounds of self-loathing. I was getting nowhere with my job-hunting, despite daily visits to the British Council, where the only new job offers on their notice-board were always for au pairs. Having been for two interviews, and each time been told I would have to share my charge's room, I decided I would rather starve in my 'loose-box': I knew the one requisite an aspiring writer needed was a room of one's own, but how was I going to pay the rent? Each time I had returned to the *pensione* with an ever-mounting sense of defeat to add to my feeling of hopelessness, and had to cling to the railings of the balcony that led to my room to fight a strong desire to fling myself into the courtyard five floors below. And in bed at night I wept with despair.

At the end of the second week two fat letters were handed me when I made my daily visit to the American Express: one was from Mother and the other from Dicky who now knew where I was.

Like a dog with a bone, I put them in my pocket and went to seek out the darkest corner of the Caffè Greco. I had finished my *cappuccino* before finding the courage to open them.

I need not have feared. Dicky's letter was forgiving and talked of a 'revelation' he had had when he heard from Francis Haskell the reaction of everyone at Aberuchill to his constant telephone calls to me there. 'In a flash,' he wrote, 'I understood the terrifying possessive obsession which has gripped me for months.' He had suddenly seen me as a person with a mind and body of my own. About my flight to Rome he said:

> Your action was brave. Had you told me face-to-face that you were going, I do not know what the consequences might have been . . . Now I trust your independence just as you have always trusted mine.

My mother's letter opened with 'My darling Lyndall' so I could safely read on. First it spoke of Dicky who seemed to her much calmer after acknowledging that I had become an obsession. Then she commented on my letter to her, saying she was touched I had made a clean breast of things: 'I do trust you now and I won't be too shaken if some "other little shocks" turn up.' She told me that my analysis of my bad side was acute, 'putting "pride" at the root of it', though she felt it was a 'good' side, 'compassionate & generous', which often got me into difficult situations. She did not blame me for lacking a 'definite sense of values', but wished I could acquire a religion or philosophy to guide me:

> My own life is no shining example to you, darling, & though I do firmly believe what I do believe, the discrepancies between what I believe and how I behave are too obvious for you not to be aware of them! But the fact remains that, however much I fail, I do know what the important things are & am therefore much more to blame than you are when I let my own weakness get the better of me. And Tom, as fathers usually are to daughters, is the most important parent to you & his own peculiar and rather changeable principles must be very confusing for you.

Mother then went on to say that, though I might find it disconcerting that the main conflict between my parents was their 'different beliefs, points of view and sense of values', it was up to me to search for my own moral yardstick and be humble.

It was in this letter that she confessed she had been 'absolutely horrified' and lost her head on finding Dorothy's affectionate letter when going through my things to discover anything she could about me, after being told by Dicky that I had entertained Tom and Dorothy at Ashburn Gardens. Now she had calmed down; she realised I could only see my father with Dorothy if I did not want to be cut off from him: 'It is very naughty of Tom himself to put you in such a horrible dilemma.'

She commiserated over my suffering and loneliness but begged me to overcome the 'put away quietly' feeling she said she knew so well. It would be a terrible blow to Tom and her, to Dicky and his mother, to Sue and Nicolette:

> No, stay with us and go through this bad patch. You are very dearly loved and have so much joy to give when you have 'found yourself'. For one small thing, my naughty sweet Pussy, I don't know how I'd have got through this year since Sue's attempted suicide & all that followed, without your sweetness and help.

She next commented on my reasons for not having told her Dicky was my lover, which had been partly because I thought, as a Catholic, she would be upset, but more because I had not wanted to discuss with her the fact that sex was becoming a problem in my life. She told me I need not have feared her reactions, knowing how she had behaved in her youth when she gave up religion. She said sex had nearly always been 'a misery' to her, too, and she understood how 'mean & prudish' one felt saying no to a man who loved one.

Then came advice and encouragement about life and writing – for I must have also told my mother that I had been trying to write and was discouraged at my first attempts. Writing, she said, came from 'experience & incessant sharpening of the eye'.

The ten-page letter ended with a request that I should write her an accusing letter without fear of hurting her feelings, then we could both feel easier with each other:

> What always hurts me most is being deceived and I am so touched and grateful to you for being honest with me in your last letter that I would like you to make the effort to bring out the resentment.

Although my mother's forgiving letter consoled me, I felt uneasy that I still had not confessed about Willy. And this guilty secret made me feel even more miserable about Dicky who had said in his letter that he trusted me. As I sat pondering how to tell him the whole truth, determined to break the habit I had formed, since living with my mother, of protecting myself with lies, I had no idea that Dicky already knew everything.

In the next lot of mail was a letter from Willy which said he had got into 'such an awful state over Dicky' that he had invited him to lunch and poured out the whole story of our affair. Dicky's reaction had been restrained fury:

> He accused me of being the biggest shit in the world and said that he supposed he should get up, slap my face and walk out; instead, he went in for a detailed grilling (the waiter meanwhile was vainly trying to get us to take some interest in ordering our lunch).

Willy's letter then went on to reminisce about Scotland, wishing we were 'back three weeks ago, to candlelight and wood fires, and walk/ rides over the moors, and the soft, cool early morning light'. How remote and romantic it now seemed. He said he would be arriving in Florence in a month's time.

There was also a letter from Sue which cheered me up by saying that all my friends and relations '(don't know about The Old Bitch)' thought I had been 'very courageous' and done the only thing possible: 'your letter to Dickie made me want to cry'. She told me not to come back for at least six months: 'You had the guts to make the plunge, don't spoil it all by turning back.' But it was her last sentence which filled me with joy, for I had never felt my elder sister took me seriously: she said my letter was 'the most wonderful' she had ever read: 'so sad and so funny'. She had read it again and again and would 'treasure it always. You sure can *write!*'

Finally there was a sobering letter from my father. He was relieved that I had ended my procrastinations over Dicky, but hoped that my falsehoods, which he thought were caused by lack of confidence, would stop. He, like Mother, was concerned that I should find a job and see things through.

There were some difficult letters to write now, particularly to Dicky and to my mother. But Antonia was right, it was 'easier and less embarrassing' to say certain things in writing, so I picked up my pen, plucked up my courage, and told my mother some of those resentments she insisted she wanted to hear about.

At the beginning of October, having finished the translation, after working 'like a steam-engine', Antonia wrote in her notebook:

The sense of a cycle closing. Lyndall has gone. But the net result of that has been the opposite of Sue's going. In spite of all the cloud of deceptions, her letters to me from Rome are more real than any I have had from her.

She had just received my 'accusing letter', with its 'interesting and unexpected' revelation that I felt she was jealous whenever I was happy, although she sympathised with my sorrows. She commented that her jealousy of me was 'trivial' compared with her jealousy of Sue; and that her 'simplest envy' of her daughters had begun when we were small children: 'their not having to be responsible for keeping themselves and always having "les Papas" or myself behind them'.

Antonia explored the same theme in her reply to my letter, and assured me she had not been jealous of me 'in any serious way' since we went to Aldeburgh together after I had tonsillitis 'except over you & Sue as an anti-me alliance'. But she admitted she had been jealous when I was little because she felt Tom cared for me more than he did for her, and that I adored Tom then and did not love her. She added, 'I would be madly jealous if you deserted me for the Kingsmill.'

Although she said it distressed her that I looked on her as the sharer of my glooms rather than of my gaiety, I seem to have been partly right about her unconscious envy of my happiness. Over the next two months, as my life began to improve, Mother's letters became colder and reverted to 'Dearest Lyndall'. After I told her I had landed a well-paid temporary job doing the night-shift as a typist for a UN Conference, when I was down to my last £2 traveller's cheque, and had met a girl at the British Council with whom I had become friends, Mother said she was relieved about the job and knew exactly how wonderful it felt to eat with someone again instead of in solitary confinement, but most of the letter described her own present 'low' state.

As I came out of the doldrums, my mother sailed into them. In her notebook she tried to trace the origin of her nervous exhaustion which was rapidly turning into a depression. Was it a symptom of the usual resistance at beginning a new book – the fourth (which would turn out to be the last) of the quartet – or was it the after-effects of the strain caused by my running away, she wondered? But later, looking back, she noticed the 'collapse' started the moment Elaine stopped working for her, for in October Elaine had left to study for an exam to enter the Foreign Office and would soon be going to work in a consulate in Germany. Without Elaine's good influence Antonia would manage to write only seven pages of the future *Beyond the Glass* over the next six months.

At the end of October, after nearly a month's silence, my mother wrote to me that her 'old head-bursting feeling' had returned. She had grown so afraid that she might be going to have a stroke ('It wouldn't worry me to die – except for the state of my soul!!'), that she had called Dr Symes, although she could ill afford the 15s for his visit. He had told her to stay in bed for a few days and not to touch any 'head work' for a fortnight.

There were other problems too: Christmas was approaching and not only could she not afford to buy presents, she did not even know where the next quarter's rent would come from.

My mother's suggesting she was on the verge of a stroke was like a threatening cloud approaching on my horizon: just as I was beginning to enjoy my new Italian life and learn the language, might I have to go back to England?

But her next letter, though still talking of pressure in the head and fear of a stroke, was less gloomy. Daisy Green-Wilkinson, her first mother-in-law who still kept in touch, had sent her £50 and she had found it 'comforting' that I had told her she could summon me if she were ill. It was one of the very few letters in which Sue's distressing behaviour was not mentioned, and, moreover, Antonia was even able to mock herself about 'peculiar' criticisms of *The Sugar House* which were still drifting in:

> One provincial paper had a big news heading over the review: 'COLOUR-LESS CLARA FADES OUT'. As that was exactly what Colourless Clara felt as if she were doing at that particular moment, I had to laugh!

Where there was humour there was hope; I thought the crisis was over and felt greatly relieved.

By December I was able to tell Mother the good news that, at the end of the Conference, I had been offered a permanent secretarial job with the Food and Agriculture Organisation of the United Nations at four times the salary I had earned in England. She tried to sound pleased about my good fortune, but it was clear that she was heading into trouble. With Christmas, her most vulnerable time of year, approaching she was feeling 'miz about absent daughters', particularly Sue who had made no sign for months.

In the same letter she told me that, by an odd coincidence, Elaine's sister, who was a nurse, had been present at the confinement of Sheila Glossop. On hearing she had been safely delivered of a girl, the new mother had said, 'I hope she grows up as pretty as my husband's other daughter.' Antonia wrote to congratulate Silas and Sheila, but her letter was not acknowledged.

I wrote Mother a long letter. It crossed with a brief and ominous one I received from her on Christmas Eve which showed her condition was by now very serious. The handwriting sprawled in all directions, and the letter was full of recrimination and cries of despair:

> Sue's cruelty is quite simply destroying me . . . I am not allowed to kill myself. If I were not a Catholic I would . . . You too had better disown me. Believe me I do understand. But believe too that I tried to do what I could. I don't know how one lives when all one's springs are broken & one is not allowed to die. Forget about me. You have always been sweet to me & I am grateful . . . I know I shd. not send this letter. I am past caring

The last words were faint and there was no signature.

Was this the summons? Should I rush back to England? What held me back, apart from the fact I could not have raised the money over the Christmas holiday, was that I noticed the envelope, presumably addressed *after* the letter had been written, was in Antonia's usual firm, round handwriting.

After Christmas, while I was still wondering what to do, another letter arrived from Mother apologising for the 'crazy' one written two days before which had crossed with mine. It began 'My darling Lyndall' and said she was trying, without much success, to pull herself together. She wished Elaine were there to get her going on the book. However, she told me she had written a poem during her pre-Christmas gloom, when my absence and Sue's exclusion made her feel she belonged 'absolutely nowhere':

> I would never have believed that it is far, far worse to be deserted by a child than by a lover. But it is . . . I simply dread hearing carols on the wireless or in the street. I think of you & Sue singing them.

The poem, '*Ubi Sunt Gaudia?*', which was published in the *New Statesman* (and later appeared in *As Once in May*), began:

> *In dulci jubilo* . . .
> Once in the candleglow

> Two faces seraph-bright
> Opened round mouths to sing
> '*Ubi sunt gaudia*
> If that they be not there?'

She was surprised when I asked to see it, and even more surprised when I told her I liked it.

I asked her why she felt so strongly that I despised her writing – which I did not. She replied that this feeling had 'crystallised to a sharp point' when Dicky told her that, after meeting Rosamond Lehmann, I remarked 'I wish my mother were like that!':

> Now that my father isn't there to disapprove, I've transferred the terror on to my children as the arch-disapprovers! . . . you two occupy a special under-the-skin position from which I shall make every effort to oust you! In bad 'states' this is not possible . . . The obvious answer is that I have somehow got to become 'detached' from my children as well as from my parents, while remaining affectionate & understanding towards both.

In fact, at the last minute on Christmas Eve, Mother told me she had received a card in Thomas's writing with 'Happy Christmas from Sue & Thomas' on the back. This had prompted her to send each of them a cheque for a guinea, so she was now post-watching to see if these would be acknowledged. But at the Speaights', where she spent Christmas Day, Bobby's wife, who had recently met Sue for the first time, told her that Sue said Mother was a 'destructive influence' and she associated Ashburn Gardens with the unhappiest time of her life.

In January 1953 Antonia began to haul herself back from the depths. She wrote to tell me she had decided to try and preserve her sanity, 'superficially at least', by isolating herself from Sue. She had had 'flu, but wrote that physical illness had brought some relief from 'the Great Depression'. The letter ended saying she was 'WICKEDLY bored' with her own and everyone else's troubles and wished Rome were nearer so that she could take me out to dinner and stand us a bottle of champagne: 'What with? The money earmarked for the 'phone bill?'

But the tone of her next letter in February was strangely altered; she hinted darkly that perhaps she should not trust me, but would continue to do so until she had 'concrete evidence' that I was still doing a little double-crossing.

Our family situation was becoming farcical as well as tragic. Antonia had seen Gerti, whose divorce from Tom had come through. Gerti, who always lacked tact, told Antonia she had been to a Christmas party given by Sue and Thomas and seen Si and Sheila there. Sheila had said she was still fond of Antonia but Sue's happiness must come first. She had also said how pleased everyone was that I too had got away from my mother by going to Rome. Sue had told Gerti, who passed it on, that I kept in touch by letter with her: Mother felt betrayed. She now told Gerti that I had seen Dorothy with Tom before leaving for Italy: Gerti felt betrayed and, Antonia told me, had 'suspended' me.

Tom's first and second wives became allies in suffering and united in their fear that Dorothy had Tom 'in her clutches'; he seemed like a person 'with no will of his own'.

Mother said more about what she called the 'Eternal Family Problems' in her next letter. She had not been able to resist writing Sue a note to ask if the Christmas cheques had arrived. There was no reply so she swore it was her last gesture to them. She had listened to Tom on the radio programme *The Critics*, where he had shown flashes of his 'old self', until, in connection with an exhibition of Mexican art, he made a strange dissertation on the importance of ruthlessness. This 'new' Tom disturbed her, particularly as she felt it was her fault he had become interested in Dorothy. She asked herself how she could have been so foolish as to get involved with Dorothy, and traced it back to 'dear old Loneliness' and the need for a friend. First she had thought Benedicta, then Dorothy, could be a substitute for Eric:

> The brute fact, my darling Lyndall, is that I'm not suited to live alone & that probably Eric is the only person with whom I *can* live happily. Well, I've paid for leaving him with over twenty years of unhappiness & I pray, my pet, you'll never make such a mess of your life as I have of mine. I wonder if lots of people have the same conflict between being 'in love' & 'loving'. I imagine you had it over Dicky.

Dicky had been out to see me after Christmas and the visit went well considering I finally had the courage to tell him outright that I would never marry him, leaving me free to continue the affair with Willy who was now in Italy. Willy and I saw each other most weekends when he either came to Rome or I stayed with him in the 'Villino' near I Tatti. My life was going well; I would soon be moving into an unfurnished flat, which I would share with another secretary from

FAO, and had bought a car. I began to meet interesting people, among them the journalist Jenny Nicholson, who was Robert Graves's daughter, and her husband Patrick Crosse who ran Reuters in Rome. Jenny became a friend and protectress, and at the Crosses' beautiful flat in the Torre del Grillo looking out across the Forum I met a succession of fascinating and famous people.

But always at the back of my mind were my mother's and my first stepmother's unhappiness – for Tom married Dorothy on 20 March 1953, three days after Antonia's letter about him. In that same letter Mother told me she had been back to Dr Symes who had suspected her continuing depression and apathy came from 'feeling abandoned by everyone so that there's no incentive to go on living'. She tried to laugh off her troubles in the ending to this letter: 'WHAT an old Misery she's becoming, your low but loving Ma!' From now on our correspondence settled into what it would remain until the end of her life: mutual commiseration and consolation.

A 'Mysterious Woman', whom she nicknamed 'M.W.', exploded into Antonia's life around this time after reading her books, and was writing as many as three letters a day to her, as well as telephoning and coming round. She told me the woman was like 'a Catholic Kingsmill' without Dorothy's liveliness and good looks: 'She's bossy and fearfully, unnecessarily unattractive.' If she had taken the advice of a priest friend at the outset to brush off this woman brutally because she was a religious maniac who had her breakdowns on other people, she would have been spared much trouble over the next few years, but she was sorry for her and felt she ought to be the last person to slam the door in a neurotic's face. So, although she did at times try to fight off this intrusion, 'M.W.' would become another of Antonia's 'dominating women'.

My mother's period of 'darkness, depression and impotence' continued into the spring. She was trying, 'with God's grace', to be more humble and more contented with her lot, and was waging 'incessant warfare' against impatience, irascibility and mental vanity; but not physical vanity, for she was now almost resigned to being 'a plain, fat ageing woman'.

At the end of March a gypsy stopped Antonia in the street and tried to sell her white heather. Normally she would have refused, but something about the woman made her stop. The woman told Antonia her initial was E (Eirene); that she had had great sorrow during the past eighteen months because a daughter was married to a man who was 'ill-disposed' towards Antonia; and that many people were jealous of her.

The gypsy also talked of a cloud over Antonia and offered to take it away; but Antonia explained she was a Catholic and could not allow this. And yet, soon afterwards, she did in fact begin to feel happier and managed to start regular daily work on her fourth novel, having first listed in her notebook the names of over sixty people who she thought wished her well (including Dicky Muir, Malcolm Muggeridge, Graham Greene, Doris Lessing and Elizabeth Bowen). I was not among them, nor, of course, was Sue. 'It is possible I have only two *real* enemies: Thomas and Dorothy Kingsmill' she concluded.

She wrote me a long letter at that time which said she was feeling a great deal better and being firm with herself. Now that she was alone in the flat (Daphne had got married and a new lodger had not yet taken her place), she was making herself overcome loneliness by inviting friends to dinner and accepting invitations, even if they were not 'madly exciting':

> Living alone, I take to scolding myself aloud . . . muttering like the White Rabbit: Now put your coat *away* . . Now *finish* the ironing before you water the flowers . . Now, now, you've nothing to grumble at. You've paid the rent, you've got a new hat, you've still got your five senses and you're going to a play tomorrow night.

But not long after things started going better, Antonia wrote me a short note – 'or rather a scream' – to say she had received a letter out of the blue from Tom's solicitor informing her that he was applying to have her maintenance order annulled. She admitted that Tom was paying her more than the legal amount of £12 a month agreed after their divorce, having increased it to £20 ten years later when he was well off and she was very hard up, but, apart from the 'appalling' financial blow, what had shocked her was that he had not written to her himself about this: 'I haven't done a stroke of work all morning and I have been working steadily, if not well, for many weeks.'

I was in disgrace with Tom, too: he had sent me a copy of his new book, *Love's Apprentice: A Handbook for Combatants in the War of the Sexes*, with a note telling me how happy he was with Dorothy who stimulated and inspired him, but he thought my thank-you letter was full of 'thinly veiled insults'.

Antonia had received a copy, too. She felt '*horribly* depressed' after reading it when she remembered what Tom had written at his best, and accepted sadly that they were now 'completely out of sympathy with each other's work'. She was horrified to hear from Tom's sister, Esther, that he had sent a copy to his father, who was now very frail and had retired to Westmorland, for, apart from analysing 'bitches' and 'cads', the last chapter was a cynical treatise on religion. The book did not get good reviews: in the second volume of his autobiography[1] Tom says 'I was deeply disappointed by this reception, but consider now that it was perfectly just', and adds that he regrets ever having written such a book thirty years ago.

Not long before, Dorothy had taken Tom to meet Meher Baba when he was on a brief visit to England. Tom was so impressed that he at once shed his agnosticism and began to study the *Discourses* of Meher Baba. Many years later he and Dorothy wrote a book, *Much Silence*, about the life and teachings of their Indian master.

The day after receiving the letter from Tom's solicitor, Antonia met Sheila in a lift at Harrods. They exchanged a stiff 'Good morning', but Antonia could not resist asking to have a word with her after they both got out on the same floor to exchange their library books. Sheila replied, 'I can't imagine anything I could possibly wish to say to you, Tony.' Antonia walked away with her knees shaking and her teeth chattering from shock. A fortnight later she still could not get over it:

> Nothing can obliterate – yet – the memory of Sheila's face & voice. Since she is kind by nature, she must think I've done something unforgivable. It is such a nightmare trying to imagine what it can be. After that, I feel Sue will *never* relent towards me.

While the alimony battle was being fought, payments from Tom had been stopped. However, Mother told me there was an element of comedy in all the beastliness: she was at last learning to become an expert in cheeseparing – 'your Ma at the moment is the meanest woman in London'. To make things worse, Eric, who had been desperate for money two months before, and had borrowed everything Antonia had set aside for the June rent, as she stood over him while he wrote out a series of post-dated cheques, now said he could not honour the first of these. The final irony, she told me, was that

---

[1] *Under the Tropic*, published by Hutchinson, 1984

Tom's solicitors were presenting her as 'bloated with "successful publications" and "clearly with moneys in reserve"', and trying to show him as 'a harassed writer, living only on his freelance earnings', with no mention of the £5000 lump sum he had received on being fired from *Picture Post*. She wished she could send him a postcard saying, 'Take back your mink: take back your poils', but knew she had to let the law fight it out as she desperately needed Tom's regular monthly cheque.

Eichholz, the trustee of her father's estate, helped Antonia contest Tom's claim. At least he managed to prevent payments being stopped altogether, but they were reduced to the original sum agreed after their divorce, which, less income tax, meant her income from Tom was to be half what it had been over the past four years.

But Antonia's greatest worry was the book which was months overdue. All she had done since starting it after Easter was '*truly* unspeakably bad'. The postscript to this letter said:

> *Do* pray for me! I can stand the Tom thing & bear the Sue-Sheila thing but I *CAN'T* make myself write decently . . . I DO miss you so.

I decided it was time to go and see Mother. I had some leave due to me and some money in the bank because I had sold my second-hand car which had proved too expensive to maintain.

Antonia said she was pleased I was coming over since she was not going on holiday because of her financial crisis. In that same letter she gave me advice on how to deal with what I called our 'cruelly disunited family', asking me not to feel I had to take sides but to have more confidence in my own judgement of right and wrong:

> Don't condone what you think is wrong for fear of annoying the one you happen to be with. The only ones who really concern *you* are Tom, Sue, me, Gerti & Amanda & Nicolette. Give us all as much affection & understanding as you can – & criticise, if you can, to our faces! For we all love you and *that's* some unity in the disunited family!!

My first attempt at being frank with a member of my family was not very successful. I wrote to Tom about my concern over Mother's finances and also about a law case he was having with Gerti over the children, for although she had been awarded their custody he wanted them to stay with him and Dorothy three times a year, a prospect Gerti and Nicolette dreaded. It was none of my business and I was duly told so. I must have been very upset for Mother wrote in her notebook that she had received 'a terribly distressed letter' from me enclosing a 'horrid' one I had had from Tom. I did not reply to Tom's letter: he did not write to me for my birthday a week later, nor send me the usual present of a cheque, so I was even more downcast. Antonia commiserated: 'I know it is agonising to be estranged from a father one loves and to feel he is disapproving of one.' She also gave me some words of encouragement:

> You're doing fine. You've learnt *far* more than you realise in the last year including the tiresome old fact that one can't eat one's cake and have it too. This is something that Tom, at 48, has never learnt . . . You also had the experience during that first bad month in Rome of falling very hard without a cushion and that again is something Tom has never had. I doubt if Tom has ever spent one week, let alone a month, quite alone, with no job, very little money and no loving, admiring, sympathising person on the spot.

An 'Anonymous Donor' – Antonia could not imagine who – had paid £50 into Antonia's bank, exactly the amount of her fee to Eichholz. It had the effect of consoling Antonia that she seemed to be being 'taken charge of'.

It was strange to be back in England again in August. Even the ugly semi-detached houses that lined the route from the airport to London seemed welcoming, and there was a comforting familiarity in Ashburn Gardens, now no longer a prison since I had a return ticket for Rome in my pocket. Antonia and I got on very well during my visit, and I was glad I was there to hold her hand when her cat had to be put down. Domina was only six, but Antonia's letters had been full of how sick the cat had been for the past months because of fur blocking her intestines: 'My vet's bill is about equal to 3 years Symes for me!'

I wanted to make a fresh start with my mother and not to lie and conceal things from her any more. I told her I was having an affair with Willy and introduced her to him. I confessed I had been to Sue's wedding, and would be seeing her, as well as the Glossops, while in London. Afterwards I was able to tell Mother that Sue had spoken about her quite affectionately and confessed she thought Sheila was building it all up into 'too much of a thing'. Antonia wrote in her notebook that I felt Sue was dominated by Thomas and that I was inclined to agree that Thomas hated Antonia. She was amazed to hear that the Chittys saw Tom and Dorothy quite often, and that through

Tom, Thomas had got a job at Shell. 'Oddest of all, Tom sent Lyndall nothing for her birthday but sent Sue £10 – double what he usually sends Lyndall!'

But that meeting had put me in a new dilemma: Sue was six months pregnant and had asked me not to tell Mother.

I went to Westmorland to see Granny and Grandfather, for my aunt Esther had said she did not think Grandfather could live much longer. In fact he hung on for another four years, but I would not see him again. I feared they must be very hard up for Granny was economising even more than during the war. Not only was it still bread with butter *or* jam, never both, but now she heated up any left-over tea from the pot in a saucepan before brewing a new lot.

I did not see Tom, for he said I was only to visit him if I 'sincerely' wanted to see him and Dorothy. Since I could not accept Dorothy on his valuation in those days, and did not want to jeopardise my chances of seeing Nicolette and Amanda, whom Gerti had agreed to my seeing on the condition I did not see Dorothy, a rift was beginning between me and my father.

The night before leaving London I told Antonia that Sue was expecting a baby, having first made her swear to keep it more secret than I had. I also told her that when Sue had heard of Domina's death she had said that if Mother wanted she would give her one of the kittens her Siamese cat was expecting. I said I would write to Sue and confess I had divulged her secret, but almost as soon as I got back to Rome I received a letter from Mother which begged me not to because it might put Sue in a difficult position: Sue's offering her a kitten had touched her deeply. In her next letter Mother said she was getting up at six every morning to pray for Sue and the baby. 'I think about it all the time but am quite calm about it now.'

Sue's baby was due in November. From the first of the month Antonia started buying *The Times*. On the fifteenth she wrote to me saying she had, that morning, received a long letter from Grandfather who thought she must be anxious about Sue's baby which was ten days overdue. 'Oh dear, oh dear! Obviously he hasn't the faintest idea I'm not supposed to know. It makes it *so* difficult to answer his letter. Sue really is making things as difficult as possible for me . . .' Here Antonia broke off her letter to me. Later she continued it, in erratic handwriting, to say she had just phoned Sue – 'I couldn't help it' – who, to her relief, was not hostile. Sue was feeling fine and expecting

the baby at any moment; she insisted she had always meant to tell
Mother when it arrived. 'I still can't believe I've spoken to her & am
shaking as I write. It is 18 months since I've even heard her voice,'
Antonia wrote.

Andrew Edward Willes Chitty's maternal grandmother learned that
he had been born in Queen Charlotte's Hospital on 20 November
1953 from the birth column of *The Times*. She at once sent a Greetings
Telegram. She heard nothing from Sue or Thomas, though she did
receive a tactful letter from Grandfather giving her details about the
baby and saying Thomas's mother had told him Sue was very well and
happy. In relaying this to me in a letter of 5 December she also said:
'Sue is almost becoming a stranger to me in my own mind.'

Antonia was now given a Siamese kitten by a friend; and Emily,
who had recently returned to England, also gave her a marmalade one
two weeks later. These were Minka and Curdy about whom she later
wrote two short novels.

Antonia managed to take Christmas in her stride that year. She told
me there had been no card from Sue, so she did nothing either, but
both Dicky and Willy had sent her cards. Her card to me was an old
photograph taken when I was about eight at Binesfield. She had found
the negative while searching through old photographs, when she learnt
Sue was pregnant, in order to make a 'sort of family album which
ONE DAY it might amuse' her grandchild to see. She was staggered
when I reminded her that the sweater I was wearing in the photo was
one she had knitted for me to wear at Brickwall, because she had no
memory of doing anything so maternal: 'I've quite got into the way of
thinking I must have been a thoroughly unnatural Ma as a result of
the "set-up"'s estimate of me!'

In her annual summing-up at the end of the year Antonia wrote:

I think the nicest thing in 1953 was having Lyn at home for a fortnight.
The most painful Sue's not telling me about the baby. The most upsetting,
that meeting with Sheila in Harrods. The most alarming, Tom's solicitor's
threat. The luckiest, the donor. Most comforting, Emily's return.

She did not mention the latest bombshell: a libel action was being
brought over *The Sugar House*. One of the minor characters in the
novel, which took place in the 1920s, had the same name as a young
living actress called June Sylvaine, and unfortunately bore a physical

resemblance to her. All copies of the book were withdrawn from sale, although the case was not heard for over two years.

For the first four months of 1954 Antonia worked flat out on *Beyond the Glass*. Two weeks after it was finished she came to stay with me in Italy for the month of May. The 'Anonymous Donor' had sent her an open-date return air-ticket to Rome for her fifty-fifth birthday.

Despite bad weather the holiday was a success. I now shared a villa on the Via Appia Antica with two friends. For the first two weeks she went sightseeing on her own by day in Rome. Antonia had always had a phobia about crossing roads, but in Rome it reached such a pitch that if the church or museum she wanted to visit was across the road from the bus-stop, she would stay on the bus until it finished its journey, wait for it to turn round, and then travel back to the place she had set out for. Unfortunately the one-way system sometimes meant she found herself further from where she was going and with more than one road to cross. But she always recounted her morning's mishaps with good humour when she came to eat lunch with me in the FAO cafeteria. She spent the afternoon resting and studying Italian.

Every day at the same time, as she stood at the bus-stop outside FAO after lunch waiting for the bus to take her to the Via Appia, an ice-cream seller bicycled past. He always stopped to try and sell her an ice-cream, and she enjoyed practising her Italian with him as they discussed his wares. However, her Italian was not yet good enough for her to understand one day that he was no longer offering her an ice-cream, but a ride home on his bicycle. Before she knew what was happening he had lifted her off the ground and put her on the handlebars, with her feet on the ice-box, and was pedalling off with his prey. They had travelled three bus-stops before she finally persuaded him to put her down. By the time she recounted her alarming and undignified adventure to me over dinner, she was in the best of spirits, and told me a similar episode had happened to her in Paris a few years before: a road-sweeper had suddenly downed his broom and waltzed across a square with her in his arms. Her outwardly soft and feminine appearance apparently still aroused primaeval instincts in robust males.

The last ten days of her holiday we spent touring round Lazio, Tuscany and Umbria in the brand new Morris Minor which Willy had given me for Christmas.

We stayed a few days with Willy outside Florence and Mother was curious to meet Berenson, who had once been married to Logan Pearsall Smith's sister. She was as awed by him as I always was.

In hotels we shared a room to save money, but the snoring that had once been a boon became a burden. 'You will wake me if I snore, won't you darling?' Mother insisted. But there was no waking her. I called her name, I whistled, I clapped my hands; all to no avail. One night in Assisi, driven to desperation from lack of sleep, because my reactions when driving by day were getting slower and slower, I threw a slipper at her. It worked, but she woke in a state of such startled fright that I never did it again.

A letter she wrote me after her holiday sounds as if she really did enjoy it:

> I feel like a boa constrictor who needs a long siesta to digest the huge (but nourishing!) rabbit of Italy. In fact I am still living in it all, from Subiaco to the baby in the bidet[1] & jump nostalgically when a Vespa whizzes by . . .
>
> And one of the very nicest things was seeing so much of you. I felt so proud of my beautiful daughter and I was absolutely dazzled by your prowess as driver & interior decorator & your general savoir-faire and savoir-vivre.

In her notebook, too, Antonia described it as 'a wonderful holiday despite very bad weather', but said that since her return she had been exhausted: 'pressure inside my head, "lead spectacles" etc. but NOT, thank heaven, depression'. In a second entry a week later she was back to worrying about Sue and me. In Italy I had shown her a snapshot of Sue with Andrew which had once again triggered off her unjustified suspicion that I was concealing something from her and making '*no* effort to bridge the situation'. Was I afraid *of* Sue or *for* Sue she wondered?

Nothing would get it into Antonia's obsessive mind that I did not know of any specific reason why Sue refused to have anything to do with her. When I had seen Sue in London I had told her that Mother had changed over the past year and I was sure she need not fear her now that she had a new life of her own.

Mother's next letter told me a strange piece of news. Before flying to Italy Mother had revised a will she had made while married to Tom, in order to make me, instead of him, her Literary Executor. I was to

---

[1] One of the advertisements on the billboards that lined the Italian roads in those days, and which fascinated Antonia.

consult with Elaine over 'any question of publishing any unpublished stuff'. She had now heard from Eichholz that because of Sue's being illegitimate, which he had not known before, she would be excluded from inheriting Binesfield because of the miswording of Cecil Botting's will, and it would one day go to me: 'I am sure she will be furious with me but it really isn't my fault . . . though of course it *is* my fault that she is illegitimate.'

She told me she would have to leave everything else to Sue but was sorry that 'precious little it's likely to be!':

> It will be a great disappointment to her and perhaps a personal blow in that it brings up the illegitimacy which I hoped would never penalise her. On the other hand, I feel Si will look after her in his will . . . It will be another nail in my coffin. I doubt if even Eichholz can make her see that I'm doing all I can (little as it is) to redress the balance.

In her notebook Antonia wrote she hoped Sue would not be too upset: 'I hope still more that it will not revive her old jealousy of Lyndall.' She said, however, that in one way she was relieved I would have the cottage if she died, since Tom had practically cut me out of his life.

Tom and I had not corresponded for months. I was feeling guilty because Gerti had persuaded both Antonia and me to write affidavits for her case against Tom. I had done so only because Nicolette hated the idea of having to live part of the time with her stepmother. In my affidavit I said Tom had always been a wonderful father, but I had reservations about Dorothy because of things my mother had told me about her. Antonia, too, had been loath to comply with Gerti's request, but felt guilty for her part in having introduced Dorothy into the family. It took her a week to write her affidavit.

The case was heard in June. Fortunately Antonia did not have to appear, but her affidavit and some 'extraordinary letters' Dorothy had written her in 1949 were used as evidence. Mine was not used, thank goodness. Gerti rang Antonia up after the hearing to say Tom had seemed 'very nervous'. He had had to pay all the costs, and his counsel had 'openly admitted that there was no defence for the way the marriage had been broken up'; but the result had been a compromise. The children were to stay with Tom and Dorothy for eight days every holidays which worried Gerti, although it was much less than Tom had hoped.

Nicolette and Amanda went to stay with Tom and Dorothy for the first time at the end of the summer holidays. Afterwards, Nicolette, who was twelve and had always been fond of Antonia, whom she called 'Aunt Tony', asked if she could come to see her. She wanted to talk about Tom and Dorothy. She was upset and almost in tears as she told Antonia that, although they both went out of their way to be agreeable, she could not bear Dorothy. While with them Tom had given Nicolette *Love's Apprentice* to read, but she had not managed to get through it. Apparently she asked pathetically, 'Aunt Tony, what IS the sex war?'

Tom was reviewing books for a radio programme. Mother reported to me that the first one was excellent, though he 'got in a queer bit about Love being a frightening thing'. And again in the second one he ended up with love: 'He said that it meant the *transformation* and even the *destruction* of the person.'

When Antonia's collection of short stories, *Strangers*, came out in the summer of 1954, she heaved a sigh of relief that Tom did not start reviewing until the very week after it was discussed in the same radio programme. The first written reviews of the short stories were 'decidedly handsome', particularly the *Observer*, *Manchester Guardian* and *New Statesman*, but then there were three attacking ones: 'the cruellest went back to *Frost* as usual', implying she had regressed over the past twenty years: '*Frost in May* hangs round my neck like a withered wreath.' One critic had dismissed the story about her insanity as a 'fantasy bearing no relation to clinical madness'. Antonia was offended and disheartened: 'Whatever my faults, I don't fake about things which I have experienced first hand.' She analysed the quality of her writing, holding herself up to other writers. Then concluded it was silly to do so:

> Nearly as silly as the way critics compare me to others. I have been compared to George Eliot, Jane Austen, Galsworthy, Compton Mackenzie and (by Julien Green) even to Dostoievsky! However, one nasty review of 'Strangers' suggested the person whom I really ought to follow was Daphne du Maurier!

In October *Beyond the Glass* came out. She wrote to me that it was getting a very good press and Arthur Calder Marshall had praised it on the wireless: 'It looks as if it *may* lay the ghost of *Frost*.'

She was beginning to contemplate her fifth novel and whether it should be a continuation of the 'Clara sequence', which would mean having to write about Eric and Silas, but since she was busy on a translation it was only in the back of her mind. The translation kept her hard at work for the last quarter of 1954 so that she wrote very little in her notebook. The only long entry was about Sue. A chance meeting with her old friend Joan Soutar-Robertson and her husband, Cochemé, in the Tate Gallery had put her into a 'trembly' state because they had seen Sue and the baby the evening before. Apparently Sue, whom Cochemé found 'brittle and tense', had asked about Antonia, giving Joan the impression that she was still fond of Mother.

They had also discussed me, and Joan had said she did not like me. Antonia reflected that 'nearly everyone prefers Sue', and that Eric and Emily, as well as Joan, disliked and distrusted me. They may have been right, but as I had not seen Joan since leaving for Rome two years before, and nothing of Eric or Emily since my childhood, I hope their low opinion of me was coloured by what my mother must still have thought of me, for she was still sure that I was the one person who could bring her and Sue together again – 'Is she afraid of annoying Sue or is there some unconscious jealousy?' Or was there unconscious jealousy on her side, for I had just written to tell her that Sue and Thomas were coming to stay with me in Rome for a few days.

Recently Mother had had a dream about Sue and me. Although she often dreamt of Sue, she had commented that it was the first time we had ever appeared together in a dream: 'However unsatisfactory a mother, I *am* a mother – and a mother of *two* daughters, not just one.'

Joan also told Antonia that the Chittys were moving to the country; when Mother wrote to tell me this piece of news, she added that it would be almost a relief 'not to start any more' every time she saw any tall blonde in the distance wheeling a pram. Normally she avoided the nearby Little Boltons, but not long before she had gone down it because a road she normally took to go to Mass in the Servite church in Fulham Road was closed. There had been a pram outside number 25 where the Chittys lived: making sure there was no one at the windows and feeling fairly safe in clothes Sue had never seen, she approached the pram '*very* circumspectly'; but it was empty.

That autumn Gerti, who had had to move out of 26 Cheyne Row, stayed with Antonia for a few weeks. She wanted to go to Austria, but there was a court order forbidding her to take the children out of the country, which, she told Antonia, made her feel England was like some kind of concentration camp. While she was looking for somewhere permanent to live, Nicolette was at boarding school and Amanda was sent to stay with a friend in Highgate, where Gerti later rented a room to be near her. Tom meanwhile had been made features editor of the *News Chronicle*.

Living under the same roof, Tom's two ex-wives had long discussions about him. One evening Gerti said: 'I wish you'd tell me *your* version of how you and Tom came to get married.' Mother told me that, having recounted her story, she could not say whose eyes opened wider, Gerti's or hers: for Tom had told Gerti that they got married 'because Grandfather *forced* us to!'

However, Antonia began to see another side to the Tom/Gerti battle. While still feeling sorry for Gerti, who was far from well and suffering from insomnia, she thought that Tom was justified in feeling that she was unrealistic about what he should be allowing her as alimony, particularly as it turned out Gerti had a little capital of her own. Antonia told me this in confidence because she thought I ought to know anything that made the picture of Tom 'a little less black'.

For the second half of 1954 Antonia received small monthly payments from the 'A.D.' into her bank account which kept her afloat. She was also being pestered by the 'Mysterious Woman' who, though she had some good points, was 'frightfully neurotic' and bullied her. But, although the 'M.W.' overwhelmed her with presents, Antonia told me she was prepared to bet her last pound '(and at this second it *is* about my last!)' that she was not the Anonymous Donor.

However, by the time she wrote her annual summing up on 31 December, she had discovered that they were one and the same person, and told me her name was Virginia Johnes. In that summing up Antonia also noted: 'miracle of miracles, a whole year without the black depression'. And, of course, talked of Sue.

When Sue and Thomas had come to stay with me in Rome I had brought up the subject of Mother. Thomas had put on his 'auntie' expression while Sue explained that the reason she avoided her was that Mother was too domineering and the Glossops did not want her to have anything to do with her. They cut short their stay and went to explore Sardinia instead of Rome. All this I had told Mother when I came to spend Christmas with her, and she said afterwards it had been a great relief and 'made some sense in this bewildering fog'.

My life in Rome continued to be pleasant, but Willy and I were now

only loosely related. Our two-year affair was more or less over because
he was openly promiscuous which made me inwardly jealous. My
mother might have thought I had savoir faire, and compared to her
perhaps I did, but I was never at my ease in the realm of the worldly-
wise. At the end of 1954 I had begun an unimportant affair with a
handsome Polish prince, but he turned out to be more promiscuous
than Willy, so by the beginning of 1955 I was growing disillusioned
with men in general, despite having a surprising number of suitors.

Antonia started 1955 with another translation because she was hard
up. But by mid-February it was done and she settled down to working
out her new novel. The interesting people in the book were Eric, Silas
and her father: 'Clara, as usual, is a bore – interesting only in her
relationships.' It was now that she read Silas's letters to get back to
the period, and wrote to me about the effect this had on her, and how
guilty she felt over having judged him wrongly for having abandoned
her at the time of Sue's birth when clearly he had not. Strangely, she
made no mention of this in her notebook.

Nor did she mention a bombshell that hit her in April either, but
spoke of it only some weeks after the event when she wondered whether
it had something to do with 'a touch of the old neurotic paralysis' over
writing that had set in in June: 'Since the only serious upheaval in my
life lately has been Lyndall's marriage, is there some connection?'

CHAPTER 20

§

A Disastrous Marriage

It may be, not Lyndall, but Bobby that I envy – having
this wonderful new start at 45.
Antonia White, 8 June 1955

Lionel Birch, known to his friends as Bobby, had been the first journalist chosen by Tom to work on *Picture Post*. Over the years he had risen to be Tom's assistant editor, and now he was the editor. Only four years Tom's junior, they had been good friends from the start. I had met him during my teens at Cheyne Row and had always been a bit in love with him.

Now, ten years later, Bobby was in Rome for Easter, and Jenny Nicholson, who was the Rome correspondent for *Picture Post*, went all out to entertain her editor. On Easter Monday she organised a picnic at Bomarzo, to which I was invited, and there, under the stony stares of the grotesque Mannerist monsters, a strange thing happened.

'I can't think why an attractive girl like you isn't married,' Bobby said to me.

'I've never met anyone I wanted to marry,' I retorted.

'Then you'd better marry me,' he said.

'All right,' I replied without hesitation.

Bobby was forty-six that very day, 11 April 1955, and I was exactly half his age. He had recently been divorced from his fourth wife, the photographer Inge Morath.

I wrote to Mother that I was going to be married, and by return of post back came her response to my impulsive folly in a long and affectionate 'My darling Lyndall' letter. It said that, though she was happy I had fallen in love, she could not help being worried that it was Bobby Birch, and begged me to wait a while before marrying him: 'You see what disturbs me most, there *seems* a fatal similarity of temperament between Tom & Bobby.'

But five days later, having had a 'tremendous' six-hour session with

Bobby, who had returned to England, Antonia was won over by him, because he had not tried to 'put anything over' on her or convince her:

> What impressed me was that I feel he genuinely loves and understands you for what you are and that your beauty, though naturally he loves it, is only a delightful accessory . . . I see now that I've been worrying about you much more than I realise for the past year. And now it's as if the solution had suddenly appeared . . . And I am very, very happy.

But now my mother had new worries: Did I want her to come to the wedding, which would mean excluding Tom, since she was sure Tom would not come without Dorothy, yet she did not want to do anything that would hurt Tom or 'make any further shadow' between him and me? Ought I not to tell Tom's parents – perhaps without mentioning Bobby's four divorces? And would I do her a favour – one which she said Bobby had already agreed to – that, after our marriage, we would go into a Catholic church and ask a blessing on it? (When the time came, three weeks later, we had completely forgotten this promise.)

Bobby had also spoken to Tom. He had telephoned him and asked him for a drink, saying he had just returned from Rome and was under the impression that Tom was 'in danger of acquiring a son-in-law', though not saying who. Tom said he would prefer Bobby to come round to the flat: 'I suppose he thinks sons-in-law are Dorothy's pigeon also.' According to Bobby, Tom, though 'shaken', was 'very controlled and very nice'. For the first time Bobby became aware how fond Tom was of him: 'In other words, two of the people he loved most were carrying each other away, and it was painful.'

Tom then asked Bobby to see Dorothy alone. He had not liked Dorothy before, but now he saw 'a new Kingsmill'. She wished he would wait six months before marrying me, but otherwise was 'all for it' and assured him Tom would be too, soon. Bobby repeated in his letter to me: 'I liked her, apart from that, and am not going to conceal the fact from you. Put your hand in mine and we will work these things out together.'

Mother and Bobby had met again, but she knew nothing of his encounter with Dorothy, only with Tom. She was still enchanted by her future son-in-law and could not get over his being so nice to her. She was too 'excited and moithered' to get on with her own book, but found translating Colette a 'marvellous dope for my excitement about your Great News'.

Meantime passionate love letters and telegrams were crossing in mid-air between Bobby in London and me in Rome. We each had our recent pasts to tidy up and gave one another mutual encouragement in facing the people we were abandoning in order to marry each other. He described an anguished meeting with a girl who had hoped to marry him; I described my farewell with Willy:

> We walked over the hills behind Tivoli on a perfect, still, warm evening, and he insisted I explain all from the very beginning, although he hated it. He listened quietly, almost angrily. Just as I was nearing the end, he said suddenly 'Look at that beautiful Judas tree,' and when I turned back from looking he was weeping helplessly.

I had not expected it to be so painful. Willy and I had seen very little of each other over the past year, and the last time we had met, a few months before, he had said I ought to marry someone older than him and that he was not the marrying type. I had taken this to be his way of saying our affair was over.

Bobby and I flouted superstition by getting married in London on Friday the thirteenth of May, and did not tell any member of our families until afterwards – both Bobby's parents were long-since dead, anyway. Only our two witnesses, Diana Graves, who was Jenny's first cousin and had been a close friend in Rome, and Mark Boxer were there. Diana is now dead; Mark Boxer I have not seen for thirty years. As a wedding present he gave us one of his drawings: a resigned-looking woman with an enigmatic smile and a feather in her cloche hat chained to a self-satisfied-looking man.

All I remember about the dismal little ceremony is that when it was over the Registrar said to Bobby, 'You may now kiss the bride.' Embarrassed, I took one step back and knocked over the waste-paper basket.

After lunch with Mark and Diana, Bobby and I went back to the furnished flat he had rented in Kensington Court to get some sleep before catching a cheap night-flight back to Rome, where we were to pick up my car and drive it back to England, stopping for a brief honeymoon on the way in a house owned by Jenny in Portofino. The only other memory of my wedding day is that on waking from a heavy champagne-induced sleep in a strange bed in a strange room, I thought a stranger was lying beside me. 'What's that old man's head with grey hairs doing on the pillow next to mine?' I had time to wonder before fully coming to and recognising it was the man I had married a few hours before who was not old and with whom I was very much in love.

We stayed a day and a night in Rome because Jenny had arranged a lunch party for us. At the end of the meal, Iris Tree, who had recently come to live in Rome, stood up, and from the depths of her pocket pulled out three crumpled pages from an exercise book. It was her wedding present, an epithalamium called 'The Ballad of Beds', which she read aloud before giving it to us.

Iris, aged nearly seventy, had always championed love in every form, and in that poem revealed the beds of her wild past rather than sketching the beds of our future. Bobby and I would never share 'Beds in sand-dunes that the wind makes over', or 'Beds of havoc – torn sheets, flying feathers'.

Of all the beds I have ever slept in, the one at Jenny's *castelletto* in Portofino was the best fitted for lovers, raised so high that you could watch the changing seascape of the Mar Ligure, and so isolated that only the nightingales and the sound of distant waves disturbed the silent nights. We had reached Portofino in the late afternoon. After a glass or two of white wine in the bar overlooking the port, we set off to climb up the steep and narrow mule-track to the *castelletto*, accompanied by bird-song which grew louder as the sounds of the port below receded with each step, and the poignant smell of *pitosforo*.

Each room at the *castelletto* was filled with vases of wild flowers; a telegram lay waiting to wish us happiness; the maid had been told to put champagne in the ice-box and to welcome us. She stayed to serve dinner on the terrace, where fireflies danced, before disappearing down the hillside before nightfall. Next morning she reappeared with the breakfast tray decorated with roses.

But there the perfect honeymoon ended.

That afternoon the weather changed. Our remaining three days were spent sheltering from the wind and rain; and I got a bad attack of cystitis.

Back in London I began at once to house-hunt. The furnished flat Bobby had taken was characterless and expensive and we could not afford to stay there long. His alimony payments, plus a weekly contribution he had to make for a recently-born illegitimate daughter, who had brought the number of his children up to four, ate away his handsome salary. So did his analyst's fees.

The first time I saw Mother after having become the fifth Mrs Birch was when we took her to dinner at her favourite local restaurant, The Barbizon, ten days after our return from our brief honeymoon. It was the first time she had seen one of her daughters with a husband and her reaction was strange:

> To see her so radiantly happy truly does please me . . . Yet is there an inevitable unconscious envy at seeing her, so really lovely as she is now – and this is not just maternal pride, everyone admits it – with an adoring husband and everything beginning fresh for her?

Then she wondered if perhaps it was Bobby, rather than me, she envied, having this new beginning in middle age. It drove home the almost unbearable monotony and loneliness of her life and reawakened those 'old longings' for the company of a man who loved her. She wrote, 'Susan's defection turns up again with a new bitterness. No one was ever less self-sufficient than I, no matter what people think.'

The irony is that while she was writing this on a Wednesday, the marriage had collapsed, for me, the Saturday before. I had fallen out of love with Bobby even faster than I had fallen into it.

Our second weekend in England, we had gone to stay with an old friend of Bobby's who was a prep-school master in Hampshire. There was to be a cricket match that weekend between the boys and masters, but a recent flu epidemic had left the grown-ups' side a man short. Bobby, like Tom, had been a keen cricketer at university and agreed to play on the masters' side.

Dutifully I went with the masters' wives to watch the match. There was a slight drizzle, never heavy enough to stop play, and the whole school had turned out to will their Davids to beat the Goliaths. When Bobby's turn came to bat, he lolloped onto the pitch rather self-consciously, then tapped the ground several times with his bat in a most professional way before settling into a Compton-like stance to face the Lilliputian opponents. A nimble ten-year-old spin bowler sped towards him and launched the ball down the pitch. Bobby overreached for it with his bat, skidded in the mud, and fell flat on his face, but not before his bat grazed the edge of the ball. As he fell, another deft little monster leapt up from behind the wicket and caught the rising ball. The catcher's mighty feat was greeted with a burst of applause, while Bobby, muddied and humiliated, picked himself up. But he nearly collapsed again when putting weight on his left leg and a chorus of soprano titterings from the boys descanted above the alto 'oh's' of the lady spectators. The skid had torn a ligament in his groin.

As Bobby limped off the pitch, he seemed suddenly absurd.

From then on, everything Bobby did or said was transformed by my mind into being ridiculous or repellent. The man I loved had been a figment of a romantic teenager's imagination; but the disparaging way I would see him for the rest of our unhappy time together was equally removed from reality. His lop-sided smile, the way he gesticulated to emphasise some point when he spoke, had lost their charm. I noticed for the first time how seedily he dressed, in frayed suits and a shabby raincoat, his shoes worn down on one side of the heels. His hands seemed too large ('surgeon's hands' he called them); his voice was too nasal. But why go into the cruel list of what I began to dislike in him, since it is obvious I never saw him for what he really was, but first over-idolised, and then over-condemned him? Just as my mother had done with the men in her life, and was now doing with Sue.

The next year was perhaps the unhappiest of my life, and a desperate one for Bobby, too. He could not remain unaware of my turncoat feelings for long when, night after night with excuses of tiredness or a headache or whatever, I turned away from him in bed because I could not bear him even to touch me. This had never happened to him, he had always been the one to cool off first, and he was at first baffled, then distraught.

Besides the irony of Antonia, and others, thinking we were in the first bliss of marital love, there was the folly of continuing to house-hunt when I knew deep down the marriage was over. But the search continued and we finally settled for the very first house we had seen as the only one our limited means could buy. At exactly the same time Gerti bought a house in Hampstead for the same price, £4,000.

Pimlico was not fashionable in 1955. Only about ten houses in Clarendon Street had been done up since the war, so white-painted number 26 stood out brightly from its shabby neighbours, some of which were still severely bomb-damaged. The street was patrolled by teddy boys on their way to smash the windows of a new housing estate down by the river. Even before we moved into the house, which was sunny and spacious and had been well renovated, I felt there was something ominous about it; perhaps because while we were waiting to sign the contract vandals broke into the basement and smeared excrement over its pristine walls.

Since coming to London in my teens I had always dreamed of having a place of my own to furnish. Now the dream was fulfilled, but in the context of a nightmare. With my presentiment that the marriage was never going to work, decorating the house made as little sense as decking a corpse for burial. With a heavy heart, I sat making curtains in the evenings – for by day I now had a full-time job as a PA/researcher for Associated Rediffusion, the first commercial television company that was preparing to go on the air. At weekends we went in search of bargains to furnish the house.

I felt guilty accepting the wedding presents we were being given now that we had somewhere to put them: a magnificent fitted carpet for the L-shaped drawing-room from the management of Hulton Press; a sofa from the staff of *Picture Post*. The Hultons gave us a set of leather suitcases from Fortnum and Mason, our identical initials gilded on them – did they suspect, knowing Bobby's record of matrimonial disasters, their very first use would be to carry our separate belongings to different destinations?

Shortly after we moved into Clarendon Street we invited Mother to dinner in our new house. It began as a pleasant evening, but after a while Bobby and I had 'a painful showdown' in front of her, 'with a great many cards on the table'. Three months after writing so enviously of our happiness Antonia wrote:

> Lyndall & Bobby are in trouble. Lyndall is the discontented one: Bobby acutely unhappy. Her old trouble ... being unable to *accept* love. He thinks analysis the only solution for her ... I am terrified of interfering ... As always, nothing to be done but pray ... The real trouble, of course, is that neither of them has any religion. Analysis cannot take the place of that but it *could* remove some of Lyndall's psychological jams: this incessant compulsion to pursue something, get it, then not want it.

It had been Bobby's analyst, Dr Klauber, who had suggested I might need treatment. So, a few days after our dinner with Antonia, I agreed reluctantly to go to an appointment he had made for me with a director of the Psycho-Analytical Society, since it was the least I could do to show I was willing to try to make amends to Bobby for my seemingly heartless behaviour.

A secretary showed me into a dimly lit room where I was surprised to find myself greeted by a kindly woman in her sixties, for the androgynous title of 'doctor' had not prepared me for a colloquy with a woman. No sooner was I seated than I apologised for wasting her time, assuring her I was not in need of treatment. Within ten minutes, after a few penetrating questions, I was reduced to a heaving heap of tears with no handkerchief to wipe them away or blow my nose on.

She got up and put a wad of Kleenex tissues on my lap. Then, giving me a friendly pat on the shoulder, said, 'We're going to have to do something about you at once, aren't we? But it isn't going to be easy because all the best analysts are fully booked.'

Weeping too much to answer, I could only nod assent.

She came back a few minutes later looking pleased. She had arranged for me to be seen by one of the most brilliant young Freudian analysts who, she said, was related to the Aga Khan. He might be prepared to fit me in before his first patient each morning.

M. Masud Khan was disturbingly attractive, straightforward and severe. He wore a dark blue blazer, which I didn't like, and a pair of dark grey flannel trousers, which I did. He agreed to take me on for five fifty-minute sessions a week before work. But when I heard the cost, two guineas a session, which would come to more than my entire weekly salary of £8, it seemed that now I was persuaded that I needed psycho-analysis it was way beyond my means and I would have to renounce it. But Masud Khan ignored my protests: 'Everyone uses that excuse, but they find the money somehow. So we'll see each other next Monday at seven o'clock.'

My chief memory of being analysed is of trying to keep awake as I lay on the couch, with the gas-fire humming, and the wintry world still dark outside his window. There were agonising silences as I tried to think of something to say, while the smell of the Gauloise cigarettes Masud Khan smoked reminded me of French railway stations, and from there my mind drifted to Rome which I was missing horribly. Whenever I had had a dream the night before, I would proudly tell it to him in great detail because I thought that was what analysis was about. If I had not dreamt, I felt defeated. After a while he told me dreams were not *that* important, and my reticence to converse was a way of expressing a resistance to being analysed. Tactfully he pointed out that I was paying for these silences which were not getting us on very far.

And money was indeed a problem. All of mine, and more, was going on analysis, so I depended on Bobby for everything. He was always broke after paying all his commitments – not just alimony and maintenance, mortgage and loan repayments, but also the hire-purchase payments on the refrigerator, the gas oven, the dining-room table etc. Also he had started drinking and, though I did not yet know it, he was gambling on horses and greyhounds in the hope of paying for this. All our careful accounting was worthless as the precious pounds flew after horses and dogs that seldom ran as fast as expected. On the rare occasions they won, Bobby would drink away his winnings to celebrate; when they lost, he would drown his despair with yet another whisky. He only confessed he was gambling when the week finally came when he could not give me any housekeeping money because a 'certain winner', a 20 to 1 outsider, instead of multiplying it into £100 by winning, had let the £5 we needed for food provide some bookmaker's fare instead.

We decided to let the ground-floor room to a lodger Bobby found through a friend. He was a man of about thirty with a double-barrelled name, who had been invalided out of the regular army after an operation to remove a brain tumour. He was so crushed with shyness and so over-polite that, if we met in the kitchen or clashed on the stairs, he would click his heels and half-bow before scuttling for the safety of his room like a rabbit heading for its burrow.

Every day, as married life in London grew more unbearable, I yearned for Italy and my lost freedom. The pall I had known since childhood, which had miraculously disappeared in Rome, settled on me tenfold as I shopped in the crowded Warwick Way market on Saturday mornings, or lugged the dirty washing to the launderette in Lupus Street before trudging back to spend the afternoon ironing the shirts of a man I no longer loved. How bitterly I resented having to concoct a meal every evening after work, especially as the *trattoria* life of a bachelor girl in Rome had not prepared me for kitchen slavery. We lived mainly on salads and soufflés I made by following an infallible recipe in the cookery book that had come free with the kitchen stove. But as Bobby lingered longer in the pubs on his way home, the soufflés sank lower until they looked like shrivelled pancakes.

Though I felt desperate and trapped in the dreariness of our life, I lacked the courage to end the marriage because Bobby insisted he still loved me and fervently believed analysis would sort out our problems.

We hardly communicated with each other directly about anything any more. Meal-time conversations were mainly Klauber v. Khan:

'My analyst says you . . .'

'How odd! *My* analyst says *you* . . .'

'That's because you haven't told him the whole truth.'

'He says you refuse to see the truth.'

Antonia and I did not see much of each other while I was married to Bobby. Meetings *à trois* were uneasy, not just because of the friction between Bobby and myself, but because Antonia's feelings towards him had become ambivalent. She decided he was 'tortuous and super-ficial', also 'slightly slick, slightly raffish'. But we kept in touch by telephone, and if I did not call at least once a week she felt it increased the state of 'curious blankness' she was in at the time – a state she blamed partly on her writing problems, and partly on Sue's estrangement which not only persisted, but which would soon be made more painful by the birth of a second child.

At the time I married Bobby, Antonia was already 'hopelessly' stuck over the novel and felt like abandoning it altogether: 'The writing of these novels is an enormous labour & that sense of squalidity, of staleness that hangs over them sometimes makes it almost unbearable to go on.' Mental strain was beginning to produce the same physical symptoms she had felt when writing *The Lost Traveller*, such as 'dead weariness', so that she could not get through a day without lying down for long rests, and feeling as if she were in a light state of hypnosis. Since she could not blame Dorothy Kingsmill this time, Antonia wondered whether Sue was the cause. As usual she pumped me for news, and as usual I tried to find a way to make her feel less personally affronted by Sue's denial of her by telling her that Sue had behaved in a cold, off-hand way with me, too, when she had come to stay in Rome the previous autumn. This had set Mother wondering whether Sue's streak of 'icy hardness' was her fault. While re-examining things she had 'pretty well clamped down on' for the Eric/Silas novel, she had had to face the fact that she had 'shirked respon-sibility' over Sue's birth: 'HOW can I blame her for her behaviour now?'

As soon as she stopped work on the book and went back to translating Colette, the 'angst completely lifted'. She finished the trans-lation in August, just in time to go to Ireland with an American friend, Dr Katherine Gurley, to whom she had dedicated *Beyond the Glass* with the words 'without whose encouragement this book might never have been written'.

While being driven through the Irish countryside, Antonia's mind turned back to 'brooding on a long-short story' she had been thinking over when on holiday in Italy the previous year. And on her return in September, she sat down and wrote it in eleven weeks, never putting it aside even to make an entry in her notebooks, as she overpushed towards the 'fierce deadline' she had set herself.

Happy Release turned into a novelette and is the story of a girl (Vanessa=Sue) who is alienated from her divorced mother (Leonora=Antonia) by her husband, her father and her stepmother (Lou=Sheila Glossop). A sentimental and venomous piece of work, it revealed all Antonia's resentments towards Thomas, Silas and Sheila for having satisfactory and happy relationships with her favourite daughter from whose affections she was excluded.

Happy Release was never published, which was just as well since it would have done Antonia's reputation little good. While admitting it was an unjust portrait of Sheila, Antonia liked *Happy Release* – perhaps because she had enjoyed writing it 'in spite of the immense technical difficulties' – and it continued to be her current obsession even after she heard of its rejection by the *Ladies Home Journal*.

It was Emily who finally removed Antonia's obsessive feeling about *Happy Release* by bluntly saying she did not like it. Although Antonia sputtered into her notebook about Emily's approach to writing being quite different from her own, she had to admit there was truth in what Emily said; and it was a clear indication that she ought not to have interrupted her 'real (agonising!) work'.

But when she returned to her novel, she was immediately faced with writer's block again. This was not helped by constant telephone calls from Virginia Johnes, the 'Anonymous Donor'. Not long before Antonia had accepted a loan of £300 which Virginia practically 'forced' on her. Now she regretted it and was desperately trying to make enough money not only to repay that loan, but also the total sum of the monthly payments Virginia made the previous year as the 'A.D.', in order to be rid of her: 'I've stood it for three years and I think that's enough. I really hope she is the last of my "dominating women".'

All through those three years since Sue's estrangement, Antonia had had curiously naturalistic dreams of reconciliation with her daughter, in which Sue was amiable to her again. She always woke from them with renewed sadness. She had another one soon after finishing *Happy Release*, maybe because Sue was on her mind, not only because she had been writing about her, but because she had received another letter from Grandfather.

Sue had kept in touch with Granny and Grandfather since her marriage, maybe because they were the only stable and conventional family contact she had to compare with the Chittys. And Grandfather, having seen that for the past fifteen years Antonia had calmed down and become a devout Christian again, and that it was his son who was now behaving contrary to his code of beliefs, had taken to corresponding with Antonia in a timid way, as if asking pardon for having once judged her so severely.

In December Antonia had a letter from Grandfather telling her that Sue's children had been baptised and revealing that I had been present. Since I had denied having seen Sue since the birth of her daughter, Cordelia, because I could not face Mother's possible reaction to hearing her grandson and his baby sister had been baptised in the Protestant parish church of West Hoathly in Sussex, where the Chittys now lived, Mother made what she called 'a little scene' about my deceit in front of Bobby. He defended my lie, saying 'What else could she do?' Just as my mother had dared to defy her father when Eric was with her, so, with Bobby backing me up, I finally stood up for myself in front of her, and she wrote down what I told her:

> I think Lyndall told the truth last night when she said it embarrassed her when I asked her about Sue & obviously longed to be given some hope which she could not give. Also that her loyalties were divided & she did not want to spoil her relationship with Sue by mentioning me. This is something I have to face and accept. I *must* not try & attach Lyndall to me at the expense of her relationship with her sister. So I am going to try hard not to mention Sue when I see Lyndall – fully realising how hard that will be. It is not fair to Lyndall to demand more than she is prepared to give: it only drives her to deceit.

Although I had told her the truth, I had not dared to upset her further by telling her that I had become Cordelia's godmother. Instead I gave her the consoling piece of news that Sue had asked the clergyman to make sure the baptismal water flowed. This appeared to Antonia as a hopeful indication Sue was 'not entirely dead' to the Catholic faith: 'Is she having a harder time repressing her Catholic side than one thinks & is that one reason why she so resolutely cuts me out?'

Antonia said I had been 'very sweet' when we parted and she did not think the scene had upset me.

But of course it had. My mother never realised that her sudden outbursts of anger, which she saw as clearing the air, to others could be mighty storms that left damage in their wake. And anyway it had not cleared the air for her either, for in the privacy of her notebook Antonia continued to feel resentment against me, and thought perhaps I did not want her to be reconciled with Sue:

> I feel Sue has somehow re-established her old domination . . . [Lyndall] is obviously desperately anxious again for Sue's approval &, in a crisis, would give me up rather than Sue . . . I wonder if I shall ever have a normal, happy relationship with those two daughters!

And a fortnight later, because she had not heard from me for a while, Antonia decided that I had turned against her and must be seeing not only the Chittys, but the Glossops as well.

When I telephoned a few days later she said it was a great relief: 'I think I worked myself up about nothing.'

How often Antonia worked herself up over nothing, and convicted someone of treachery or negligence by building up some unimportant incident in her imagination until it became proof that the person had committed a crime against her, only to make a short and casual correction in a notebook later when she discovered her condemnation of their guilt was based on a false premise.

Apart from the fact that, with Sue living in Sussex, tied by two small children and her writing, and me in London tied to an unhappy marriage and a time-consuming job, we never saw each other, I was not seeing the Glossops in London either: Sheila was busy with her small child and she and Silas had not taken to Bobby.

My silence was because I had been sent abroad to do some research, and, before that – in fact ever since a few days before 'the little scene', which took place on the last day of 1955 – I had been living a drama of my own that made my mother's and sister's feuding insignificant.

During Christmas week, when his analyst was away on a short holiday, Bobby had tried to commit suicide. If a member of his staff, who happened to be waiting on the same crowded underground platform, had not realised what was happening, and hauled him back as he was about to throw himself under a tube train, Bobby would have been killed. At Bobby's request, his saviour escorted him to my analyst, since his own was out of town. Masud Khan then telephoned and asked me to come round.

It was Khan himself who opened the door when I arrived at his house that Christmas Eve. He told me it was against Freudian ethics for an analyst to see someone else's patient, particularly when that patient is the husband of one of his own, but Bobby had been delivered to his doorstep in such a piteous state, shaking and muttering incoherently, that he could not turn him away. He was now much calmer, Khan said, but I was not to let him out of my sight over the Christmas holiday.

He took me up to his consulting-room where Bobby sat huddled and shivering in an armchair beside the gas-fire, then left us alone. Bobby looked so much older that he seemed a stranger in front of that familiar hearth. As I approached, he opened his mouth to speak, but no words escaped. By the time I reached him, his shoulders were heaving with sobs. He stretched out his arms and pulled me towards him onto my knees with my head on his lap. Weeping too by now, I was horrified that I had brought a fellow human being to such a degree of despair, and resolved that come what may I must overcome my antipathy for him and somehow make this marriage work.

When I next saw Khan in a session he told me that he had been astonished when the sad figure on his doorstep said he was Lionel Birch: from my descriptions he had imagined someone quite different. He told me, 'I found him charming, you know.'

'I know,' I said sadly. 'That's why I haven't the heart to leave him.'

Three weeks later Bobby left me.

In January, Associated Rediffusion had sent me to Monte Carlo and San Remo to research a programme on casinos for the programme I worked on, This Week. Bobby drove me to the airport. We parted sadly, for his near-suicide had brought us closer; united in distress, an unexpected tenderness had sweetened our rapport in a way which would have been unthinkable before Christmas. He offered to meet my return flight and promised he would not waste money in pubs during the week of my absence so that we could dine at our favourite Soho restaurant the night of my return.

I actually missed him in Monte Carlo where it seemed a waste to be living in solitary splendour at the Hôtel de Paris. I missed him in San

Remo too, wishing he were there to share my excitement at being back on Italian soil.

On my return he was not at London Airport but, since it was *Picture Post*'s press day in Watford, I assumed he was working late. He was not at Clarendon Street when I got home. After a while I was hungry and went to see if there was anything in the house to eat. The kitchen was surprisingly tidy, without the mess of unwashed plates and greasy frying pans I always found after even a couple of nights away. This was explained when I opened the refrigerator to find all the food I had left for Bobby untouched.

After supper I was tired and went upstairs to go to bed. I had just got into the bath-tub when I heard footsteps running up the stairs and then Bobby hammering on the door. Before I had had time to ask where on earth he had been, he said, 'I've fallen in love with Venetia Murray. I'm leaving you. I'll call you in the office tomorrow,' and was gone.

My reaction was wild and unexpected. For weeks I had been wishing there were some way to leave him without hurting him. But now that *he* had found so swift a solution which exonerated me of any guilt, I was outraged and smitten with unreasonable jealousy. Wide awake from shock, and in a state of nervous agitation I had never known before, I quickly dried myself, put my clothes back on and set off in my car to Thurloe Square where, I remembered, Venetia and Timothy Jones, her handsome lover with a wooden leg, had once given a party to which we had been invited.

As I sped through the semi-deserted streets of Chelsea at midnight, memories of Venetia scuffled in my mind. I had first met her dressed as a newspaper at the Chelsea Arts Ball. Then, while passing through Rome, she had appeared at the picnic at Bomarzo where Bobby and I decided to get married. When I told him afterwards how attractive I found her fiery Latin good looks, Bobby commented, 'What odd taste you have! She's got no neck.' But, not long after we were married, he gave her a job as a staff writer on *Picture Post*.

I spotted Bobby's green-and-white office Ford parked in Thurloe Square, but could not remember at which number Venetia lived. Frustrated, and driven beyond reasoning by jealousy, I did something mad and pointless. Just before going abroad, I had noticed a coincidence almost too odd to be believed: Bobby's new Ford, bought in England, and my two-year-old export Morris Minor, bought in Italy, had ignition keys with the same serial number. In that moment of post-Christmas optimism that our marriage might yet be saved, I had even taken it as an omen that perhaps we were meant for each other after all.

I got out of my car and went to see if the key would unlock the Ford. It did. So I turned on the engine, moved the Ford round the corner and left it there. Then I drove my own car back to Pimlico and went to bed, but not to sleep.

The next morning at analysis I broke down and wept and wept and wept. 'Why do I feel like this if I don't love him any more?' I sobbed out. 'That's something you're here to work out,' said the imperturbable Masud Khan.

When Bobby telephoned me in the office, I confessed what I had done with the car. He was furious and made me fetch him in the lunch hour to go and pick it up. From Fleet Street to South Kensington he refused to mention Venetia, and would only question me about Monte Carlo. Finally, as he was getting out of my car, he said, 'We'll discuss our future this evening.'

'You mean you're coming home tonight?'

'Of course,' he said, surprised that I was surprised.

The next six months are hazy in my mind. Bobby usually slept at Clarendon Street, though I never knew whether he was coming home or not. Maybe this was because Timothy Jones had not given up his claims on Venetia.

One evening I came back from work and found blood stains trailing up the stairs and a bloody hand-print smeared on the drawing-room wall. The dark red stains continued up the stairs and, dreading what I might be going to find, I followed them into the bedroom. Bobby lay fully dressed on the bed, his face and clothes a mess of blood. Apparently Timothy Jones had come round to have it out with him over Venetia; and when their verbal row had turned into a physical fight which Bobby looked like winning, Timothy had whipped off his wooden leg and thrashed Bobby with it.

Another episode I remember clearly was our decision to give up our analysts. Over breakfast one Sunday morning Bobby expounded on our critical financial situation to me; he was getting deeper and deeper in debt trying to find twenty guineas each week for our analysts' fees. If we ditched them, I would have my salary to live on, so Bobby could give me less housekeeping money. The next morning I announced to

Khan that I would be giving up analysis at the end of the week. For the first time he did all the talking. He told me that for a man of Bobby's age analysis could help only in a limited way, but for someone young with my sort of problems, it could be really beneficial. The more he spoke, the more I recognised that I needed analysis, but knew there was no going back on my pact with Bobby.

On the Friday morning, as always, I wrote out a cheque to pay for the week's sessions. 'Well,' I said as I handed it over, 'this is goodbye, and thank you.'

Khan looked dumbfounded. He had thought his arguments at the beginning of the week had convinced me to stay on. For three months I had never seen him anything but calm. Now, for the first time, he betrayed emotion as he tried persuasion to put pressure on me not to renounce analysis.

'But I have no choice,' I kept repeating, 'Bobby was paying and he just can't afford it any more. He's giving up his analyst too.'

When Khan saw there was no reversing the situation, he recomposed himself and accepted his dismissal. He shook my hand and wished me well. When I had already started to descend the stairs, he called after me: 'You may be intelligent enough to sort things out for yourself and pull through on your own.' Although I suspected those words were said in order not to send me away without hope, in moments of utter despair later in my life, I would recall them to give me the courage to keep going.

Normally he left a ten-minute interval between patients. That day, because of the time spent on leave-taking, a youngish man was on the doorstep just about to ring the bell as I walked out of Khan's front door for the last time. Unnerved, he had leapt back down the steps and tried to hide behind a dustbin, knocking the lid clattering to the ground. He was still crouching there when I rounded the corner of Harley Street to have my last breakfast at the French café in Marylebone High Street where I had always consoled myself with a *café-au-lait* and croissant after analysis. 'At least,' I reassured myself, 'I'm not a quivering neurotic like that poor man.'

Since it was pay day, and I had my salary all to myself after three months of skimping, I bought a bottle of Italian wine and food to cook a special dinner for Bobby and me to celebrate the untimely end of our analyses, though a more responsible side of me was suffering a sense of loss and felt more like mourning.

Bobby came home late. He was slightly drunk, wore his most sheepish expression and ate nothing. After telling him how the parting with Khan had gone, I asked how he had fared with Klauber. He finished the last of the wine, then admitted he had not given Klauber notice and, what's more, did not intend to.

From then, until his departure in July, my memory is a blank; but on 13 May, our wedding anniversary, Antonia wrote in her notebook that I had called to say Bobby had resigned from *Picture Post* and intended to sell the house. He was thinking of going abroad to live by writing. Antonia commented this would leave me practically destitute and that I had therefore decided to go back to Rome.

Poor Lyndall! I feel it would be wiser of her, instead of rushing abroad (no job in sight) to keep on in TV and camp out here until she can make other plans. I think we can manage somehow.

But I had no intention of returning to live with my mother again, though I did soon have to spend a few nights under her roof.

One evening in early July, as I pulled out my nightdress from under the pillow before going to bed, a note fell to the floor. It was from Bobby and said he had left that morning with Venetia to go and live in the South of France. It ended: 'Goodbye. You are the only person I have ever loved. Bobby.' Now that he had left for ever, I felt strangely bereft and abandoned, despite having been the one who had turned away from his love. And those last words reawakened my guilt.

He told me he had left everything in the hands of a lawyer who would be dealing with all the bills until the house was sold; in the meantime I could continue to live there; and the lodger would pay his rent to the lawyer.

On discovering that Bobby had left for ever, the silent lodger sprang into my bedroom one night and burst into speech, babbling about how he had always known that we were meant for each other. I managed to escape and spent the night in the car. The next day I told him he must leave, but he turned nasty and refused, saying he had an agreement with Bobby and would only go if told by him to do so. So while Bobby's lawyer dealt with the lodger, I asked Mother if I could take refuge at Ashburn Gardens. Those few days under her roof brought back all my memories of how oppressive it was living with her. In our after-dinner talks she could not resist discussing Sue; and it was painful to see how her writing and money problems were as bad as ever, for she had not enough to live on, having somehow managed to pay back Virginia Johnes in the vain hope that she could be rid of her. It seems we also talked of religion, for she noted I had said I thought I believed in God, but was less sure about Christ: 'He frightens me.'

I had already written to FAO to see if they could give me a job again, but resolved that even if they could not I would return to Rome and look for some other work. As soon as the lodger left I went back to live at Clarendon Street and started packing up my things.

Before leaving I went to say goodbye to Sue and Thomas in Sussex. I managed to talk to Sue on her own for a few minutes and asked if she could bring herself to make it up with Mother. She said she had never meant the rift to be permanent, and would like to see Mother and show her the children, but was afraid of getting tied up emotionally with her again. She finally agreed that, if she could persuade Thomas to accompany her, she would see Antonia on the condition no reference was made to the past and that the meeting was not at Ashburn Gardens. I told Mother this when I spent the last night there before driving to Italy. She wrote in her notebook that, although she dared not hope Sue would do anything so definite, it was a relief to learn she was 'not as actively hostile as she appears'.

Before I left, Mother noted that she was glad I had gone to say goodbye to Tom, whom I had not seen for months. According to her, he and I found nothing to say to each other.

Three days after my departure my mother wrote:

When the daughter in Mrs Dale's diary told her mother she was off to Wales with her husband, I nearly wept. Lyndall's going, I suppose, which I haven't really had time to take in yet . . . I am terribly fond of her: more so every year.

Bobby married Venetia and they had a son, but the marriage did not last long.

His seventh marriage, which lasted until his death, was to a woman who, like me, had loved him since being a young girl. Their child, his sixth and last, was the only one he watched over from infancy onwards with a paternal pride and affection he had never shown before; she was in her teens when he died of cancer in 1982.

When I got back to Rome, Jenny confessed something to me. In that short time between Bobby and my falling in love at Bomarzo and getting married in Kensington Register Office, he had had a drink with his previous wife, Inge Morath. Jenny had seen Inge the next day and asked her what she thought about Bobby and me getting married. Inge was thunderstruck. Not only had he told her nothing about us, he had taken her to all their old haunts and, at the end of the evening, asked her to remarry him. Thinking it over after Bobby left, Inge was on the verge of accepting, and would have told him so the next day if she had not met Jenny first. Some time later, she became – and still is – Arthur Miller's third wife.

When I told Antonia that Jenny had been in a quandary at the time whether to divulge this piece of information to me, she wrote back: 'Why, why, why didn't Jenny tell you at the time? It might have saved you much misery.'

CHAPTER 21

❧

Reconciliations and Separations

I had at last given up hope. The restoration of it is almost
more painful than what I had grown used to.
Antonia White, 20 March 1956

Antonia and I settled back into our correspondence of recounting our own and consoling the other's woes, of which there were plenty.

In September there was a fire in Antonia's work-room which destroyed the furniture and several chapters she had done of a Colette translation. She had to begin again on the Colette, and the insurance paid only some of the damage, making her already bad 'finsit' desperate. I was having trouble finding somewhere I could afford to live, and my new boss in FAO was unpleasant and literally twisted my arm if I did not comply with all his wishes.

The libel suit over *The Sugar House* was heard in October. Antonia, or rather her publisher, lost, despite Graham Greene and Compton Mackenzie giving evidence to support her. She told me it was a 'really horrid' experience, which had often reduced her to tears, but Mary Siepmann held her hand throughout.

In December I got hepatitis which put an end to what might have been a new career before it even started. A fashion designer called Fabiani, married to Simonetta, had seen me across a room at a party and, to my astonishment, asked me to model their spring collection. I had been going every evening after work for fittings, and to learn how to walk in a less awkward manner. The month in hospital was vile, but I did not regret my lost second job because, as the time for the showing approached, I had grown more and more apprehensive about my role as a fashion model.

After a lonely Christmas – the Siepmanns had invited her for Christmas, but she was too broke to pay the train fare to Devon where they now lived – Antonia cracked a rib, but told me, 'I count it as the last tweak of 1956, not a bad beginning to 1957.'

However, 1957 had unpleasant things in store for both of us. Bobby, who had returned to England and to analysis, took to writing me vicious, accusing letters and posted back my original love letters. Antonia was still being persecuted by Virginia Johnes who, she told me, continued to have a certain power to upset her; and a close friend, Alick Schepeler, was dying of cancer.

Writing was going so badly on her novel, whose working title was *Clara IV*, that Antonia abandoned it for a while to write the first book about her cats. It took her sixteen days to write *Minka and Curdy* and she actually enjoyed it: 'It is a delicious change to write about cats instead of human beings; their psychology is simpler and more dramatic.' But she was not optimistic that it would make money: The Harvill Press, who had brought out *Strangers* which had only made her £85 in three years, offered her the worst contract she had ever signed.

In January Mother confessed she had committed her 'annual folly' of writing to Sue for Christmas and as usual had received no reply, so she had resolved '*definitely*' never to get in touch again. On the first of February she rushed to get Thomas's second novel from Harrods the day it came out. It was called *Happy as Larry* and she told me she could not follow the plot and found it '*very* rum – all hangovers, people being knocked out, incredible squalor'. There was a girl in the book who had a dreadful mother from whom the hero rescued her:

> I guess this is M E. Larry is just Thomas all over again, ever so sensitive & intelligent & misunderstood & seeing through hypocrisy & knowing all about life & death etc. etc. And, of course, never washing.

But she entirely agreed with one reviewer that Thomas had 'a marvellous eye & ear'.

Articles by Sue were appearing weekly in *Punch*. Antonia found them extremely funny and wished she could write to say how much she enjoyed them. But she was firmly holding on to her resolve not to give any further sign: 'For whatever reason, Sue wants to be rid of me for good. So she shall have her way.'

In her next letter a month later, after a paragraph about our financial worries from which I had been saved by a gift of £20 from Granny towards my hospital expenses, and she by £30 from Daisy Green-Wilkinson – 'it certainly is a miracle people like us somehow don't quite drown in the sea of financial troubles' – there was an astonishing

piece of news. Mother was still numb with shock after receiving a
letter from Sue three days before. It said she had decided that old
wounds had probably healed by now and that it would be nice if they
could meet again, but no reference must be made to the past as their
'versions of what had happened would never agree'.

The very day that Mother and Sue were reunited, 13 April 1957, I
was rushed into hospital for appendicitis. The letter from Mother
describing their meeting was brought to me by Jenny, who came almost
every day to the hospital bearing flowers and gifts:

> I can't tell you how odd that day was. Exactly like a very pleasant, very
> vivid dream. Both she & Thomas were extremely pleasant and hospitable.
> And yet all the time, though I KNEW this was Sue . . . I couldn't, or didn't
> dare, think of her as my daughter, in case the dream vanished.

Mother was '*crazy* about' the children. She found them natural and
easy to get on with:

> All Sue's sweetness comes out as a Mamma. And I must say Thomas is
> marvellous with them too – I've never liked him so much as that day. Sue
> looked radiant – more than I've ever seen her. It is amazing to see her
> *happy*, and so calm, managing everything so marvellously. We walked to
> the field she rents to keep the Exmoor pony in – she's just bought it AND
> broken it in. I was in bliss (but not *believing* it) pushing Cordelia in her
> little cart with Andrew trotting beside me, holding on to my arm.

Antonia also met her co-grandmother, Lady Chitty, and found her
'nice, quiet & shy'.

Her letter telling me all this ended: 'Now I just LONG to see YOU
happily married as soon as you have cleared away the obstructions.'

Just before getting appendicitis I had started what turned out to be
another unhappy love affair – the first one where I would be left before
wanting to leave. In less than two months, the first Italian I ever loved,
a handsome prince called Andrea, had abandoned me. I signalled my
distress to Antonia who sent back words of sympathy, and a warning:
'He might try and break into your life again. If he does I hope, hope,
hope you'll be strong and not let him.'

He did; and I could not resist his call to drive over a hundred miles
to dine with him and be back at my desk in FAO by eight o'clock the
next morning, which started the whole cycle all over again.

Mother began to worry that I had an awful sense of a void inside
me which I filled by falling in love: 'It stops you from being able to

use your many talents because as soon as "love" comes along, nothing else matters.'

I was becoming aware of a split in my nature. It was first revealed to me when Andrea and I spent a few days in Ischia, racing across the sea in a friend's speedboat to swimming parties and late lunches, and dining and dancing till dawn in an outdoor nightclub in an orange grove. But in the mornings, unable to sleep till midday as he did, I used to slip out of his bed and wander off to a lonely beach to swim. There, by chance, I met Iris Tree who had rented a tumbled-down farmhouse only a kilometre from the luxurious hotel where we were staying. As I lay in the hot sand, listening to her poetry and enjoying her reminiscences, I felt at ease and happy, something I never did in Andrea's disturbing company. But, like Cinderella in reverse, as midday struck on a distant church tower, I would hurry back to my other life and leave Iris and her dog to enjoy their freedom.

And it was Iris who tried to console me when Andrea abandoned me the second time. She noticed my heaving shoulders as I sobbed silently while listening to a classical guitarist one summer night at a party on Jenny's terrace, and came over to sit beside me. 'He wasn't worthy of you, Lyndall' was all she said.

After the final break-up with Andrea my mother wrote telling me not to feel humiliated. But one thing worried her: I seemed to be attracted by trouble-makers, or men with 'some extraneous "glamour"', such as money or a title. Yet she said she did not think I was '*fundamentally* worldly', otherwise I would have married Dicky or Willy.

In her next letter Antonia described staying with Elizabeth Bowen at Bowen's Court. She was falling in love with Ireland and had been tempted to 'chuck everything' and, for £100, to buy a Georgian house overlooking an estuary. But, apart from the fact she did not have £100, she realised it would have been 'crazy'.

Mother also told me Gerti had brought another court case against Tom and lost. Her alimony had been cut drastically, and Nicolette, not yet sixteen, was to be given £200 a year for her education until she was eighteen: 'then FINISH'. This would mean her ambition of going to university would depend on getting good enough exam results in order to be awarded full grants. (When the time came, Nicolette not only managed to support herself by grants at Girton, but was the only Hopkinson ever to achieve a double first.)

Antonia also reported that since her meeting with Sue she had received several friendly notes: it was a great relief to her to have this 'remote, but pleasant, association' with Sue and her family.

Many things happened to our family around this time. Grandfather, whose mind had been growing more confused in his old age, died in a mental home at the end of 1957. Shortly after his father's death, Tom accepted a job in Johannesburg, encouraged to do so by Dorothy. He was to run a magazine for black African readers and train a staff to work on it. Not long after he left, his mother died.

On his way out to South Africa in January 1958, Tom stopped over in Rome. He was alone: Dorothy was to follow when she had dismantled their flat and found a home for her daughter, Dorothy.

I enjoyed introducing Tom to my Roman friends and showing him my Roman haunts. When I drove him to catch his plane to Johannesburg after forty-eight hours together, our five years of undeclared feuding had reached a silent truce.

Shortly after Tom left, I was offered a small part as a nun in a film to be made by Fred Zinnemann, *The Nun's Story*, and took unpaid leave from FAO for a month. And in the spring I accepted a proposal of marriage from Edward Montagu.

I had first seen Edward, though he did not remember it, when I was working for Bernard Miles. Self-assured and handsome, he had rushed into the Mermaid, dictated to me a list of possible sponsors, and rushed out again. Our second meeting had been a week before the party/picnic where I met Bobby in 1955, when Edward was travelling Europe to escape being hounded by the British press after having served a prison sentence for homosexuality. A mutual friend had given him an introduction to me. We got on well and dined together every night during his Roman holiday. While I was married he came to a dinner party we gave for the Hultons, and, after Bobby left me, Edward had invited me to stay at Beaulieu for my last weekend in England.

Now, in March 1958, he came to Rome for a specific purpose: to suggest we should get married as soon as I was free. I had never felt so happy; he had always attracted me and I had never realised the attraction was mutual. He said he had wanted to ask me to marry him in Rome three years earlier, but had felt it might look as if he were using marriage as a cover-up so soon after coming out of prison, and had been upset when I married Bobby shortly afterwards. To celebrate our engagement, which had to be secret until my divorce came through, we drove to Naples to hear Verdi's *La Forza del Destino* at the San Carlo.

The next few months were the happiest of my life, though I could not confide this to anyone yet. Edward and I exchanged lengthy love letters, in which we planned our future and explained our pasts. When the filming of *The Nun's Story* ended, Edward sent me an air ticket to come over to England for two days to speak to a solicitor who might be able to speed up my divorce; and to a doctor about the pain in my right side which persisted despite the removal of my appendix. I could not tell Antonia of my quick visit since our engagement still had to be kept secret.

Antonia's fifty-ninth birthday on 31 March was a significant one. She had reached the age at which her father had died, and Sue and Thomas had invited her to go to a cinema with them to celebrate her birthday. Mother told Sue I had a part in a film and her 'poise was momentarily shattered. She recovered quickly but for a second we were back in the nursery!!' Yet, until my engagement to Edward, I had been envious of Sue: her *Punch* articles were soon to come out as a book, she was to appear in a series of television programmes, *and* she owned a horse.

Although Mother's problem with Sue was happily solved, her old problems of writing and money continued. She had started 1958 with a lecture to herself in her notebook: 'You can't be extravagant in ANY way but you can manage . . . So stop fussing and be CHEERFUL.' But by February she was desperate: the book seemed absolutely beyond her capacity. Would it be cowardice or common sense to go back to translating Colette? In the end she did neither, after having had a two-day collapse when her brain just would not function, which had frightened her. She redecorated the flat instead. Since this meant spending money, there was no choice but to go back to the translation, particularly as her rent had just been raised substantially.

In May Mother wrote to tell me the papers were full of a strange piece of news: Eichholz had died a few months before and it was now revealed that he had steadily been embezzling his richest clients' money since 1926. The Law Society's Compensation Fund did not have the half a million pounds needed to pay all the damages. Ironically he had always been very strict with Antonia about her over-spending: 'I had almost to go on my knees to get him to advance me enough of Daddy's money to buy a black coat for my mother's funeral.'

Eichholz's death was fortunate for Sue. In her next letter Mother told me she had been to see his partner, who had worked with him for thirty years and never had the least suspicion of what Eichholz was up to – it would take years to discover the clever and devious ways he had used of investing clients' money in non-existent companies and properties. The partner thought there was a way for Sue to inherit Binesfield, if I would sign away my rights to it. When I had suggested this to Eichholz three years before he had said such a thing would not be legal. Mother asked me whether I was still prepared to do so, adding, 'I am sure this IS the right decision – it will make both you & Sue much happier.'

Although I could not see why this should make *me* happier, I signed the Deed of Gift when it arrived a few months later. By then Sue and her family had set sail for Africa, because Thomas had been sent to Nairobi by Shell, for whom he still worked: and by then my relationship with Edward, which both our mothers now knew about, was in trouble.

The doctor to whom Edward had sent me had diagnosed an ovarian cyst. Worried that this might interfere with my chances of bearing an heir, Edward arranged for me to have an operation in London in July. Then I went to convalesce at Beaulieu, not at Palace House but in the house of his widowed mother, Pearl, who lived nearby. She could not have been kinder. When I arrived she took me up to a flower-filled bedroom where a present of a pink silk nightdress was laid out on the bed. But I began to feel, as I had when Dicky's mother had given me pearls, that I was being trapped in a world to which I did not belong.

Now that the first part of my divorce was over, and I was waiting only for the decree nisi to come through in October to set me free to marry him, Edward introduced me to his sisters and some of his closest friends, as well as to his estate manager, as the future châtelaine. Again, they could not have been more friendly and welcoming, but again I heard my inner voice saying 'You're an outsider, you don't belong here.'

In those two weeks at Beaulieu staying with my future mother-in-law, I saw another side of Edward. There was a restlessness in him; he could not stay still for more than five minutes without having to rush off and busy himself with something. He had already opened Palace House to the public, and, with his collection of veteran cars and other attractions, Beaulieu would soon be near the top of the list for attendance figures at English stately homes. There was also something in him which, although he was in no way a show-off, seemed to enjoy being in the limelight. I remember him playing tennis one afternoon, apparently unperturbed by the ogling visitors in the grounds of Palace House watching him play. Since I was still recovering from the operation I was luckily on the side-lines, but I knew that I could not live always in view of prying strangers.

Edward wanted us to be married with pageantry in November; I was to arrive at Beaulieu Church in an open veteran motor car. When I asked why we could not be married quietly – after all I was a divorcée and he had been in prison – he said the estate workers expected a spectacular occasion. He wanted to give me a veteran car and a mink stole as a wedding present; I said I would prefer a piece of land by the sea in Italy (which in those days cost far less than a mink stole) where one day we might build a small holiday house. He insisted that I would need a mink stole for the social events we would have to attend.

I went back to Rome in August with grave doubts. Was I marrying for love, or to escape from my dreary job as a proofreader in FAO? I became obsessed with the same idea I had had when engaged to Dicky – that I would only know the answer if I achieved something on my own before marrying. I pleaded for the autumn wedding to be postponed to the spring, for I was in the middle of rewriting a novel and wanted to finish it first.

Mother tried to keep pace with my confused feelings and thoughts, and to see both Edward's side and mine in endless conversations with him and letters to me. His directness impressed her each time they met, and she liked him. She told me she felt that there was something suspect in my wanting to prove myself before marrying him, and she feared it came partly from my 'terrible' lack of self-confidence – 'the idea people cannot value you for what you *are*'–and partly from old nursery rivalries with Sue, who was establishing herself as a writer. She pointed out that if I really cared passionately about writing, I would have concentrated more on it before: 'This sounds harsh, and I realise how hard that would have been for you with no money & all the temptation of being a desperately pretty girl with an appetite for life.' She wondered whether this 'success' I sought was 'a kind of chimaera luring you to look for it now in this place, now in that, but never where you are, preventing you from *real* fulfilment'. One letter concluded: 'As long as you regard marrying Edward as a pis-aller, a kind of confession of failure, of course it will NEVER work.'

I had just persuaded Edward to agree, reluctantly, to a spring wedding, when one of his friends leaked the news of our engagement to the press.

Edward knew what it was like to be hounded by journalists, but I had no idea how to deal with it. When my telephone rang at three o'clock one October morning, waking me out of a deep sleep, and a reporter from the *Daily Express* said that Lord Montagu had just told him we were engaged and he would like my comments on this statement, I did not know this was a well-known trick. Not wanting to contradict Edward, I admitted it was true. All hell broke loose.

Edward said I must come back to London and together we would decide what to do and face the press. I refused. He wrote to me saying he thought it better to break everything off. His letter arrived on the day John XXIII was elected Pope. As the church bells pealed out joyfully over Rome, I sat weeping in my room, feeling more desolate than ever before at having thrown away a chance of happiness and security with someone whom, in an odd way, I loved. The future seemed a pointless blank.

I even considered pretending I had not received the letter and rushing to England to find Edward. I booked a place on a night plane and Jenny lent me the money to pay for the ticket. But a couple of hours before leaving, around midnight, a dog which had been left in my care, and which I was to leave with a friend on my way to the airport, started to whelp. She was in great distress as one puppy after another was born dead, so I could not abandon her, and took it as a sign I should not go back on my decision.

Edward now made such emphatic denials to the press that it sounded as if we had never even known each other. I appeared in the papers as a publicity-seeking adventuress out to ensnare a rich peer. As the story had reached Italy, too, my life in FAO became almost unbearable, with people either making sarcastic comments to my face or whispering behind my back. My only consolation was that my real friends who had known of my dilemma for some time, like Iris and Jenny, remained staunch allies.

I told Mother I was trying to forget my misery by completely rewriting my novel: 'But it is still just as ghastly so this makes me even more despondent.' I was tempted to take one of two jobs I had been offered in America, working for the conductor Thomas Schippers in New York or for David O. Selznick in Hollywood, but did not have the money for the fare, particularly as I now had to repay Edward for my operation and for the divorce lawyer's fee.

Two months later, in January 1959, Edward became engaged to a girl he had known since childhood, and they were married in the spring. Meantime I had started the first of what would be a chain of disastrous affairs, where the end result was always the same: either I was left by the ones I thought I loved too much, or I left those whom I could no longer love because I thought they loved me too much. Over the next three years it would have needed a Leporello to catalogue the poets and painters, princes and playboys, pianists and producers, in whose embraces I sought to escape from myself, for sex in itself did not interest me.

But I continued to suffer over the loss of Edward. In the summer I typed a letter to Mother from the office in which I told her that I could not concentrate on reading the proofs of *Fish Farming in the Philippines* because my mind kept wandering back to memories of the previous summer with Edward at Beaulieu: listening to music in the ruined abbey, picnicking in the New Forest with ponies roaming nearby, boating at Buckler's Hard. But for my pride and stupidity I might now be expecting our first baby. This was made worse when I was asked to be an extra in Fellini's *La Dolce Vita*. A fellow extra was a fortune-teller who sighed and shook his head as he read my cards because, he said, I had recently taken a hugely wrong decision.

This feeling that I had made a wrong decision would haunt me for the next eight years. Every time I saw a picture of Edward in a newspaper, or read about the births of his children, it was like being stabbed in the heart.

Mother continued to console me in her letters; her friend Sonia, George Orwell's widow, who also knew Edward, told her that his wife was finding the strain of keeping up with all his activities very exhausting. But Antonia's letters were more concerned now with her preparations for going to America in the autumn to teach creative writing for one semester at St Mary's, a Catholic Women's College in Indiana. She had only accepted the invitation because the fifth novel was still proving impossible to write, and after a run of twenty-one translations – ranging from Colette to a political biography of General de Gaulle – she needed a change. She also wanted to get away from

Virginia Johnes whose indefatigable pestering still continued after five years of 'persecution'. Nine months before her departure she told me she was in a 'Proper State' about going to America, and already planning her wardrobe and making lists of what to take.

In May 1959, four months before sailing on the *Liberté*, she started 'dieting and exercising like mad to try and get *physically* fit for the ordeal'. She had '*awful* cold feet about plunging into such an utterly unknown life & being unable to escape till I've done my time (viz 4 months)!!'

In fact Antonia enjoyed her time in the United States. She felt well and her tightly written air-letters were filled with how amused and interested she was by every aspect of the New World: 'England seems completely unreal, like another planet I once lived in.' Her problem was not loneliness, as she had feared, but how to have a moment alone. She did the most unexpected things, such as becoming a supporter of the American Football team of St Mary's brother college, Notre Dame; every Saturday afternoon she joined in the tribal rite of the girls 'bawling out incantations ordered by the cheer leaders, worked up before at a "Pep Rally"'.

Antonia told me she was surprised to discover she did not mind that her destiny to be a schoolmarm had caught up with her: 'I seem to be good at it! I adore my students, find the work thrilling & absorbing, & am getting results already beyond my wildest hopes.'

One pupil, in particular, would remain a friend for the rest of her life. Her name was Lyn Cosgriff and she became another 'dream daughter', like Elaine. But after Antonia's death Lyn told Sue:

I did try hard to be a good friend to Antonia . . . but I always knew I had to stay clear of her temper. The few times she showed it were enough to let me know that I never wanted to provoke its full force! Still, one's friends are never perfect, and she gave me much of herself. Perhaps in a way I, and her other 'adopted daughters', were a kind of revision of her failures with her real daughters . . . However, as far as Antonia was concerned, the one thing I knew right away was that I wouldn't have wanted to be her born daughter.

However, after four months, Antonia was glad to come home. On her return to Ashburn Gardens in February 1960 she wrote to me describing her leave-taking from St Mary's College:

There were actually *tears* when I left – even from the 80-year-old she-dragon who ruled the Faculty Table with an iron hand, & from the severe Classics

Mistress who will be my lifelong friend & from my 'lambs' – my darling students. I was overwhelmed with presents and found flowers in my cabin on the boat . . . Even the waitress in the canteen cried when I left and the coloured maid who cleaned my room.

Mother also told me she had made enough money to last her until the autumn, which meant she could concentrate solely on *Clara IV* for the next six months.

It is sad to see from her notebooks, and from her letters to me, how quickly her neurotic symptoms returned as soon as she started work on an autobiographical novel again, right down to the physical and mental exhaustion accompanied with anxiety dreams bordering on nightmares, until by July she felt it was like the 'bad old days'.

By then Sue and her family had returned from Africa. In a letter Mother told me she felt Sue had been really glad to see her again, though they only talked 'surface chat'. She also enclosed a newspaper cutting about what she called Tom's 'splendid act of heroism' – he had saved an African from being stoned to death by confronting an angry mob alone.

After having worked for five months on *Clara IV*, Antonia confessed in her notebook that she was suffering from not being able to discuss the book. Although she seemed to be attracting more affection than ever before in her life, and people sought after her company, it was to discuss their problems and not hers. Only Elaine seemed to care about her writing – and Eric on the rare occasions she saw him. She noted that over the last ten years all the people who had wanted her friendship were women – 'the Lord's little ironies!' She wondered whether God had been trying to drive something into her 'thick head' during these months of 'impotence and failure': was He trying to show her that her role in life was to listen to other people's problems rather than write about her own?

> The older I get, the *sadder* I find people and the more courageous. You listen to someone boring you, yes, to tears & yet you love them – you listen to something underneath.

By the autumn, when it was time to turn back to translating to earn some money, Antonia was desperate. She wrote to me that she had flogged herself on until she was 'on the edge of some kind of crack-up', but all she had to show for it, after throwing away nearly two hundred pages, was 'a hideous mess of some 80 scribbled, pasted up, not even consecutive pages' which she would probably scrap when she saw them typed up:

> Over & over again these last few weeks I would find myself milling over & over one perfectly simple sentence, think I had spent maybe an hour on it, look at the clock & find 4, 5 or even 6 hours had gone by. It became a little frightening. I would go out & walk about the streets in a kind of hypnotised misery, my mind quite blank.

Finally, one Sunday in September, after walking round Kensington Gardens for an hour or two in a trance, 'but in a sort of calmness of despair', she asked herself, 'What is the worst that can happen?' and the answers were:

(a) 'You can't write this particular book.'

(b) 'You may never be able to write *any* book again.'

I too was trying to write another novel – I had long since thrown away the first one. This one was about a love affair with an Italian journalist and adventurer from which I had been trying to extricate myself for over a year. He had turned out to be an alcoholic and had reduced me to near suicide by his schizophrenic behaviour, alternating pathetic pleas for tender love and forgiveness with sadistic threats and perverse demands.

No longer could I confide even to my mother all that was happening to me with 'the fiend' (as we called him), nor how estranged I had become from myself as well as from any hope that a God existed. When I came over on a surprise visit at the end of 1960, and went straight to the Chittys where Mother was to spend Christmas Day, she did not even recognise me, and afterwards described me in her notebook as an 'uncertain quantity'. She also said in that last entry of the year that she was beginning to feel her age and could not 'take in' things as she used to. She was nearly sixty-two, and feared she had come to the end of her talent.

A few months later, just before my thirtieth birthday, 'the fiend' found the first chapters of my book: he destroyed them and tried to kill me. To escape from him, I sold my car and bought a one-way ticket to New York where a friend had offered me the loan of her apartment while I looked for a job. I had resolved to become a career girl, whatever I thought that meant, and was determined never to fall in love again. I chose 16 September as the day to set sail from Naples, since that was the date I had fled to Italy nine years before in 1952.

CHAPTER 22

༷

Antonia White's Old Age

*Without realising it, one has developed a different point of
view which I suppose is what old age is.*
Antonia White, 31 December 1962

Shortly before I left for America, Antonia moved into a new flat
because her landlady at Ashburn Gardens had refused to renew her
lease for longer than three months at a time. She persuaded the trustees
to let her sell Binesfield and reinvest exactly the same amount in buying
a flat in nearby Courtfield Gardens. All writing was put aside for three
months as she packed up her belongings and sold off her excess
furniture to pay for refurbishing the new place. She wrote to me
apologising for having had to sell off the things she had meant to leave
me:

> the Bechstein piano, my darling blue Coalport basket, my diamond ring
> inherited from poor Alick, my pretty candlesticks – everything I can get a
> few pounds or even shillings for. WILL YOU FORGIVE ME? I FEEL
> AWFUL. I wouldn't have done it if I weren't up against the crisis of all
> time and the *desperate* need to have a home. I sold the aquamarine ring
> this morning for £5. If you are angry, I will pay you the £5 if you like, only
> PLEASE not yet.

The aquamarine ring had been Tom's engagement present to her;
and she had given it to me on my twenty-first birthday.

I did not demand the £5. Instead, I see from her next letter, I sent
her £25 as a present.

She had had no regrets about leaving the flat where so many
important years of her life had been lived: 'Much suffered in it, much
experienced in it, books written in it, friends made in it, crucial
decisions taken in it.' But although she was at first delighted with her
new, very own, home, she felt guilty over 'the enormous step' of having
sold Binesfield, which had been an 'assertion of independence – of my

father, of course'. She hoped this fresh start would remove the jinx on her writing, but it did not, and *Clara IV*, which would never be finished, caused her just as much pain and agony over the last eighteen years of her life at 42 Courtfield Gardens as it and its predecessors had in her eighteen years at 13 Ashburn Gardens. But this did not happen at once, for as soon as she had settled in she had to get down to another Colette translation to earn some money quickly to cover her overdraft.

My New York life started with an ill omen. As I walked into my bedroom of the apartment in Park Avenue something dark hurtled past the high window: the doorman later told my hostess that a man had thrown himself off the roof. And a desire to commit suicide was the strongest emotion I had during the chaste nine months I was there. After getting my first 'depressed' letter, Mother, who had just received a letter from her American 'dream daughter', Lyn Cosgriff, by the same mail, saying her father had been killed in a car crash, noted that she wished I had some of the honesty of 'the other Lyn'. She decided that in some ways I was the most dishonest person she had ever known because I said in my letter that 'the fiend' was telephoning me constantly. This, she assumed, meant that I was not really running away from him since I must have given him my address. (In fact it was his mother who had almost blackmailed Jenny into divulging it, saying he was threatening suicide if he could not speak to me; but I knew there was no danger of his turning up in New York, because a few years before he had been involved in some incident which prevented him from being allowed an entry visa to the United States.) Finally Antonia wrote in her notebook:

> You can't call her dishonest in one sense; she is acutely aware of her shortcomings ... I am too like Lyndall myself – hoping for something outside to solve all my problems. It won't.

Her last letter before I left for New York had been full of sympathy, saying how much she worried about me, and prayed for me every day, because a state of mind I had described to her compared 'almost word for word' to things she had written about herself in old diaries. She felt more strongly than ever that it was a lack of a centre – 'yes, I *do* mean religion' – that made life seem so meaningless to me. Now, not surprisingly, my mother was getting tired of my moanings. She sent me a stern letter saying I should try harder to appreciate New York, and suggesting a visit to the Empire State Building which had greatly impressed her two years before.

Mother made a new will (not her last) because of her changed situation. Sue would get the flat instead of Binesfield. She would also get the contents 'so that the flat is there completely furnished for her to let'. We were to share any royalties that might come in from her books – though she feared we were more likely to inherit debts than earnings. Sue and Elaine now replaced me as Literary Executors.

A month later Mother heard from a friend that something she had prayed for daily for ten years had come about: Sue went to Mass every week. Six months later, while spending a Sunday with the Chittys, Sue told her in person she had become a practising Catholic again and that her marriage with Thomas had been 'regularised'. Cordelia, aged seven, took Antonia to see the little chapel in their village. As she realised that her daughter and granddaughter had been to Mass there together that very morning, Antonia had the same dreamlike feeling, as when she first saw the grandchildren five years before, that this was too good to be true. Antonia wrote that she could 'die happy' now that Sue had become a whole and real person again:

> I feel a deeper responsibility to her than to Lyn because of all I deprived her of and all the complications I caused in her life. Darling Lyn, I love her just as much but in a different way. I suppose because there has never been such a deep, painful bond between us & I have never suffered over her as I have over Sue . . . The older I get, the more my children mean to me.

Some time afterwards, Mother and Sue spent an evening alone together, which they had not done for over ten years. Antonia noted that Sue was more than just her daughter: 'She is the person to whom I feel closest.' They had even discussed 'the breach':

> She said she had to get away, to be herself. That Thomas saw me as a rival powerful influence. What surprised me was that she said she felt 'inferior' because of having such a 'clever' mother. This seemed extraordinary to me, because I always felt Sue to be as intelligent as myself, if not more so, as well as having many gifts I have not, including beauty.

A week after Sue told Mother of her return to the Church, I returned from nine months in America. I had been working for the Festival of Two Worlds as Gian Carlo Menotti's assistant. The job was interesting and I liked Menotti, but my depression never lifted the whole time I was in America, indeed it worsened because I was so homesick for

Italy. The greatest advantage of my badly paid job was that it took me back there for the Spoleto Festival.

With the money FAO repaid me for what I had put into a pension fund during my five years there, I bought a brand new Volkswagen convertible, and with Sue I drove it across Europe, spending a few days en route riding horses in the Camargue. I had forgotten what happiness felt like, indeed I had never felt so happy as I did that May galloping across the deserted sand dunes to the seashore, as startled flamingoes flapped their wings preparing for take-off, and the herds of small black cattle edged nervously away. Sue and I got on well, she was much more approachable than she had been for the past few years and I was sorry to see her train pulling out of Turin station, where we parted.

We had both spent the night before leaving at 42 Courtfield Gardens with Mother. It was the first time I had been there and the first time for eleven years the three of us had slept under the same roof. Antonia, who had been going through a period of disliking the new flat, said afterwards that our staying there had suddenly made it seem her home.

Before setting off, I had left on her desk the manuscript of the novel about 'the fiend', which I had re-written from scratch in New York. I was nervous about showing *The Solitary Lemming* to her, for there was a portrait of the heroine's mother which she could not fail to recognise: on the other hand, it only said things I had already hinted at when we started our frank correspondence after I left for Rome in 1952; and she was the person I most wanted to read it.

She sent me a long and flattering letter to Spoleto about my '*terribly sad book*', insisting I could write and that the landscape was 'admirable'. Of course I was pleased, but suspected at the time she was being kind; however, I see from her notebook that in some ways the book had impressed her – 'A terrifying book. Wonderful things in it.' It haunted her as a 'terrible picture of despair'. She thought it a miracle that I had not gone out of my mind or killed myself because of my 'lack of any centre', and 'desperate isolation'. She understood, perhaps better than I realised, what it meant to have a 'sense of not existing unless involved in some violent emotion'. She found the portrait of the mother in my novel highly unflattering:

But it is very probably how she saw me in her 'teens & early twenties. An embittered frustrated woman, devoured with jealousy . . . I think the only thing I could ever have been said to 'envy' was her beauty, not that it has brought her much happiness ... If she'd married a rich man, I would probably, at times, have envied her for being financially secure.

When the first publisher turned the book down, Antonia told me not to be discouraged. She insisted I had talent, despite obvious flaws in my novel: 'Whether you eventually become a "writer" depends *entirely* on if you think it is worth all the misery, of which there is plenty!'

But when, a year later, my agent found a publisher who showed an interest, if I was prepared to revise the book, I never followed up the offer because I felt it was too much an exposé of my past, and realised the book had not been written so much with a view to publication, as to prove something to my mother.

That year, 1963, Sue had a book published: *White Huntress*. As soon as she had read it, Mother told me that, although she had enjoyed the 'dash and gusto', she wished Sue would write a 'straight book' one day instead of a 'hilarious farce'.

Thomas's seventh novel, *The Day the Call Came*, was published soon afterwards. Antonia wrote to me enthusiastically about it. She was praying that he, as well as I, would become a Catholic, particularly after he took Cordelia's First Communion 'wonderfully well' at the end of 1964. It was a moving occasion for Antonia: she had the 'happy feeling' of belonging to a family, and at last was beginning to like Thomas and feel more at ease with him. On returning home she wrote:

> Sue is wonderful. I love her so much, admire her so much & *respect* her so much. Lyndall wrote Cordelia the sweetest, most touching letter. My last from her was so sad.

After the first euphoria of returning to Italy had worn off, I sank into a state of despair. Spoleto, which ought to have been an earthly paradise – music and the arts in a beautiful Italian hill-town – only drove home to me what an outsider I was in every way. As I climbed Spoleto's hilly streets, the scent of the linden trees sweetening the summer breeze, the sound of pianos and string instruments floating out from open windows in Renaissance palaces, I felt my heart would burst from sadness. I had gone beyond the stage of being tempted to commit suicide into a state of apathy where everything was a uniform shade of grey. If a fairy godmother had appeared and offered me three wishes, there was not a single thing I desired: no place where I wanted to be, no person I wished to be with, no object that would have given me any gratification. Migraine headaches returned after a thirteen-year truce. Although I had no money and no job, I could not face returning to America with Menotti, and stayed on in Italy, intending to sell my car to exist. Instead, some kind American friends invented a job for me with them as secretary/au pair in Rome.

Then, in the late autumn, I met Wolfgang Reinhardt.

Wolfgang, who was twenty years older than I, had wanted to be an art historian, but circumstances – having to leave Germany in the thirties because of the Nazis and make a career in America – and the influence of his father, Max Reinhardt, had forced him into the world of entertainment as a film producer. He was married with three sons in their twenties, but had been separated from his wife for many years and had just come to live in Rome after having written and produced *Freud*, directed by John Huston, in Vienna. He was looking for someone to work on a new filmscript with him: we met through Iris Tree and, after reading my novel, he employed me.

Not one of the three scripts we worked on over the next few years ever became a film, but Wolfgang became the most important person in my life – as influential as Eric had once been in Antonia's, except we also became lovers and that, in the end, was what caused us to separate.

His interest in psychology – he had spent three years researching the Freud script – made him question every remark I made, and forced me to look at myself as I had never done before.

Antonia thought Wolfgang one of the 'most charming and *sympathique*' people she had met for years – 'the nicest of any of your men friends I've so far encountered' – when he took her out to lunch after we had been living together for a year.

About this time Antonia became certain she did not want to write any more novels, though she was still attempting to finish *Clara IV*. Six months before, Lyn Cosgriff, who had inherited part of a fortune after her father's death, had 'implored' Antonia 'with tears' to accept enough money to keep her until the end of the year: 'She wanted me to feel free for a few months, not to have to take on a translation – not even to feel I *had* to work on my own brute of a book – just to be able to "stare at the wall" as she said.'

Of course Antonia had not been able to resist spending extravagantly, particularly on the flat – for she had taken against it again and kept reading the property columns of the papers and 'dreaming idly' of other places. Two months after receiving Lyn's gift she had transformed her work-room at Courtfield Gardens enough to be able to write one July evening that she had finally begun to love it.

Before getting this money Antonia had been so broke that she had not only sold all her manuscripts for £50 to a man called Schultz, but, since she had not kept the original of *Frost in May*, had agreed to his suggestion to copy it out by hand for a fee of £35. Transcribing her first novel made Antonia realise she had lost that quality of 'simplicity and freshness' in her writing, and turned her even more strongly against her present work. (Three years later Antonia discovered from Olivia Manning that Schultz resold one of Olivia's manuscripts, for which he had paid her £25, to an American university for the sum of £1500.)

A few months after Lyn's gift-money ran out Antonia was due for her old age pension, but it did not even keep her in cigarettes. Old age was now a recurrent theme in her notebooks. She noticed a slowing down in movement and mind, and soon climbing the five flights of stairs with heavy shopping became 'a real ordeal'. Physical ailments started in her sixties: first rheumatism and stiffness of the joints; then agonising attacks of lumbago, which gave her an insight into how pain can alter one's life; the beginnings of deafness, and, in 1965, the oculist's warning that she had incipient cataracts which would one day mean undergoing an eye operation, something she dreaded all her life.

Several important things happened to Antonia in 1965.

At the beginning of April she received a note from Dorothy in Nairobi, where Tom, who had had enough of living close to apartheid for five years, was now training African journalists. Dorothy wrote that there was to be a Press party for Tom's sixtieth birthday on 19 April at which telegrams would be read out, and she was sure it would give him pleasure if there was one from Antonia. Mother sent a telegram because, she told me, 'I certainly do wish Tom well.' She then received a friendly letter from Tom saying how glad he was they had renewed contact, which had heartened her enough to write him a long reply. Back came an answer from Nairobi saying he had to attend a conference in London at the end of May and hoped she would dine with him. She accepted, and it was not until she read Tom's next letter – saying the only 'obstacle' to clear away was Antonia's 'bitter injustice to Dorothy in the affidavit' – that she realised it was to be a 'dîner à trois'. However, she was prepared to face that – 'after all Dorothy is his wife & has obviously made him very happy' — and to think of it as a dinner with 'a new entity, Tom-and-Dorothy'. But she was in a quandary as to what to do about his reference to the affidavit.

Finally Antonia decided to write to Tom giving her reasons at the time for writing the affidavit, and explaining that the doubts she had expressed about Dorothy were based on a letter she had received from her in 1949, when Dorothy was probably almost out of her mind with worry over Hugh's last illness and financial problems. Since she was sure they had all changed in fifteen years, she would be happy to meet them both if they still wished. Back had come a typewritten note saying it was clear their points of view on Dorothy were still opposed. Tom would only believe that Dorothy had written what Antonia had interpreted as a heartless and menacing letter if he could see it. He told her:

> Dorothy's 'weakness' has been, not a drive for power, but a drive for service — a passion for helping other people. Being myself a worldly character, I know how intense an enmity this provokes. I wrote to you as I did with the idea that fifteen years might have made some difference to your own attitude — as it has done to mine on almost every subject.

Mother told me that even if she could find the letter, which had been seen by several people, including Gerti's solicitor, she would never show it to Tom, though it hurt that he thought her a liar.

Tom and Dorothy were to stay with me in Rome on their way to England. I had seen Tom several times on his way through from Africa to England or America, but this would be the first time for ten years I had seen him with Dorothy and I was apprehensive. Antonia told me not to worry: Edmée, Dorothy's daughter who lived round the corner and whom she sometimes met in the street, had told her that her mother had become 'milder and less domineering'. Antonia added that, in his letters to her, Tom said it meant a great deal to him to be on good terms with me again.

The visit went well. Dorothy, who was suffering from back trouble, spent most of the time sitting on my terrace knitting a black skirt, and answering my questions about their African life. Like Antonia — whose name neither of us mentioned — she was much mellowed in her sixties. From then on my relationship with the Tom-and-Dorothy 'entity' grew easier and more affectionate, now I accepted that the father I had known as a child no longer existed. Many years later the three of us would travel to India together to stay near Meher Baba's ashram. Unfortunately, he was no longer alive, but I was impressed by many of his followers and their work with the sick and needy.

In 1965 Thomas was offered a teaching job at an American University, so he, Sue and their family left England for two years at the end of the summer. Antonia missed Sue.

In the spring of 1965 Antonia had received a £400 grant from the Royal Literary Fund. At the time she thought, 'How wonderful! I can refuse a translation this year and concentrate entirely on my own work!' Her 'own work' was no longer *Clara IV*, but an attempt at her autobiography following a suggestion by Malcolm Muggeridge that she should write it. But a few months after getting the grant she wrote to me that from the time she had received it she had never been free of some kind of accident or ailment:

> First I fall down in the street, cut my knee and it goes septic. Then I crack a rib. Then I have a violent and prolonged attack of lumbago. Then I have a mysterious, eczema-like rash on my face and neck – still not gone. Finally, in the course of a violent cold, I wake up with my eyes swollen and inflamed and am literally *unable* to read or write.

A young National Health doctor, whom she had consulted about her eyes, spent an hour talking to her and came to the conclusion she might be on the verge of another crack-up. He agreed to see her every week for fifteen minutes and prescribed an anti-depressant. For a while his treatment worked; instead of her usual nervous panic when she was stuck over a sentence, Antonia found herself saying, 'Maybe it'll go better tomorrow and it doesn't matter if it doesn't.' But the effect did not last, and she had to go to a National Health psychiatrist. She spent a year being treated by Dr Ployé, who delved far more than Carroll into her relationship with her mother: even suggesting some of her problems might be traced back to a pre-natal shock connected with her father's drunken 'rape' of her mother three months before her birth. She was sad when Ployé could not see her any more because of overwork, since he impressed her and she felt he had helped avert a third mental breakdown.

At the end of 1965 *The Hound and the Falcon* was published. The subtitle for her collected letters to Peter Thorpe in 1940–41 was 'The Story of a Reconversion to the Catholic Faith'. The critics were enthusiastic and she received numerous marvellous and moving letters from friends and strangers: 'It is a most extraordinary feeling to be having a success of the kind I'd most like,' she told me, 'for it seems that this queer book actually *helps* people.'

It is ironical that it should have been published just as she was beginning to lose her belief in 'a good God'. For the rest of her life she would live in a state of conflict as her religion became more and more meaningless. Christ seemed to her so contradictory; and much of the Catholic religion was now repellent to her, such as the 'horrible idea' of drinking Christ's blood. She wished there were some 'gaiety' in Christ, 'a *smile* somewhere in the Gospels'. By the end of 1968 religion had become a greater problem even than writing. Whether the story of Adam and Eve was literal or myth grew into an obsession which filled pages of her last notebooks. But she made herself go to Mass almost daily however much she doubted; and she forced herself to attend Child of Mary meetings at Roehampton, though she nearly always lost her temper there with someone.

Yet the weakening of her faith seems to have made her increasingly aware of other people's problems. In the last quarter of her life Antonia became more sensitive to the misery in other lives. She started giving a small part of any sums she received to charity. She befriended an unmarried cousin, Helen White, who, after her retirement, had aspirations to become a writer. Antonia would sit with her for hours trying to explain how to put a short story into shape; and, later, when Helen developed senile dementia, visited her almost daily until things became so bad that Helen had to be put into a home. Antonia wrote the equivalent of a short novel in her notebooks about her trials and tribulations with Helen.

At the time her doubts began again, Antonia 'adopted' a prisoner in Pentonville: George. It was a relief to her when he was moved to Dartmoor, which he preferred, so that she did not have to visit him, but she still 'sweated over' a weekly letter to him. Her reward for befriending George for more than five years was that during one of his brief spells out of prison he came to call and stole some money from her.

Money was to be a problem almost to the end of her life, so that Antonia always had to have a lodger occupying the spare bedroom at Courtfield Gardens. The first one, a charming middle-aged homosexual, turned out to be so convincing a liar that he reminded her of Dougal, her first lover, and disappeared one day owing her £80 in back rent. From then on she rented to duller, but safer, tenants; but, whenever there was a gap between lodgers, it was a welcome luxury for her to have the flat to herself.

One inevitable sadness as she grew older was the death of friends. From the death of Fr Victor White onwards there seemed to be a relentless crescendo of loss. Eric, the person whose death most affected her, died in January 1972. The full force of what she had lost hit her first at his cremation: as Eric's ex-wife and his widow clutched each other's hands while the 'Recordare Jesu Pie' from Verdi's *Requiem* was played, they both wept. Georgie gave Antonia Eric's watch which she wore as a 'comforting' memento of 'the most important person' in her life.

I understood Antonia's loss better than she suspected. A few years before, I had 'lost' Wolfgang to another woman because of my reluctance to continue our affair, although I still loved him as my mentor, and had been desolated. It had also meant the loss of a job, and for several months I had been in a worse state than when I had met him, bombarded with migraine headaches, which the homeopathic doctor who cured them said were caused by 'grief'. But I had been lucky, for just when I was certain my life was over in every sense (I was thirty-five) I had been given a job in FAO as a documentary scriptwriter; and, far more important, a few months later had met Lorenzo Passerini, the man I would eventually marry. But, much as I loved Lorenzo, I could not confide in him as I had with Wolfgang. When I told Mother this, she said Eric and Wolfgang (though not a homosexual) had the same analytical minds and were so interesting to talk to that they spoilt one for the company of other men.

But Antonia was compensated in some ways for the death of friends by meeting new ones, such as Elizabeth Sprigge and 'the dear Marnaus' – Fred and Senta – as well as by the return of old friends from the past, in particular Kathleen Raine, Charlotte d'Erlanger, Emily Coleman and Phyllis Jones.

Kathleen had reappeared in 1962 when Antonia noted, 'It is very good having K. back in my life: someone I can *talk* to.' For the rest of her life Antonia's most serious religious discussions would take place with her: she was amazed, and a little envious, that Kathleen dared to believe in reincarnation and had no qualms about thinking the Fall of Adam a myth, while still practising her Catholicism.

Antonia described her reunion with Charlotte d'Erlanger, 'Léonie' in *Frost in May*, in a letter to me. A guilty conscience had made her avoid Charlotte for forty years, although she had 'longed to see her all this time': at the time of her marriage to Reggie she had borrowed £80 from her which she never managed to pay back. When Antonia had her 'wonderful windfall' from Lyn Cosgriff in 1963, she was at last able to send Charlotte a cheque, which she refused:

> She said it was always meant to be a present (quite untrue!) & asked me to lunch . . . She hasn't changed essentially – all the old edge is still there . . . it's wonderful to find her undimmed. Still a little frightening, I admit!

At a second meeting, Antonia noticed a profound melancholy in Charlotte who told her she had not believed in God since her twenties: 'She does not feel it necessary that the universe should have any purpose or explanation.' Although she continued to remain in awe of her, Antonia would occasionally see Charlotte in London, and twice stayed with her in Cornwall.

Emily Coleman reappeared and disappeared in Antonia's life. Her behaviour became even more erratic than usual after she developed a brain tumour, which caused all her friends, particularly Phyllis Jones who was looking after her, much anguish until she died.

And Phyllis Jones was the person closest to Antonia for the last years of her life. Seeing these two old ladies hunched over *The Times* crossword together, it was odd to imagine that Phyllis, before becoming a Catholic, had once been wilder than Antonia. But, although she now looked the picture of a staid spinster, her handsome legs betrayed that she had been a beauty: those legs had often been used in advertisements, as had Antonia's beautiful hands, when they both worked in advertising in the 1930s. It was Phyllis who typed the chaotic chapters, all to be discarded, of *Clara IV* and the autobiography, sometimes for nothing, although she was poorer than Antonia. Somehow she even managed to help Antonia out with money, and was always willing to hop on a train, first from Sussex, then from Devon, to come and stay on the work-room couch to lend a hand in an emergency.

One such emergency was at the beginning of 1970 when Antonia developed double pneumonia and was rushed to hospital seriously ill. At the time Sue was in America with Thomas and her family (now increased to three after the birth of Miranda in 1967). Afterwards Antonia said what 'a loyal standby in trouble' Phyllis, who always insisted she was absolutely worthless and hid sweetness behind a sardonic façade, was. Antonia also wrote how moved she was by everyone's kindness at the time. Sue had called from Boston, and I from Italy, 'each wanting to come over'; Tom had written a 'stiff, formal little note'; and Silas had telephoned – it was the first time she had heard his voice for nearly nineteen years.

A few months earlier Sue and I had celebrated Mother's seventieth birthday with her. Afterwards she wrote in her notebook that she felt '*singularly* blessed' in her daughters. She said how much she admired Sue who had 'developed a great sweetness'. I too was 'sweet' and 'an angel daughter' – maybe because as a birthday present I had given her a small allowance to continue for the rest of her life.

Antonia now entered the final run of her old age. Already she had had two cataract operations and wore heavy glasses. Despite the hearing aid she now had to wear, her deafness caused her much inconvenience. She had started to develop a hunch back from osteoporosis, which would soon give her excruciating pain in the spine. Rheumatism and lumbago continued to assail her, especially in wintertime.

But even so she came twice to stay with my husband and me in Italy. She and Lorenzo liked each other, but after staying she wrote in her notebook that she would no more want to be married to him than to Thomas. The highlight of her first visit was seeing Venice for the only time; and of the next one, meeting Iris Origo.

In the 1970s many things happened to Sue. She had her fourth and last child, Jessica. She had two biographies published: one of Anna Sewell and one of Charles Kingsley. Then Thomas took her and the children on a two-year trek from Spain to Greece – a journey recorded in a book called *The Great Donkey Walk* which came out in 1977 – shortly after which she had the first of two serious nervous breakdowns.

Nineteen seventy-seven was an eventful year for Antonia.

In April I was able to tell her that finally I believed in God. The story, partly recounted in her notebook, is too long to tell here. It came as a revelation, and for a month afterwards I lived through what I have since discovered is a quite common phenomenon, for which some psychologists have a name: 'peak experience'. During that month I saw everything as good; it seemed to me that nothing could be interpreted as evil. Of course it ended, and I returned to my old pessimism, but now that I finally believed in some sort of higher divinity nothing would ever be quite so black and purposeless again. Of her own fading faith Antonia said around that time: 'I just moulder quietly away, going round and round in circles about the eternal religious question.'

In October 1977 Antonia had what she described as an important meeting with Carmen Callil, the founder of Virago Press:

Dark, good-looking, 39 but looking much younger. I took an instant liking to her & we talked for 2 hours . . . I've a feeling that C.C. will be 'in my life'. She interests me extremely . . . We have a lot in common. She was at a convent school for 13 years in Australia . . . We like the same books & have the same passion for cats (she has 3). She made me *want* to write again.

But it was too late for writing; the only work Antonia had had published since living at Courtfield Gardens (apart from *The Hound and the Falcon*) was the second volume of *Minka and Curdy* shortly before Curdy died. Minka had to be put down a few years later, leaving Antonia sadly catless for the last years of her life. The 'kitty litter' was too heavy to carry up her many stairs.

However, through Carmen Callil, Antonia would finally make some money from her books when Virago reprinted most of them. Suddenly the media took an interest in Antonia White; Carmen, who had also become her agent, managed to sell the TV rights on all four novels which were later made into a four-part *Frost in May* series. But, pleased and amused as she was at having recognition, and being fêted, worldly success had come too late for Antonia to enjoy. Trying to survive her painful physical ailments took up nearly all her energy in her late seventies, and she did not live to see her works on television.

But Carmen's most important role in Antonia's life was as a friend in her old age: she often did shopping for her on the way to work, and called in on the way home. Antonia knew she could telephone her at any time of the day or night if she was in trouble – though Carmen did tell Antonia she had gone too far when she once made her drive across London to pour out a glass of water. It was Sue, as our mother's financial heir under her final will, who would benefit from Carmen's having relaunched Antonia as a writer; for Antonia's works brought in far more in the five years after her death than they had in her entire lifetime.

In 1977 Antonia saw Tom and Silas each once more before she died.

Strangely and appropriately, Sue was present at her meeting with Silas, and I at the one with Tom. Silas and Antonia had not seen each other for twenty-six years when Sue 're-introduced' them at the opening at the Royal Academy of the John Tunnard exhibition, to which each had loaned a painting. Silas was very amicable and asked Antonia what she thought of her grandchildren. She replied, 'They are yours too, you know!' before praising them.

The tea party which took place not long afterwards at Courtfield Gardens on 27 November (the day before Antonia's marriage to Tom 47 years before), and at which I was also present, was a more formal occasion, where conversation between Antonia and Dorothy revolved mainly around whether it was necessary to use a tea-strainer. Antonia had in fact seen Tom at my half-sister Amanda's confirmation a few years before, but had not met Dorothy for nearly thirty years. She wrote in her notebook after the tea party that Dorothy could not have been more benevolent; 'Tom seemed genuinely pleased to see me: we talked *almost* naturally.' When Tom received a knighthood for his services to journalism in the next New Year's Honours, she was relieved there was no dilemma about whether she should write to congratulate him. Antonia, too, had had a small accolade in old age: on her seventieth birthday, the Queen gave her a Civil List Pension for her services to literature.

In the last three years of Antonia's life a strange, almost telepathic, bond developed between us. My husband had nearly died in 1976, and for the rest of his life could not manage on his own, making it difficult for me to go away just at the time when Antonia most needed someone, for she was seldom without pain or fear from one of her ailments. But she never called on Sue, who had small children, or me with an invalid husband, for help. However, every so often I would get an insistent urge to fly to London and see my mother, which meant finding someone at short notice to stay with Lorenzo.

Each time, I arrived when there was a crisis.

The first time I found her in the throes of an attack of pain in the back caused by the osteoporosis. Her elderly doctor had said he was too busy to visit her, so I stormed his surgery and came away with a prescription for morphine to get her through the night. The next day, when he still refused to come, I had her moved to a private nursing home. As the ambulance men carried her in a chair down five flights of stairs, she cried so loud from the pain that I cried, too. When she came out of the nursing home, Sue and I convinced her to change her doctor.

The next time I came over she had just heard she had cancer. I was in time to go with her to the Royal Marsden for the first radiotherapy treatment which she was dreading. As we sat waiting, holding hands, I felt like a mother taking a frightened child to the dentist, and a wave of tenderness suffused me as a nurse led away the hunched little figure when her turn came.

But the third time was the most fortuitous.

In the summer of 1979 I had heard from Sue before she and Thomas went on holiday to France that Mother was in hospital again, but well looked after. Knowing how much she loathed hospital life, particularly St Mary Abbots where she was expected to join in the therapy sessions for geriatrics and where, during her last confinement, her hip broke as she was being turned over in bed, I decided to fly over for a few days to visit her. I arrived on a Friday afternoon and went straight from Heathrow to the hospital, only to be told she had insisted on being discharged a few hours before.

On entering Antonia's flat in Courtfield Gardens I heard moaning. I found my mother propped up at her desk, where she had told the ambulance men to deposit her, unable even to reach the telephone to call Carmen for help. When she saw me she wept from shame as much as relief, for she had wetted herself several times. Somehow I got her to the bathroom and undressed and washed her before putting her to bed. Then I rang a nursing agency to find a night nurse. I suppose Mother would have died if I had not found her, for the health worker was not due to call until Monday to check if she was all right.

When Sue returned from France, the two of us finally persuaded Mother to agree to go into a home if a suitable one could be found, for she refused ever to go back to hospital and realised that her Virago royalties would soon be eaten up in paying a day nurse and a night nurse.

While I was in London that July, I heard that Wolfgang had died of cancer. His death was the first in what I came to call my 'Plutonic phase', for in less than three years ten people who had been important in my life died, including Antonia, Gerti, Bobby and, in August 1981, Lorenzo.

In October Sue sent me the good news that she had found a place for Antonia at St Raphael's, a pleasant nursing home in Sussex only a few miles from where the Chittys lived. I agreed to fly over and accompany her there.

I spent the night before Mother left Courtfield Gardens in the flat with her. She could not get to sleep, and asked me to read aloud her favourite piece of prose: the opening chapter of *Adam Bede*. Twice in the night I was woken by her screams. The first time she was in pain; the second time she had had a nightmare. As I tried to soothe her, I asked her what she had dreamt. For the first time in her life she would not answer my question: 'It's too obscene to tell you,' she said; 'It was about my father.'

The next morning, before the ambulance came to fetch us, she wanted to explain some things to me concerning the flat, which was not to be sold, but rented to lodgers. She pointed to some boxes which she said were to go to Carmen, and contained, among other things, Silas's love letters. 'I've thrown all your and Sue's letters away,' she said. My expression must have showed dismay, for, as if to console me, she added: 'Except for the best ones from Sue' – presumably the 'Kolbsheim letters'.

She clutched my hand throughout the journey in the ambulance, yet managed to see black humour in the fact that, near the beginning of her life, her father had delivered her into the hands of nuns and now, near the end, her daughters were doing the same.

Sue was waiting at St Raphael's where we settled Mother in. It was then Antonia said, to our great relief, that she was happy to be there, and I was free to return to Italy under the illusion that this was so.

Only after her death, five months later, did Carmen Callil and Phyllis Jones show me pathetic letters they had received from Antonia which show how miserable she felt. They visited her; so did Isabel Quigly, and a truly good new friend, Perpetua Ingram, who spent many long hours at her bedside listening to reminiscences and comforting her. And Thomas went once a week to see she was all right and to deal with any practical problems. But those letters said she felt abandoned by her daughters, which saddens me.

Epilogue

This story which ended before it began is over. But there is a postscript.

A year after my mother's death I received a note from Kathleen Raine. She was at that time one of the two Vice-Chairmen of the College of Psychic Science and had recently been to see a medium called Ena Twigge. While there, a message came through that someone called 'Eileen or Irene' was trying to get in touch with her. Unable to recall ever having known anyone of either name, she did not pay much attention and the medium did not persevere in making contact. But on the way home Kathleen suddenly remembered that Antonia's real name was Eirene and wondered if she were the person trying to reach her? So Kathleen wrote to me saying that, if I were interested in following this up, she could fix an appointment for me to see Ena Twigge the next time I was in England – not an easy task, for Mrs Twigge was world-famous and booked for months in advance. Although the idea of communicating with a dead person was daunting, I was too curious to refuse the offer.

It was the medium in person who opened the door of her semi-detached house in a distant suburb of London. She looked like any homely middle-aged matron as she led me into an over-furnished room. We sat down, and after a few minutes of friendly conversation she asked, 'Well, dear, do you want trance or not?'

'No, no, not trance,' I said quickly, at once regretting my cowardice.

Mrs Twigge told me to turn on the tape recorder. Then she took a deep breath, lifted up her left arm to tug at what seemed like an invisible lavatory plug, and began to tell me things from my past she could not possibly have known about. It could not have been telepathy because she was not saying anything that was in my mind. All the way on the tube train, and since sitting in her chintz-covered chair, I had been half hoping for and half dreading a possible 'encounter' with my mother; instead she was giving me messages from an ex-lover. Not only did she describe Wolfgang physically, but every time she said 'He says to tell you . . .' out came some piece of information pertinent to the past, the present and, as it would turn out, to the future. One statement in particular astounded me: 'He says to tell you that you'd like it here. No sex and no socks!' Even if she had sensed that sex had become a problem between us, without it having been mentioned, she could not have known that Wolfgang changed his socks twice a day and would not entrust their laundering to a maid or a washing machine. If I ever went away I used to return to a mound of socks waiting to be washed in cold water, and I complained mightily.

Suddenly Wolfgang was interrupted. 'There's somebody else here,' said Mrs Twigge, 'a small woman. She had a great many books. She's written the letters K E A T S over your head in luminous writing. Does that make sense?'

Before I could answer she continued without stopping: 'Perhaps it's a name. Do you know someone of that name? She says she's completely adjusted but looks back at her life and sees a great many omissions: "Too self-occupied" she's telling me. She seems very worried about her hair. She says to tell you, "Don't feel unequal: you have the gift. I love you more as I understand you more." I wonder why she keeps patting her hair? She says to tell you, "Nothing to forgive: it was meant that way."'

There was a pause at last. 'Oh dear,' said Mrs Twigge, 'she's gone. Well that was sudden. Very sudden indeed.'

The session was over.

Antonia had many books. Keats was one of her favourite authors. Anyone reading her notebooks could not fail to agree that she was too self-occupied. But it was the reference to her hair that was to me the most convincing proof that Mrs Twigge had been communicating with my mother. She was always preoccupied with it: one of the things that troubled her most during her terminal illness, and which she complained about more than the pain, was not being able to get to a hairdresser.

I went home joyously. Any lingering self-pity from the past had gone. If fate, or karma, had meant things to be that way, then of course there was nothing for either of us to forgive.

Sources

Published

AM = *As Once in May* by Antonia White (ed. Susan Chitty). Virago 1983
BG = *Beyond the Glass* by Antonia White. Reprinted Virago 1979
DGJ = *Journal 1936–1937* by David Gascoyne. The Enitharmon Press 1980
FM = *Frost in May* by Antonia White. Reprinted Virago 1978
GM = *God to Man and Man to God* by Meher Baba. Sheriar Press 1975
HF = *The Hound and the Falcon* by Antonia White. Reprinted Virago 1980
LT = *The Lost Traveller* by Antonia White. Reprinted Virago 1979
NM = *Now To My Mother* by Susan Chitty. Weidenfeld 1985
OC = *Out of this Century* by Peggy Guggenheim. Andre Deutsch 1979
OT = *Of This Our Time* by Tom Hopkinson. Hutchinson 1982
SH = *The Sugar House* by Antonia White. Reprinted Virago 1979
SS = *Strangers* by Antonia White. Reprinted Virago 1981
UT = *Under the Tropic* by Tom Hopkinson. Hutchinson 1984
(All page numbers refer to the published editions above.)

Unpublished

AWLL   = Letter from Antonia White to Lyndall
AWLSL   = Letter from Antonia White to Susan and Lyndall
AWLT   = Letter from Antonia White to Tom Hopkinson
AWN   = Antonia White's notebook
BRLAW   = Letter from Bertrand Russell to Antonia White
EESLAW = Letter from Eric Earnshaw-Smith to Antonia White
HTHLAW = Letter from Tom Hopkinson to Antonia White
HTHLL   = Letter from Tom Hopkinson to Lyndall
HTHN   = Tom Hopkinson's notebook
MHL   = Letter from Mary Hitchcock to Lyndall
SGLAW   = Letter from Silas Glossop to Antonia White

Taped Interviews

AWTC   = Antonia White talking to Carmen Callil
HTHTL   = Tom Hopkinson talking to Lyndall

CHAPTER ONE

HF   pp.xvii, 24, 62
LT   p.90
Queen Magazine, April 1974
AWLL   17 & 25 September 1952; 12 & 25 January, 1 April, 20 May,
            21 June, 3 August, 16 October 1953; 21 March, 5 July 1954
AWN   27 June, 24 July, 15 August 1937; 27 August 1938; 24 June
            1964
AWLSL   26 December 1979

CHAPTER TWO

AM   pp.188, 200, 204, 206, 208, 209, 216, 286
LT   pp.20, 31, 100, 121
AWN   13 October 194(8?); 23 August 1961; 6 September 1968;
            11 November 1970

CHAPTER THREE

AM   pp.58, 82, 162, 163–176, 209, 243, 244, 258, 259, 288, 311,
            314, 317, 319, 320, 321, 329
FM   pp.145, 173, 177, 181, 209, 217, 219
HF   pp.65, 82
LT   pp.24, 35, 36, 68, 78, 96, 110–115, 179, 235
SH   pp.28, 57, 59, 161, 162, 168, 188
AWN   24 June, 3 September 1938; 1 March, 4 April 1939; 12 May
            1941; 3 & 12 October 194(7?) & 18 October 1947; 26 May,
            31 October 1948; 25 March, 2 May, 25 July 1949; 12 July 1950;
            11 May 1951; 18 February, 8 October 1952; 2 & 22 February,
            12 March 1953; 16 August 1954; 18 February 1956; 9 August
            1959; 3 September 1960; 23 August 1961; 12 May, 21 Nov-
            ember 1962; 23 & 26 April, 10 October 1966; 12 April, 9 June
            1967; 25 January 1970; 26 May, 16 June 1975
AWTC   1979

CHAPTER FOUR

AM   p.39
BG   pp.78–81, 86–7, 89, 113, 120, 127–130, 142, 143, 168, 189,
            203, 204, 263, 271
HF   pp.25, 37, 53

LT   p.178
SH   pp.119, 120, 125, 143, 153, 154, 155, 156, 157, 196, 197, 209,
            220, 237, 244, 253
SS   pp.45, 46, 47, 59, 62–3, 119–156
AWN   24 August, 15 September 1937; 25 June 1938; 12 May 1941;
            19 & 25 March 194(9?); 12 July 1950; 23 February, 13 & 17
            September 1951; 26 January, 4 November 1952; 17 & 21 June
            1954; 17 September 1955; 9 & 19 January, 11 August 1956; 21
            February 1958; 22 February 1959; 4 June, 11 August, 3 & 28
            September, 13 December 1960; 22 March 1962; 9 December
            1965; 8 October 1968; 9 February 1969; 12 August 1970; 23
            August 1971; 25 January 1972; 20 April 1973
Letter from Dr Percy Smith to Tom Hopkinson, 22 November 1930

CHAPTER FIVE

AM   pp.34, 61–66, 132
BG   p.89
HF   pp.25, 30, 67
AWN   1926; 26 May 1948; 25 March 194(9?); 18 October 1952; 2
            February 1953; 17 June 1954; 11 August 1956; 5 & 21 February
            1958; 22 February 1969; 12 August 1970; 26 January, 12
            February 1972; 20 April 1973; 8 September 1974
BRLAW   Undated; 22 January, 29 April, 13 July, 2 September 1926; early
            1928
EESLAW   16 July 1928; 16 July 1934

CHAPTER SIX

HF   p.26
AWLL   3 October 1952; 16 & 18 February 1955
AWN   25 June 1938; 12 May 1941; 1 February 1948; ? November
            1948; 8 October 1952; 17 June 1954; 21 February, 18 October
            1958; 3 October, 27 December 1960; 8 January 1962; 8 January
            1966; 12 April 1967
BRLAW   2 September 1929
EESLAW   16 & 18 August 1929
SGLAW   Undated, 22 & 30 September, 2 & 3 & 4 & (8?) October, 14
            & 26 November, 11 December 1928; 8 & 14 June, (?) July, 3
            & 20 August, Undated (pre Mexico), Undated (Los Pilaros), 2
            & 27 & 28 October, 16 & 18 December 1929

CHAPTER SEVEN

OT   pp.12, 16, 18, 41, 44, 65, 66, 67, 74, 76, 88, 92, 97, 104, 105, 108, 110, 119, 124
C. Day-Lewis by Sean Day-Lewis (Weidenfeld), p.38
AWN   2 December 1939; 12 March 1953
HTHN   19 May, 29 July 1935; 1 June, 20 September 1936; 8 November 1939; 31 December 1942; 10 & 11 & 30 January, 8 & 27 February 1943

CHAPTER EIGHT

HF   pp.1, 26
LT   p.41
NM   p.40
OC   pp.116, 131–5
OT   pp.127–129, 137, 143
Recollections by Geoffrey Grigson (Chatto & Windus), p.5
Introduction to *The Shutter of Snow* by Emily Coleman (Virago), p.ii
AWLL   16 & 18 February 1955
AWLT   14 November 1931
AWN   25 & 26 & 30 & 31 January, 8 & 9 February, 7 & 20 June, 31 July, 8 & 10 & 14 September, 16 October 1933; 1 & 4 & 23 January, 19 March, 16 June 1934; 9 January, 14 March 1935; 11 August, 1 & 15 & 27 September 1937; 25 June, 3 September 1938; 13 February 1939; 11 September 1947; 1 & 2 February, 2 & 3 April, 26 May, (?) November 1948; 25 March 1949; 12 September 1951; 17 June 1954; 18 February 1956; 21 February 1958; 12 April 1967; 23 August 1970; 12 & 14 February 1972
BRLAW   13 July 1929
EESLAW   18 August 1929
HTHLAW   20 April, 8 June, (?) July, (?) & 22 August, 26 September, (?) October 1930; (?) May, 24 July, (9?) & 13 November 1931; 19 December 1933; (?) June, (?) July, (?) August 1934
HTHN   20 April, 28 June 1932; 31 December 1942
MHL   28 February 1986
Letter from Dr Percy Smith to Tom Hopkinson, 22 November 1930

CHAPTER NINE

OT   p.151
SS   pp.23, 36, 40–44
AWLT   (?) December 1934

AWN   25 July, 2 & 5 & 10 & 17 August, 27 September, 28 & 30
             December 1934; 3 & 6 & 9 & 11 & 20 & 25 & 29 January, 9
             & 12 & 14 & 16 & 17 March 1935
HTHLAW   (?) & (?10) August, Undated, 4 December 1934
HTHN   16 & 17 January, 1 & 25 February, 12 & 22 March 1935; 3 &
             22 February 1937
HTHTL

CHAPTER TEN

OT   p.154
AWN   23 January 1934; 15 August 1937; 17 October 1954
HTHN   4 September 1932; 15 December 1935
MHL   28 February 1986
HTHTL

CHAPTER ELEVEN

NM   pp.45, 52
OT   p.149
AWLT   (?) August, 12 December (2) 1935; 22 March, (7?) & 11 & 16
             April 1936
AWN   9 January, 31 March, 14 April, 26 & 28 May, 1 & 4 & 14 &
             26 June, 7 & 28 August, 19 September, 6 October, 20 November
             1935; 4 & 7 & 17 & 28 January, 16 February, 9 & 15 & 23
             March, 12 May, (?6) June, 6 & 9 & 11 July, 22 October 1936;
             8 January 1937
EESLAW   20 April 1936
HTHLAW   (?30) March, 14 April, 19 & 23 August 1936
HTHN   22 & 23 March, 13 & 19 & 30 April, 19 & 26 May, 4 & 27
             June, 3 & 29 July, 5 & 11 & 29 December 1935; 4 & 13 & 14
             & 24 January, 18 February, 9 March, 1 & 7 & 27 June, 31
             August 1936; 31 December 1942
HTHTL   1982

CHAPTER TWELVE

AM   p.330
DGJ   22 & 25 & 28 September, 9 & 22 October 1936; 17 & 19
             March, 4 & 6 April, 10 May 1937
NM   p.90

OC   p.342
OT   p.167
AWLT   9 August 1937
AWN   31 August, 10 & 18 & 28 September, 22 October, 16 November,
            4 December 1936; 8 & 27 January, 2 & 15 & 25 & 27 May, 7
            & 19 & 20 & 24 & 26 & 27 & 28 June, 1 & 8 & 12 & 14 &
            15 & 21 & 25 & 28 & 31 July, 3 & 5 & 9 & 12 & 15 & 24
            & 27 August, 1 & 2 & 4 & 6 & 15 & 22 & 25 & 27 September,
            6 October 1937; 21 May 1948; 19 February 1953
HTHLAW   31 July 1937
HTHN   31 August, 7 & 20 September, 29 & 30 December 1936; 22
            February, 14 March, 11 & 31 July, 28 August, 9 September, 17
            October 1937; 22 April 1939

CHAPTER THIRTEEN

LT   p.128
NM   pp.84, 106, 117
AWLT   12 April 1938; 24 May 1940
AWN   8 October 1935; 15 & 21 August, 30 November, 4 December
            1937; 31 January, 1 & 23 March, 14 & 15 & 18 & 21 April,
            22 & 29 May, 12 & 15 & 16 & 18 & 19 & 20 & 25 & 28
            June, 5 & 6 & 7 & 10 & 12 July, 3 & 4 & 27 & 28 & 29
            August, 3 & 11 September, 25 & 26 & 29 October, 13 December
            1938; 13 February, 1 March, 4 & 31 December 1939; 17
            January, 15 March, 13 May, 8 & 12 June 1940; 12 May 1941;
            1 February, 3 April 1948
EESLAW   16 July 1933
HTHLAW   (?) March 1938; (?2) & (?8) & mid November, 31 December
            1939
HTHN   21 December 1935; 14 March 1937; 5 & 31 December 1939;
            29 December 1941

CHAPTER FOURTEEN

HF   pp.33, 62, 102, 113, 134, 141, 146
AWLT   19 January 1941
AWN   12 May, 29 July, 18 August 1941; 2 February, 22 April 1942

CHAPTER FIFTEEN

HF   29 August 1941

NM   p.128
OT   p.231
AWN   22 February, (?) September 1942; 8 June 1955
HTHN   1 June 1936; 20 April, 26 July, 17 November, 23 & 29 December
            1941; 25 December 1942; 30 December 1944; 5 August 1945;
            19 February 1948

CHAPTER SIXTEEN

GM   Back cover
NM   pp.139, 144–5
The Land Unknown by Kathleen Raine (Hamish Hamilton), p.182
AWN   4 June 1943; 5 August 1944; (?) October 1945; 14 & 15 & 19
            & 21 & 28 & 31 March, 3 & 4 & 5 & 6 & 8 & 9 & 10 &11
            & 13 & 14 & 15 & 16 & 18 & 19 & 20 & 21 & 24 April, 2
            October 1947; 23 March, 3 & 27 April, 5 July, 12 October
            1948; 7 & 11 July 1949; 12 September 1951; 17 June 1954; 18
            February 1956; 29 June 1964

CHAPTER SEVENTEEN

GM   p.133
NM   pp.154, 161
AWLL   12 July 1965
AWLT   11 July 1947
AWN   1 March 1939; 31 December 1947; 5 January, 1 & 7 & 16 &
            19 & 21 & 29 February, 2 & 3 & 6 & 8 & 9 & 18 & 20 & 23
            & 27 March, 3 & 4 April, 19 May, 24 & 25 & 27 July, 1 & 2
            & 3 & 18 & 25 August, 9 September 1948; 31 January, 25
            March, 5 & 12 & 15 & 19 April, 23 May, 2 & 6 June, 4 & 7
            July, 8 August 1949; 26 February, 19 & 22 April, 12 July, 9 &
            19 September, 5 November 1950; 21 & 22 January, 1 & 23
            February, 5 March, 14 May 1951; 4 October 1952; 26 January
            1972

CHAPTER EIGHTEEN

AWN   10 & 14 & 15 & 26 May, 5 June, 3 & 20 & 26 & 27 & 30
            August, 16 & 17 November, 5 & 25 & 28 & 29 & 30 December
            1951; 23 & 26 January, 12 March, 18 May, 9 & 14 August
            1952; 1 January 1956

HTHN   1 June 1936

CHAPTER NINETEEN

UT   pp.17, 29
AWLL   17 & 25 September, 3 & 9 & 31 October, 13 November, 14 &
            20 & 22 December 1952; 1 & 12 & 25 January, 1 & 22
            February, 17 March, 1 & 12 & 17 April, 3 & 20 & 27 May, 10
            & 21 & 23 June, 20 & 23 July, 21 September, 15 November, 5
            & 31 December 1953; 4 January, 19 April, 8 & 15 June, 5 &
            19 July, 8 & 12 August, 5 September, 17 October, 9 November
            1954; 1 & 16 January, 16 & 18 February 1955
AWN   4 & 18 October 1952; 12 March, 15 April, 27 July, 20 August
            1953; 13 & 15 June, 27 July, 16 & 18 & 21 August, 11
            September, 31 December 1954; 23 February, 8 June 1955
Letter from Susan Chitty to Lyndall, September 1952
Letter from Willy Mostyn-Owen to Lyndall, September 1952
Letter from Richard Temple Muir to Lyndall, 25 September 1952

CHAPTER TWENTY

AWLL   8 June 1954; 19 & 25 April, 5 May 1955; 4 June 1957
AWN   8 & 10 & 12 June, 17 September, 31 December 1955; 9 & 29
            January, 1 & 6 February, 3 March, 13 May, 15 July, 11 & 14
            August 1956
Letter from Lionel Birch to Lyndall, 18 April 1955

CHAPTER TWENTY-ONE

UT   p.26
AWLL   9 January, 10 February, 15 March, 20 April, 4 June, 14 July, 14
            September 1957; 30 & 31 March, 16 May, 8 & 31 August, 25
            September 1958; 26 January, 9 May, 28 August, 8 October
            1959; 19 March, 20 July, 27 September 1960
AWN   20 March 1956; 21 January, 5 & 7 & 11 & 17 February 1958;
            6 September 1959; 3 June, 23 July, 3 September, 1 October, 6
            & 27 & 28 December 1960
Letter from Lyn Cosgriff to Susan Chitty, 20 June 1986

CHAPTER TWENTY-TWO

NM   p.182
AWLL   11 March, 3 April, 9 August 1961; 1 June 1962; 19 February,
          5 June, 30 September, 5 November, 28 December 1963; 14 June
          1964; 1 March, 23 May, 7 & 14 October, 21 November, 11
          December 1965; 26 January, 19 February 1972
AWN   7 May, 21 June, 29 & 31 July, 6 & 11 October 1961; 27
          February, 13 March, 1 & 12 May, 30 June, 9 August, 31
          December 1962; 22 July, 18 & 30 December 1963; 24 June, 3
          August, 28 October, 3 & 20 & 23 December 1964; 26 April, 22
          & 27 May, 30 December 1965; 8 October 1966; 12 March, 20
          November, 28 December 1967; 8 October 1968; 4 April 1969;
          20 January 1970; 25 January 1972; 27 January, 17 February
          1974; 15 October, 31 December 1975; 26 October 1977
HTHLAW   May 1965

Index

Novelist

(Eirene Botting)

1899-1980

LIVED HERE
1899-1921